THE ROUTLEDGE (
TO FILM HIS....

The Routledge Companion to Film History is an indispensable guide for anyone studying film history for the first time. The approach taken presents a substantial and readable overview of the field and provides students with a tool of reference that will be valuable throughout their studies.

The volume is divided into two parts. The first is a set of 11 essays that approaches film history around the following themes:

- History of the moving image
- Film as art and popular culture
- Production process
- Evolution of sound
- Alternative modes: experimental, documentary, animation
- Cultural difference
- Film's relationship to history.

The second is a critical dictionary that explains concepts, summarizes debates in film studies, defines technical terms, describes major periods and movements, and discusses historical situations and the film industry. The volume as a whole is designed as an active system of cross-references: readers of the essays are referred to dictionary entries (and vice versa) and both provide short bibliographies that encourage readers to investigate topics.

William Guynn is Emeritus Professor of Art (Cinema) at Sonoma State University, California. His previous publications include *Writing History in Film* (Routledge, 2006).

Also available from Routledge

The Routledge Companion to Children's Literature
Edited by David Rudd
978–0–415–47271–5

The Routledge Companion to Critical Theory
Edited by Simon Malpas and Paul Wake
978–0–415–33296–5

The Routledge Companion to English Language Studies
Edited by Janet Maybin and Joan Swann
978–0–415–40338–2

The Routledge Companion to Gothic
Edited by Catherine Spooner and Emma McEvoy
978–0–415–39843–5

The Routledge Companion to Postcolonial Studies
Edited by John McLeod
978–0–415–32497–7

The Routledge Companion to Postmodernism (Second Edition)
Edited by Stuart Sim
978–0–415–33359–7

The Routledge Companion to Russian Literature
Edited by Neil Cornwell
978–0–415–23366–8

The Routledge Companion to Semiotics
Edited by Paul Cobley
978–0–415–44073–8

THE ROUTLEDGE COMPANION
TO FILM HISTORY

Edited by
William Guynn

Routledge
Taylor & Francis Group

LONDON AND NEW YORK

First published 2011
by Routledge
2 Park Square, Milton Park, Abingdon, Oxon OX14 4RN

Simultaneously published in the USA and Canada
by Routledge
711 Third Avenue, New York, NY 10017

Routledge is an imprint of the Taylor & Francis Group, an informa business

Typeset in Times New Roman by Book Now Ltd, London

British Library Cataloguing in Publication Data
A catalogue record for this book is available from the British Library

Library of Congress Cataloging in Publication Data
The Routledge companion to film history / edited by William Guynn.
p. cm.
Includes bibliographical references and index.
1. Motion pictures—History. 2. Motion pictures—Dictionaries. I. Guynn, William Howard.
PN1994.R5735 2010
791.4309—dc22   2010014852

ISBN 13: 978–0–415–77656–1 (hbk)
ISBN 13: 978–0–415–77657–8 (pbk)
ISBN 13: 978–0–203–84153–2 (ebk)

CONTENTS

CONTRIBUTORS

Cynthia Baron teaches at Bowling Green State University. She is the co-author of *Reframing Screen Performance* and co-editor of *More Than a Method*, with essays in *Journal of Film and Video*, *Quarterly Review of Film and Video*, *Women Studies Quarterly*, *Food, Culture and Society*, and elsewhere.

Jay Beck is Assistant Professor of Cinema and Media Studies at Carleton College. He has co-edited *Lowering the Boom: Critical Studies in Film Sound* with Tony Grajeda, and *Contemporary Spanish Cinema and Genre* with Vicente Rodríguez Ortega.

David Desser is Emeritus Professor of Cinema Studies and Comparative and World Literatures, University of Illinois. He is the author and editor of nine books, including *The Samurai Films of Akira Kurosawa, Eros Plus Massacre: An Introduction to the Japanese New Wave Cinema*, and *Ozu's "Tokyo Story."*

Wheeler Winston Dixon is the James Ryan Endowed Professor of Film Studies, Professor of English at the University of Nebraska, Lincoln, and, with Gwendolyn Audrey Foster, Editor-in-Chief of the *Quarterly Review of Film and Video*. His newest books include *Film Noir and the Cinema of Paranoia* and *A Short History of Film*, written with Gwendolyn Audrey Foster.

Robin Griffiths is Course Leader and Senior Lecturer in Film Studies at the University of Gloucestershire, UK. He is editor of *British Queer Cinema* (Routledge, 2006) and *Queer Cinema in Europe* (2008), and author of *Cinema and Sexuality* (forthcoming).

William Guynn is Emeritus Professor of Art (Cinema) at Sonoma State University (California). His work on the theory of nonfiction film appears in *A Cinema of Nonfiction* (1990) and *Writing History in Film* (Routledge, 2006), and as chapters in collaborative books and in translation.

Erkki Huhtamo is Professor of Media History and Theory at UCLA, Department of Design | Media Arts. He holds a Ph.D. degree in Cultural History. His new book, *Illusions in Motion: An Archaeology of the Moving Panorama*, is forthcoming.

Norman M. Klein is a professor at the California Institute of the Arts. Among his books are *Seven Minutes* (on animation); *The History of Forgetting* (on urban erasure); *The Vatican to Vegas* (on special effects environments); and *The Imaginary 20th Century*.

Marcia Landy is Distinguished Professor of English/Film Studies at the University of Pittsburgh. Her books include *Cinematic Uses of the Past, Italian Cinema, The Historical Film: History and Memory in Media*; *Monty Python's Flying Circus*; *Stardom, Italian Style*, and *Screen Performance and Personality in Italian Cinema*.

Hilary Radner holds the Foundation Chair of Film and Media Studies at the University of Otago, New Zealand. Her publications include *Shopping Around: Feminine Culture and the Pursuit of Pleasure* (1995) and, as co-editor, *Film Theory Goes to the Movie*s (1993), *Constructing the New Consumer Society* (1997), *Swinging Single: Representing Sexuality in the 1960s* (1999), and *Jane Campion: Cinema, Nation, Identity* (2009).

Charlene Regester is Assistant Professor of African and Afro-American Studies, University of North Carolina, Chapel Hill. She has contributed essays to the *Encyclopedia of African Americans and Popular Culture* (2008) and *Thomas Dixon and the Making of Modern America* (2005), among other publications.

Rosemarie Scullion is Associate Professor of French, Gender Studies and Film Studies at the University of Iowa. She has written on political cinema in several national and historical contexts and is currently writing a book on film censorship in France during the Cold War.

Brian Winston is the Lincoln Professor of Communications, University of Lincoln, UK. He has been involved in documentary production since 1963, winning an Emmy in 1985 for documentary scriptwriting. Among his extensive writing on documentary is *Claiming the Real II: Documentary: Grierson and Beyond* (2008).

Prakash Younger is Assistant Professor of Film Studies in the Department of English at Trinity College. He has published articles on André Bazin and Jean Renoir (*Offscreen*), *The Harder They Come* (*Social Text*), and the reception of MTV India (*Frontiers*; reprinted in *Television: The Critical View*, seventh edition).

Part II A critical dictionary: history, theory, technique

Cynthia Baron [CB]
Jay Beck [JB]
David Dresser [DD]
Robin Griffiths [RG]
William Guynn [WG]
Erkki Huhtamo [EH]
Norman M. Klein [NMK]

Marcia Landy [ML]
Hilary Radner [HR]
Charlene Regester [CR]
Rosemarie Scullion [RS]
Brian Winston [BW]
Prakash Younger [PY]

EDITOR'S INTRODUCTION

AN ANALYTIC APPROACH TO FILM HISTORY

The Routledge Companion to Film History is designed as a basic text for under-graduate students in film studies. It may serve either as a primary text in introductory or more advanced undergraduate film history courses or as an ancillary text that complements and enriches traditional textbooks in film history. It provides a substan-tial and readable overview of the field that is accessible to students in the early stages of their studies and will continue to serve them as a valuable tool of reference throughout their undergraduate careers.

The *Companion* is not intended to substitute for film histories that cover the field chronologically in long narrative accounts. Narrative histories are essential texts in film studies, but they tend, in our view, to overwhelm the beginning student because they need to be chronologically comprehensive while attempt-ing to describe and explain movements, periods, aesthetic history, individual styles, modes of production, industrial history, and so forth. Whence their fre-quently daunting length. What is often sacrificed in the student's experience is a deeper understanding of historical complexity and a meaningful encounter with film texts. In our view, students in film history courses should not passively acquire knowledge of the development of the medium. They should be actively involved in investigating the history of the medium and in developing the critical and analytic skills that are the foundation of creative research. This volume attempts to provide the tools that will make such an approach possible.

We are aiming, therefore, not so much for historical comprehensiveness as for depth of historical analysis. To this end, the *Companion* recognizes the diversity of approaches to film studies that has always characterized the field. Therefore we are against orthodoxy—for example, the attempt to reform film history according to traditional art historical methods—and prefer to remain open to all modes of inquiry. We embrace the innovative methods of interdisciplinary and new historical work, but we also advocate for the theoretical and philosophical approaches that have dis-tinguished film studies since its inception. We hope to demonstrate the relevance of all these approaches to the study of film history.

THE STRUCTURE AND SCOPE OF THIS VOLUME

As you will discover, *The Routledge Companion to Film History* is divided into two nearly equal halves. In the first half, the student is introduced to film history through a series of essays on themes crucial to the understanding of the discipline. The essays are both theoretical and historical in their approach: they address topics in their generality; demonstrate their importance in describing and explaining historical developments; offer the foundation for historical analyses focused on specific moments and film texts; and provide a short set of references for students who want to explore the topic in more depth. The essays cover the cultural history of the moving image, the stages of the production processes, the evolution of sound, the status of film as art and popular culture, the alternative practices of experimental, documentary, and animation cinemas, the concept of cultural difference, and the relationship between film and historical events and situations.

The critical dictionary explains unfamiliar concepts, summarizes significant philosophical and theoretical debates, defines technical terms, identifies major periods and movements and emerging fields, and briefly evokes historical events that have had a major impact on the cinema. It supports the essays by clarifying terms and, in general, facilitating the student's reading. Moreover, the dictionary functions as an active system in which the student is encouraged to develop a train of thought through references the entries give to other entries in the dictionary, to the essays, and to other basic works of scholarship. We decided to present even quite sophisticated concepts in simple language so that the dictionary entries would continue to be useful as students progress into more advanced studies. The dictionary is of course a selection. Given the scope and approach of this short introductory volume, we could not be exhaustive. Thus, while acknowledging that we were excluding much that is important to the study of film history, we have chosen what we think are essential concepts or terms that students need to make a part of their critical vocabulary.

Taken together, the two halves of the *Routledge Companion* provide the student with theoretical and historical perspectives and the tools of analysis for understanding:

- how and why the medium (its forms, styles, and techniques) has changed over time;
- how historical periods of film production can be defined;
- how films relate to social history and the culture within which they are produced;
- how different modes of production and distribution have been organized and for what purposes;
- how the practice of filmmaking can be described in different periods and cultures, and under different modes of production; and
- how the spectator's experience and the conditions of reception have evolved over time.

We hope instructors will find *The Routledge Companion to Film History* a flexible instrument for curriculum design and that its open structure will encourage them to develop units of study that are at once historically specific and centered on readings of film texts.

How to use this volume

The essays and the critical dictionary are intended to interact with each other. Thus in the process of reading an essay, the reader's itinerary is shaped by the system of cross-references the essays contain. Terms or topics that appear in bold type in the essays refer to entries in the critical dictionary. For example, the essay on "Film as art" discusses the notion of **aesthetics**, which appears in **bold** in the text indicating that the reader will find a definition of the term in the critical dictionary. Within the entry on aesthetics there are also terms in bold— **auteurism** and **formalism/neoformalism**, for example—referring to other entries that discuss the aesthetic character of specific critical and filmmaking practices. (Please note that the term in bold may be a cognate of the actual entry title: **auteurism** and **auteurist**, for example, refer to the entry titled **auteur**.) Many of the entries in the dictionary refer the reader back to the essay where the term appears and may be discussed in more depth. Others present concepts which are not discussed elsewhere in the volume but were judged important enough to include on their own, often in the form of brief essays. At the end of each major essay and most dictionary entries, students will find a short list of suggested readings intended to guide them in beginning to research a topic.

The way the volume is organized is not intended to impose an order of reading. Students may begin with any one of the essays, increasing their knowledge of the topic by following the system of cross-references and suggested readings. The critical dictionary may be used as a resource for understanding terms and notions encountered elsewhere, but it is also conducive to intelligent browsing. We are hopeful that this less linear and more analytical approach to film history will stimulate curiosity and independent thinking in our students while providing them with a solid foundation in film history.

Part I

FILM HISTORY: A THEMATIC APPROACH

1

NATURAL MAGIC

A short cultural history of moving images

ERKKI HUHTAMO

It was not a very long time ago that the history of moving images was considered to go back barely a 100 years. Their hundredth anniversary was celebrated either in 1994 or 1995. The former year was chosen in the United States, using the public introduction of the Edison Company's *Kinetoscope* in 1894 as the landmark, while in France, the latter year was selected to commemorate Louis and Auguste Lumière's first public screenings of films both shot and projected with their *Cinématographe* in 1895. As it often happens in the history of inventions, other candidates to the title of inventor of moving images were also suggested and the dates were adjusted along national, cultural, or technological lines. Yet whoever the "true inventor" may have been, the dates varied only slightly. The 1890s were, it was generally agreed, the period that gave birth to moving images.

There were a few voices that did not join the chorus. In 1995–6, Laurent Mannoni curated in Paris an exhibition carrying the provocative title *Trois siècles de cinéma de la lanterne magique au Cinématographe* ("Three centuries of cinema from the magic lantern to the Cinématographe"). It highlighted **magic lanterns**, **peepshows**, and other pre-twentieth-century devices from the fabulous collections of the French Cinématheque. Mannoni's aim was to present an "archaeology of cinema," emphasizing that its "long history is complex, full of surprises, mysteries, and extraordinary findings" (Mannoni, 1995, p. 13). In 2009 he went even further by organizing another exhibition with Donata Pesenti Campagnoni from the Turin Film Museum. Titled *Lanterne magique et film peint: 400 ans de cinéma* ("Magic lantern and painted film: 400 years of cinema"), it focused on magic lantern slides and extended the history of moving images by yet another 100 years (Mannoni and Campagnoni, 2009).

The celebration of the hundredth anniversary of moving images has begun to feel more and more spurious. Since then, there has been a flurry of books and articles that have not only questioned and gone beyond prevailing ideas about moving images but also pointed out links with other media forms and hitherto neglected cultural contexts within which they developed.[1] The emerging picture is very different from the one routinely found in cinema histories of just a few decades ago. The developments that preceded the appearance of the Kinetoscope and the Cinématographe used to be lumped together under the title "pre-cinema" and briefly presented as a succession of steps leading to the climax: the classical cinema, epitomized by narrative feature film, movie palaces, the star cult, and the Hollywood dream factory.

The recent shift of emphasis reflects fundamental changes within audiovisual culture itself. Cinema is no longer its uncontested fulcrum. A multitude of other media forms, channels of distribution, and modes of presentation have emerged that vie for attention. Labeling all the developments that took place before the emergence of cinema as pre-cinema has begun to feel unjustified, not the least because early forms considered so far as "primitives" of the cinema are now seen to have contained seeds of very different media forms than the ones generally projected via cinema. If the dominance of the cinema was really just a stage in a much longer and broader trend, it is time to rethink the history of moving images. In his preface to a massive collection of sources bearing a problematic title, *A History of Pre-Cinema* (2000), Stephen Herbert stated the challenges ahead with admirable clarity:

> Perhaps the most useful way to look at these problems is to recognize that cinema is just one of the many time-based visual media that have existed over a number of centuries. Because it is so familiar to us, we naturally relate the previous time-based media to it, and these recognizable similarities can, to some extent, help us to understand those media. But new time-based media continue to be invented and developed, and since cinema is no longer the dominant form of time-based media—television, video, computer games and the internet have overtaken it to a large extent—we can no longer expect to consider all of the earlier media as precursors of cinema alone.
>
> (Herbert, 2000, vol. 1, p. xii)[2]

What is the "shape" of the history of moving images? What are its ingredients, and how have they been related with each other and to other developments? In what kinds of cultural conditions have moving images developed, flourished, and perished? It is impossible to provide conclusive answers in a short introduction, but guidelines can be laid out. Above all, one should avoid considering the history of moving images as a single linear development. There are multiple trajectories that don't necessarily run neatly side by side; they often intermingle in confusing and unpredictable ways. Motives and ideas disappear and reappear again. Dead-ends occur, but outlets are found, too, perhaps decades, or even centuries, later. Media hybrids are repeatedly formed and dissolved. Tracing the paths of moving images across centuries is a fascinating adventure without closure.

THE CONTINUING SPELL OF NATURAL MAGIC

Ancient cave paintings depicting animals with more than four legs have been proposed as the earliest representations of living beings in motion. Likewise,

4

references to optical phenomena scattered in ancient texts have been considered as primitives of moving pictures. Aristotle, and, centuries later, medieval savants, like Roger Bacon, and the eleventh-century Arab scientist, Ibn Al-Hazen [Alhazen], are said to have known the principle of the camera obscura. Empedocles developed a theory of vision and perception, anticipating the nineteenth-century theorizing on "afterimage" (see Zielinski, 2006, pp. 47–50), and the ancient Chinese developed an optical science of their own, discussing, among other things, the idea of the camera obscura (see Needham, 1954–2004, vol. 4, p. 98).

For millennia, knowledge about optical phenomena existed, but had little impact on the lives of ordinary people. It was limited to theoretical discussions and observations by savants. Apparitions and perceptual illusions (later often linked with optics) were evoked but more often in relation to mythology, religion, folklore, and poetry, rather than communication, science, and technology. Why it took so long for a more widespread desire for practical visual media to develop—in spite of the fact that some applications would have been easy to realize—is a complex question that cannot be answered here. What is clear is that it was only during the transition from the Middle Ages to the early modern era in Europe that optical media began to gain more prominent roles in people's lives.

The decisive developments extended from "natural magic," an intellectual current prevalent among the Jesuits, to the early modern experimental science represented by figures like Galileo Galilei, Johannes Kepler, and Christiaan Huygens. For the Jesuits, practicing natural magic was a way of investigating and explaining the God-created universe. An important part of natural magic was "artificial magic," the use of human-made contraptions to demonstrate phenomena found in nature. Applied by polymaths like Giambattista della Porta and Athanasius Kircher, such demonstrations often tended to slip into pseudoscientific showmanship, where explanations of rational causes were overshadowed by a desire to impress, mystify, and exercise power. The Jesuits also exported marvels of Western science into other parts of the world as part of an effort to gain political supremacy and ideological dominion.

The repertoire of objects displayed by the Jesuits included optical devices, among them mirrors inside "catoptric theaters" (endless reflection cabinets), peepshow boxes, **camera obscuras**, and magic lanterns. All of them had by no means been invented by Jesuits. The origins of the magic lantern, for example, point in the direction of the Dutch savant Christiaan Huygens, one of the beacons of the emerging experimental science. Huygens's knowledge of optics, as well as his mastery of the art of lens grinding, allowed him to project hand-painted glass slides already around 1659—a device he had constructed himself (Mannoni, 2000, pp. 38–9). Lens grinding was also a precondition, although not the primary cause, of the invention of the telescope and the microscope. These devices played tangential roles in media culture but had a momentous influence on human understanding, extending its reach into macroscopic and microscopic dimensions.

Optical instruments became an indispensable feature of the "cabinets of physics" amassed by savants. However, attitudes toward them were not uniform, which reflected the raging scientific and ideological debates of the time. Concerned about its potentially ruinous impact on his career, Huygens disavowed his association with the magic lantern (which he may have invented), allowing unscrupulous experimenters like the Danish mathematician Thomas Walgenstein and Kircher himself to popularize it across Europe. Huygens feared the magic lantern would associate his name with the kind of charlatanism that natural magic represented for him. His fears were justified, because the magic lantern did not remain a privilege of the learned for long. Already by 1700 it had been introduced to common people by touring showmen, who used it for colorful, coarse, and sensationalist amusement (Rossell, 2008).

The influence of natural magic has been felt in an enormous number of popular "how to" handbooks, courses, and demonstrations up to the present day. The Scottish scientist Sir David Brewster still used the concept in his popular *Letters on Natural Magic* (1832), an easy-reading manual that covered, among other things, optical devices like the magic lantern and the camera obscura. By that time the impulses of natural magic had been merged with the discoveries of Newtonian experimental science. The spirit of natural magic appears whenever new media technology is introduced, be it the widescreen Cinerama in the 1950s, or Apple's iPhone or Nintendo's Wii today. Ads laud the awe-inspiring, near-uncanny quality of such "breakthroughs" but ultimately attribute it to human ingenuity. Special effect films and the fan cultures surrounding them are another example of the continuing appeal of natural magic.

Interestingly, there are aspects of media culture that purport to retreat back to the occult. In the eighteenth century, magic lanterns were not only used to provide "rational entertainment" but also to create horror in séances of necromancy. In phantasmagoria, a form of the magic lantern show that became popular in the late eighteenth century, "fantascope" projectors were hidden behind the screen to invoke ghosts whose identity was left deliberately ambiguous (Heard, 2006). Audience members may have resorted to a "willing suspension of disbelief," but this did not fully dissipate the uncanny aura surrounding the spectacle. A similar uncertainty prevailed in the nineteenth-century debate about spirit photography. Belief in occult interventions has persisted in later media contexts as well (see Sconce, 2000).

VARIETIES OF MOVING IMAGES

The misconceptions behind the hundredth-anniversary celebration of moving pictures were partly based on the idea that images started moving only when celluloid film became available. The introduction and quick adoption of film by industrial experimenters like Edison and Lumière helped to create the false impression that all preceding visual forms had been static, little different from the 35-mm holiday slides projected in countless twentieth-century living rooms with the slide projector (a descendant of the magic lantern). Early cinema rarely referred to media cultural forms that had anticipated it, contributing to the impression of a sudden technological and cultural rupture. This coincided with the idea of a sharp break between the Victorian and the modern society, extolled in its most extreme form by the manifestoes of the Italian **Futurists** calling for the destruction of past culture and the erection of a new one amidst its smoldering ruins.

However, the moving images made possible by running exposed reels of celluloid film through a film projector represent just one possible form among many. Ever since their origins in the mid-seventeenth century, lantern slides had been made to move. The first existing piece of evidence about magic lantern slides, a sketch by Huygens depicting a "dance of the death" motive, a skeleton removing and replacing its skull, is already animated (Mannoni, 2000, p. 39). Many types of animated lantern slides were described in handbooks of optics as early as the early eighteenth century. The tricks included brass levers, rotating rackwork mechanisms, and superimposed sliding glass plates. In the nineteenth century, the selection of effects was enriched by chromatropes (abstract kaleidoscopic rackwork slides), moving astronomical diagrams, and other innovations. From around 1870 onward, slides known as the "Beale Choreutoscope" and the "Ross Wheel of Life" could even be used to produce continuous moving images by means of shutter blades rotating in front of a few sequential views—directly anticipating mechanisms used in moving picture projectors of the celluloid film era.

Even when lantern slides did not contain actual movable elements, they were animated by the projectionist. Pushing a long slide of a wide landscape or many painted figures through the slide stage of the magic lantern could create an impression of a moving procession or sweeping panoramic gaze. The optician Philip Carpenter suggested in the 1820s that a small magic lantern could be attached to the projectionist's belt; by moving behind the screen, the projectionist could make the figures "come alive" (see facsimile in Mannoni, Campagnoni, and Robinson, 1995). After their introduction in the 1820s–30s, the "dissolving views" made smooth transitions from day to night possible. Such effects were realized by a pair of identical magic lanterns provided with a mechanical shutter that revealed and blocked their lens tubes in turn. Two slides with identical views but depicting different times of the day could be made to dissolve into each other. Later, such effects would be made even more impressive by a biunial, a magic lantern with two optical tubes and adjustable oxy-hydrogen gas jets as illuminants.

Magic lantern slides were not the only type of imagery that provided sensations of movement or passing time; such effects were also realized with the peepshow box—another popular optical device that seems to have had its origins in the world of natural magic. Peepshow boxes were exhibited by itinerant showmen already in the eighteenth century. Changing the direction and amount of light falling on the translucent perspective views placed inside the box (by opening and closing panels on the sides of the box) caused atmospheric transitions: the day could be seen to turn into the night. The camera obscura also contributed to the culture of moving images. It is often considered just as a pre-form of the photo-graphic camera and, therefore, associated with still images. However, one should not forget that the scenes transmitted by the rays of light entering a darkened room or box through a pinhole are actually in motion. This fact was appreciated by early commentators such as della Porta who described in his *Magia naturalis* (1589 edition) how a room-sized camera obscura could be used for spectacles staged outside in real time. His stupefied friends did not believe that the spectacle they had witnessed inside the dark chamber had been produced by natural causes until della Porta opened the panels and "demonstrated them the artifice" (see facsimile in Mannoni, Campagnoni, and Robinson, 1995, p. 51).

There were many types of optical illusions capable of effecting transformations in images when perceived by an observer. Distorted anamorphic images could be rectified by viewing them from a curved mirror or slanted angle. Experiments were also made by spinning glowing sticks in the dark and observing the momen-tary traces they left behind. When scientists began exploring the physiology of vision in the early nineteenth century, they could build on earlier visual forms and experiments. Scholars like Peter Mark Roget, Michael Faraday, Charles Wheatstone, and Joseph Plateau became interested in the afterimage or "persistence of vision," the idea that a time-lag existed between a visual phenomenon and its perception by a human (see Crary, 1989). They created devices to study and demonstrate this phenomenon that was initially attributed to the slow response time of the human eye rather than to the operating principles of the nervous system.

Although devices such as the thaumatrope, anorthoscope, stereoscope, phen-akistiscope, and zoetrope were introduced as scientific instruments, they were commercialized and marketed as fashionable philosophical toys. All were based on the same phenomenon, but their effects were different. Thaumatrope and anorthoscope used spinning disks to create illusions of static images, while stereoscope produced an impression of a deep three-dimensional space. In spite of their seemingly different configurations (picture disks vs. animation strips placed within a rotating drum), both phenakistiscope and zoetrope used sequences of images in motion viewed through a series of slots functioning as a "shutter." When the image impulses were received at a certain rate, the observer began to experience them as a continuous, cyclically repeated image in motion. Later inventions such as the flipbook (John Barnes Linnett, 1868) and the Praxinoscope (Émile Reynaud, 1877) refined their effects but did not fundamen-tally change them, except for the fact that the flipbook's animations offered a linear miniature narrative sequence in place of a repeating cycle of images.

An important intermediary stage between the invention of these devices and the cinema was chronophotography, an international phenomenon that emerged in the 1870s. Although the motives behind its explorations varied (from scientific and ideological to commercial and aesthetic), the basic occupation of chronophotography was the production of sequential photographs of humans and animals in motion. By means of instantaneous photography, movements were frozen and transformed into a series of photographic still images. Eadweard Muybridge, Étienne-Jules Marey, Ottomar Anschütz, and others focused their attention more on stopping and analyzing motion than on reconstructing it. However, the sequences of photographs they created were also reanimated with zoetropes or, in Muybridge's case, shown in public with a Zoöpraxiscope, an adapted magic lantern that projected phenakistiscope-like glass disks based on the photographic sequences he had produced (see Herbert, 2004, pp. 97–100).

The importance of devices like the phenakistiscope and the zoetrope in the history of cinema has been universally acknowledged. However, such devices are generally considered primitive because they were only capable of presenting short looped sequences of hand-drawn images. The cinema's success, it has been stated, was based on linear sequences of photographed (or cinematographed) moving pictures, made possible by celluloid film. However, it could be argued that short repeated animation sequences do not necessarily make a device primitive—they represent a different mode or "series" of moving images (see Gaudreault, 2006, pp. 227–44). Cyclical animation loops have been revived numerous times, for example, by techno-videojockeys and creators of tiny Flash-animations for web pages, as well as by artists like the Japanese Toshio Iwai, for whom phenakistiscopes, zoetropes, and other early devices have provided models for questioning and rethinking the history of moving images.

THE FOUR PRACTICES

The history of moving images unfolds around a set of practices that not only provide access to moving images but also condition their reception and interpretation. These practices are connected with the notion of the **apparatus**, which is understood here as a configuration of technological, psychological, and cultural-ideological conditions for the moving image experience. The cinema theater, for example, is an apparatus consisting of elements like the auditorium with its rows of seats, the screen, projectors and their light beams, and so on. As a material-mental "viewing machine" the apparatus imposes predetermined conditions upon the viewer. Early psychoanalytically oriented apparatus theory thought that there was no way of avoiding or countering their effects; they constituted a mental straitjacket that conditioned the identity formation of the spectator (see de Lauretis and Heath, 1980). Nowadays, it is more commonly suggested that the cinematic experience is based on negotiation between the givens of the viewing situation (including, of course, the moving images themselves) and the viewer who uses learned and inherited codes to reach his or her stance (Sturken and Cartwright, 2001, ch. 2).

It could be claimed that there are four basic practices that have manifested themselves in the course of the history of moving images: "**screen practice**," "**peep practice**", "touch practice", and "mobile practice". These are not absolutely separate; rather, they often coexist and influence each other. The culture of moving images evolves through their interactions and mergers. The earliest and geograph- ically most widely distributed may well have been screen practice. The notion of screen practice was first suggested by the silent-film scholar Charles Musser in an effort to point out links between silent-film exhibition practices and the preceding tradition of magic-lantern projections (see Musser, 1994, ch. 1). However, the idea could also be applied in a much broader sense to the enormously rich realm of visual storytelling (for the best general account, see Mair, 1988).

The shadow theater has been a particularly prevalent form of visual storytell- ing in Asian cultures from ancient times. Whether performed for religious, social, political, or cultural purposes, its manifestations use moving shadows and light to visualize stories on a screen. No matter how primitive it may now seem, it does use an apparatus to communicate representations to an audience. Western forms of visual storytelling such as *Bänkelsang* ("bench-singing") and the mov- ing panorama could also be considered screen practices. The former was per- formed by modest, itinerant, show people singing broadside ballads while pointing at series of pictures. The latter was an elaborate public performance of large and long rolls of paintings accompanied by a lecture, music, and sound effects (see Huhtamo, forthcoming); although moving panorama did not, strictly speaking, use a "screen," the moving paintings were experienced through a pro- scenium arch-like frame. The configuration of the apparatus likened it to the magic lantern show, its chief rival in the late nineteenth century.

One of the most basic characteristics of screen practice is the distance separat- ing the screen from the viewers, who remain motionless during the performance. This distance is—partly—abolished in peep practice, which refers to visual experiences gained by peeping at hidden images. These images are often accessed through peeping holes on the side of a dedicated box-like device. Countless variations have been produced, including showboxes of all kinds, anamorphic images, seductive objects containing hidden pictures, kaleido- scopes, stereoscopes, phenakistiscopes, zoetropes, Mutoscopes, Kinoras, View Master 3D viewers, and so on. What distinguishes these from the apparata encountered in screen practices is the more intimate nature of the experience. Images are peeped at by a single viewer, at a time, or, at most, by a small group (often taking turns). Some forms of "peep media" are personal handheld devices, while others are public viewing machines transported from place to place. Yet others are installed in permanent locations such as amusement arcades.

Trajectories of peep practice have run side by side with screen practices for centuries (see Huhtamo, 2006a, pp. 74–155). Both were already part of the world of natural magic. It is not surprising to discover that the earliest film pio- neers also pondered which one to choose. Edison's Kinetoscope was meant just for one viewer at a time, peeking into an eyepiece on the top of its oak viewing box. As novel as this device may have seemed for the contemporaries, it joined the long trajectory of peep practices, while the Lumière brothers projected their films for a seated audience from the beginning. In the short term, screen practice was the undisputed winner—even Edison soon abandoned the peepshow

Kinetoscope and launched a Projecting Kinetoscope (a combined film and lantern slide projector) instead. With the cinema theater as its focus, projection came to dominate commercial film exhibition—and, consequently, the culture of moving images—for decades. Eventually, however, peep practices began questioning its hegemony. The TV set is a kind of peepshow box, though not purely so; in the era of large, flat, wall-mounted displays, it seems to have moved closer to the realm of living-room screen practices. Yet peeping at even smaller moving images has become commonplace in the era of the internet, multimedia mobile phones, and pocket game consoles.

"Touch practices" sometimes overlap with peep practices. However, in the latter case the link with the media remains ocular—the images are inside a device and often behind a glass lens as well. They are accessed by the eyes only. Touch practice introduces a tactile relationship to the media machine which transforms the viewer into an "interactor" (see Huhtamo, 2006b). Within touch practices moving images are controlled, manipulated, and also created by the user. The camera obscura was already an apparatus supporting touch practice. In room-size camera obscuras, the view from the outside is normally projected (via a lens-and-mirror combination at the top) on a horizontal "table." Its strange, silent, nearness, and hand-level position invites viewers to touch the moving figures. Portable box camera obscuras turned this gesture into a productive act: armed with a pencil, the hand of the user could sketch the view on paper. Even after photography made its breakthrough in 1839, camera obscuras were still used as intimate and tactile sketching tools by artists.

Persistence of vision devices such as the phenakistiscope and the zoetrope can also be linked with touch practice. While peeping through slots is a prerequisite for perceiving the images in motion, the user operates the device by hand—speeding it up, slowing it down, and choosing the visual "software" (that can even be produced by the user). These features associate such seemingly primitive devices with personal interactive media such as personal computers, game consoles, and multimedia phones. Contrary to what is often claimed, interactive media does not constitute an absolute rupture with earlier media forms—its coming had been anticipated by touch practices for centuries. The hand-cranked cast-iron Mutoscope (1897) placed on an amusement pier may seem very different from a twenty-first-century Blu-Ray player or iPhone, but its operational principle links it with the same lineage, as the rich cultural imaginary surrounding it also testifies (see examples in Bottomore, 1995). Touch practices seem to be turning increasingly mobile—we often use media devices like mobile phones while we are in motion, walking, or driving.

"The mobile practice" refers to situations where the observer him or herself is in physical motion. The mobility of the observer became a precondition of the media experience at the circular wrap-around panoramas that were introduced in the late eighteenth century (Oettermann, 1997). The panorama medium was invented and patented by the Irish-born landscape painter Robert Barker in 1787. To be fully able to experience the gigantic 360-degree painting that surrounded them, the spectators had to walk around the viewing platform. The idea of mobile spectatorship had already been raised by Chinese and Japanese landscape gardens that can be considered highly artificial and coded "media texts." As the visitor moves from place to place along either predefined or individually chosen paths, she or he encounters "pictures" and even sound environments that have been designed by the garden architect and often refer to other landscapes, history, poetry, and visual arts.

In her *Window Shopping* Anne Friedberg argued that in the evolution of media culture the physical mobility of the observer was increasingly replaced by virtual mobility on the screen (Friedberg, 1993). As further evidence, one could refer to the experience of playing computer games like *Grand Theft Auto*, where the player navigates inside a simulated city. However, one could also argue that mobile practices flourish in phenomena such as theme-park attractions, media art installations, and all kinds of everyday practices that evoke media spectatorship. In audiovisual theme-park "rides" like Douglas Trumbull's *Back to the Future—the Ride* at Universal Studios, the spectators are placed in simulated vehicles and are violently jolted physically, their bodily motions synchronized to events on the screen. Media art installations often require exhibition visitors to walk around the space to be able to experience the interplay of their elements.

In the context of everyday life, walking the city streets is a mobile multimedia experience where giant screens, recorded sounds, and one's own mobile phone compete for the "flaneur's" attention. Instead of walking, the subject may be traveling through "non-places" (Augé, 1995) on a moving walkway, escalator, or elevator. At the Paris Universal Exposition of 1900 a *trottoir roulant* transported visitors through the exhibition grounds, turning the city itself into a panoramic attraction. Scenes seen through the windshield of a car or from the window of a moving train have also been compared with media experiences (Morse, 1998; Schivelbusch, 1986). Such mobile practices may be smoothly transformed into screen practices. This happens at the drive-in theater, where the car is stopped and turned into an "auditorium." The film is viewed through a kind of double frame: it is surrounded by the edge of the giant screen as well as by the frame of the windshield (Friedberg, 2002).

INSTITUTIONS AND MOVING IMAGES

In the realm of classical cinema the system of institutions dedicated to **producing, distributing, and exhibiting** moving images was—in spite of its internal complexity—relatively easy to grasp (see Gomery, 1986). The issue became much more complex with the advent of radio and television broadcasting; battles were fought and complex institutional liaisons were forged between the film industry and the newcomers, eventually leading to the formation of giant industrial conglomerations operating across media platforms and attempting to market cross-over products through different channels. Media convergence became a buzzword for this development. Moving pictures were no longer presented solely in cinemas or television broadcasts; they could be purchased as digital disks or downloaded as files from the internet to be viewed with a personal computer or an iPhone. Spin-off products like video games were also created and marketed as parts of global branded franchises.

If we look at the culture of moving images from an extended historical perspective, we notice that no institutional model has been absolutely dominant. Early visual media like the magic lantern were not initially exhibited in any single context. Magic lanterns were not only used for scientific and educational purposes but were also exhibited by itinerant showmen. The same applied to peep media—already in the eighteenth century peepshow boxes were used in diverse social sites from market squares and popular fairs to the homes of the nobility. The public exhibition culture remained nomadic, partly because of the scarcity of media devices and their "software." Because no distribution or rental networks existed for lantern slides or perspective prints (*vue d'optique*) used in peepshow boxes, traveling showmen were unable to renew their offerings very often. This made them seek ever-new audiences, joining the age-old world of itinerant merchants, knife-grinders, and other journeymen.

In the nineteenth century itinerant visual media remained a cultural force, reinvigorated by more sophisticated magic lantern shows and moving panoramas that reached audiences in both urban and rural areas. However, in the late eighteenth century permanent media institutions had begun to appear in great cities like Paris and London. Étienne-Gaspard Robertson's Fantasmagorie, Robert Barker's **Panorama**, Abbé Gazzera's Cosmorama, and Daguerre and Bouton's Diorama all became influential exhibition institutions, inspiring others elsewhere. The success of these enterprises encouraged the creation of simplified "roadshow" versions as well. The formula behind Fantasmagorie was adapted from the offerings of touring magic lantern showmen and necromancers. The Panorama presented huge circular paintings that did not move but challenged others to compensate for this lack. The Diorama drew inspiration from illusionistic stagecraft, while the moving panorama set the panoramic canvas in motion, adding the dimension of time. Cosmorama was an urbanized and refined version of itinerant peepshows and anticipated later institutions such as the Kaiser-Panorama and the Kinetoscope Parlor.

The evolution of these institutions was closely linked with social, cultural, and economic factors. The rise of commercial capitalism inspired financial speculation with media ventures. Urban growth created potential audiences for permanent attractions. Most of them were originally meant to appeal to members of the wealthy upper and middle classes. Gaining access to affordable public media attractions took much longer for people such as office and factory workers and immigrants who belonged to the lower social strata. However, the entrepreneurs who mounted magic lantern shows and moving panoramas began reaching out to them as well, realizing their commercial potential. Toward the end of the century, amusement piers, parks, and arcades began catering to large and mixed crowds, preparing the ground for the appearance of the cinema theater during the first years of the new century. Cinema came to be seen as a great equalizer, to the dismay of some commentators who saw its mixing effect as socially and politically dangerous.

Parallel with these developments, the home began to turn into a nexus for moving-image consumption earlier than is usually thought. Devices like peep-show boxes and zograscopes appeared in upper-class homes already in the eighteenth century, though it was also common to invite itinerant showmen to give indoor presentations for domestic audiences. The development of the middle-class home into a safe haven segregated from the outside world inspired family-oriented pastimes that included playing with optical toys and scaled-down versions of the magic lantern. Soon after 1850 the stereoscope made a massive breakthrough in Victorian homes, becoming the first true domestic media machine. It did not present moving images but prepared the ground for them as well. Very soon after celluloid film-based moving images made their break-through, small film projectors for home use appeared on the market, followed by other devices for the home, such as the Kinora, a hand-cranked peep viewer that used Mutoscope-like flip reels. Along parallel tracks, home phonographs and gramophones—and from the 1920s also the radio—appealed to the ear, prepar-ing the ground for an audiovisual synthesis—television.

The most interesting institutional development of the past decades may well be the abandonment of traditional institutions by consumers of moving images. Media machines have become portable and are used in what Marc Augé has called "non-places": spaces we cross as part of our daily lives but don't inhabit (see Augé, 1995; also Urry, 2007). Laptop computers and multimedia phones are used in airport lounges, supermarket cashier lines, streets, classrooms, even where their use has been officially forbidden. Media has become itinerant again but in ways that differ from the activities of the touring magic lanternists and peepshowmen of the past. From exhibition the focus has shifted to private communication. We may not send moving images files to each other constantly, but we often pass on tips about something interesting that has just appeared on YouTube—which we of course can view wherever we happen to be. Certainly, such developments don't represent the final stage, or "the end of history," of the culture of moving images. It is likely the near future will bring more parallel developments, mergers between traditions, and reconnections with the past.

NOTES

1   Among the most significant general works are Laurent Mannoni, *The Great Art of Light and Shadow: Archaeology of the Cinema*, trans. and ed. Richard Crangle, Exeter: University of Exeter Press, 2000, orig. French 1994; many articles by Tom Gunning; *Ich sehe was, was du nicht siehst! Die Sammlung Werner Nekes*, ed. Bodo von Dewitz and Werner Nekes, Göttingen and Köln: Steidl & Museum Ludwig, 2002; *Encyclopedia of the Magic Lantern*, ed. David Robinson, Stephen Herbert and Richard Crangle, London: The Magic Lantern Society, 2001; Deac Rossell, *Living Pictures: The Origins of the Movies*, Albany: State University of New York Press, 1998.

2   I developed a similar argument in my book and television series combination titled *Elävän kuvan arkeologia* ("Archaeology of the Moving Image"), produced for the Finnish Broadcasting Company, Helsinki: YLE, 1996.

FURTHER READING

Balzer, Richard (1998) *Peepshows: A Visual History*, New York: Harry N. Abrams.
A richly illustrated book about the history of peepshows.

Crary, Jonathan (1989) *Techniques of the Observer: On Vision and Modernity in the Nineteenth Century*, Cambridge, MA: MIT Press.
A controversial but essential exploration of the history of visual media in relation to philosophy and theory. Contains much information about the camera obscura and the persistence of vision theories and devices of the early nineteenth century.

Hammond, John (1981) *The Camera Obscura: A Chronicle*, Bristol: Adam Hilger.
Still the most extensive and reliable study about the history of the camera obscura.

Heard, Mervyn (2006) *Phantasmagoria: The Secret Life of the Magic Lantern*, Hastings: The Projection Box.
So far the most extensive book about the history of the phantasmagoria.

Hecht, Hermann (1993) *Pre-Cinema History: An Encyclopaedia and Annotated Bibliography of the Moving Image before 1896*, ed. Ann Hecht, London: Bowker-Saur with British Film Institute.
Huge collection of material and bibliographical data on many aspects of early visual media.

Herbert, Stephen (ed.) (2000) *A History of Pre-Cinema*, 3 vols., London: Routledge.
An essential collection of source material on the history of early visual media reproduced in facsimile, including a reprint (vol. 3) of Olive Cook's pioneering book *Movement in Two Dimensions* (1963).

Mannoni, Laurent (2000, orig. French 1994) *The Great Art of Light and Shadow: Archaeology of the Cinema*, trans. and ed. Richard Crangle, Exeter: University of Exeter Press.
The most extensive and best-researched "archaeology" of the moving image, entirely based on archival research.

Mannoni, Laurent, Campagnoni, Donata Pesenti, and Robinson, David (1995) *Light and Movement: Incunabula of the Motion Picture 1420–1896*, Gemona: La Cineteca del Friuli/ Le Giornate del Cinema Muto.
An extensive collection of hard-to-find source material on the history of moving images, reproduced in facsimile.

Oettermann, Stephan (1997) *The Panorama: History of a Mass Medium*, trans. Deborah Lucas Schneider, New York: Zone Books [orig. 1980].
The most extensive history of the panorama and related visual spectacles.

Robinson, David, Herbert, Stephen, and Crangle, Richard (eds.) (2001) *Encyclopedia of the Magic Lantern*, London: The Magic Lantern Society.
Essential collection of information on the history of the magic lantern.

Rossell, Deac (2008) *Laterna Magica—Magic Lantern*, vol. 1, Stuttgart: Füsslin Verlag.
Well-researched and detailed history of the magic lantern, based on extensive first-hand archival research from the origins to the early nineteenth century.

Sturken, Marita and Cartwright, Lisa (2001) *Practices of Looking: An Introduction to Visual Culture*, Oxford: Oxford University Press [new edition 2009].
Sophisticated introduction to visual culture, including its theory and analysis.

2

FILM AS POPULAR CULTURE

HILARY RADNER

Ars gratia artis, art for art's sake, is the motto of MGM, one of the major
Hollywood studios, yet from the beginning the business of cinema was to produce entertainment for a popular audience, at a price. The significant debates
surrounding film as a popular form, rather than an **art** form, revolve around a
number of questions: is cinema as an institution shaped largely by industrial
forces or by cultural forces? Does cinema give expression to a democratic vision
of the world—that is "popular," as in "of the people"? Or is cinema the purveyor
of an **ideology** imposed by the captains of industry that transforms the active
citizen into a passive cultural dupe, who then buys into a system of beliefs and
practices that are contrary to his or her own interests? There is no single answer
to this question. Depending on what dimension of cinema we examine, we may
come up with different assessments of cinema's role.

In terms of its history, we can define film in two different ways. First of
all, it is a medium involving the projection of images using a celluloid strip
that was initially developed in the last decade of the nineteenth century.
More importantly for the purposes of this chapter, cinema is a cultural,
social, and economic institution involving an ever-increasing range of new
technologies and viewing practices, many of which do not involve projection
at all.

Film's destiny as a cultural form was not apparent at its inception. Proto-
filmic forms were frequently used as parlor games. **Early cinema**, in its initial
incarnation, often referred to as "the cinema of attractions" by historians
(Gunning, 1995, p. 121), was treated as a novelty or curiosity, enjoying a status
not unlike that of the illusions produced by a theatrical magician. At first, films
were not shown in theaters but at fairgrounds and exhibitions. Later, particularly
with the development of storefront theaters or **nickelodeons**, they formed part
of longer programs that included a variety of materials. On one hand, film technology was (as it is today) quickly put to work in the service of science, in
particular with a view to understand the dynamics of human and animal motion;
on the other, the Lumière brothers, among the first to project films for a public
(to advertise their invention, the Cinématographe), developed what was basically a home movie system, with the camera doubling as a projector. Although
their camera/projector was too expensive for individual use, the Lumières recognized its commercial potential, and moved into film **production, distribution, and exhibition** (being careful to retain exclusive ownership of their
apparatus).

It is this commercial dimension that distinguishes popular cinema from other uses of technologies involving the visual image, such as home movies. While home movies, having been made possible by the advent of cheaper cameras, are certainly a "popular" form (in so far as they are made by ordinary people, reminiscent of folk culture), they are not mass-produced. Home movies are made for private, limited use rather than for a general public. In contrast, cinema as an industry (as opposed to the camera industry that served the amateur film market) was, and is, characterized by its investment in the presentation of a story or narrative as a public spectacle aimed at the largest possible audience. Its closest ancestors are the plays and novels of the nineteenth century—which perhaps explains the significant tradition of **adaptation** that characterizes cinematic narrative.

We do not know who first recognized the possibility of cinema as a public storytelling device—some say it was the French director Georges Méliès, whose charming short films owe as much to the conventions of the music-hall magician as to the novelist or the playwright. Certainly by 1904 (ten years after the Lumière brothers had their first public demonstration of the Cinématographe), film's narrative potential was well recognized, though it would take at least another five to ten years before it gained respectability on a par with the popular theaters of the day. By the mid-1920s, if not earlier, movies had ceased to be a curiosity having replaced theater, music hall, and variety shows as the dominant form of mass entertainment, with scenarios and scripts that developed new heroes and myths, drawing upon the past as a source of inspiration. Plays, novels, Biblical tales, and epic poems were all revisited in cinematic narratives.

What struck the great thinkers of the early twentieth century was not simply that movies were a popular art form but rather that they were part of a new kind of culture—what is now commonly referred to as "mass culture"—that is grounded in inventions like "the transoceanic cable, the linotype, the phonograph, the wireless, inexpensive photographic equipment" of which cinema "was the most spectacular" (Naremore and Brantlinger, 1991, p. 5). Some early film scholars and critics, such as Hugo Munsterberg (1863–1916) and Vachel Lindsay (1879–1931), saw these new technologies, cinema in particular, and the new mass literacy that accompanied them, as holding out the promise of an enlightened mass citizenship and an emancipated society. The majority, such as economists Karl Marx (1818–83) and his co-author Friedrich Engels (1820–95), followed by sociologist Thorstein Veblen (1857–1929), cultural critic and film theorist Siegfried Kracauer (1889–1966), philosophers Theodor W. Adorno (1903–69) and Max Horkheimer (1895–1973), as well as the great social historian G. M. Trevelyan (1876–1962), feared the effects of the culture industries on the larger population; the extreme left and the extreme right both expressed suspicion and disdain for the new leisure activities of the postindustrial era, deemed the result or even the cause of social and cultural decay. "[T]he culture industry theories of the Frankfurt Institute philosophers" (which included Adorno and Horkheimer) proved especially influential, underlining "both the difficulties and the desirability of a liberation from forms of oppression that liberals ordinarily do not acknowledge, including the nearly universal false consciousness which, they argue, is the main product of the mass media" (Brantlinger, 1983, p. 247). Frequently, this condemnation of contemporary culture, and the ideology that it disseminated, was accompanied by nostalgia for earlier cultural forms, such as folk culture.

Industrialized mass culture distinguishes itself from pre-industrial folk culture by the way it is produced and consumed. Folk culture is generated by traditions passed down from generation to generation, often informally (as in the case of household arts, e.g. embroidery) or through apprenticeship (in which a novice imitates a master). The folk art object is made by one person, or group of people, from start to finish, usually for her or his or the group's own use (as opposed to exchanging it for other things such as money). In the case of storytelling, for example, the teller learns the tales as a child, perhaps from his or her mother or perhaps as part of a religious training, but each time the story is told the teller will introduce variations that speak to his or her own concerns and also to those of the audience at a given moment. The role of audience and storyteller is not fixed; one evening's storyteller may be the next evening's audience. While the story draws upon traditional formulas and characters, each telling of the tale is unique, reflecting the individuals involved.

In contradistinction, mass culture, it is argued, is based not on tradition but on technological innovation that is motivated by the constant search for the new. It is associated with the advent of modernity (Hansen, 1999, pp. 59–77), with production and consumption developing as separate activities. In the case of movies, for example, the audience does not participate in any way in the making of the films they watch. Mass culture is mass-produced; works of art are no longer unique but rather can be reproduced indefinitely as a theoretically infinite number of copies without an "original." Two audiences separated by time and geography can watch the same film, with each film remaining an "original" production. Audiences may be inclined to adopt their own perspectives on a film; subtitles may be added or, even more commonly, different audiences may interact differently with the film, producing a different cinematic experience with each viewing. Nevertheless, the motive of making and distributing movies is profit, with the goal being to attract the largest possible audience. Movies may have other functions (which explains why audiences flock to see them), but in essence, as asserted by the US Supreme Court decision in the case of *Mutual Film Corporation* v. *Industrial Commission of Ohio*, 236 US 230 (1915), they are a business—neither religion nor art. As such, films are not protected under the US Constitution as free speech because their purpose is commercial. While this decision was overturned in 1952, the view that cinema was a fundamental part of the culture industries continued to influence public thought, in particular because movies themselves were mass-produced. They were copies without an original.

When we buy an original work of art we want to be assured that there are no others like it. When we watch a movie, we assume that it is as close as is possible to all other copies of that film, in contrast with traditional folk culture artifacts, which bear the mark of the individual maker, in spite of the fact that one object may resemble another. In mass culture, goods are neither unique, nor made by individuals. Mass culture presupposes a certain system of production requiring a capitally intensive assembly line process that employs a variety of specialized workers (known as division of labor). Such an arrangement can produce large quantities of virtually identical objects with a view to maximizing the profits of the factory owner. With the development of mass production, the cultural (as opposed to practical) function of objects inevitably underwent a transformation.

In the pre-industrial era, culture functioned largely in terms of class stratification and identity, being "designed to preserve an agrarian society by preventing social and geographical mobility" (Slater, 1997, p. 68). People holding different positions dressed differently and used different objects; these distinctions were prescribed and regulated by society in the form of sumptuary laws. With the rise of industrial society, wealth rather than "tradition, birth or breeding" came to confer legitimacy and power, transforming the nature of culture (Slater, 1997, p. 69). On one hand, with the development of consumerism, the folk were encouraged to improve their status through the acquisitions of various objects and clothing as well as through the pursuit of activities in which the ostentatious display of wealth was the norm. On the other, the elite sought to display their status through the acquisition of unique (and costly) objects, while the common folk were obliged to consume cheap, mass-produced objects that were identical to one another. Mass culture, then, as scholars like Adorno and Horkheimer have argued, was not an organic expression of the people, but rather a contrivance of the elite, designed to entrench and perpetuate class stratification in a context where change was economically desirable.

It would be a mistake to see this process as a simple linear progression; the shift from a popular folk culture to a popular mass culture took place in fits and starts. By the second decade of the twentieth century, however, the shift from home and individual to mass production was firmly entrenched in American culture (Ewen, 1977, p. 116). This new dependence on a wage economy, in which the individual's primary needs were met through purchases (rather than home production), was part of a general shift from an agrarian culture (which was often largely self-sufficient) to an urban culture, of which the rise of cinema was an integral part.

While the development of cinema was a product of modernity, the movie business also facilitated and profited from the new metropolitan society. To become economically viable, movies required large audiences, which the concentrated populations of the new industrial centers provided. They were also a response to the necessity of occupying the new urban masses whose shorter working weeks permitted (for, perhaps, the first time in history) unstructured leisure activities as part of the many attractions endemic to city life. Movies initially developed as a lower class form of entertainment directed at working-class men, gradually expanding to include their families before finally reaching the more discerning (and more affluent) middle classes.

As a business, however, movies were motivated to expand their audiences by producing more and more ambitious and expensive productions with a view to ever-increasing profits. Film companies were not alone in seeking to develop their business. Theater owners, for example, were keen to provide surroundings and ameni-ties (culminating in the creation of movie palaces) that would allow them to charge higher admission prices and sell further spin-off products, such as elaborate souvenir programs for special events. From the very beginning, movies were a cultural form that depended on knowledge of demographics for its survival—that is to say, on the producer's ability to target certain groups with common tastes in order to create the broader paying audiences necessary to cinema's survival and expansion. While the second two decades of the twentieth century saw the cinema industry seeking to appeal to the affluent middle and upper middle classes with new, flashier movie palaces, and longer, more elaborate narratives, very early in its history, the industry learned to diversify its products in order to reach different audiences. Apart from making "A" films (more expensive prestige films), studios also produced "B" films (cheaper pictures), such as the "weepy" or "hanky-pic," directed at housewives in town for an afternoon of shopping and an afternoon movie. These low-budget films were often produced by less powerful studios, known as **B Studios**.

In the United States, cinema also attracted a large number of upwardly mobile immigrants who were seeking to familiarize themselves with a way of life, and this provided a fertile environment in which to initiate Americans into a new consumer-culture lifestyle, based on the consumption rather than the production of goods. The good worker (and citizen) was not only productive, but also a smart and up-to-date consumer, as evidenced through clothing, appliances, and vehicles, automobiles in particular. Movies, proselytizing and circulating the American way of life on a global scale—offered a vision of bourgeois affluence that was, through the miracle of mass production, accessible to all; however, while movies gained a stronghold on public imagination, they were also denigrated as popular and "trashy" entertainment.

Later in the century, as movies lost much of their mass audience in the United States because of the rise of television in the 1950s and 1960s, new audiences were needed. The industry countered by concentrating on a few big-budget mov-ies, subsequently known as blockbusters or event movies, and also by targeting more upscale, sophisticated audiences through films that, if less expensive, focused on acting and dialogue. The recognition of an urban elite, a demographic category of people who were educated, wealthy, and enjoyed a significant amount of discretionary income to spend on leisure activities, encouraged the movie industry to incorporate types of filmmaking initially associated with the **avant-garde**, or **experimental, cinema**, which is often considered a counter-Hollywood cinema. The ability of mass culture to appropriate the strategies of artists, who are hostile to its very nature, in order to reach a niche market, attests to its resiliency. Marketing, then, including niche marketing, has always been at the heart of cinema, which has adapted over time to the changing tastes and demographics of its audiences. This has led some scholars to describe film as a demographic, rather than a democratic, cultural form.

The growth of the movie industry in the twentieth century is inseparable from the development of **Classical Hollywood Cinema**. Until the **First World War**, the

French had dominated world cinema production, sending directors and crews to the four corners of the earth, with the aim of producing small-scale films directed at a local audience (many of which are now lost), and of returning to Europe with exotic documentary footage. Cinema was largely still part of music-hall entertainment, which characteristically included comic skits, acrobats, singing, and dancing as well as films, though the same period saw the rise of the feature-length film (between one and two hours) and the development of movie-palace culture.

With the disintegration of the global French cinema industry as a result of the First World War, California, in particular the area of Los Angeles and its surroundings known as Hollywood, came to dominate worldwide production and distribution—and with this shift came a significant change in the place of cinema in the public imagination. Increasingly, cinema was viewed as giving shape and voice to the fantasies and desires of its audiences through elaborate sets, spectacular plots, and glamorous stars. Only a few studios could afford to create the lavish productions that the wider public had to come to demand—and most of these were located in Hollywood. In the post-Second World War era of **globalization**, Hollywood ceased to control world screens in the same manner that it had in the first half of the century; however, the cinema industry today, in which many Hollywood studios remain major players, is marked by the legacies of the studio system.

In Hollywood itself, the **studio system** was more or less in place by the late 1920s. Worldwide production of movies was controlled by a limited number of companies or studios, known as the Majors, through a system of **vertical integration** that united production, distribution, and exhibition. At the height of the Hollywood studio system, Hollywood films would occupy conservatively 70 percent of the world's cinema screens (Schatz, 1981, p. 6). The American film industry secured its hold on the international market by recovering its costs within a national market, which enabled it to charge foreign distributors a lower rate, virtually ensuring the demise of **national cinemas** that did not enjoy protective tariffs.

The **studio system**, releasing 400 to 700 pictures per year in its heyday (Schatz, 1981, p. 6), was based on the principles of industrial organization that governed mass production more generally: it did not promote a family-business ethic, and the cinema industry was frequently at odds with labor unions. Decisions about production were strictly governed by concerns of economic viability. Each studio relied on product diversity for its stability, with low-budget pictures entailing less risk and lower returns and prestige pictures enjoying both a higher level of risk and a potentially higher (or lower) profit margin. Hollywood employed what was known as a decentralized management system, borrowed from companies like General Motors and often referred to as Taylorization, Fordism, or deep division of labor. No single individual controlled the product, in this case, the film. A team of highly specialized workers under the supervision of a line producer developed different aspects of the picture, often relying upon formulas, with the line producer answering to the studio head, whose own perspective was shaped by marketing specialists and the sales team.

21

The *Paramount* decree, *United States* v. *Paramount Pictures, Inc.*, 34 US 131 (1948), forced the Majors (in a process often referred to as divorcement) to relinquish their control over exhibition by giving up theater ownership and other monopolistic practices such as **block booking** and blind booking, which had ensured that the Majors, rather than the theater itself, had had control over what was screened, pushing smaller studios out of business. In the second half of the twentieth century, the film industry attempted, more or less successfully, to regain its economic stability through what is known as synergy or **horizontal integration**—with Time Warner, Inc., as a primary example. Created as a result of a 1989 merger, the global media conglomerate's financial viability now depends upon the success of entertainment franchises, such as *The Matrix* movies or the *Harry Potter* series (with their potential for the endless licensing of ancillary products), as well as the activities of its subsidiaries such as the cable movie channels HBO and TCM. Those studios still in existence enjoy a privileged position within the new media conglomerates, by brokering the creation of blockbusters that serve as the lynchpins in many entertainment franchises. Power, nonetheless, resides with the parent company, and not with the studio itself as it did in Classical Hollywood Cinema.

Beginning in the 1950s, television grew increasingly important to the film industry, especially after the development of home VCRs and DVD players, and the rise of pay television in the form of cable and satellite delivery systems. Each of these new technologies competed with theatrical attendance at movie screenings, which declined during the postwar period, stabilizing in 1965 at 25 percent of its high and rising since 1985 (Maltby, 2004, p. 124). These innovations, however, also offered new venues through which the industry could distribute its ever-expanding range of products: from music videos, television ads, to miniseries, and even video games. Feature-length fiction films, pioneered by directors, such as Thomas Ince and D. W. Griffith, in the second decade of the twentieth century, continued as a programming staple: Web-based culture might not only provide consumers with new competing forms of leisure activities, but broadband also enabled home viewers to access a wider range of feature-length films.

If the feature-length fiction film remains a viable mass-culture form, its success is tied to another less tangible Hollywood product: the star, created and managed through the **star system**. Early studios attempted to suppress the identity of actors and actresses in order to contain their growing influence over cinema audiences as the primary source of revenue. In spite of these efforts, producers were ultimately unable to control or limit the star's power, because he or she was often the most important factor in determining a film's performance at the box office. A number of them even created their own studio, United Artists, in the classical era. In post-Paramount Hollywood, the status, visibility, and economic clout of the star continued to grow with many (such as Clint Eastwood and Warren Beatty) generating their own production companies as well as moving into directing.

Film stars were not the first celebrities to be vaunted by the mass media; however, their fame was distinct in that it derived neither from their place in a hereditary system (as in the case of kings or queens) nor from any particular activities or accomplishments (as in the case of politicians, explorers, or inventors). In addition, their visibility as celebrities was global in its dimensions, supported not only by the movies in which they appeared but also through the wider efforts of the culture industries—newspapers, magazines, and radio as well as the music recording industry, and, in time, television and the Internet. The celebrities of stage and music hall of the nineteenth century, actresses, singers, and dancers, were limited in comparison to Hollywood's idols of consumption because they could only be in one place at one time.

Stars and the star system are frequently the target of mass culture's most virulent critics because of the way they are associated with a consumer-culture dream world tied to the rise of global capitalism, manifested, in particular, through the pursuit of fashion and the cultivation of the body. Paradoxically, stars are also vaunted as giving expression to the hopes and fears of their fans, their personae, and the stories that surround them constituting an authentic expression of the popular. Stars, from this perspective, are viewed as the vehicle for self-understanding and for the expression of desires that may resist the ideological frameworks that the culture industries attempt to impose. For example, scholars like Jackie Stacey, influenced by **feminism**, argue that women audiences' relations with stars entail "active negotiation and transformation of identities which are not simply reducible to objectification" (Stacey, 1998, p. 208). Under the **studio system**, producers and studio heads were acutely aware that the success of most films was dependent on its star (or stars) and her or his ability to attract an audience. The major studios cultivated stars whose lives (both public and private) they sought to control, more or less successfully, through a system of formal legal contracts supported by a subtle and not so subtle manipulation of the press and that star's private life. Communication between fans and stars in the form of fan letters gave expression to audiences' views about the star's behavior, acting capacities, roles, and future possibilities, providing a crucial source of information to the studios. With the rise of new technologies and cultural practices, from the paparazzi with their fast film and mobile cameras to the Internet where fans can log on to blogs and chat rooms dedicated to individual stars and even receive daily messages from their favorite media figure, the celebrity industry (devoted to circulating stories and images about stars) has burgeoned, though film actors and actresses now share the limelight with other media luminaries. As a result, in spite of his or her dependence on a notoriously fickle public, the star of postclassical Hollywood constitutes the single most powerful force in the cinema industry.

While the event film depends less upon its stars than the prestige "A" film, stars remain the primary focus of film narrative. In the classical era in particular, stars would be associated with particular genres. In turn, this association would contribute to the persona cultivated by the star in question. This phenomenon continues today, supported by franchises for which the initial James Bond films provided the model in the early 1960s. Like the star system, Hollywood's use of

genre or formula storytelling, though attacked by those who define culture as the province of the individual artist, singled out by her or his unique vision, is often, paradoxically, defended as a dimension of the cinema industry that provided an outlet for authentic popular expression. Early genres or types of film, such as the Western, were associated with traditional folk forms. The repetitive structure of the genre, its focus on an individual hero, it is argued, follow transcultural patterns that mark all traditional mythologies, predating mass culture. Further, the success and repetition of specific variations of this formula depended upon audience support in the form of box office receipts, creating a "reciprocal relationship between artist and audience" (Schatz, 1981, p. 6) that resulted in the representation of a collective consciousness. The observation that "the Hollywood Genre film is . . . both produced and consumed collectively" gave rise to theories about its ritual function (Schatz, 1981, p. 12). "By offering a representation of a society's value system codified in rules and functions that are known by all, a genre helps viewers to recognize themselves as members of that society," claim scholars who support this perspective (Moine, 2008, p. 83).

Anthropologists, such as Joseph Campbell (1904–87), influenced by the theories of Carl Jung (1875–1961), a Swiss psychoanalyst, argue that movies function as contemporary myths, addressing fundamental human questions such as: "Who am I?" "Where did I come from?" "Where am I going?" (Campbell, 1949). This perspective has been the target of significant criticism as typifying a bowdlerization, or dumbing down, of anthropological history for the purposes of mystifying mass culture, which seeks to implicate cinema's audience into a consumer-culture system in which movies are an important product. These critics point to how the demise of the vertically integrated studio system and the rise of the horizontally integrated studio conglomerate have facilitated the range of products tied together for which a film provides an initial shop window—ranging from product placement within the film to the creation of ancillary products such as video games, clothing, toys, and so on. In some cases, as with *Lara Croft: Tomb Raider*, a successful film franchise, the video game preceded the film itself. Conversely, there is a strong dimension in feminist film criticism that argues that these same films, like the women's weepies of the 1930s and 1940s, offer potential counter-discourses, positions that challenge a dominant patriarchal model of culture, to its women viewers, under the guise of consumer pap (Deuber-Mankowsky, 2005).

Critics of genre film tend to turn to **national cinemas** as a means of finding an authentic voice of the people; however, much of national cinema is funded internationally with a view to attracting an audience comprised of the urban elite through the international **art cinema** circuit. Paradoxically, then, national cinemas that do offer an opportunity to hear voices, accents, and languages other than those promoted by global Hollywood are nevertheless at the mercy of an international industrial system. There are instances of what might be termed vernacular popular cinema—comprising films whose audience constitutes a specific national group but which fail to attract international audiences on the art cinema circuit. For example, the most popular French film with French audiences during the French New Wave period was Gérard Oury's *La Grande Vadrouille* (*Don't Look Now, We Are Being Shot At*, 1966) (Jeancolas and Marie, 2007, p. 88). Largely unknown outside of France, the picture's appeal depended upon a demotic dialogue style and the promotion of French comic stars, whose humor is nationally marked. Other examples of vernacular cinema include what is known as "Bollywood" films from India, which developed a vertically integrated **studio system** comparable to that of Classical Hollywood Cinema but which distributed films in a range of different dialects and languages. These vernacular forms depend, however, upon government support as well as protective tariffs and repressive cultural climates that often exhibit a degree of state-mandated hostility toward Western culture, and American culture in particular.

In conclusion, cinema illustrates the paradoxes of mass culture. Mass culture arises out of the industrial revolution, which created a society where economic rationalization became the primary social principle. Culture did not escape the industrialization that has come to characterize other human activities. The cinema industry is a business run for profit, yet at the same time if it did not manage to produce stories and stars that held significance for its audiences it would not survive. In a certain sense, a scholar can choose which dimension of cinema he or she wishes to investigate—its economic dimension as a culture industry or the meanings that it creates with its audiences; however, a scholar who focuses on one dimension at the expense of the other will lose sight of the essence of cinema as a cultural form, arising out of a productive and, for the most part, happy marriage between the desires of audiences and the demands of business.

FURTHER READING

Patrick Brantlinger in *Bread and Circuses: Theories of Mass as Social Decay* (1983) offers an introduction to the primary issues of what are known as the mass culture debates. See also Max Horkheimer and Theodor W. Adorno, *Dialectic of Enlightenment* (1972), and Walter Benjamin, *The Work of Art in the Age of Its Technological Reproducibility, and Other Writings on Media* (2008). For a definitive description of Hollywood cinema in its many dimensions, see Richard Maltby, *Hollywood Cinema* (2004). Patricia Zimmermann in *Reel Families: A Social History of Amateur Film* (1995) describes the import and impact of home movies while John Trumpbour offers an account of how American movies maintained their world dominance in *Selling Hollywood to the World: U.S. and European Struggles for Mastery of the Global Film Industry, 1920–1950* (2002). Janet Staiger's *Bad Women: Regulating Sexuality in Early American Cinema* (1995) and Karen Mahar's *Women Filmmakers in Early Hollywood* (2006) give a sense of women's roles (both on and off screen) in the development of the cinema industry. There is a wealth of material on stars; the work of Richard Dyer (*Heavenly Bodies: Film Stars and Society*, 2005) is a good starting point. Diane Negra is one of the few scholars to focus on ethnicity in *Off-White Hollywood: American Culture and Ethnic Female Stardom* (2001). Gorham Kindem's *The American Movie Industry* (1982) examines the business side of cinema and Janet Wasko in *Hollywood in the Information Age: Beyond the Silver Screen* (1994) describes the new industrial organizations that characterize movie-making today. Toby Miller's *Global Hollywood* (2001) introduces the important elements that define post-Paramount international popular cinema; Jim Hillier's *American Independent Cinema: A Sight and Sound Reader* (2001) documents the counter-tradition or anti-Hollywood thread that also emerges out of the demise of the studio system. Daniel Slater's *Consumer Culture and Modernity* (1997) summarizes the major perspectives defining academic discussions on this topic. Genre as a concept and phenomenon has been widely discussed by film scholars of the past and the present. Raphaëlle Moine's *Cinema Genre* (2008) synthesizes the breadth of research on the topic; Barry Keith Grant's *Film Genre Reader III* (2003) contains a range of examples. *Theorising National Cinema* (2006), edited by Valentina Vitali and Paul Willeman, offers a similarly broad compendium of approaches to national cinema as well as a good list of further sources. Jim Collins in *Uncommon Cultures: Popular Culture and Post-Modernism* (1989) asserts that cinema provides a source of resistance and counter-discourses to its audiences in a re-examination of the mass culture debates, characteristic of a cultural study. Similarly, Jackie Stacey in *Star Gazing: Hollywood Cinema and Female Spectatorship* (1998) argues that stars of the Classical era provided vehicles for multiple and ongoing negotiations about identity among female fans, while Jeanine Basinger in *A Woman's View: How Hollywood Spoke to Women, 1930–1960* (1993) analyzes the woman's film as an expression of proto-feminist sentiments. The exhaustive four volumes of the *Schirmer Encyclopedia of Film* (edited by Barry Keith Grant) include extended discussions by prominent film scholars about many issues raised in this chapter.

3

FILM AS ART

PRAKASH YOUNGER

INTRODUCTION: THE OUT-OF-SYNC DISCOURSE OF CINEMATIC ART

In a general sense, we call something "art" when we attribute a high cultural value to it. Thus, in principle, and from a historical perspective, no film has an intrinsic, universally valid, artistic value. Its value depends on it (and us) being embedded in cultural **discourse** that gives it value, that tells us why it is good. Cultural discourses are the networks of words and images that mediate and interpret our experience, and it is from these networks that critical narratives of cinematic art—reasoned accounts that explain why certain films are good—emerge. Thus, formal or informal critical narratives of the cinema, based in collective or personal memories of what films have achieved as art, create expectations that govern the ways in which we experience and value films. These critical narratives are themselves grounded in explicit or implicit theories of what the art of the cinema can and should do, and it is ultimately these theories that determine whether or not a film is defined as a "work of art." Though films are created by filmmakers and enjoyed (or not) by their audiences, their creation and enjoyment do not in themselves give films aesthetic value: the historical status of films as art is always dependent on the cultural discourses which define them as such. Thus, some films are only recognized as art long after they first appeared; others, once celebrated as eternal masterpieces, suddenly plummet in value and disappear from the critical narrative. It is as if the history of film as art is always, and perhaps necessarily, out of sync with its object, trying to catch up with the unceasing evolution of the cinema itself.

It is for this reason we can say that the history of film as art has been determined by major historical shifts in the way film has been defined as an art form. Each of these paradigm shifts has involved the recognition of new **aesthetic** values and created new **canon**s, bringing certain aspects of the cinema into sharp relief while allowing others to fall into the shadows. Each shift also represents a reconfiguration of the audience for film as art, either valorizing the breadth of the national and global communities created by film as a popular art or, conversely, privileging the exclusive appeals and refinement of an avant-garde, a cinema of quality, a modernist cinema, or an art cinema. In addition to being informed by a concern with the social function of films, almost every definition of film as an art form is also the product of theoretical reflection and debate about the aesthetic possibilities of the medium. Each stage in the narrative that follows tells us how the art of film was defined at the time and offers a set of critical values that can, in principle, be applied to films today.

STAGE ONE (1895–1915): THE SIDE-SHOW VERSUS THE SEVENTH ART

Within a year of the first screenings of Lumière Brothers films in 1895, the projection of film as a form of commercial entertainment had spread around the globe. But the recognition of the cinema as an art form equal in dignity to the traditional arts was much slower in coming and faced several challenges. Early cinema's immediate and tremendous success as a form of mass entertainment was, due to the dominant class-based aesthetic discourses of the time, something that was held against it. Any art worthy of the name was supposed to be elevated in its content (deal with a "serious" subject and themes) and elevating in its form (sublimating our desire by focusing on the "refined emotions" of "refined people"). **Early cinema**, with its direct appeal to the working-class spectator's desire to see cinematographic reproductions of celebrities, curiosities, attractive human bodies, comic gags, exotic locations, special effects, chases, and so on, was considered to be "vulgar" and "lowbrow": it was devalued the way we today might devalue supermarket tabloids or reality TV. During the first half of this period those who wished to raise the new medium to the level of the traditional arts did so by borrowing the prestige of those arts via literary and theatrical **adaptation**s. The most ambitious and influential model in this regard was the Société Film D'Art, founded in France in 1908 with the aim of presenting celebrated actors of the **theater** in filmed adaptations of well-known stage plays. These films were successful with both critics and middle-class audiences and led film production companies throughout Europe and the United States to adapt classic works of literature, theater, opera, and ballet. But the appeal of these adaptations derived mainly from the predetermined prestige and interest of their subject matter, not from the way in which that subject matter was filmed or presented. Dramatic scenes were typically filmed in one continuous long take, as if to reproduce the point of view of a live theater spectator. Thus, while they did succeed in making the cinema more respectable, the films d'art and their many imitators left unanswered the question as to where the aesthetic possibilities specific to the cinema itself lay: beyond simply recording the achievements of other arts, what could the art of the cinema do for itself?

Though there are many other figures we could point to, it was above all the work of two revolutionary American filmmakers, D. W. Griffith and Charles Chaplin, who, during the second half of this period, demonstrated to the world what the cinema could do for itself. By 1915 these two directors had achieved popular success with a global audience and critical success with intellectuals, and it is no exaggeration to say that their films were crucial to giving the cinema an aesthetic dignity equal to that of the traditional arts. Prominent in his films for the Biograph company since 1908, Griffith's interrelated innovations in **narrative** structure, staging, editing, and acting were a decisive break with the theatrical modes that dominated both early cinema and the films d'art. By rendering any scene into a series of separate shots edited in accordance with narrative concerns and character **point of view**, by cross-cutting between separate scenes linked by narrative concerns, and by using the full range of shot scales from extreme close-ups to extreme long shots, Griffith redefined the concepts of cinematic acting and cinematic action, which now ranged fluidly from the most subtle change in a facial expression to the grand movements of armies in battle. The net result was that the ability of spectators to engage with characters and stories was greatly enhanced. Griffith also progressively extended the running time of his films, establishing the norm of a feature-length narrative film as being between 90 and 120 minutes. Though Griffith was not entirely alone in developing any of these innovations, he stands alone for the way in which he integrated and maximized their effects. By the time he released his controversial epic, *The Birth of a Nation* (1915), his style was in the process of being adopted worldwide as the standard language of narrative filmmaking.

While his influence on other filmmakers was not as immediate or as direct as that of Griffith, Chaplin's tremendous global popularity was recognized during this period to have created an audience for the cinema that was unprecedented. On an aesthetic level, Chaplin's refinement of the **gag** structures of early cinema and his sophisticated use of ellipsis were seen to have allowed for an economy of expression in acting specific to the cinema. Like Griffith, Chaplin was widely credited with having used the cinema to create a "universal language" that transcended the boundaries of nation, language, class, and culture. This idea of cinema as universal language was to become a key element of the aesthetic discourses that dominated the next stage in the history of film as art.

STAGE TWO (1915–30): EXQUISITE SILENCE: THE PURE AND UNIVERSAL ART

The impact of Griffith, Chaplin, and other filmmakers working during the second half of Stage One led to the consolidation of what we now call the classical Hollywood style of filmmaking and other distinctive styles of narrative filmmaking throughout Europe and Asia. By the beginning of Stage Two, the feature-length fictional narrative was on the way to establishing itself as the mainstream mode of film production worldwide. During this period, the discourse about film art took a theoretical turn, as the art of the cinema was largely defined in terms that reflected the contemporary trend toward modernism and abstraction in all the traditional high arts. Working with a normative ideal of music as a "pure" (i.e. non-representational) and "universal" (i.e. culture-and-language-independent) art that has a direct effect on the listener's emotions and thoughts, film theorists sought to identify instances in which the cinema utilized its unique formal potentials and minimized any limits to its universality (e.g. the use of written language in intertitles). But since there was no agreement about what the unique formal potentials of the cinema actually were, critical discourse was focused on the achievements of a diverse and competing group of aesthetically ambitious "movements," some working within the mainstream of feature-length narrative filmmaking, and others working outside it, and appealing to the much smaller audience for modernist painting, theater, and music, with all of them claiming, explicitly or implicitly, to have discovered the pure essence of the cinema.

Two of the movements working within the domain of feature-length narrative filmmaking, **German Expressionism** and **Soviet Montage**, gained wide international prominence during the 1920s, and each of them has exerted a powerful influence on subsequent filmmaking that continues up to the present. Reflecting current trends toward expressionism and abstraction in painting, German Expressionism took the vocation of the cinema to be the expression of human subjectivity and emotion through narratives of fantasy and paranoia, extreme visual stylization (e.g. sets constructed and painted to express the emotional state of characters, the use of low-key, *chiaroscuro*, **lighting** design that employs strong contrasts between light and dark areas of the image), and superimpositions and other special effects designed to replicate hallucinations and dreams. Following closely in the wake of Robert Wiene's masterpiece of paranoia, *The Cabinet of Dr. Caligari* (1919), the films of Fritz Lang and F. W. Murnau exerted a strong influence on contemporary filmmakers. Years later, when many European filmmakers fleeing Nazism and war emigrated to Hollywood, the effects typical of German Expressionism were extended into **film noir**, one of the dominant American genres of the 1940s. Its continued influence on cinema worldwide can be recognized whenever its array of techniques for the expression of human subjectivity and emotion are deployed.

Building on what they took to be the main lesson of Griffith's work, the theorists and filmmakers of the Soviet Montage movement took the power of editing to be the most important key to the art of film. After the famous experiments of the film teacher Lev Kuleshov demonstrated that shots combined by editing had a meaning and emotional impact not found in their individual components, his students Sergei Eisenstein and V. I. Pudovkin worked out the logical consequences of this discovery in their theoretical writings and a series of celebrated films. Though the French term "montage" simply means "putting together" and refers to film editing in general, Eisenstein's theory of the cinema synthesized a rich and diverse group of influences, including the dialectical principles of **Marxist** philosophy, the aesthetics of Japanese printmaking, theater, and poetry, and research into cognitive psychology. As Eisenstein conceived it, montage is the principle of dynamic conflict between elements of the film image that produces both meaning and emotional effects for the spectator. This principle governs the visual/spatial composition of individual shots (the conflict or tension between lines, shapes, and volumes within a shot), the relationships between shots (the conflict or tension between the visual/spatial composition of one shot and another), and the rhythm of the editing (designed to maximize the violence of the conflict between visual/spatial elements). Since the narratives of Eisenstein's films were themselves based around various conflicts from Russian history, they can be seen to represent a seamless blend of cinematic form and content. Films such as *Battleship Potemkin* (1925) and *October* (1928) were widely recognized to have visceral effects on the spectator, and they have continued to function as conclusive demonstrations of the power of dynamic visual compositions and rapid, rhythmic editing for ambitious filmmakers ever since.

German Expressionism and Soviet Montage were only the two most prominent of many movements that, like them, claimed to have discovered the essence of cinematic art. With the achievements of these movements and those of many other individual filmmakers in mind, formalist theorists such as Rudolf Arnheim and Béla Balázs could put forward the view that the silent cinema had realized its aesthetic essence in a pure or direct effect on the spectator's emotions analogous to music. Whatever the representational content of a film, its value as art stemmed from the effect of certain close-ups, compositions, camera movements, or rhythms of editing. In one sense the art of the cinema was understood to be a form of abstract art that emerged from and transcended its documentary or fictional content, that is, the characters, stories, and worlds which it represented.

But just as this critical narrative of cinema as a pure and abstract art was being consolidated toward the end of the 1920s, it was suddenly put in question by the advent and popular triumph of sound cinema. Though the addition of sound could in principle be theorized and practiced in accord with formalist aesthetics (as Eisenstein did in his later films) or simply refused (as Chaplin did by continuing to make non-talking films into the 1930s), filmmakers and audiences worldwide immediately embraced the technology of **synchronous sound** recording as a means of making the characters, stories, and worlds represented on film more real. While the cinematic achievements that had been sponsored by the pure art discourse continued to be recognized and valued after this period, and while the impact of movements like German Expressionism was integrated into the style of sound cinema, the cinema-as-pure-art discourse was out of sync with the vast majority of sound films that were being made – films that were, in terms of its standards and values, impure and theatrical. The discourse itself thus lost its relevance to the mainstream of narrative filmmaking and has only survived as a theoretical justification for the more marginal practices of avant-garde or experimental cinema.

STAGE THREE (1930–45): QUALITY AND TWO FORMS OF REALISM

From the beginning of the 1930s until the Second World War serious discussions of film aesthetics were hampered by a lack of critical concepts relevant to the achievements of the sound cinema. Critical discourse fell back into old habits of describing and evaluating films in extra-cinematic terms. The use of spoken language in films turned the singular object cinema as a global and universal art into a multiplicity of nation-based cinemas, and critics addressing these cinemas during the 1930s typically distinguished two types of films within them as significant.

Films of the first type were distinguished by their elevated subject matter and the high-culture affiliations of those involved in their production—their "quality." In France, for example, the cultural prestige of **Poetic Realism**, the dominant movement of the 1930s, derived mainly from adaptations of French literature and the participation of writers and actors from the world of French theater and literature. Though film historians today recognize the stylistic richness and diverse cinematic influences at work in Poetic Realist films, critics writing at the time lacked both the categories and terms to describe that style and the historical perspective to recognize those influences. Thus, a film such as *La Grande Illusion* ("Grand Illusion," Jean Renoir, 1937) was valued for having a complex and ambitious subject (i.e. the illusions of nationalist ideologies that lead to war) rather than for the cinematic style that articulated that subject. In the absence of a critical vocabulary to describe what was new and original about the sound cinema of the 1930s, critics often celebrated those elements which seemed to carry forward or perpetuate the values of Stage Two. Thus, *The Informer* (John Ford, 1935) became one of the most critically celebrated American films of the decade because it used the moody low-key lighting and other effects typical of German Expressionism, while the many Westerns which the same director made in a popular American idiom were treated as mere entertainment.

The second type of film recognized as art during this period dealt directly with contemporary social reality. The gritty style and aspiration to represent social problems of a Hollywood film like Mervyn LeRoy's *I Am a Fugitive from a Chain Gang* (1932) were valued by critics for raising the social awareness of the audience: the conjunction of a realistic approach to subject matter and style (topical narratives, idiomatic dialogue, location shooting, etc.) with a clear social or political purpose (influencing public opinion about an issue) was considered to raise a film from the realm of mere entertainment to that of art. The career of Frank Capra offers another convenient example in this regard. From *It Happened One Night* (1934), which blended the conventions of romantic comedy with a realistic treatment of Depression-era conditions, the scope of Capra's subject matter grew over the course of the decade and culminated in powerful analyses of American politics and media such as *Mr. Smith Goes to Washington* (1939) and *Meet John Doe* (1941). While they would not necessarily strike us as realistic today, Capra's films were celebrated as art because of their unmistakable ambition to engage and elevate the social conscience of the American audience. During the 1930s critics around the world applied the criteria of realism and social purpose to distinguish art from entertainment. Thus, and for example, films that forcefully addressed women's issues—Kenji Mizoguchi's *Osaka Elegy* (Japan, 1935) or V. Shantaram's *Duniya Na Mane* ("The Unexpected," India, 1937)—were valued very highly within their national film cultures.

The 1940s saw the emergence of critical approaches capable of recognizing the aesthetic value of the mainstream genre films produced during the sound era.

Robert Warshow in the United States and André Bazin in France recognized the cultural significance of **genre** films and put forward the first strong and clear definitions of the cinema as a popular art. For these critics a popular genre like the Western was a form of modern mythology with deep roots in American history and culture, a mythology that gave vivid and imaginative shape to the experiences and aspirations of modern life for both domestic and global audiences. Both critics recognized the value of the stable dialogical relationship between studio-based, commercial film industries and the desires of the mass audiences to which they catered; giving the people what they wanted was not necessarily vulgar, lowbrow, or escapist but could now start to be valued as an organic cultural expression of modern democratic societies.

On a theoretical and stylistic level, Bazin's conception of cinematic **realism** allowed him to identify tendencies of aesthetic achievement that bridged the rupture in critical values created by the advent of sound and thus set the stage for the recuperation of the entire history of the cinema after the war. For Bazin, the essence and historical vocation of the cinema was not to be found in the specific techniques celebrated by the proponents of the pure art discourse, nor did it reside in the extra-cinematic values of quality or social purpose that were emphasized by critics during the 1930s. He argued instead that the technology of cinematographic images and synchronous sound had a power to compel belief in the reality of the world represented and that the aesthetic mobilization of this capacity satisfied a fundamental need of human psychology. For Bazin realism was more an issue of style than it was of subject matter. By identifying a lineage of filmmakers whose style was built around the cinema's photography-based power of conviction, that is, its capacity to produce an engagement with the image analogous to our engagement with real life, he created an evolutionary narrative that connected the work of filmmakers from the silent era (Erich Von Stroheim, F. W. Murnau, Charles Chaplin) to that of the most ambitious contemporary directors (Jean Renoir, Orson Welles). Bazin's critical narrative of the cinema was the first to take into account the complete history of the medium, and it set a standard of comprehensiveness and critical precision that was a powerful and productive challenge to the generation of critics that followed him in Stage Four (see **film language**).

STAGE FOUR (1945–75): CINEPHILE REVOLUTION: NEOREALISM, MISE-EN-SCÈNE, AUTEURS, MODERNISM, POLITICAL MODERNISM

The period from the end of the war to the mid-1960s saw the triumph of a revolution in critical values, the results of which continue to dominate any serious discourse about films today. Though the narrative of this revolution is typically centered in Paris and features the critics-turned-filmmakers of the film **journal** *Cahiers du cinéma* ("Cinema Notebooks") as stars, a full appreciation of its significance would have to recognize the existence of similar developments taking place in metropolitan centers around the world. Educated in film history by being exposed to new and classic films in film clubs, repertory theaters, and film museums such as the *Cinémathèque française*, a new generation of **cinephiles** (film lovers) arose who were both aware of the cinematic achievements of the past and excited about the prospects for the future embodied in contemporary movements such as Italian **Neorealism**.

The appearance of Neorealist films at the end of the Second World War represented a dramatic break with the conventions of the **classical narrative cinema**s that had dominated mainstream film production since Griffith. Abandoning the traditional conventions and production methods of studio filmmaking, directors such as Roberto Rossellini and Vittorio De Sica employed episodic narratives, location shooting, available light, and non-professional actors to create films that had a more immediate, documentary approach to the representation of the contemporary world. For Bazin and his followers, these films represented an extension and confirmation of his theory of the cinema's realist vocation, and their new aesthetic emboldened filmmakers around the world (Satyajit Ray and Bimal Roy in India, Nelson Pereira dos Santos in Brazil) to adopt their methods. Beyond their combination of realistic subject matter with a clear sense of social purpose (i.e. their reaffirmation of critical values already recognized in Stage Three), Neorealist films also exemplified the creative freedom of the filmmaker to approach any subject without recourse to the dramatic, generic, and stylistic conventions established by the mainstream of studio-based filmmaking. They represented a more direct and dynamic model of the relationship between the film artist and the subject matter he or she chose to represent, and as such, they offered powerful support to the critical concept of the *auteur* that was emerging at the time.

With a historical relevance that far transcended their immediate moment, the two critical premises that effected the cinephile revolution were that of **mise-en-scène** and the **auteur**. These concepts allowed the *Cahiers* critics and their counterparts elsewhere (Andrew Sarris in the United States, critics writing in the British film journals *Sequence* and *Movie*) to describe how a director's precise and coordinated use of mise-en-scène (i.e. details of the script, set design, cinematography, editing, direction of actors, etc.) resulted in a unique and personal expression of his or her response to the subject matter of a film (considered to be the mark of an auteur or film author), even when this subject matter was itself determined by the commercial constraints of mainstream studio-based filmmaking (e.g. the use of stars, genre conventions, etc.). Though the *Cahiers* definition of mise-en-scène as the personal style of an auteur director is not the only definition, it played a crucial role in restructuring the existing canon. The critical elevation of **style** over the subject matter of a film was both a sweeping rejection of the canons of quality and seriousness and the means to recover a fresh and greatly enlarged history of the cinema as an art. While reaffirming many of the achievements recognized under the critical rubrics of Stages One and Two, auteurist critics also celebrated genre filmmakers such as John Ford, Alfred Hitchcock, Samuel Fuller, and Howard Hawks, who had hitherto been considered merely entertainers, and also globalized the canon by recognizing the work of Japanese directors such as Kenji Mizoguchi and Akira Kurosawa. In the process, longstanding class-based and nation-centered definitions of film as art gave way to a much broader, more inclusive, conception in accord with Warshow and Bazin's ideal of cinema as a global and popular art form.

Their broad education in film history and the singular concept of mise-en-scène as style also allowed cinephiles and critics to recognize historical patterns of influence both within and across national boundaries and to thus recover the conception of the cinema as a single, continuous, and universal culture that had been lost since the coming of sound. From the early 1960s on, the historical self-consciousness of this cinephile culture with regard to film style generated a prominent tendency toward **modernism** within the mainstream of film production, especially in Europe. Established auteurs were emboldened to push against or play with the boundaries of existing film conventions and create a modernist language of the cinema in films such as *L'Avventura* (Michelangelo Antonioni, 1960), *8 ½* (Federico Fellini, 1963), *Persona* (Ingmar Bergman, 1966), and *Belle de Jour* (Luis Bunuel, 1967). The younger cinephile generation itself began to make films which combined their knowledge of film history with the creative freedom and freshness they inherited from Neorealism. The first films of the French **New Wave** created by *Cahiers*-critics-turned-filmmakers such as Francois Truffaut (*The 400 Blows*, 1959) and Jean-Luc Godard (*Breathless*, 1960) both inspired young filmmakers and helped to create a growing audience for a cinema of auteurs. During the second half of the decade, and in the charged climate of the **Cold War**, modernist cinema also developed a more oppositional, political, tendency ("political modernism") evident in the work of Godard (*Weekend*, 1967), Miklós Jancsó (*The Red and the White*, Hungary, 1967), Glauber Rocha (*Land in Anguish*, Brazil, 1967), and Nagisa Oshima (*Death by Hanging*, Japan, 1968). By the early 1970s the many successes of the cinephile revolution in critical values—its recuperation of the movements and auteurs of the past, its affirmation of cinema as a popular art with a social and political function, its creation of an expanding film-educated audience, and its direct impacts on the modernist forms of contemporary filmmaking—allowed cinephiles to imagine that ongoing destiny of "the Cinema" was the most vital and important aspect of global culture.

STAGE FIVE (AFTER 1975): AFTER POSTMODERNISM: ART CINEMA, ATTRACTIONS, MELODRAMA, AND THE NEW CINEPHILIA

Over the course of the 1970s, the cinephile revolution's ideal of a universal culture and singular object ("the Cinema") slowly began to disintegrate. On one level, this disintegration or crisis of belief was the result of the historical failure of political modernisms on either side of the Cold-War divide to reach a mass audience or effect social and political change. After the social and cultural movements that culminated in the political crises of 1968 failed to achieve their aims,

Stage Four's cinephiles were forced to acknowledge the unrealistic nature of their high expectations and recognize that the social base of their revolution was not in fact as broad as they had liked to imagine. The aesthetic differences between modernist auteurs and more popular mainstream cinema came back into sharp relief and were now recognized to reflect the class differences between two distinct audiences. During Stage Five the limited size and class basis of the audience for what was now called "art cinema" hit home; while cinematic modernism continued to thrive during the 1970s and 1980s, anticipated and celebrated at film festivals and art-house theaters around the world, both critics and audiences now had diminished expectations about its social and political functions. Though aesthetically ambitious movements continued to arise (e.g. the New Hollywood and New German Cinemas of the 1970s, the Fifth Generation of Chinese filmmakers during the 1980s), they were always shadowed by, or in danger of being absorbed by, a mode of mainstream entertainment filmmaking that reaches a much larger audience. In a very general sense, there are two main types of critical values that dominate Stage Five: traditions of populist aesthetics, which would run, in the American context, from *Jaws* (Steven Spielberg, 1975) and *Star Wars* (George Lucas, 1977) to the latest successful blockbuster, and the more diverse and fragmented traditions of cinephile aesthetics (the ongoing legacy of Stage Four).

From the mid-1970s on, the critical values and practices of Stage Four's cinephile revolution were institutionalized and disseminated through the growth of Film Studies programs in universities. While continuing to focus on and extend the understanding of the movements, auteurs, and genres recognized in preceding stages, and while applying the concepts of movement, auteur, and genre to new objects, certain groups of academic scholars also worked to recognize the aesthetic qualities of modes of popular cinema that had been devalued in the past. Tom Gunning and other scholars argued for the value of early, that is, pre-Griffith, filmmaking, demonstrating that it involved unique techniques and effects that were different from the effects and techniques of narrative filmmaking that succeeded it; this period of filmmaking that had hitherto been considered to contain only primitive attempts at narrative was now seen quite differently. Around the same time, **feminist** scholars such as Linda Williams began to recognize the social importance and aesthetic values of **melodrama**, a mode which has played a crucial role within film cultures ranging from Hollywood to Germany and India. By eliciting identification with its socially marginalized victim-protagonists (women, members of the lower classes, and/or people of color) melodrama can be seen to exercise an important, politically subversive, function. In these two cases, and in a more general sense, academic film scholarship continues to expand our understanding of film as art by developing paradigms that recognize the aesthetic qualities and value of new objects. Equally important, the teaching of Film Studies within the academy continues to introduce successive generations of students to the canonical films and canon-expanding theories that have traced the out-of-sync evolution of film as art.

Finally, since the mid-1990s there has also been a "rebirth" of cinephilia (out of the ashes of critical pronouncements regarding its "death"). Just as the original revolution was fueled by the excitement around Neorealism, in this case the global buzz around movements and auteurs such as Abbas Kiarostami (in Iran) and Hou Hsiao-Hsien (in Taiwan) revived hopes that the art of the film could transcend the predictability and limited audience implied in the concept of "art cinema." Though there is a global critical consensus about the aesthetic value of these new movements and auteurs (they are already part of the cinephile canon taught in universities), it is also unlikely that they will ever attain the global popularity of a Charles Chaplin or a Steven Spielberg.

CONCLUSION: FILM AS ART IN THE DIGITAL AGE

What defines a film as a "work of art" today? Though the answers to this question would obviously be as diverse as the group of people one asks, it is nonetheless possible to identify the general factors that would determine the answers people might give. The single most important of these general factors is that today the vast majority of films are not being watched in movie theaters. Though mainstream films have been regularly screened on network television since the 1950s, it was above all the advent of home VHS tape technology in the 1980s and DVD technology in the 1990s that has led to a wide-ranging fragmentation of the audience for film as art. No longer determined by what happens to be playing at local movie theaters, the films that people choose to watch reflect their specific tastes for film as art. A person schooled in the populist American tradition that began in the 1970s might choose to watch *Star Wars* on DVD several times a year and find that her appreciation of the movie grows with each viewing. Another person with a taste for Hollywood musicals could systematically exhaust his local video shop's selection of titles in that category while eagerly awaiting the appearance of restored versions on the cable channels devoted to classical Hollywood. A third person with roots in both "old" and "new" cinephilia will scan the critical discourse in online journals and blogs for news of the latest DVD release of a classic Renoir film or a brand new film from Hou Hsiao-Hsien, while a fan of Bollywood cinema can pick up the latest DVD releases from their local Indian grocery store and, if they wish, educate themselves by reading the growing amount of academic scholarship on this topic. Each of these people may feel that he or she is deeply engaged with the art of the cinema without necessarily being concerned as to whether their definition of that art has a more general or universal currency. As suggested by the French philosopher Jean-Francois Lyotard, the main fact of the **postmodern** condition is that there are no longer any "master narratives" capable of creating a consensus as to what the art of the cinema is; though most of the critical values, narratives, and canons that arose during Stages One through Five continue to play a role in contemporary culture, none of them can claim to play a dominant role. The dynamic international cross-fertilization of contemporary cinema and the secondary effects of Stage Four's cinephile revolution (e.g. the ongoing impacts of Film Studies programs) means that the self-conscious audience for film as art is undoubtedly much larger than it was during its late-60s heyday. While today's audience is fragmented and no longer has the utopian hopes of that earlier generation, it has far greater access to the films it values and to critical tools and categories it can use to enhance its appreciation and understanding of "the art of the cinema."

FURTHER READING

Bordwell, David (1997) *On the History of Film Style*, Cambridge, MA: Harvard University Press.
Bordwell is a film scholar with a comprehensive understanding of the history of film as an art form and this book presents his version of the critical debates on the topic from the silent era up to the present.

Braudy, Leo and Cohen, Marshall (2004) *Film Theory and Criticism: Introductory Readings*, 6th edn., New York: Oxford University Press.
An invaluable anthology of primary critical and theoretical essays that includes contributions from key figures in the five-stage meta-narrative above such as Arnheim, Balász, Eisenstein, Bazin, Warshow, and Sarris, as well as important essays by academic film scholars such as Tom Gunning and Linda Williams.

Casetti, Francesco (1999) *Theories of Cinema 1945–1995*, Austin, TX: University of Texas Press.
This book offers a comprehensive and detailed review of the many different paradigms that theorists have used since the Second World War, both aesthetic and non-aesthetic; treating the cinema as a field contested over by a variety of critical discourses, it provides an exciting narrative of this revolutionary period.

Thompson, Kristin and Bordwell, David (2003) *Film History: An Introduction*, 2nd edn., New York: McGraw-Hill.
Probably the best single-volume history of the cinema as an art form. In addition to presenting and illuminating all of the most important movements, many of the best-known auteurs, and dozens of canonical films, all in great detail, the authors give considerable space and attention to lesser-known but fascinating aspects of global cinematic history.

4

THE STAGES OF THE FILM
PRODUCTION PROCESS

WILLIAM GUYNN

This chapter will attempt to describe a model of the production process as it has developed in the narrative film of live action in most commercial cinemas. I will discuss the tools and techniques of each phase of production and how they contribute to the structures and meanings of the story. Because I am focusing on the dominant model of narrative cinema, I will not directly address other modes of filmmaking (Chapters 6, 7, and 8 on experimental, documentary, and animated cinemas take up questions of production methods specific to those modes).

Admittedly, what I am offering here is an abstraction. There are significant variants on the model: "transgressive" cinematic movements or filmmakers, **national** or **postcolonial** cinemas, among others, may quite consciously attempt to overturn the norms of film practice and establish an oppositional or idiosyncratic style. Moreover, production systems vary enormously. For example, Hollywood in the era of the great studios operated very differently from the artisanal approach—small, short-lived companies that produced a single film or a short series of films—characteristic of the French cinema of the 1930s. I will try to give a sense of differences in production methods through examples drawn from different cultural contexts and historical periods. However, most modes of narrative filmmaking, even outside the hegemonic Hollywood practice, do not depart radically from the model I will be presenting. Even where departures are significant, much can be learned about other forms of cinema by comparing them to the dominant paradigm.

Film theorists conceptualize the production of the fiction films as a set of processes divided into four successive stages:

1   the activities of writing involved in the production of the film's *script*;
2   the various techniques by means of which an action is staged in front of the camera, the film's *mise-en-scène*;
3   the choices filmmakers make in the process of *shooting* the film, including the camera set-up that determines the distance and angle of the camera—its framing of the image;
4   the successive stages of *editing* that shape the filmed material into a cohesive narrative structure composed of a chain of shots.

This four-part chronological model is of course theoretical. The reality of the production of a film can often be less linear and the relationship between the stages more complex. (1) One stage may anticipate a subsequent one. For example, the **shooting script** often describes in specific terms the continuity of a sequence of shots, which will receive its definitive form in the final work of **editing**. Similarly, while shooting a scene, the director and the cinematographer are constantly mindful of creating elements of **continuity** between takes that will make the editing of the scene possible. (2) Production may "regress" momentarily to a prior stage. For example, the rewriting of a scene in the process of shooting is a common occurrence in all types of narrative filmmaking. Or the editor may notice a "gap" in continuity that requires additional "filler" material to be shot.

Each stage involves nonetheless specific tasks and a specific art. Let's look at each in the order of production.

FROM SCREENPLAY TO SHOOTING SCRIPT

Storytelling is a way of making sense of human experience that has existed in every known culture, historical or contemporary. Stories, whether "real" or imagined, may take on different forms: they may be written, told orally, danced, mimed, communicated in sign language, or produced in one of the audio-visual media. All stories share one attribute: they have a "life of their own" that is distinct from the way we experience our daily lives. No matter how close a story may be to lived experience (e.g. the account you give of what you did last night), it is unlike lived experience because it looks back on events and shapes them; it has a beginning, a middle, and an end, that is, a narrative structure.

When we talk about the script, we are referring to the narrative design in written form that passes, in the tradition of studio production in the classic period, through several stages. Typically, a studio producer options a script—either the more or less developed story idea that a scriptwriter or his or her agent pitches to the studio executive or a "property" (often a novel) the rights to which the studio has purchased. The studio then employs a writer to develop a treatment—an outline of the basic events of the plot. The script undergoes significant modifications often through collaboration between the scriptwriter, the director who accepts or is assigned to shoot the film, and/or the producers in charge of production. There is, finally, the shooting script, which, in the Hollywood tradition, but not exclusively, is a more or less elaborate breakdown that specifies the content of the shots, the dialogue and indications for the camera, including the **scale of shots**, whether there is **camera movement** or not, and so forth. In the following discussion, we will talk about the script as a fully realized narrative project in the tradition of the classical Hollywood era. This model is broadly applicable to other commercial cinemas.

CONSTRUCTING THE FILM'S PLOT

The classical film typically opens with an *exposition*—what Syd Fields refers to as the Set-Up (2005). The exposition identifies the major (or some of the major) characters, the setting, and the pertinent circumstances the spectator needs to be aware of before the film's action begins. It is a moment in which an immense amount of information is communicated, and many manuals for scriptwriters warn that the exposition should not look like what it is. Information should be communicated through dramatic situations, not through static dialogue between characters.

The exposition presents a state of equilibrium that is disrupted. To take a classic example, John Ford's *My Darling Clementine* (1946) begins with a sequence showing Wyatt Earp (Henry Fonda) and his brothers herding cattle to market in the landscape of Monument Valley, images of exhilaration and happiness. A second sequence begins with the appearance of the Clintons in a buckboard: their dour look and a disturbing musical cue tell us that they threaten the peace and well-being expressed in the first sequence. Wyatt refuses to sell his cattle to Pa Clinton. The Earps set out for an evening in Tombstone, leaving the youngest brother, Jamie, in charge of the camp. During that evening, we are introduced to a fearful community beset by random violence: Wyatt's shave at the barbershop is interrupted by wild gunfire unleashed by a drunken Indian, Ford's figure of uncivilized nature. Wyatt disarms the Indian, but refuses the mayor's offer to take over as sheriff. When the Earps return to their encampment they find their youngest brother murdered and the cattle rustled. At the end of this very dramatic exposition, Wyatt assumes his double narrative mission: revenge the murder of his brother and return Tombstone to a more civilized state, both of which depend on his accepting the job as Tombstone's sheriff.

Some films choose an exposition *in medias res*: plunging the spectator "into the middle of things," that is into an already evolving event, depending on dialogue to fill us in on the origins of the action. In some cases, the full exposition may be delayed so that the audience gradually fills in the missing information as the developing story provides it. Such an exposition can be characterized as suspenseful and enigmatic. Contemporary filmmakers frequently use a *hook* or *teaser*: a striking or enigmatic event that takes place before the main action begins, often before the titles appear, in order to capture the attention of the audience. The hook was a constant feature of the television series *The Wire*.

Film narratives share many characteristics with other forms of narrative. Narratives have been described as resembling staircases; they move progressively up (narrative theorists call this the *rising action*), increasing in intensity with each step until they reach a *climax*. This pattern is often referred to as the narrative line or curve, and, as Michel Chion (2007) observes, films can be divided into acts and scenes, even if these divisions are less obviously marked and exist "more below the surface." (DVD releases of films often divide films into "chapters," making their scene structure more apparent.) The climax is the highest moment of tension in dramatic and emotional terms and usually occurs near the end of the film. It is followed by the *falling action*, in which the conflicts that have come to term in the climax are brought to resolution. This unknotting of the plot is called the *denouement*, and it establishes a new equilibrium, parallel to but different from the equilibrium that existed in the narrative world in its beginning, before the first disruptive action. At the end of *My Darling Clementine*, Wyatt Earp and his remaining brother are leaving Tombstone, which they have returned to a state of peace. Wyatt encounters Clementine, Doc Holliday's fiancée from the East, who, after Doc's death in the shootout at the OK Corral, has decided to be the town's schoolmarm. A new equilibrium exists: civilization and its institutions have taken hold.

Let's return now to the rising action, the most developed and complex part of the narrative. Along the way to its final climax, a narrative moves through a series of moments of mounting tension. The tension is often the result of dead-lines that characters face (appointments to be kept, time-related dangers to be defused). These moments reach peaks of action, localized climaxes that are called **plot points** in the language of the scriptwriter. Narrative theorists call these peaks of action *peripety*, critical points at which a major change affects characters and their actions. *Reversals* are turns of the plot that change one situation into its opposite: the unexpected, brutal murder of Sonny in *The Godfather* (1972) signals a downturn in the power of the Corleone family in relation to its rival; in *recognition* the protagonist (or the antagonist) becomes aware of a crucial piece of information (the "aha!" moments in Hitchcock's films); *confrontation* is a scene in which a long-simmering conflict is played out: the moment in *Citizen Kane* (1941) in which the long-abused Susan Alexander leaves the domineering Kane. Localized climaxes are often followed by moments of release of tension before the next ascent.

THE CHARACTER

One of the tasks of the scriptwriter is the work of creating a dramatis personae: a set of characters who will carry the story's action. Characters are subjects or objects of action in narratives (they perform actions or actions are performed upon them). In general, fictional characters are products of the narrative: they emerge out of the telling and "come to life" as a result of several techniques the storyteller uses. First, the author—novelist, dramatist, filmmaker—describes or shows the characters' appearance: their individuated faces and bodies, their tone of voice, their gaits and postures, their costumes, their age and sex, and so forth. From this physiological information we make judgments about the characters' personalities. The notion that physical characteristics translate into moral and psychological traits (the gangster's flashy suit not only signals his prosperity but also his moral depravity) is an ancient one and an important tool of characterization. Second, the author places characters in settings (a lonely hotel room, a bowling alley, a Park Avenue apartment) that "speak" about their inner being. The same can be said of the objects (props) that surround them. This correspondence between human subjectivity and non-human phenomena is termed the pathetic fallacy and is particularly characteristic of the nineteenth-century novel, from which film inherited many of its techniques of characterization. Third, the author defines characters through the decisions they make and the actions they take. We come to understand characters through their behaviour, particularly in the cinema, the most "behaviorist" of narrative forms, where we have limited direct access to the characters' inner emotions and thought processes. We watch and judge the actions the characters perform and the gestures they make, and we listen to the words they say and how they say them. Finally, characters define themselves in relationship to other characters: by contrast (one character serves as a foil to another), by similarity (as a basis for comparing the behavior of two characters), by opposition (as in the melodramatic figures of hero and villain). Supporting characters often exist simply to bring out the character traits of the central protagonists.

In classical cinema, there is typically a small configuration of characters featuring one or two central protagonists. Protagonists set themselves goals to attain in relation to the events that motivate their mission (one of the tasks of the exposition, as we saw in the example from *My Darling Clementine* above). In the course of the narrative action, the protagonists encounter opponents and obstacles that obstruct their mission: antagonists (like Pa Clinton) or natural phenomena (such as a blinding snow storm) that hinder the protagonists' progress and over which they attempt to triumph. They also encounter "helpers" that enable or abet the protagonists in their mission (the police informer or the wind rising in the sails of a stranded ship). In the Hollywood film, there are typically two strands of action: the mission to be accomplished (the principal action) and the relationship to be worked out between the central male and female protagonists (the romantic action).

In the classical, and indeed in the majority of commercial, films, events are typically arranged in a linear chronology (A happens, then B, then C) and in causal sequence (A happens and causes B to happen... it is because the older Wyatt brothers decide to go into Tombstone that the Clintons are able to rustle their cattle and kill Jamie). The individual characters' actions and reactions are the vehicles of the narrative. Every action should have its motivation: the character's drive toward a goal, the character's psychological needs or impulses (the need to seek revenge, a fateful attraction to a woman), or the character's need to deal with emerging circumstances. Motivation supports the plot's plausibility: once we accept a situation and the characters' goals and motivations, the plot seems to unfold of its own accord. A "good" script avoids actions that appear eccentric, that lack **verisimilitude**: actions that don't correspond to the spectator's expectations about how things should happen in the "real" world or in the conventional world of a **genre**. Characters should be consistent, but they are open to change as long as the change is foreshadowed (hinted at beforehand) and doesn't take the spectator by surprise. Thus, characters reveal aspects of their personalities that may not be anticipated but are nonetheless credible.

In constructing characters and situations, the scriptwriter also constructs the characters' relationship to the spectator. In classic films, he or she solicits the audience's **identification** with the protagonists. The scriptwriter gives his sympathetic characters positive traits that elicit admiration—for example, forth-rightness, self-assurance, or devotion—but often balances strengths with weak-nesses that underscore the character's humanness. The scriptwriter places characters in situations of danger or reversals of fortune that generate empathy and anguish in the spectator. Although film rarely attempts to give the equivalent of the first-person narrative, we often see the action from one character's posi-tion because we sympathize with the character and spend more time in scenes in which he or she plays a central role. It has often been observed that, even in the case of characters who are performing a reprehensible action, we can identify with their predicament. The classic example is the gang of robbers alone in a bank who hear an alarm and realize they have x minutes to complete the heist and escape. Because the story places us with them in the circumstances, we place ourselves—willy-nilly—in their position and identify with their fear of getting caught.

Some critics make a distinction between films that center on story ("action films") in which characters are relatively *flat* (simply drawn and predictable in behavior) and those that center on characters who are *complex*, nuanced, and capable of surprising us. François Truffaut saw American cinema as a cinema of action and plot, in which characters are seen principally through their actions (as in the films of Hitchcock), and the French cinema as a cinema of character, which allows for moments of character development that aren't immediately absorbed into the plot.

NARRATIVE TIME IN FILM

Theorists have often reflected on the sense of time the spectator experiences while watching a film. Cinematic images give a strong impression of presence ("being there" at the scene). **Flashback**s, properly cued, for example, by the close-up of a face and a dissolve, are initially understood as belonging subjec-tively to the character, but they quickly slip into the present in the spectator's mind as their action unfolds. Film has no tenses, as they exist in the novel, for example. It has had to develop techniques for specifying relationships in time. A return to the past may be specified by an intertitle ("a year ago") or a line of dialogue, an elliptical jump into the future by clichés such as pages flying off a calendar.

There are two fundamental times in narrative films: the time of the story (the duration of the events recounted), and the time of the telling (the time of the film's projection). A 2-hour film that recounts events transpiring over a period of a sin-gle night develops more continuously than a 2-hour film recounting the history of two generations of a family; their narrative *speeds* are radically different.

In constructing a narrative, the scriptwriter decides which aspects of the action are to be recounted but also which will not. The gaps between narrated actions are called ellipses. In the ellipsis, a narrative skips over events that are not pertinent to the plot or character development and are sacrificed in the interest of economy, or because the narrator wants to "hide" them temporarily from the spectator (for the purposes of suspense) only to reveal them later when they will have maximum impact. Ellipsis is one of the basic tools of narrative rhythm.

HISTORY OF THE SCRIPT

Early cinema (1895–1917) looked to the novels and plays of the past, particularly the nineteenth century, as sources for scripts. The earliest literary **adaptation**s took the form of static *tableaux* (theatrically staged scenes from a single camera position at considerable distance from the actors). Little thought was given to cinematic transposition, and the script was simply a synopsis of the action borrowed directly from the literary model. This would change as film-makers became increasingly aware of the difference between the literary and the cinematic. Literature uses the verbal powers of language and is unrivaled in its ability to *tell* stories; its power to give concrete representations of fictional worlds is, however, limited. The cinematic image, on the other hand, *shows* the world in phenomenological detail; the filmmaker's problem then is how to shape the sequence of images so that they *tell* a story. Thus, the modern script developed as filmmakers "discovered" new resources in the medium: multiple camera set-ups within a single scene, the ability of the ubiquitous camera to intercut shots from different locations and times, among others. As the film became a more complex visual text, and particularly as it grew into the feature film, the script evolved as an increasingly important tool of organization.

We know that by the end of the period known as **Early Cinema** the emerging Hollywood studio system had established scenario departments, whose mission was to produce shooting scripts that broke the films into scenes and individual shots. This process is known as **découpage**, the "cutting-up" of the narrative into small pieces, the last stage of written preparation before shooting. The **shooting script** was conceived as a plan of attack and a basic reference for the various technicians and the set designer, allowing them to organize their work in relation to each other. This organized work of specialists is one of the hallmarks of the Hollywood **studio system**, and the **continuity** system spread to other national film industries, particularly in Europe, during the 1920s. Jacques Aumont calls the classical shooting script the "first version of the mise-en-scène" because it negotiates between the script and its transformation into images and sounds. It remained the dominant form of the script in the West at least until the 1940s.

We know that historically the script has taken forms radically different from the working blueprint of the studio tradition. This is particularly the case of self-conscious artists working outside (and often in opposition to) the "industrial" model. At the moment of **German Expressionist** cinema in the 1920s, for example, the script often reflected the tendency of the films to present strong, even violent images as outward projections of characters' inner conflicts. Thus, Carl Meyer's scripts for F. W. Murnau weren't technical documents, but poetic works that evoked mood and psychological state. Important film movements—such as Italian **Neorealism** and the French **New Wave**—tended (at least in theory) to devalue the script because it compromised cinematic **realism**: it organized the world through the word instead of allowing the world to speak for itself. Throwing off the tyranny of the shooting script left space for happenstance and improvisation (and often lessened the control exercised by the producer). Independent filmmaker John Cassavetes made a series of films based on his actors' improvisations (e.g. *Shadows*, 1961, and *A Woman under the Influence*, 1974), as did Mike Leigh, particularly in his early work (e.g. *Bleak Moments*, 1972). However, we should remember that there are limits to "raw realism," and even oppositional films depend to some extent on scripting. We tend to forget that Vittorio De Sica's *The Bicycle Thief* (1948)—emblem of Italy's new realism—was produced following a detailed shooting script.

MISE-EN-SCÈNE

Origin of the term

The French word **mise-en-scène** comes from theater and designates the craft of staging a play. It assumes a theatrical space, the stage on which the play's actions are represented: a painted backdrop or constructed set, actors playing characters and moving about, the lights that make the scene visible. In the Western tradition, the stage is occupied by a box set, with the side toward the proscenium (the arch that frames the stage) "removed" so that the members of the audience, located in that other space, the auditorium, can follow the action from the fixed position of their seats. In addition, there is a third space, the wings: the fictional space where characters go when they leave the represented space on stage or from which they emerge, and the real space where actors retire to the backstage world. As Jacques Aumont observes, "... since the *skéné* of Greek antiquity, [the stage] has been for the theater what the frame has been for painting: the artifact that permits us to create, to isolate, to design a particular space that escapes from the laws of everyday space in order to substitute other laws that are perhaps artistic and certainly artificial and conventional" (Aumont, 2006, p. 8). Mise-en-scène as a fundamental notion of the art of staging emerged in the nineteenth century as the theater began to designate an individual responsible for the coherence of the representation, the *metteur-en-scène*, the stage director.

Mise-en-scène in film has come to mean all the activities that prepare the actors and the sets for the shooting: rehearsing the actors for their performance in front of the camera, including blocking their movements, organizing the exchange of looks among them, rehearsing dialogue and gesture, and fashioning the actors' appearance through costume and make-up; constructing the set and dressing it; and designing the lighting that illuminates actors, set, and action. Mise-en-scène is the audio-visualization of the narrative. Thus, we could say, using narrative theory, that if the script is the preliminary phase of *telling* events—characters and actions are narrated and described in words—mise-en-scène is the phase of *showing* the events: the characters are embodied in actors and the actors move through the concrete space of the scene. Actors and set become audio-visually concrete phenomena to be filmed.

The film's director is in general responsible for the look of the film and supervises the work of the other professionals of mise-en-scène: the art director, who designs and decorates the sets; the costume and make-up designers; the cinematographer, who at this stage works on the film's lighting and color design, among others.

Early models of mise-en-scène

It is easy to apply the term mise-en-scène to the earliest production of fiction films when the staging of the film maintained a close parallel to theatrical staging. Léon Barsacq observes that the great French "primitive" filmmaker, Georges Méliès, staged his films (1896–1912) in a building enclosed in glass but otherwise much like a theatrical stage: "In Méliès's studio the shooting was done with a stationary camera set up in a special recess at the far end of the theater, and the actors played facing the camera as though facing an audience" (1977, p. 6). Indeed, Méliès was more concerned with the visual look of his work than with the story. The camera distance from the action mimicked the spectator's distance from the theatrical stage, and the actors were positioned frontally and performed their actions and gestures against elaborately painted flats. Thus, whole scenes often unfolded in a single take. Most narrative films before 1908 did not attempt to construct a plot but were content to present dramatic scenes lifted from stage productions of the period: a series of "views" or "tableaux" that reproduced the play's strongest or best-known scenes, without attempting to tell the complete story.

In the period preceding the First World War, many European directors continued to work in a style of mise-en-scène that was based on the static position of the camera and the **long take** and shaped the narrative through subtle effects of staging, especially the blocking of actors' movements. Some film historians have found this style archaic because it makes insufficient use of "cinematic language," in particular the multiple camera set-ups, impossible in theater, which came to characterize the American cinema. However, a case can be made that cinematic mise-en-scène is fundamentally different from its theatrical counterpart.

Film historian David Bordwell draws a clear distinction between theatrical and cinematic mise-en-scène. Theatrical staging fits the play's action into the wide rectangle of the constructed set and tends to spread the actors out laterally across the stage so as to preserve unencumbered sightlines from anywhere in the house. Cinematic mise-en-scène, by contrast, works within a pyramidal space defined by the optical perspective of the camera, "with the top of the pyramid at the lens and the playing space radiating out from there" (Bordwell, 2005, p. 60). Cinematic space is, therefore, much narrower and deeper than theatrical space. During a long take, the camera has a fixed point of view, and the director who stages the action is able to lay out a complex configuration of actors in the space of the scene. This kind of mise-en-scène was typical of European films in the 1910s, which exploited the resources of the great **depth of field** of the image; all planes of the image, from foreground to background, were sharply focused, and, therefore, all the activities and centers of interest were clearly visible to the spectator. Thus, the filmmaker could create a layered mise-en-scène that set up relationships between foreground and background activities. Moreover, European filmmakers strove for a strong pictorial quality. As the word *tableau* (French for painting or picture) suggests, there was a stronger sense of framing the action in the manner of academic art of the period. Europeans tended to place the actors in the foreground of a scene at a greater distance from the camera (10, 12, or more feet—the so-called French foreground) than what was typical of the American practice of about 9 feet; they found the American foreground too tight and constricting because it cut off the actors at the knees or hips.

In the 1920s Europeans continued to experiment with expressive mise-en-scène. Most notable was the **German Expressionist** movement, which began in 1919 with the appearance of Robert Wiene's *The Cabinet of Dr. Caligari*. The film was a sensation because it seemed to turn its back on "cinematic realism." Expressionist mise-en-scène in film, borrowed initially from Expressionist theater, is heavily stylized and emphasizes the graphic character and cohesiveness of all elements of composition: distorted sets, full of oblique angles and sharp contrasts between light and dark; similarly stylized costume and make-up design that reflect the set design; non-naturalistic acting, often involving sudden and awkward gestures and choreographed movement. In the *Nibelungen Saga* (1924), Fritz Lang had his set designers construct landscapes in the studio or on back lots: "... for a film to become a work of art nature had to be stylized. ... Only when a director builds his own landscape can he give it a soul and make it play an active role in the plot" (Rudolf Kurtz quoted in Eisner, 1973, p. 152). F. W. Murnau, three of whose films (most importantly, *Nosferatu: A Symphony of Horrors*, 1922) are usually attached to the Expressionist movement, was less inclined toward stylized painted sets and often shot in real locations. He was, however, preoccupied with the pictorial design of the space of the scene, which he achieved through his sensitivity to the chromatic effects of light and shadow and the expressiveness of the point of view chosen for the camera. The most important moments in Murnau's films occur within the single shot, and not as a result of editing.

The art of mise-en-scène would ultimately be displaced by the art of the American editing style that would dominate production practice until at least the early 1940s.

Mise-en-scène in the American cinema

It would be a mistake, however, to think that the Europeans created a cinema of mise-en-scène while the early American cinema relied exclusively on editing.

D. W. Griffith's American Biograph films (1908–13), for example, reveal Griffith's interest in layered mise-en-scène in depth. In interiors and particularly in exterior shots this meant staging a relationship between foreground and background actions. Moreover, the early American cinema developed increasingly "realistic" sets, gradually abandoned the theatrical traditions of melodramatic gesture and pantomime that compensated for the lack of dialogue, and made significant advances in the use of artificial lighting. American Biograph studios from 1903 to 1913 were artificially lit, and by 1911, Biograph began experimenting with the potential of lighting for expressing mood and reflecting character emotion (Bowser, 1990, pp. 235–6).

Mise-en-scène became a crucial moment of production in the Hollywood studio system. It allowed the director (who was charged with transforming the shooting script into images) to work with the real bodies of actors and in the actual sets or locations. He or she could eliminate the unforeseen (major gaffes in the **continuity** between shots, disappearing props, inconsistency in placement of actors within the scene), thus saving time and money at the moment of shooting. Alfred Hitchcock, for example, was famous for his tight control over mise-en-scène, which he prepared with fastidious precision, so as to eliminate the slightest "accident" at the moment of shooting. To this end, by the mid-1950s he visualized each shot before shooting through elaborate *storyboards*.

Mise-en-scène in the sound era

During the early moments of the talkie, the "capturing" of sound brought a sudden end to the pre-eminence of the image: the camera became the prisoner of a soundproof booth. Because all sound had to be recorded at the same time as the image, whole scenes were shot in continuity, with actors grouped around a hidden microphone. Mise-en-scène in most films was reduced to keeping the speaking actors centered in the frame. Although the camera soon regained its mobility, dialogue remained primary. Cutting was very often cued by the exchange between speaking actors, and **reverse-angle shooting** became the classic editing pattern in dialogue scenes. This was the case especially in the American cinema, and expressive strategies of mise-en-scène played a lesser role through the end of the 1930s. There were, of course, many exceptions: in the 1930s the films of Josef von Sternberg, French poetic realism with its emphasis on the symbolic in sets, lighting, and props, among others. In Japan, Kenji Mizoguchi developed a style that opposed the contemporary dominance of editing, preferring very long takes and a mise-en-scène strategy that integrated "bold and intricate visual design with the demands of narration and emotional expression" (Bordwell, 2005, p. 90).

The year 1941 has become a symbolic date in the renewal of the art of mise-en-scène in the Western tradition: the release of Orson Welles's *Citizen Kane*. With his cinematographer Gregg Toland, Welles shot in great **depth of field**, organizing the planes of the image from foreground to background to achieve dramatic effect. He thus abandoned the techniques of **analytical editing**, which created dramatic emphasis through cutting (e.g. the cut to a close-up that signals an intensification of emotion), and shot in very long takes, even **sequence shots** (entire scenes taken from a single continuous camera set-up). Placing characters in depth at different distances from the camera often suggested relationships of power or alienation. In the first flashback of the film, recounted by Kane's guardian, we see Kane's mother in the foreground of a long take, her face grim with the determination to send her son away, her back turned to the other characters; in the middle ground, Kane's weak father paces and protests ineffectually; and in the distant background seen through a window, the young boy Kane, unaware that his fate is being sealed, plays with his sled in the snow. A quite different effect is achieved in the sequence shot of the music lesson: Kane's wife, the untalented Susan Alexander, stands in the foreground taking a lesson from her singing coach at the piano, humiliation written on her face; Kane enters the room as a relatively small figure in the background, but his forceful stride toward the piano, emphasized by the wide-angle **lens** that exaggerates the depth of the set, establishes his dominance over his wife.

Kane inaugurated a return to the use of **deep-focus cinematography** in the American cinema that spread throughout the industry in the 1940s and 1950s. Welles's films became models for an influential theory of "realist mise-en-scène," championed particularly by André Bazin, who asserted that shooting in depth and in long takes brought cinematic representation closer to the reality of the world as it exists (see **realism**).

While it is true that there are no films without mise-en-scène, there were those experimental filmmakers who rejected the commercial practice. Already in the 1930s, French filmmaker Jean Renoir resisted the idea that mise-en-scène was simply the realization of the shooting script; for him, the script was a partial and tentative document, and the moment of shooting, when the actors came together in the location or on the set, should be open to improvisation by both actors and director. This tendency reveals a radically different perspective on the creative process, an emphasis on the moment of shooting, most fully expressed in the work of Italian filmmaker Roberto Rossellini. In his films before the 1960s, Rossellini worked from minimal scenarios, thus avoiding pre-planned mise-en-scène. He preferred to discover the film's location with his actors: he lay in wait to "trap" the real, to use his expression. His films played down drama since he rejected the techniques necessary to produce it: "I don't describe the [dramatic] point, but the wait, and I arrive suddenly at the conclusion." In *Stromboli* (1949), one of the films he made with Ingrid Bergman, Rossellini proposed an encounter: in a starkly beautiful place (the isolated volcanic island of Stromboli), a refugee from the Second World War (Bergman, the only professional actor in the film) makes a marriage of convenience with a fisherman (tuna fishing was the island's only industry), and, because of an experience she has on the brink of the volcano, comes to accept her husband's love. Such films of revelation incorporate elements of chance and anticipate experiments in mixing documentary and fiction and contemporary work using digital cameras.

Lighting

Before closing this discussion of mise-en-scène, we should look more closely at the techniques of lighting. Lighting always affects the quality of the image we perceive by creating patterns of light and dark. Let's start with the manner in which sets were lit in Hollywood in the studio era. The classical formula is called the *three-point lighting system* and, as the term suggests, consists of three sources of light:

1   The *key light*, placed to the side of the camera, gives the shot its overall illumination, highlighting the body or the face of the actor. The lighting may be *high key* if the key light is bright. This is typical of certain genres such as the romantic comedy or the musical. *Low-key* lighting means that the key light is turned down in the interest of creating more expressive areas of light and shadow, as in the classic **film noir**.
2   The *fill light* is less bright than the key light, is set at an angle from the key, and functions to soften the "hard" shadows created by a bright key.
3   The *back light* is set behind the actor, opposite the key light, and functions to detach the body and head of the actor from the background. It is sometimes used to create an "aura" around the head particularly of female stars.

If the classical Hollywood film for the most part chose the three-point system, other traditions and individual filmmakers have preferred more "expressive" lighting. *Source* lighting emphasizes particular sources of lighting in a scene: a desk lamp in a darkened room, light filtering through venetian blinds. *High-contrast* lighting creates stark patterns of light and shadow. Both source and high-contrast lighting were used by Orson Welles in films such as *Citizen Kane*, *Lady from Shanghai* (1947), and *Touch of Evil* (1958). In a completely different spirit, some filmmakers have preferred to shoot in *available light* (as documentary filmmakers do by necessity in uncontrolled shooting). Some of the films from the Italian **Neorealist** movement (*Rome, Open City*, 1945; *The Bicycle Thief*, 1948) acquire a veristic style by choosing to shoot in real locations, interior and exterior, using available light.

THE SHOOTING PROCESS

The shooting of a film involves another set of professionals, all under the supervision of the director. The *cinematographer*, or director of photography, is responsible for the photographic look of the film—the choice of cameras, lenses, and film stock, the camera set-ups and movements, the consistency of photographic quality from one shot to the next—and he or she supervises the work of the camera crew, including the *camera operator*. Other technicians include the *gaffer*, who sets up the lighting, and the *key grip*, who manages the props. The *sound mixer* is responsible for coordinating sound recording during the shooting process and supervises the sound crew: a sound recorder, a boom operator, and others.

French filmmaker Eric Rohmer describes the art of shooting the film as "knowing where to put the camera and how long to leave it there" (quoted in Aumont, 2006, p. 46). Knowing where to put the camera implies two essential choices the filmmaker faces in establishing the camera's point of view: at what *distance* (see **scale of shots**) to position the camera from the subject he or she is filming and what **angle** the camera should take in relation to the subject. By convention, distance has been determined by the size of the human figures in the frame: a *long shot* shows the full bodies of the actors and at least some of the surrounding context; in the *medium shot* the body of the actor, taken from knees-up or waist-up, fills the screen and makes pose and gesture prominent; the *close-up* isolates the face, site of thought and emotion, or an object of dramatic importance, and usually shows little of the surrounding context. These broad categories are refined by modifiers: very long shot, extreme close-up, medium-close shot, for example.

The **camera's angle** is also predicated on a convention: eye-level framing that emulates the "normal" sight line of the standing human adult. Thus, when angles deviate from this norm, technicians talk about *low angles* that look up at the subject and *high angles* that look down on it. Angles often have an expressive (**connotative**) function: most conventionally, a low angle lends power or menace to the human figure; a high angle suggests relative weakness. Extreme high and low angles are unusual and strike us as self-consciously expressive. *Canted* framings are askew, out-of-level shots that often suggest instability.

Framing and on- and off-screen space

Choosing the camera set-up, its distance and angle, is the act of **framing** the image. The choice is significant on several levels. First, the frame, in the manner of the frame in painting, sets the image and the events it depicts apart from the world we inhabit, in particular from the auditorium where we are seated looking at the film. The image may be convincingly realistic and the events compelling and credible, but our experience of the image (and the sound) remains an experience of "art" or of the "imaginary," and not of life.

Second, the framing determines the composition of the image in the pictorial sense: it organizes the different planes of the image in relation to each other; it places us at an "appropriate" distance from the action and directs our attention to focal points in the visual field; and it may design the space within the frame, in the manner of composition in other visual arts, through linear patterns, zones of light and shadow, the placement and movement of actors, and so forth. Pictorial composition is more apparent when long takes allow us to scan the image at a more leisurely pace, much less so in more rapidly edited sequences where we are occupied for the most part in reading the narrative information the shot gives us. Thus, as we saw, composition is a crucial expressive element in the work of F. W. Murnau (1888–1931), whereas it is much less so in a classic Hollywood film where the major compositional concern is to center the dramatic action within the frame and avoid any formal element that might detract from the story.

Third, framing determines what part of the fictional scene is visible to the audience (*on-screen space*) and what is invisible (relegated to an imaginary *off-screen space*). Because the filmic image appears as if cut out of a broader "reality," we are called upon to imagine the space as extending beyond all four edges of the frame, as it does "beyond the set" and into the space behind the camera. In deciding to shoot at a certain distance and a certain angle, the filmmaker involves us in the complex play between what is included in the image and what is excluded from it. In constructing the film's story, the existence of off-screen space can be as important as the space the image shows us (e.g. the off-screen murder we can't see but hear). Although off-screen space is almost always in play in most films, our awareness of it fluctuates. The more an off-screen space is animated by unseen action, the more it contributes to the basic narrative tension of the story.

The techniques for evoking off-screen space are so common that we sometimes forget how crucial they are. We imagine the landscape or the room that extends beyond the frame; we have perhaps already seen a broader view of the space in a previous shot and are aware of a narrative element developing there (e.g. Indian warriors aligned along a hillside in the Western). Or something from a space we have not previously seen in a wider shot that may protrude into the frame (e.g. the slashing knife in the horror film infers the unseen slasher, who is off screen). The element that frequently lends off-screen space its sense of presence and calls our attention to it is "off-screen" sound, or more accurately, sounds whose source is not visible in the image but, we imagine, exists off screen. An actor's entrance into or exit out of the frame brings into play the space from which he or she comes or is going to. The off-screen space thus evoked may simply be another part of the set we have already seen or a more distant place the actor is headed for, often established by the dialogue. The look off-screen immediately brings that other space into play, a space we have previously seen and recall, or a space we haven't yet seen but anticipate seeing. When we add the moving camera, the relationship between what the camera gives us to see and what it holds back becomes even more complex. The tracking camera continuously transforms the visual field, what we can see becoming what we can no longer see. Moreover, multiple set-ups in a single scene shift the parameters of the visible (e.g. cutting to a wider shot to reveal some element of the drama that was hidden from view in the closer shot).

All these techniques of framing lead us to construct a plotline and a fictional universe through the articulation of what we see, what we imagine to exist, our memory of what we have previously seen (and what we have been told), and what we anticipate seeing. Film criticism employs the term **diegesis** to refer to what the film represents to us, or, rather, what we collaborate in representing in response to the information the film communicates to us. To use French theoretician Christian Metz's definition, the diegesis is the whole work of **denotation**: the story that develops in fictional space and time, the characters, settings, and events.

53

Let's return to the second aspect of Rohmer's description of the art of shooting: how long to leave the camera there. To avoid confusion when talking about the *duration* of a shot, we refer to **take**s that are more or less long: whereas a long shot refers to the spatial scale, long take refers to the time the shot remains on the screen. Camera movement or lack of movement may affect a shot's duration: a take may be relatively long if the camera is moving to keep characters within the frame, and relatively short, if characters are stationary and shown in close-up. **Camera movement** can be divided into several techniques. In the *tracking shots* the camera moves through space by means of tracks laid out in studio or on location or by means of a *dolly*, a camera platform on wheels. The *pan* is a lateral movement of the camera on its stationary axis; the *tilt* is like the pan, except that the camera moves vertically rather than horizontally. The *crane shot* uses a hydraulic machine that allows the camera, perched on its platform, to "swoop" in any direction and to very high angles. Although not an actual camera movement, the *zoom* (see **lenses**) emulates the forward or backward tracking shot by changing the lens's focal length during the take. The *hand-held camera*, originally a technique used by ethnographers to film in the field, became part of **Direct Cinema** documentary practice and found its place in the work of innovative filmmakers of the 1960s and 1970s. The *Steadicam* is an apparatus attached to the body of the camera operator to allow for smooth movement during hand-held shots.

Camera work may be quite conventional or highly idiosyncratic, but it is one of the keys to describing the visual **style** of a work, a body of works, or even a whole period. A style of camera work may be the result of that emblematic creative moment when the filmmaker (director or cinematographer) looks through the lens and assesses the effects produced by a certain distance and angle; or it may be part of established patterns of filmmaking that legislate, for example, that a shot should be held for just the time necessary for the spectator to take in the narrative information it provides. Thus, a style may be personal to a filmmaker, who asserts his or her freedom from conventions, and purposely transgresses against certain codes of filmmaking. The style of the modernist Hungarian filmmaker Miklòs Janscò, for example, is considered transgressive, particularly in its use of very long takes and extreme depth of field. Style may also be collective, defined as a set of conventions and codes that characterize a movement or a period. The French New Wave was a rather eclectic movement but shared certain features particularly in the early period 1959–62: the production of lightweight camera and recording devices, developed for use in documentary films, allowed the New Wave directors to shoot on location, particularly in city streets, where the camera was set free to pursue its characters amid the crowds and simultaneously record ambient sound and dialogue.

The choice of lenses for shooting a scene also contributes to determining the shape of the visual field and the planes of the image that receive special emphasis. The phenomenon of **depth of field**, for example, is determined by the construction of the lens. It refers to the zone of the image that is sharply focused and is measured on the axis of the camera: for example, an image might be in sharp focus between 9 feet and 14 feet from the camera. The areas closer than 9 feet and further than 14 would be more or less out of focus. The depth of field of an image becomes particularly apparent in shots, fairly common in contemporary cinema, which show an actor out of focus who approaches the camera until he or she comes into focus. Similarly, *rack focus* changes the depth of field during a shot, for example, by showing a foreground figure in sharp focus, then shifting to a sharp focus of a figure in the relative background.

As we saw, early cinema with its short focal lengths produced images of great depth of focus. However, from the advent of sound through the 1930s, a reduced depth of field or relative *shallow focus* became the norm in shooting, with notable exceptions: Jean Renoir's work in France in the 1930s and Kenji Mizoguchi's in Japan. This long hiatus in the use of deep-focus images explains why the work of Orson Welles and William Wyler in deep focus in the early 1940s appeared so revolutionary and had such an immediate impact on shooting strategies.

Lenses can also shape the contours of the image. A "normal lens" doesn't distort the relationship between the planes of the image: they appear to be staggered in depth as they are in our perception of real visual space. The wide-angle lens (as used by Welles and Toland in *Citizen Kane*) broadens the foreground and exaggerates the distance between foreground and background. This results in the distortion of actors or objects in the immediate foreground (becoming grotesque in certain shots in *Kane*) and creates the impression of outsized sets and of the precipitous movement of actors from background to foreground or the reverse. Long-focal-length *telephoto lenses* produce quite the opposite effect: they visually collapse the difference between foreground and background so that actors or objects in the foreground appear much closer to those in the background. If the wide-angle lens broadens and deepens space, the telephoto lens flattens it. There are many examples of the "expressive" use of such lenses in film history (uses that "violate" the effect of the "normal lens"). In the 1960s and 1970s there was increased use of telephoto lenses, even in relative close-ups—a trend that went counter to the emphasis on depth that resurfaced in the 1940s. We find systematic use of these long-focal-length lenses in the work of **modernist** filmmakers in Europe and in Hollywood, for example in Michelangelo's *Red Desert* (1964) or Robert Altman's *The Long Goodbye* (1972).

EDITING

In current practice, editing refers to the final phase of production in which the fragments of film (the takes) to be included in the film are chosen, trimmed of unwanted footage, and assembled (glued together) in a certain order. In commercial production, this function is performed by a specialist (the editor) who works under the guidance of the director or the producer. It is important to realize, however, that editing is part of a long process of **découpage** (breaking the film's story into significant pieces). As we saw, the script or scenario divides the action of the film into its various sequences and scenes; the shooting script breaks the sequence or scene into shots; the film's action, thus prepared, takes concrete form in the shooting process (during which several takes may be made or several simultaneously shooting cameras may give different points of view on the same action). The various takes constitute the *rushes* or *dailies*, the unedited footage from which the final editing makes a coherent whole. This process begins with the exclusion of footage that will not be used (the outtakes): the *rough cut* that places the takes in their approximate order, and the final editing that establishes the film's finished form. In the postproduction phase, the editor works in collaboration with a sound mixer, who mixes the different elements of the sound track—dialogue, sound effects, and music—recorded during shooting or in postproduction (see **production sound** and **post-production sound**).

The emergence of editing is a crucial aesthetic event in film history. The editor's art consists in creating meaning by placing a given shot in sequence with others. The single shot doesn't have intrinsic meaning but takes on its value in the context of the other shots that are associated with it. Although not the sole province of the American cinema, editing became its most salient feature by the time of the emergence of the feature film (*c.* 1914). Film historians have paid much attention to this early period in order to follow how a practice so important to the future of the medium developed. Film historian Tom Gunning's close analysis of D. W. Griffith's Biograph films (1908–13) demonstrates that, although Griffith didn't invent film editing as early historians had asserted, he played a central role in establishing the consistent use of editing techniques he had received as a heritage from earlier filmmakers (Gunning, 1994).

The art of editing emerges from the intuition that film is not necessarily wedded to the structure of theatrical representation in which the actors come together in a theatrical space where all action takes place in absolute continuity (see **theater**). In its radical departure from the constraints of the theatrical scene, the art of editing recognized the value of discontinuity: that a film may be made up of fragments (shots) that the audience is still able to piece together and read as narrative continuity. Basically, editing opened up two very productive kinds of discontinuity. First, the interval(s) between two or more shots might include breaks in time: ellipses that allow the film to skip over "unimportant" moments, condensing the time of an event and increasing its speed, or hold back information to be revealed at a later point. This manipulation of time distinguishes film from theatrical representation and brings it closer to the narrative flexibility of the novel. Second, discontinuity allowed the film to break a continuous scene into multiple shots, with each change in camera set-up changing the camera's point of view on the scene. The same could be achieved by editing together footage taken by more than one camera operating simultaneously. Such a shift in point of view is obviously impossible in the classical theater, where the audience has none of the ubiquity it gains from the camera's mobility.

How is it that this discontinuous discourse doesn't compromise the impression of continuity the spectator needs in order to construct the film's story?

It is difficult for us now to imagine the extent to which the d'
between shots was perceived as a violation of a rational (theatric;
space and time. Indeed, in the earliest films, the shift from one shot to ს.
was justified as a trick. The telescope at the eye of an observer, for example,
could be followed by the "magnified" view of what the observer saw, a cinematic "joke" that showed what the technology could do. The edited narrative
film, on the other hand, established a dynamic relationship between the film and
the spectator and required the development of a set of techniques of **continuity**
that would, over time (1908–13), become codified, that is, accepted by the audience as conventions underpinning a new form of **verisimilitude**. The following
is a partial inventory of some major techniques of matching shots in sequence.

1   *Match on screen direction.* If the trajectory of a character or an object is to be
    perceived as representing a continuous movement, it must cross the screen in
    the same direction in all shots that make up the sequence. Thus, in a battle
    scene, all the shots of the combatants on one side are shown advancing from
    screen left to screen right (or the reverse).
2   *Match on action.* Two shots showing the same gesture should give the appear-
    ance of uninterrupted movement. For example, a character who begins to rise
    from a chair in a medium-close shot may be shown completing the movement
    in a longer shot. Transitions are smoother if the two shots divide the gesture into
    distinct moments.
3   The match on action is particularly smooth if the camera remains on the same
    axis in relation to the character (*axis match*); changes of angle on a subject
    should be significant enough "to make a point," at least 30 degrees.
4   *The eyeline match.* A first shot of a character looking off screen is followed by
    a second shot representing what he or she is looking at in the immediate off-
    screen space. A *point-of-view series* is a more elaborate form of the eyeline
    match: in the first shot, we see the observer looking off screen; in the second
    the camera adopts the *optical point of view* (or close to it) of the character to
    show what the character is looking at. In the second shot the audience has been
    placed in the position of the observer so that the spectator sees as if through the
    character's eyes. This pattern can be repeated at length, as in Hitchcock's
    Vertigo (1958).
5   *Analytical editing.* Analytical editing is a method for breaking down a scene
    into multiple shots in order to preserve a sense of continuity. The classical pat-
    tern begins with an *establishing shot* (or *master shot*) showing the positions of
    the characters in a broad view of the scene of action. The establishing shot is
    then followed by closer views of actors and activities within the scene. The
    closer shots maintain the same orientation of the detail to the camera previously
    established in the broad shot and focus the audience's attention in order to pro-
    vide narrative and psychological information. If a new element is introduced
    (e.g. a character not seen in the first establishing shot enters the room), a second
    broader view (a re-establishing shot) reorients the spectator to the new arrange-
    ment of characters in the scene. Analytic editing is associated with the emer-
    gence of the classical American style in the 1910s and became a dominant

editing pattern in the full-blown **classical Hollywood** style (1914 to at least 1940) (see **continuity editing**).

6 *The 180-degree rule*. In classical filmmaking, this rule sets the parameters for camera set-ups in scenes that take place in a single location. Take the example of **reverse-angle shooting**. Two characters are shown in conversation, looking at each other—character A on the left and character B on the right. The imaginary line that connects their gaze is called the *axis of action*. Once the axis is established, the camera may take up positions within the space on the same side of this axis but must not cross over it. The 180-degree rule ensures that character A will continue to appear looking right and will appear on the left in shots that include both characters. Character B similarly maintains his or her position from shot to shot.

7 *Cross-cutting*. An alternation of shots represents two or more separate aspects of the action that are occurring more or less simultaneously and are usually described by the pattern a/b/a/b. The classic example is the last-minute rescue. In Griffith's Biograph films a frequent situation involves three spaces: (a) the interior of a building where a young woman becomes aware that (b) outside the building there are miscreants attempting to break in and (c) in a third, more distant space the male protagonist learns of the danger and begins the ride to the rescue, with each alternation approaching closer to the moment of salvation.

These techniques of continuity editing emerged in response to specific problems of representation posed in early cinema by the desire to rival the length and complexity of works of nineteenth-century novel and theater. Ambitious directors and producers, like Griffth, who sought legitimacy for the new art, understood the need to appeal to the tastes of new audiences from the middle and upper classes. Although it is important to recognize that "progress" toward new narrative forms was not always conscious and not without backsliding, filmmakers sought to resolve problems of the following kinds:

1 The static long shot, which brought into play various areas of activity in the depth of the image, offered limited choices for guiding the spectator's attention to what was narratively important to see.

2 In such scenes, the camera remained subservient to the theatrical character of the dramatic event, which dictated that the first cut (like the rising theatrical curtain) reveal the scene opening and that the second mark the closure of the scene's action.

3 The long shot that framed the actors with space both below their feet and above their heads was an obstacle to the spectator's identification with characters; indeed in the very early cinema, even the recognition of actors as individual characters was problematic.

4 The lack of language, particularly the voiced dialogue of theater, made it cumbersome to communicate narrative information (whence the reliance on **intertitles**) and express characters' states of mind and intentions; very early cinema consequently depended on the broad artifice of mime or melodramatic gesture.

The basic impulse of innovative filmmakers was to create a new, dynamic relationship between the camera and the staging of events. The notion that one could begin a scene *in medias res* (in the midst of an already evolving action) or that one could cut away from an action before its completion (the basic mechanism of suspense) was revolutionary. Moreover, the edited sequence allowed the filmmaker to shape the spectator's understanding of the story by isolating and centering the focus of action. The position of the spectator also becomes dynamic as he or she becomes the active instrument for constructing a coherent narrative out of the edited pieces. Likewise, the power of analytical editing and point of view was to bring the spectator into a more intimate and knowledgeable relationship with characters. As Eileen Bowser observes, there was an increasing public demand for closer views of the actors and an acting style that corresponded to the illusion of reality the medium was capable of producing (Bowser, 1994, pp. 87–102). Griffith's direction of actors at Biograph began to stress restraint as a positive value, and the smaller, subtler gestures he elicited required the camera to move closer, eliminating the "empty" space below the actors' feet and the expanse of set that rose above their heads. Such closer view gave spectators access to characters' reactions and involved them in the intimate reading of state of mind and intention. Indeed, character psychology became an essential motivation for shot changes and one of the motive forces of narrative.

Let us note, finally, that editing, particularly in the commercial cinema, had the advantage of economy that derived from the ability to shoot out of sequence. It became common practice, for example in reverse-angle shooting, to do all the takes of one of two characters engaged in conversation before shooting the takes of the second.

There are, of course, other styles of editing. Many of them were developed by filmmakers in response to the dominant model of classical filmmaking I have just described. Although a comprehensive historical account of editing is beyond the scope of this short discussion, I would point to several theoretical conceptions that mark radical departures from classical practice.

1   The Soviet filmmakers of the 1920s, who worked in the genres of the documentary and the historical film, elaborated theories of montage that sought to overturn the classical notion of continuity, so closely allied with fiction. Instead of effacing the spectator's awareness of the cut through the techniques described previously, they emphasized the cut as a primary creative moment in which the filmmaker stimulates audience reaction and gives meaning to the world. Dziga Vertov proposed the notion of the *interval*, the gap between two shots that may play on such factors as their differing **scale** or **angle**, contrasts in **camera movement**, changes in lighting, among others. The interval is thus at the origin of the meaning and emotion produced in the spectator. Sergei Eisenstein's theories of montage are complex and developed over a long period of time. They are based on the notion of the fragment, which is broken off from the real in order to take its place as a signifying element in a **discourse** about the world. Eisenstein was

not interested in film as a simple record of real phenomena, nor was he interested in the practices of editing that produced fictional worlds. Eisenstein's notion of *intellectual montage* argues for an art of editing that creates meanings through the juxtaposition of shots or the juxtaposition of elements within the shot. What interested Eisenstein was a cinematic *language* in which the montage of images produces a level of abstraction comparable to verbal language. The key notion is *conflict* rather than continuity. Thus, two visual fragments (two shots, for example) placed in juxtaposition produce an *idea* that transcends their material signifiers.

2   There is a current of thought, among critics like André Bazin (1918–58) and filmmakers like Andrei Tarkovsky (1932–86), which advocates the rejection of editing as a discursive tool, such as we find in the theories of the Soviet montage school. Bazin argued, for example, that editing was "forbidden" if it involved "cheating" on reality (as in the tiger hunt composed of the hunter and the hunted who never meet in real space but only on the editing table). Further, Bazin believed the cinema, with its ability to capture reality without creative human intervention, should preserve the ambiguity of the real and respect its resistance to the meaning effects that Eisenstein advocated. Tarkovsky, for his part, argues that the spectator comes to see a film in order to have a certain experience of time: the machinery of cinema reproduces the time of an event, the kind of time we experience in our lives. The movement of time within the take—shot and then projected at 24 frames per second—is preserved in what Tarkovsky thought of as a state of purity. The role of editing, for Tarkovsky, is reduced to "sculpting" time: shaping the material of time that is deposited in the shot. The aesthetic of the long take characterized more experimental work, particularly in Europe, through the 1970s.

Contemporary film practice since the 1980s, particularly in the American commercial cinema, has revalorized a style of editing that no longer entirely conforms to the continuity system typical of Hollywood filmmaking in the classical period. Indeed, there is a marked tendency in commercial films to rapid and often flashy shot changes, once reserved to more experimental work. It is as if filmmakers needed to avoid spectator boredom at all cost through perpetual visual titillation. David Bordwell has termed this stylistic tendency in Hollywood filmmaking "intensified continuity," the filmmaker's urge "to convey constant motion—through cutting, character movement, or camera movement" (Bordwell, 2005, pp. 22–32). A prime example, Bordwell observes, is the conventional rhythm of takes in contemporary television and movies for shooting conversations: on the one hand, in the figure called "stand-and-deliver," short takes and repeated camera set-ups piece together close-ups of individual characters in conversation; on the other hand, the figure of "walk-and-talk" uses relatively long takes in which the camera tracks back from the conversing characters moving toward it.

In the dominant practice today, the aesthetic of "**transparence**" in commercial filmmaking has given way to visual nervousness. Indeed, there is no universally accepted mode of editing. Each aesthetic tendency adopts its own.

THE PRODUCTION PROCESS IN THE DIGITAL AGE

What has been the impact of digital technology on the model of the production process I have thus far elaborated? On a technical level, it has been enormous. In the phase of script writing, word processing has made the written text highly malleable. The powerful tool of computer imaging generates video sequences of still or moving images that have begun to replace the hand-drawn or photo-graphed images that constitute a film's story boards. It is now possible to "pre-visualize" an entire film before any of the takes that will be used in the film have been shot, creating an interface between literary representation and cinematic visualization.

Fast-forwarding to the final stage of the production model, electronics have transformed the craft of editing. So-called non-linear editing, which emerged in the late 1980s, allows the editor access to all the filmed material, digitized and stored on a hard drive, in any order he or she chooses. Image and sound can thus be manipulated at will, trimmed, and sequenced; edit-decision-lists can be recorded, and optical effects can be experimented with, without causing any damage to the original material. Powerful electronic editors like the Avid Film Composer or the Lightworks Off-line have now largely displaced the flat-bed editing machine that worked directly on celluloid.

As computers developed faster speed and larger storage capacity, Computer Generated Imagery (CGI; also known as Computer Animation)—images or parts of images created through computers and digital systems—began to pro-duce, by the mid-1990s, very credible special effects. Not only did CGI displace older special-effect processes, it showed itself capable of producing images that formerly could only be achieved through mise-en-scène (the placement and movement of actors within a setting). Digital **compositing** combines images that may come from quite different sources. For example, digital matte-painting can create "photorealistic" environments that can be integrated with live-action foot-age, or newly shot live action can be integrated into previously shot material (footage of Tom Hanks in *Forrest Gump*, 1994, is inserted into documentary footage to produce his meeting with JFK). CGI can thus create the illusion of three-dimensional worlds (as in the *Lord of the Rings* cycle); digitally multiply extras to produce crowd scenes, making the spectacle film once again an afford-able genre (e.g. Ridley Scott's *Gladiator*, 2000); or make one figure *morph* into another (as in Ron Howard's *Willow*, 1988; *Judgment Day*, 1991). Although characteristic of Hollywood genre production—sci-fi, disaster films, fantasy— digitally created effects are not unknown in the art cinema (e.g. in Eric Rohmer's recreation of historical settings in *The Lady and the Duke*, 2001). See also **digital sound**.

George Lucas, founder of Lucasfilm Computer Development Division (LCDD), declared that the cinema of the twenty-first century would be entirely digital; that is, digital technology would govern every phase of production: digital cameras, digitally manufactured images, digital editing (and of course digital projectors for exhibition). Cinema would become a medium of simulation where there is no analogue (a "reality" that pre-exists the image) and no celluloid. As in Jean Baudrillard's notion of *hyperreality*, the digitalized signs would seem to float free of the world and give the public a disembodied simulation of real experience.

Some scholars have called into question the presumably revolutionary character of digital. John Belton in a piece entitled "Digital Cinema: A False Revolution" (2002) argues that digital is poised to overthrow 35-mm technology but that it offers little in the way of an aesthetic revolution. In this view, digital has had none of the impact of other "revolutions" in the history of film, like the advent of sound or the conversion to color. Electronic devices, for example, have become the powerful assistants to the editor, but they have not brought about a significant change in the art of editing: editing effects produced by electronic means do not appear significantly different to the audience, nor does digital projection change the audience experience, particularly since its goal is to reproduce the image quality of 35 mm.

Digital manipulation of images in the commercial feature film seems, to this point in time, aesthetically conservative. Digital effects aspire to reproduce the "realism" of celluloid—that is, celluloid's ability to produce an image of the world that is rich in phenomenological detail—and fabricate images appropriate to both cinematic and HD TV screens. The ambition of Cooper and Schoedsack's *King Kong* (1933) and Steven Spielberg's *Jurassic Park* 60 years later is the same: to "convince" the audience. And the audience is willing to be convinced— suspend their scepticism—if the "illusion" is adequate, that is, proximate to cinematographic realism. If digital effects in the feature film are grounded in **animation**, they possess none of animation's **reflexivity**: the spectator's awareness that the animated film is a hybrid of materials (it is drawing, sculpture, puppetry before it is cast in film). Digital manipulation in the feature film conforms to the aesthetics of **transparence**: its visual and auditory effects may be dazzling but the audience is not intended to see the telltale signs of their compositing.

FURTHER READING

Aumont, Jacques (2006) *Le Cinéma et la mise en scène*, Paris: Armand Colin.
Essential study of mise-en-scène, unfortunately only available in French.

Bazin, André (1967) "The Evolution of the Language of Cinema," in *What Is Cinema?*, vol. 1, Berkeley, CA: University of California Press.
One of the most important and influential analyses on the development of editing from the silent era to the 1950s.

Bordwell, David (2005) *Figures Traced in Light: On Cinematic Staging*, Berkeley, CA: University of California Press.
Excellent study of art of staging, including close studies of work by four major filmmakers.

Bordwell, David, Staiger, Janet, and Thompson, Kristin (1985) *The Classical Hollywood Cinema: Film Style and Mode of Production to 1960*, New York: Columbia University Press.

Based on thorough research, key work on the studio system, including styles of narration, mise-en-scène, and shooting.

Bowser, Eileen (1994) *The Transformation of Cinema: 1907–1915*, vol. 2, Berkeley, CA: University of California Press.
Ground-breaking research on the evolution of film practice in Early Cinema.

Burch, Noel (1973) *Theory of Film Practice*, New York: Praeger Publishers.
Important pioneer study that examines, among other things, the principles underlying classical editing.

Chion, Michel (2007) *Écrire un scenario ("How to Write a Script")*, Paris: Editions Cahiers du cinéma.
In French, but perhaps the most intelligent analysis of the functioning of the screenplay.

Eisenstein, Sergei (1988) *Selected Works*, ed. and trans. Richard Taylor, London: BFI Publishing.
Key texts of the great Soviet filmmaker and theoretician on the fragmentary nature of film materials, their organization into a discourse through montage, and their impact on the spectator.

Eisner, Lotte (1973) *The Haunted Screen*, Berkeley, CA: University of California Press.
Classic work on Expressionist mise-en-scène.

Field, Syd (2005) *Screenplay: The Foundations of Screenwriting*, New York: Delta Trade Paperback.
A classic screenplay manual, formula driven and repetitive, but typical of the genre.

Gunning, Tom (1994) *D. W. Griffith and the Origins of American Narrative Film: The Early Years at Biograph*, Urbana, IL: University of Illinois Press.
Now classic text on the development of the Narrative System in Early Cinema focused on the most important filmmaker of the period.

Reisz, Karel and Millar, Gavin (1953–68) *The Technique of Film Editing*, London and New York: Focal Press.
Classic study of the craft of editing.

Tarkovsky, Andrei (1987) *Sculpting in Time: Reflections on the Cinema*, trans. K. H. Blair, New York: Knopf.
Profound reflection on the essential element of cinematic time in relation to the shot, the spectator, and the past.

5

THE EVOLUTION OF SOUND IN CINEMA

JAY BECK

General histories of the relationship between **sound** and image in cinema tend to perpetuate an ocular-centricity (emphasizing vision over the other senses) that dates back to the very earliest experiments in "moving pictures"—a term which itself serves to confuse historians. The vast majority of cinema histories tend to relegate the subject of sound in cinema to a subordinate position by studying the transition to the sound period in the late 1920s and early 1930s, only to drop the subject of sound and to emphasize the visual nature of film. Yet as long as cinema has existed, sound has been a part of it—both in its presence and in its absence. A generation of new film historians has revealed that the interplay between sound and image in cinema is quite complex and a number of presiding assumptions about film sound need to be re-examined. For example, "detonating celluloid" was a popular slang term dating from a 1930 industry guidebook for "talking cinema," and it encapsulated a crucial misconception in the history of early sound film ("Studio Slanguage," 1930, p. 125). As an expression, it emphasized the radically transformative effect that sound was perceived to have had on the film industry in the late 1920s. However, the term obscured the fact that sound films had been produced in small numbers since the advent of cinema while it supported the popular myth that sound cinema emerged fully grown from the mouth of Al Jolson in *The Jazz Singer* (1927) when he uttered the now-immortal expression, "You ain't heard nuthin' yet!" In fact, the transition to sound in cinema was quite orderly and not nearly as explosive as the term implies, and the history of film sound follows a winding path from the earliest experiments in sound and image synchronization to today's digital cinema systems. The function of this chapter is to apply a corrective filter to film history and to amplify how film sound has aided the development of modern cinema.

SOUND AND IMAGE RELATIONS DURING THE "SILENT ERA": 1895–1926

Perhaps the greatest misnomer in the history of sound and image relations is the term "**silent cinema**." During the period commonly referred to as the "silent era" (roughly from 1895 to the end of the 1920s), films were never called "silent," nor were they even called "cinema" for the first decade of their existence. In fact, from the very earliest experiments in the 1890s—such as Thomas Edison's Kinetoscope and the Lumière brothers' Cinématographe—through the rise of **Nickelodeons** in 1904–5, films were always part of other mixed-entertainment forms such as vaudeville shows, traveling lectures, magic lantern presentations, song–slide performances, phantasmagorias, and even circuses. Despite these numerous divergent practices, there is general consensus that the earliest moving pictures were accompanied by some form of acoustic presentation. In the case of the first projected films in the United States, at Koster and Bial's Music Hall in New York City on April 23, 1896, Thomas Edison's films were shown with accompaniment by Dr. Leo Sommer's Blue Hungarian Band. And two months later when the Cinématographe made its American debut at Keith's Union Square Theater, it was accompanied by lecturer Lew Shaw and the use of live sound effects. In later presentations of the Cinématographe, this was expanded to include pre-recorded sound effects, such as the sounds of a train engine starting, played back via a phonograph in the auditorium. Although these models seem diverse from a twenty-first-century perspective, it is because films were interpolated into pre-existing entertainment forms as part of a variety bill. Therefore, much of the early history of cinema can be understood as multiple attempts at establishing a sense of accord between image and sound.

After the turn of the century, as moving pictures began to be used more regularly in vaudeville shows, their musical accompaniment grew from the lone pianist to the inclusion of small orchestras. The most versatile member of these orchestras was the trap drummer, who specialized in "catching" the pratfalls of stage comedians with a well-timed cymbal crash or kettledrum hit. As an extension of his art, the trap drummer also was responsible for providing synchronous sound effects for films. Because musical accompaniments were often done without the benefit of previewing the films, they would regularly vary from show to show and theater to theater. Therefore, visual cues within the films would often trigger related sound effects (see a cow, rattle a cowbell) or musical passages (generally relying on the recognition of lyrical passages from popular songs) that would either augment or hinder an audience's experience of a film.

Although films were just one part of an evening's entertainment, in their first ten years they grew from 1- to 2-minute actualities and trick films to 5- to 10-minute narrative pieces. In early cinema, traveling lecturers like Lyman Howe used moving pictures to augment their slide show presentations, and to add an extra dimension, a team of sound-effects men—often stationed behind the screen—were employed to bring the image to life through the addition of **synchronous sounds**. This led to vocal "impersonators" like LeRoy Carleton, who would use his voice to provide sound effects during his lectures, and immersive sensorial experiences like Hale's Tours. Utilizing a trailer that had been converted to look like a railroad car, Hale's Tours would project "phantom" train films (shot from the perspective at the front of the engine) on the front wall as live sound effects were played and the trailer was jostled to mimic the experience of movement. Intriguingly, these formats did not emphasize the now-common narrative function of the film; instead they used both image and sound to convey a sensorial experience.

Cinemas, based around the exclusive viewing of moving pictures, did not arrive until the Nickelodeon boom between 1904 and 1908. And with the fundamental rules of editing working to construct narrative trajectories in the films, the lecturer's role of explaining the content of the films became less necessary. Thus, with the Nickelodeon's piano accompanist providing music for the illustrated song slides and sing-a-longs, the films were shown in silence as often as they were shown with some form of acoustic accompaniment. Despite this, Nickelodeons were far from silent. Projectors were noisy mechanical devices that were located at the back of the room. Audiences were encouraged to sing along with the slides and were not discouraged from conversing during the film presentations. In addition, ballyhoo music was often played on phonographs directed out into the street to draw patrons into the theater. The result is that early cinema was a heterogeneous experience where events within (and outside of) the space of the theater demanded the audience's attention as much as the films being projected.

Even though live musical accompaniment became the main form of sound in early cinema, the idea of synchronous sound and image correlation was a concern from the earliest days in the development of cinema technology. Even in the first Kinetograph experiments, Edison sought to combine sound and image by using musical recordings on cylinder to accompany film shorts. Although most historians are quick to invoke Edison's words about the Kinetoscope as "an instrument which should do for the eye what the phonograph does for the ear," few bothered to include the full quote, which explains "and that by a combination of the two all motion and sound could be recorded and reproduced simultaneously" (quoted in Dickson and Dickson, 2000, p. 14).

The synchronous reproduction of sound and image had been a goal of Edison, as well as most of the early inventors, from the very start of moving images. However, the maintenance of synchronization while using disks or cylinders, which could easily get scratched and skip, with hand-cranked cameras and projectors proved to be very difficult. In addition, recordings had to be amplified acoustically, which meant that they could be heard clearly in a small room but did not provide sufficient volume for larger auditoriums. Despite numerous attempts at synchronous sound and image devices—like Edison's Kinetophone (1895), Gaumont's Chronophone (1902), Messter's Kosmograph (1903), Norton's Cameraphone (1908), and the modified Kinetophone (1913)—both the difficulties surrounding synchronization and the lack of amplification stood in the way of success for any one system.

This difficulty in providing synchronization between sound and image recording devices led to the development of varying strategies for combining sound with the projected image. As the presentational methods for early cinema changed—from Nickelodeons to movie palaces—so too did the interplay between the image and accompanying music and sound effects. With the emergence of stable systems of cinema production and distribution, and the development of visual techniques such as editing and **intertitle**s, came new sound and image relationships: from the orchestral accompaniments in large movie palaces and scores specifically composed for feature films, to the continued use of narrators to enhance the narratives with dialogue and sound effects in the tradition of the Japanese *benshi* and Québecquois *bonimenteur*.

THE TRANSITION TO SOUND: 1926–35

The earliest experiments to add synchronous sound to films had failed outright or met with little success with exhibitors; however, in the second half of the 1920s, an alignment of specific determinants allowed sound film to take root and flourish. Film sound became a practical reality only with the invention of electrical amplification in the 1920s, and the development of new technologies in the radio and telephone industries had a direct impact on cinema. Lee De Forest, who revolutionized early radio with his Audion vacuum tube, was one of the first individuals to apply the notion of electrical amplification to film sound when he developed the Phonofilm system for recording **sound-on-film** in 1922. Unlike most preceding film sound systems, the Phonofilm did not rely on a synchronized disk recording; instead, the sound waves were recorded on film as oscillating light and dark wave patterns. The Phonofilm boasted perfect synchronization, even if the film were to break and be repaired, but it initially suffered from poor sound quality. After a less than successful debut in April 1923, De Forest started filming synchronized film performances by several of Broadway's brightest stars and he signed up engineers Theodore Case and Earl Sponable to fix the problems with the system's sound. With the addition of Case's light-valve technology, the sound quality of the Phonofilm was improved and De Forest started marketing his films directly to theater owners. By 1924 the Phonofilm system was installed in over 50 theaters and De Forest was regularly producing a number of shorts that highlighted Broadway performers and vaudeville routines. In contrast with the advanced editing patterns and complicated camera movements of "silent" cinema, these sound shorts were static single-takes shot with a fixed camera. Although the shorts were successful in presenting synchronized sound and image, De Forest was unable to interest any of the major film studios in using the technology. By 1926, Case and Sponable had left the company and Phonofilm had been relegated to a novelty.

Even though De Forest's system had failed to provide a model for the successful representation of sound and image, it was not due to the technology. Concurrent with De Forest's work in sound-on-film, AT&T's Bell Laboratories was developing a **sound-on-disk** system called Vitaphone, and in April 1925, this new system was introduced to the Warner brothers. Despite a long-standing wariness of "talking cinema," they were overwhelmed by the impact of synchronized voice and music. After expressing his reservations about using the system for the reproduction of voice, Harry Warner noted:

> We can use it *for musical accompaniment to our pictures*! We can film and record vaudeville and musical acts, and make up programs for houses that can't afford the real thing or can't get big-time acts.
> (Green, 1929, p. 50; emphasis in original)

Their goal was not to make talking pictures, but to obviate the need for theater orchestras.

After the June 1925 merger between Warner Bros. and AT&T, two divergent paths of sound usage were followed: the first concentrated on recording sound and images live for the shorts, while the second confined itself to adding semi-synchronized musical scores to already completed feature films. Through this two-pronged approach, Warner Bros. was able to test their new equipment in the lower-priced shorts, incorporate technological advances into their feature films, and market the Vitaphone equipment by ensuring smaller theater owners the same program quality and content as higher-priced venues. The new Vitaphone team conducted several tests to perfect the art of live recording in which, unlike the films of De Forest, they understood that cinematic elements were equally as valuable as the sound recording. They used multiple cameras, electrically synchronized, to capture different angles on the action being recorded. The takes were then edited together into one master film that preserved synchronization with the disk recording while allowing for changes in visual perspective. However, most of the shorts filmed were either musical or theatrical performances, which created an **aesthetic** that foregrounded sound synchronization often at the expense of visual expressiveness.

Vitaphone made its public debut on August 6, 1926, when a program of Vitaphone shorts preceded *Don Juan* with its recorded score by the New York Philharmonic Orchestra. Although the presentation was deemed a success, it is interesting to note that, aside from an introductory message, neither the shorts nor the feature film emphasized the synchronization of the spoken word. Instead, over the next year Warner Bros. and Vitaphone continued to release films with recorded scores and dozens of musical shorts, yet dialogue was rarely emphasized. By the time *The Jazz Singer* debuted on October 6, 1927, audiences had been conditioned by nearly a dozen sound features that contained semi-synchronous sound effects and occasional dialogue. While there is no contesting the fact that Al Jolson's improvised dialogue sequences were impressive to audiences, it should be noted that when the film was released only a few theaters had been wired for sound and in the course of the film's run more people saw it *silent* than with sound. Furthermore, after the success of the dialogue sequences in *The Jazz Singer* it took over a year of hybrid "part-talkies" before *The Lights of New York* (1928), the first "100 percent talkie," was released.

The result is that, even though Warner Bros. and AT&T had made a carefully calculated business investment in the transition to sound films, the actual creation of the films introduced a host of technical and stylistic challenges. The presentational aesthetics of the single-take sound shorts and hybrid "part-talkies" contrasted with the highly developed narrative logic and editing strategies used in the late silent period. For example, the length of the disks dictated that feature-length films had to be shot in 10-minute increments, where all dialogue, music, and sound effects were performed live on the set. This required actors from the stage to be brought in to accommodate the long dialogue sequences. In addition, with cameras in soundproof boxes and microphones fixed in place, the actors were very limited in their movements and nearly all action was restricted to shooting in studio. The ultimate effect was a cinematic "staginess" that was in great contrast to the fluidity of the films of the late silent period.

Even though Warner Bros. was the first studio to introduce sound into cinema, the Vitaphone's exclusivity was short-lived. After leaving Phonofilm, Case and Sponable shopped their sound-on-film technology to other studios, and Fox Film Corporation decided to buy the rights to the sound system under the name Movietone. At the end of 1926, the studio signed a cross-licensing agreement with Vitaphone which gave Fox the use of amplification technology and AT&T the rights to market sound-on-film. Like Warner Bros., Fox studio started releasing its feature films with "canned" musical scores that were synchronized to the films but featured no dialogue. However, instead of providing a bill of synchronized entertainment shorts, in April 1927 Fox started to release synchronous sound newsreels called Fox Movietone News. These not only featured important figures of the day recorded speaking in the studio but sound trucks were also outfitted to record newsreels on location. As a form of product differentiation, the Movietone newsreels stood in stark contrast to the staged performances of the Vitaphone shorts, yet each was providing the same function: to use sound as a form of spectacle to attract cinema audiences.

Despite their differences in shorts, both Warner Bros. and Fox made an orderly transition to sound feature films by adhering to the prior codes of silent cinema, first dabbling in hybrid "part-talkies" before embarking on all-talking pictures in 1928. The five major studios initially took a wait-and-see strategy to film sound and signed an agreement in February 1927 that they would all act together in any transition. To make matters more complicated, in 1927 the research division of the Radio Corporation of America started shopping its own Photophone sound-on-film system to studios. By May 1928 the major studios decided to use Movietone sound-on-film technology, and in October 1928, RCA merged with the Film Booking Office and the Keith–Orpheum theater chain to create the Radio–Keith–Orpheum studio to use its Photofilm technology.

In the midst of the confusion regarding varying sound technologies, the idea of talking pictures rapidly caught on with audiences. Although *The Jazz Singer* may have introduced the idea of talking pictures to the public, it wasn't until September 1928 with *The Singing Fool* that Warner Bros., and the film industry, had their first bona fide sound-film hit. In the months and years that followed, the American studios worked at refining the awkward style of the early talkies to an aesthetic that was in line with the demands of narrative. Whereas early sound cameras had to be contained in stationary padded booths to limit their noise, innovative filmmakers equipped the booths with wheels so it was possible to have moving camera shots. In addition, the fixed carbon microphones that were attached to the ceiling of sets were replaced with lighter and more sensitive condenser microphones mounted on moveable boom poles. And with the industry's preference for sound-on-film came the capability of recording and editing the soundtrack separate from the image track, something that was not possible with the Vitaphone disks. The result is that, after a period of awkward transition from 1926 to 1929, by the 1930s the American cinema entered into a new era of film sound that served the narrative and representational demands of filmmakers and audiences.

In the rest of the world the transition to sound was dominated by the American sound systems and the development of competing sound systems like the Tri-Ergon sound-on-film system owned by German company Tobis-Klangfilm. In a July 1930 agreement, both AT&T and Tobis-Klangfilm decided to split up the remainder of the global cinema market between the two systems. As a result the transition to sound occurred rapidly around the world in the early 1930s, yet many international filmmakers resisted the models of film sound being exported from the American studios. In particular, a number of directors like Alfred Hitchcock in the United Kingdom, René Clair in France, and Dziga Vertov in the Soviet Union resisted the redundancy of synchronous sound by experimenting with the use of **subjective** sound, **off-screen** sounds, the "doubling" of voices, and manufactured sound effects. Due to the inability to dub the language tracks in early sound films, several European studios started producing "**multilingual**" **versions**. These were made by utilizing the same sets and stories, but casting actors of different languages to play the same roles. Often, an English-language cast would shoot the scenes in the morning, a French cast in the evening, and a German cast overnight. This ensured a steady stream of film releases, but it also meant that they were "fixed" in certain languages without the ability to dub them into others. The practice of filming multilinguals continued in Europe until the development of efficient dubbing technology in the mid-1930s.

CLASSICAL FILM SOUND AND THE RISE AND FALL OF MULTICHANNEL: 1935–70

With the end of Vitaphone disk recordings in 1933 and the adoption of 35-mm monophonic optical sound as a global standard, the period from the mid-1930s to the early 1950s saw sound film find its equilibrium. Even though international standards meant that sound film would be distributable and compatible around the world, the era also saw gradual changes in sound and image relationships. In the hands of innovative filmmakers (such as Mamoulian, Lubitsch, Hawks, and Welles in the United States; Hitchcock in the United Kingdom; Clair and Vigo in France; Lang and Pabst in Germany; Eisenstein, Pudovkin, and Vertov in the Soviet Union; and Ozu and Mizoguchi in Japan), sound film was able to evolve from its fragmented origins into a stable narrative system. Filmmakers moved away from a logic that demanded a match between sound scale and image scale to a more flexible system of sound recording where dialogue intelligibility was more important than spatial fidelity. Additional aesthetic changes occurred with the creation of new industrial developments such as Foley (a technique for creating synchronous sound effects), sound-effects libraries, magnetic recording, and dubbing techniques. However, the most significant change occurred in the early 1950s with the introduction of widescreen cinema with multichannel film sound and its effect on cinematic presentations. Widescreen formats such as Cinerama, Vistavision, and ToddAO created complications for **framing**, **composition**, and **editing**, in addition to narrative. The inclusion of multichannel sound with each of these systems allowed for new aesthetic possibilities, but it also meant an increase in cost and labor. As a result, the period for multichannel film releases was relatively short during the 1950s, yet it offered a model for future sound and image relations.

Although experiments in **multichannel sound** had been conducted since the advent of sound recording, it wasn't until the 1950s that the advent of magnetic recording allowed for multichannel sound in cinema. Not only did magnetic recording allow sounds to be recorded, erased, and rerecorded on the same tape (optical sound could only be recorded once) but it also allowed for instantaneous playback. This revolutionized the recording of sounds during production and their rerecording and editing in postproduction, but the introduction of magnetic playback in theaters did not meet with as much success. In 1953, Twentieth Century Fox introduced their own widescreen format, CinemaScope, which utilized four-track release prints (Left, Center, Right, and a fourth "Surround" channel) with magnetic stripes running along the side of the filmstrip. CinemaScope sound recording was done by placing three fixed microphones on the set at a distance that would roughly correspond to the spatial limits of the image. This left the camera free to move around while the microphones constructed an acoustic plane across the screen. In order to mix the fourth surround channel, separate effects tracks were combined and added in **postproduction**. The trend in many early CinemaScope films was to favor **long take**, single-camera set-ups over multiple cameras and shorter shots. Films like Henry Koster's *The Robe* (1953) and Jean Negulesco's *How to Marry a Millionaire* (1953) suffer from a stylistic stiffness that is imposed by the technical demands of the widescreen framing and the sound-recording apparatus. It is because CinemaScope sound systems patterned its technology after a model of "realistic" matching sound and image scale that it came into conflict with the highly constructed mode of representation established in monophonic narrative cinema.

Thus with the development of CinemaScope and the use of multichannel sound in narrative feature films, the spectacular demands came into discord with the need for dialogue comprehension. A common complaint of the CinemaScope system was about sounds and voices "traveling" across the screen. Because of the previously established modes of close-miked dialogue and monophonic theater sound, audiences in the 1950s found it distracting if sounds, especially dialogue, moved across the screen or extended beyond the frame line. However, the multichannel reproduction of a musical performance's spatial qualities was not considered distracting, but preferable over monophonic reproduction. It is, therefore, not surprising that a third form of multichannel sound recording emerged using "pseudo-stereophonic" sound.

Perspecta Sound was a system that recorded all of the individual audio tracks monophonically and mixed them into a stereo field during postproduction. It was developed as a response to the other multichannel sound systems' inability to reproduce the established function of close-miked monophonic cinema. When the Perspecta Sound system was engaged, the control signals sent the monophonic sound information to any or all of the speakers behind the screen while also raising or lowering their volume levels. In this way Perspecta Sound could provide "pseudo-stereo" with an expanded dynamic range from a standard monophonic optical track. Moreover, the US$900 cost of installation and backward compatibility was a major appeal to exhibitors who wanted stereophonic sound without the price or complexity of the Fox system. But the major advantage of the Perspecta Sound system was an unstated one. Because the system was designed to re-channel the information on a monophonic soundtrack into a stereophonic presentation, the "effect" of multichannel sound needed to be considered only in the very last phase of soundtrack construction: the mix. This meant that all other aspects of sound recording and rerecording carried on as before: dialogue tracks were close-miked and mixed in mono, rather than "fixed" in stereo during the recording process. Consequently, the Perspecta Sound system delivered the multichannel "effect" while adhering to both the narrative demands of a pre-existing monophonic code of representation. It is for this reason, more than any economic advantage, that Perspecta Sound rapidly became the exhibitor's stereophonic format of choice in the last half of the 1950s. Thus, the contradictory modes of multichannel sound achieved equilibrium with the general acceptance of this constructed method of soundtrack creation. By 1958 all production sound was recorded monophonically and a move was made back to single-channel film sound which had taken on a code of realism on the basis of its previously privileged narrative status.

Further codes of **realism** were explored with the development of lightweight 16-mm cameras and portable quarter-inch magnetic tape recorders. Starting with the growth of **Cinema Vérité** and **Direct Cinema**—two models of documentary that moved away from the standard voice-over to let the subjects and events narrate the stories themselves—there was a move toward the use of direct sound in cinema. In the documentaries, sound recording was as important as the image for fully chronicling events and for creating a sense of **verisimilitude**. The 1962 introduction of the Nagra III recorder, which featured a crystal-driven synchronization unit, meant that both sound and image were recorded by separate devices yet perfect synchronization could be achieved in postproduction. This gave documentarians a freedom to follow their subjects and to film in ways that had never been possible when using 35-mm cameras and bulky sound recorders. The result was an enhanced sense of realism in documentaries that rapidly made its way into feature film techniques.

Coincident experiments with film sound were occurring in the narrative feature films of "**new wave**" directors from France, Cuba, Czechoslovakia, and Japan, where the filmmakers sought to manipulate and reconfigure standard sound practices to provide new models of film style. During the late 1960s in the United States, sound practitioners also started to explore new methods of constructing film soundtracks in an attempt to rethink regimes of seeing and hearing in narrative cinema. Formal alterations appeared in multi-microphone mixing, the use of radio microphone transmitters, location sound use, and the dismantling of hierarchically structured systems of film sound editing and mixing. Filmmakers like Robert Altman, Francis Ford Coppola, Arthur Penn, and George

Lucas resisted models that dictated certain accepted structural aspects of how to correctly make a film and proceeded to challenge audiences with films that required spectator/auditors to engage with the cinematic action on new, visceral levels. These changes made the gap between the uniform address of classical Hollywood and the emergent cinematic forms of the period more palpable. However, changes that took hold in the latter half of the 1970s—specifically the introduction of Dolby Stereo—introduced a new Classicism into cinema and derailed many of the formal and aesthetic experiments initiated in the late 1960s.

MODERN SOUND PRACTICES AND THE RETURN OF MULTICHANNEL: 1970–92

In the 1960s, road show pictures, like *The Sound of Music* (1965) or *My Fair Lady* (1964), regularly used multichannel sound as part of their presentation; yet the majority of theaters still relied on optical sound reproduction that sounded scarcely better than it did in the 1930s. After leading the sound industries in terms of new technologies and new presentational styles in the 1950s, by the 1970s commercial cinema had become woefully behind the times. Although some experiments in "spectacular" sound like Sensurround—a low-frequency sound system that would literally shake the viewers in their seats—met with modest success on films like *Earthquake* (1974), it was not until the introduction of Dolby Stereo that the basic nature of film sound was changed.

Delivering high-quality multichannel sound in the same space as the standard 35-mm monophonic optical soundtrack, the Dolby Stereo was comprised of a stereophonic optical recorder, dual noise-reduction units, and a processor that derived a third "center" channel of sound from the left and right optical tracks. The result was a realistic field of sound that matched the wide-screen visual field of the film where sounds could be placed precisely in relation to their location on the screen. Moreover, the use of noise reduction circuitry resulted in a greater frequency range as well as improved dynamic range over regular monophonic optical sound. Dolby Stereo made its commercial debut in 1975 with the releases of Ken Russell's *Tommy* and *Lisztomania* and the three channels provided adequate coverage of the screen space. However, at the request of director Frank Pierson and producer Jon Peters, the next Dolby Stereo film, *A Star Is Born* (1976), also included a fourth "surround" channel.

At the heart of the system was a "matrix" converter, a remnant of the quadraphonic music boom, which made it possible to mix left, center, right, and surround channel information onto two optical tracks. This allowed for four channels of sound to be encoded into the space of the optical soundtrack, obviating the need for the more expensive magnetic "road show" formats and allowing for backward compatibility of the prints. Its effect was a constant field of sound that surrounded the audience from all sides, similar to the experience of attending a live musical performance. This was crucial to a film like *A Star Is Born*, which wanted to immerse the audience in concert ambience for the majority of the film. However, when dialogue and sound effects were recorded in Dolby Stereo, the system did not function as well. Certain frequencies and moving sounds would confuse the matrix, which would then send these erroneous sounds into the surround speakers. This required that all dialogue be mixed into the central channel to ensure comprehension. Sound effects could be positioned anywhere across the space of the screen, but moving effects needed to be monitored carefully so that their acoustic motion matched the on-screen motion. **Music**, however, provided few problems because it was rarely anchored to an on-screen image. While music and effects were occasionally deployed to the surround speakers, dialogue was strictly avoided.

Moving away from the earlier emphasis on music-based films, the first major successes for Dolby Stereo were in a number of late-1970s science fiction films: *Star Wars* (1977), *Close Encounters of the Third Kind* (1977), *Invasion of the Body Snatchers* (1978), and *Altered States* (1980). In the hyperbolic worlds of science fiction, manufactured sound effects and acoustic ephemera could be assimilated into the genre without disrupting the narrative. Specifically, the use of the surround channel to introduce narrative elements and the ability to envelop an audience in ambient sound proved very popular with filmmakers and audiences alike. But just as the genre assimilated the use of Dolby Stereo, so too did it rapidly impress its own representational codes onto the technology. After the inspired use of the surround channel to convey the horror of the pods from the *Invasion of the Body Snatchers* or the alien drag races in *Close Encounters*, future uses were regularly entangled with either the portent of the sinister or the uncanny. Conversely, the surround channel was rarely used to give a sense of acoustic realism.

Despite their advances in 35-mm optical sound, Dolby Laboratories recognized that the six-channel 70-mm magnetic format still provided the best sound quality available for theaters. Starting with *Star Wars* in 1977, they improved the sound in the 70-mm format by rechanneling two of the tracks to provide enhanced low-frequency "baby-boom" tracks. (This was the first example of low-frequency enhancement in cinema, a technique still in use today with the addition of sub-woofers to most theater sound systems.) Unlike the 35-mm system, 70-mm Dolby Stereo utilized six discrete channels and followed the same mixing patterns as the road-show films of the 1950s and 1960s. Simultaneously marketed as Dolby Stereo, alongside the 35-mm system, it was actually the 70-mm system that was responsible for many of the earliest successes of Dolby Stereo. The Dolby Stereo systems were praised in part due to the popularity of *Star Wars* and *Close Encounters*, and the "baby-boom" sound created a young audience base for the films; however, this aesthetic had far more to do with emulating the volume and dynamic range of home stereo systems and rock concerts than it did with accurate sound representation and verisimilitude. Like the magnetic sound systems of the 1950s, the primary attraction of Dolby Stereo was acoustic "spectacle."

A final change in Dolby Stereo occurred in 1979 when director Francis Ford Coppola decided that he would use 70-mm Dolby Stereo as the primary release format for *Apocalypse Now* (1979). Coppola wanted a sound mix that would emulate the quadraphonic musical recordings of the early 1970s: in both the multichannel location of the speakers and their psychedelic sounds and style. According to sound editor Walter Murch, this required a greater measure of control over the soundscape, as well as the ability to position sounds anywhere within a 360-degree area. To achieve this, Murch placed all the low-frequency enhancement on one track, thereby freeing up another for use as a second surround channel. By doing so, it made it possible to position a sound anywhere in a 360-degree sound field in the auditorium. The result was a truly immersive model that could be expanded or contracted according to the needs of the narrative. Its effect was completely original and this model of five-channel discrete sound with low-frequency enhancement became the template for 5.1 sound in the digital era. However, due to its lower cost and "spectacular" nature, the 35-mm Dolby Stereo system was adopted as an industry standard for multichannel optical presentations by the 1980s and became the dominant format until the introduction of DTS and Dolby Digital sound in 1992 and SDDS (Sony Dynamic Digital Sound) in 1993.

DIGITAL TECHNOLOGIES AND CONTEMPORARY
SOUND DESIGN: 1992–PRESENT

With the development of new film sound technologies and their acceptance around the globe, the 1980s and 1990s represented a period of both standardization and a reconsideration of the significance of sound and image relationships. Specifically, the transitions in the film industry brought on by the advent of video and eventually digitization meant that films could circulate further than ever before and have a greater influence on emergent filmmakers. The result is that the aesthetic experiments inaugurated in the 1960s and 1970s finally came to fruition. Even though the use of Dolby Stereo as a standard for optical sound in the 1980s meant that filmmakers had to adapt to a new technology, by the end of the decade directors such as David Lynch, Jean-Luc Godard, Jonathan Demme, and Steven Spielberg were each using the technology to better serve their films.

In conjunction with the standardization of multichannel sound came a shift in the conception of sound, one that put sound on equal footing with the image. Drawing on his experiences making *Apocalypse Now*, Walter Murch described his role of placing sounds throughout the three dimensions of the theater as analogous to what the production designer does when dressing a set. Hence, he called this art of integrating the sound of a film with its dramatic demands "sound design." Conceptually, the sound designer's role was to work with the director to see how the sound of the film could best help to tell the story. In a way this was a radical concept, since sound had traditionally been broken into two entirely separate domains—**production sound** and **postproduction sound**—and there was little, if any, communication between the two. The sound designer was a bridge between these two domains and would work with the director in both the shooting of the film and afterward as it was being edited. With the development of low-cost digital editing and mixing equipment, the full potential of sound design is now coming to fruition and a generation of filmmakers now think of cinema in terms of its visual as well as its acoustic capabilities. In addition, it has meant that creative sound work has been decentered from Hollywood by global directors such as Aleksandr Sokurov (Russia), Carlos Reygadas (Mexico), Isabel Coixet (Spain), Takeshi Kitano (Japan), Lynne Ramsay (Scotland), Tsai Ming-Liang (Taiwan), and Lucrecia Martel (Argentina), a trend which points toward the use of film sound in the varied expressions of cultural identities.

On the home front, the development of digital theaters and DVD technology has allowed the living room to mimic the theater. While this is a vast improvement over prior forms of home viewing, especially the limitations of videotape, it means that paradigms for theatrical sound are dictating the aesthetics of personal listening practices. In a way, DVD sound has become a kind of "options package" for the home film viewer. In addition to the standard two-channel Dolby Stereo and 5.1 mixes available on most DVDs, home theater sound systems also offer a variety of adjustable listening environments. Indeed, most home theater listeners are now able to replicate the low-frequency enhancement and moving stereophonic effects of early Dolby Stereo in their own living room. And with the application of multichannel sound to television broadcasts, musical recordings, and video games, the home listening environment has now become the prime platform for sound and image interplay. Finally, not only are digital technologies transforming sound and image relations in contemporary cinema and home viewing but media convergence is also changing the very nature of cinema itself, making it necessary to consider the future of moving image technologies and the ongoing evolution of sound and image.

FURTHER READING

Altman, Rick (ed.) (1992) *Sound Theory, Sound Practice*, New York: Routledge.
A collection of important case studies of film sound and theoretical discussions of its function.
Altman, Rick (2004) *Silent Film Sound*, New York: Columbia University Press.
The most comprehensive examination of the multiple forms and functions of sound in American silent cinema.
Beck, Jay and Grajeda, Tony (eds.) (2008) *Lowering the Boom: Critical Studies in Film Sound*, Urbana, IL: University of Illinois Press.
A collection emphasizing the theory, history, and cultural effects of film sound.
Crafton, Don (1999) *The Talkies: American Cinema's Transition to Sound, 1926–1931*, Berkeley, CA: University of California Press.
The most complete assessment of the industrial and aesthetic changes in American cinema's conversion to sound.
Sergi, Gianluca (2005) *The Dolby Era: Film Sound in Contemporary Hollywood*, Manchester, UK: Manchester University Press.
An excellent study of the changes in cinema sound practices since the 1970s.
Weis, Elisabeth and Belton, John (eds.) (1985) *Film Sound—Theory and Practice*, New York: Columbia University Press.
A compilation of many important historical and critical tests.

6

EXPERIMENTAL CINEMA

WHEELER WINSTON DIXON

In the beginning of the cinema, all films were, by definition, experimental. The Lumière brothers were making 1-minute films that documented real life in the late 1800s; Thomas Edison was concerned primarily with commercial projects, as evidenced by such exploitational short films as *Electrocuting an Elephant* (1903), as well as the first advertisement created for the cinema, *Dewars Scotch Whiskey* (1897). Alice Guy, Edwin S. Porter, R. W. Paul, Georges Méliès, and others were making early stabs at narrative formats, creating such film genres as the Western (*The Great Train Robbery*, Porter, 1902), the science fiction film (*Le Voyage dans la lune* ["A Trip to the Moon"], Méliès, 1902), and the fantasy film (*La Fée aux choux* ["The Cabbage Patch Fairy"], Guy, 1896).

Soon, however, the narrative impulse began to take hold in the cinema; audiences wanted films to tell them a story. *The Great Train Robbery*'s compelling and violent narrative was a sensation; Méliès's *Trip to the Moon* had the same electrifying effect upon the public. Soon, films were being made in two-reel, then four-reel, lengths (or roughly 40 minutes' screening time), and narrative structures seemed designed to fit these longer films. With D. W. Griffith's epic *The Birth of a Nation* (1915), and the move west to Hollywood, the narrative format seemed firmly fixed in the public's mind as the ideal structure for mass, commercial cinema. **Experimental cinema** was born as an oppositional cinema, a cinema made by and for artists, and not for mass audiences, a cinema that broke all the rules of narrative convention, and did so with a style and panache that soon captivated critics and more discerning audiences on an international scale.

Early pioneers in experimental cinema included animator Emile Cohl, whose bizarre transformative abstractions such as *Fantasmagorie* ("Fantasmagoria," 1908) captivated audiences, and the first wave of French experimental cinema, including Marcel L'Herbier's *L'Inhumaine* ("The Inhuman Woman," 1923), Dimitri Kirsanov's impressionistic tale of two young sisters caught up in a family tragedy, *Menilmontant* (1924), Fernand Léger and Dudley Murphy's nearly Structuralist *Ballet Mécanique* (1924), Marcel Duchamp's intentionally absurd *Anémic cinéma* ("Anemic Cinema," 1926), and Man Ray's notorious Dadaist abstract film, ironically titled *Le Retour à la raison* ("Return to Reason," 1923), all of which caused a public sensation.

Germaine Dulac, a pioneering feminist avant-garde filmmaker of this period, also made substantial contributions of her own to the experimental cinema, with her abstract films *La Souriante Madame Beudet* ("The Smiling Madame

Beudet," 1922) and *La Coquille et le clergyman* ("The Seashell and the Clergyman," 1928). René Clair's *Entr'acte* ("Intermission," 1924) intercut a funeral procession with a rollercoaster ride shot from the first person perspective; and Salvador Dali and Luis Buñuel's **surrealist** short *Un chien andalou* ("An Andalusian Dog," 1929) consisted entirely of a series of scandalous, disconnected scenes, the most famous of which is a woman's eyeball being slit with a straight razor.

This first great wave of experimental filmmaking also included Germany's Ernö Metzner's Impressionistic short film *Polizeibericht Überfall* ("Police Report! Assault," 1928), Hans Richter's *Vormittagsspuk* ("Ghosts Before Breakfast," 1928), *Filmstudie* ("Film Study," 1926), as well as *Rhythmus 25* (1925), *Rhythmus 23* (1923), and *Rhythmus 21* (1921), ranging from pure abstraction in the *Rhythmus* series, to surrealist "anti-narrative" in *Ghosts Before Breakfast*, and Viking Eggeling created the abstract animation film *Symphonie diagonale* ("Symphony Diagonale," 1924).

When sound arrived, the poet Jean Cocteau jumped right in with his own bizarre "dream film," *Le Sang d'un poète* ("The Blood of a Poet," 1930), a homoerotic 55-minute fantasy in which statues come to life, a poet enters a mirror and walks into the shadow world it contains, and characters appear and vanish with equally unsettling abruptness. The film's producer, the aristocratic Vicomte de Noailles, also backed Luis Buñuel's *L'Âge d'or* ("The Golden Age," 1930), a savagely anti-clerical and brutally violent film that so upset French audiences and censors that it was abruptly withdrawn from circulation after its initial premiere. In England, Len Lye's experimental short films *Colour Box* (1935) and *Rainbow Dance* (1936) gained wide circulation, and used a combination of optical printing techniques and hand-painted images to bring a world of color and motion to life.

After this great outpouring of cinematic brilliance in France in the 1920s and 1930s, the next wave of truly experimental cinema came in America, which would later be dubbed "The New American Cinema" or the "Underground Cinema" by its foremost proponent and polemicist, the critic and filmmaker Jonas Mekas. This new wave was essentially pioneered in New York and Los Angeles in the 1940s and 1950s by a small group of artists, foremost among them Maya Deren, an intense young woman whose ritualistic dream films include *Meshes of the Afternoon* (co-director, Alexander Hammid, 1943) and *Ritual in Transfigured Time* (1946).

Kenneth Anger, who began making films while still in his teens in Los Angeles, with the **Queer** classic *Fireworks* (1947), followed by the ambitious, phantasmagorical, and nearly feature-length *Inauguration of the Pleasure Dome* in 1954, was another important early innovator. He later created the homoerotic outlaw classic *Scorpio Rising* (1964), which links the members of a biker gang to Christ and his apostles. In New York, Harry Smith worked on a series of intensely complicated animated films in conditions of almost paranoid secrecy between 1939 and 1946, releasing a compilation of his works under the umbrella title *Early Abstractions* (1964).

By the 1960s, an entire new filmic movement had developed in New York and San Francisco, as a part of the emerging counterculture of the period. Of necessity, experimental films of the 1960s often employed hand-held camera work, used minimal crews, were often shot silent on a 16-mm spring wound Bolex camera, with music added after the fact, and displayed a strong Romanticist bent. Romanticism in the early 1960s experimental cinema means an extravagance of vision—multiple superimpositions, frames jammed with color, light, and movement, and images of lush extravagance in costuming and design—coupled with a celebration of the body, especially in matters of sexuality, so that the films burn with the desire not only to make cinema, but also to reclaim from the stagnant and repressive 1950s the erotic nature of human existence. Many of the films were, in fact, diaries of the lives of their makers; Jonas Mekas's *Diaries, Notes and Sketches* (1969) is one of the masterpieces of the movement, and in reality is simply an inspired recording of Mekas's life during this turbulent and dramatic era.

West Coast filmmaker Bruce Conner specialized in rapidly edited collage films, using found footage with original material to create *A Movie* (1958), *Cosmic Ray* (1962), a 4-minute visual assault on the viewer, and *Report* (1967), a brilliant compilation film that interrogates the assassination of John F. Kennedy. James Whitney's *Lapis* (1966), one of the first computer-generated films, featured mathematically precise, circulating geometric forms set to a background of Indian sitar music.

Jack Smith's Queer classic *Flaming Creatures* (1963) is a transgendered orgy set in an Orientalist fantasy world. Shirley Clarke directed numerous short films, as well as several features, the most famous of which is *The Connection* (1962), based on the play by Jack Gelber, in which a group of jazz musicians in a loft wait for their "connection," a heroin dealer, to arrive. Marie Menken was the most poetic of the New York movement, and her short, epigrammatic films *Visual Variations on Noguchi* (1945), *Hurry! Hurry!* (1957), *Glimpse of the Garden* (1957), *Dwightian* (1957), and *Andy Warhol* (1965), a silent portrait of the artist at work, are some of the most personal and gently evocative works of the era.

The most famous filmmaker of this movement was undoubtedly Andy Warhol, who began turning out films at a staggering rate in the early 1960s, beginning with a series of 3-minute silent "screen tests" of celebrities and fellow artists who passed through his New York studio, dubbed "the Factory," and then moving on to the epic *Sleep* (1963), a 5-hour, 35-minute film of the poet John Giorno sleeping, and *Empire* (1964), an 8-hour film of the Empire State Building from dusk to dawn, all silent films. Later sync-sound films, such as *Vinyl* (1965), Warhol's version of Anthony Burgess's novel *A Clockwork Orange*, and *Chelsea Girls* (1966), a three-and-a-half-hour, split-screen, color and black-and-white voyage into the depths of the New York art world scene, are vigorously framed, nearly formalist works, part documentary and part fiction.

Warren Sonbert, the most romantic of the experimental cineastes, directed a group of bracingly personal films beginning with *Amphetamine* (1966), and then moving on through *Where Did Our Love Go?* and *Hall of Mirrors* (both 1966), before abandoning soundtracks on his films altogether, and embracing the **Structuralist** movement (see below) with such rigorous films as *Carriage Trade* (1971), *Rude Awakening* (1976), and *The Cup and the Lip* (1986). A different vision is that of Ron Rice, whose anarchic, entirely improvised feature film *The Flower Thief* (1960), starring underground icon Taylor Mead, was shot in 16-mm black and white using 50-foot film cartridges left over from aerial gunnery equipment used during World War II.

In San Francisco, Scott Bartlett was one of the first to mix video and film in his dazzling *OffOn* (1967), while Stan Brakhage, based for most of his career in Rollinsville, Colorado, was easily one of the most prolific members of the movement, directing the epic *Dog Star Man* (1961–5), *Scenes from Under Childhood* (1967–70), and the sensuous, shimmering ode to physical love, *Lovemaking* (1968), along with literally hundreds of shorter works. Bruce Baillie, another major West Coast artist, created a moving series of works linked closely to nature, with *Mass for the Dakota Sioux* (1964), *Castro Street* (1966), and the feature-length *Quick Billy* (1970). San Francisco filmmakers Dorothy Wiley and Gunvor Nelson's *Schmeerguntz* (1966) and *Fog Pumas* (1967) are early feminist classics about the "ideal" vision of the American woman, contrasted with the reality of being female in American society.

Carolee Schneeman is best known for her film *Fuses* (1964–8), which explores human sexuality in a frank and direct manner, unashamed and devoid of self-censorship. Barbara Rubin's taboo-shattering *Christmas on Earth* (1963) documents an omnisexual orgy in a New York apartment with clinical detachment and a sense of corporeal abstraction; Rubin projected the film on two reels simultaneously, one inside the other, and further manipulated the images by flashing colored gels in front of the lenses at irregular intervals.

During this period, experimental filmmaking "cooperatives"—loose gatherings of filmmakers and exhibition facilities—spread out across the globe, leading to experimental movements in Canada, Rome, Paris, and London, where Jim Haynes and David Curtis helped to found the New Arts Lab, one of the most influential venues for filmmaking in Europe during the 1960s. Located in Drury Lane, the Arts Lab presented nightly screenings in three theaters simultaneously, mixing film, theater, and music, with a restaurant in the back of the theater. A number of influential filmmakers surfaced at the Arts Lab during this period, including Jeff Keen, whose *Marvo Movie* (1967) was a paean to pop culture, and Anthony Scott, whose film *The Longest Most Meaningless Movie in the World* (1968), composed entirely of outtakes, commercials, strips of undeveloped film, academy leader, and other filmic castoff material, received its world premiere at the Arts Lab in the Summer of 1968.

It was also during this period that Yoko Ono (originally a New York artist with the Fluxus movement, a Dadaist group of artists and filmmakers founded by George Maciunas) began to make her most prolific mark as a filmmaker, often working with John Lennon, on such challenging and playful films as

Apotheosis (1970), a long ascent by a camera in the basket of a hot air balloon into the sky; *Fly* (1970), a fly crawling slowly over the body of a model; *No. 5* (aka *Smile*, 1968), a brief smile of John Lennon's slowed down through ultra-high-speed cinematography to 51 minutes in length; and *No. 4* (aka *Bottoms*, 1966–7), made before Ono met Lennon, in which the buttocks of a group of friends and associates fill the screen in serial progression, walking on a circular treadmill, for 80 minutes.

As the 1960s came to a close, a new form of experimental filmmaking—**Structuralist** cinema—emerged on the scene with Canadian Michael Snow's 1967 film *Wavelength*, a 45-minute zoom across an empty New York City loft while Snow manipulates the image using various stocks and color filters. Snow's *Back and Forth* (1968–9) is equally rigorous; the camera pans back and forth across an empty college classroom, gradually increasing in speed until the image becomes a blur, then abruptly shifts into an up and down movement, and slows down until the image again becomes recognizable. His epic *La Région Centrale* ("The Central Region," 1971) is a 180-minute series of camera arabesques on a mountaintop in which the earth and the sky seem to meld into a seamless flow of color and motion.

Snow's films created a sensation when first released, and attracted an entire school of filmmakers in their wake, such as Ernie Gehr (*Serene Velocity*, 1970), Hollis Frampton (*Surface Tension*, 1968; *Zorn's Lemma*, 1970), Joyce Wieland (*Sailboat*, 1967; *Hand Tinting*, 1967), and others, who made films that were concerned primarily with the formal properties of the film medium, such as grain, duration of shots, framing, light, color filters, and camera movement. Structural cinema was embraced by such filmmakers as Malcolm LeGrice (*White Field Duration*, 1972–3) and Peter Gidal (*Room Film*, 1973), who also created austere, **formalist** works that questioned the plastic and physical properties of the moving image. Structuralist cinema dominated the world of experimental film from the late 1960s through the early 1980s.

But for many younger artists, Structural filmmaking was too essentialized, and slowly but surely, a backlash began to form. This led to the rise of the "punk" filmmaking movement, also called "no wave" cinema (an ironic reference to the French **New Wave** of the late 1950s and early 1960s), which flourished in New York in the late 1970s through the mid-1980s. Pioneered by such artists as Beth B. and Scott B., whose brutal *Black Box* (1978) depicted a man being tortured in a sensory deprivation device, along with the filmmakers Nick Zedd, Richard Kern, Vivienne Dick, and others, "punk" films were usually shot in Super 8-mm sound (in the days before video was truly portable), and dealt with themes of despair, loneliness, and isolation, in direct contrast to the halcyon films of the 1960s.

In London, the Black Audio Film Collective was making politically engaged films that called for direct action, such as *Handsworth Songs* (1986) and *Testament* (1988), while the members of Sankofa Film Collective, especially Isaac Julien and Maureen Blackwood, also questioned the racial politics of the era in their work. The Queer activist filmmaker Derek Jarman, who would tragically die of AIDS after a blisteringly brilliant film career in 1994, started on the fringes of the experimental film movement before moving into mainstream cinema with a series of Super 8-mm diaries, which were collected after his death in the anthology film *Glitterbug* (1994), with a soundtrack by Brian Eno.

At the same time, a new **feminist** filmmaking movement exploded in both New York and San Francisco, with such lesbian activists as Su Friedrich (*Scar Tissue*, 1979; *Gently Down the Stream*, 1984; *The Ties That Bind*, 1984; *Damned if You Don't*, 1987; *Sink or Swim*, 1990; *Rules of the Road*, 1996; and many others) and Barbara Hammer (*Nitrate Kisses*, 1992; *Tender Fictions*, 1995; *History Lessons*, 2000; and numerous other films) leading the group. Sadie Benning, who started out using a primitive Pixelvision video camera to create her earliest work, directed a group of playful and childlike films that effectively interrogated the boundaries of socialized behavior in *Flat Is Beautiful* (1998), *German Song* (1998), *The Judy Spots* (1995), and *It Wasn't Love* (1992).

This leads us to the present, and for the moment, the future of experimental cinema and/or video is unclear. Film schools throughout the world have wholeheartedly adopted a commercial model for instruction, discouraging experimentation in students, and concentrating on mainstream genre filmmaking. At the same time, the rise of YouTube and other video-sharing websites makes it possible for anyone to "post" anything online, and reach literally millions of viewers, something that earlier generations of experimental filmmakers could only dream of being able to do. Much of what appears on the Web is instantly disposable, but a great deal of interesting work is also being created, and through a variety of web portals, the spirit of truly experimental cinema survives and flourishes.

FURTHER READING

Blaetz, Robin (ed.) (2007) *Women's Experimental Cinema: Critical Frameworks*, Durham, NC: Duke University Press.
An excellent text on women in the world of personal filmmaking.

Curtis, David (1971) *Experimental Cinema*, New York: Universe.
A superb overview of the entire movement from the 1920s to 1970.

Curtis, David (ed.) (1996) *A Directory of British Film and Video Artists*, London: John Libbey.
The best book on British experimental cinema.

Dixon, Wheeler Winston (1997) *The Exploding Eye: A Re-Visionary History of 1960s American Experimental Cinema*, Albany, NY: State University of New York Press.
The most encyclopedic volume on 1960s American "underground" film.

Dixon, Wheeler Winston and Foster, Gwendolyn Audrey (eds.) (2002) *Experimental Cinema: The Film Reader*, London: Routledge.
Perhaps the best reader on the subject of experimental cinema, with a collection of articles, essays, and interviews.

Mekas, Jonas (1972) *Movie Journal: The Rise of a New American Cinema, 1959–1971*, New York: Macmillan.
A classic history of the New York underground film.

Renan, Sheldon (1967) *An Introduction to the American Underground Film*, New York: Dutton.
The Best overview of the early days of the movement.

Sargeant, Jack (1997) *The Naked Lens: An Illustrated History of Beat Cinema*, London: Creation Books.
The Beats get their due in this superbly detailed volume.

Sitney, P. Adams (2002) *Visionary Film: The American Avant-Garde, 1943–2000*, Oxford: Oxford University Press.
A classic text, newly revised.

Youngblood, Gene (1970) *Expanded Cinema*, New York: Dutton.
Examines West Coast filmmakers especially, along with film and video hybrids.

7

DOCUMENTARY FILM

BRIAN WINSTON

The term "**documentary**" to describe a particular class of non-fiction film comes into general use in English by the early 1930s, but film having the characteristics of what would come to be regarded as documentaries pre-existed the application of the word. The concept of the photograph as a document—in the sense of the image being accurate and faithful evidence of what is before the camera's lens—dates from the outset of the introduction of the technology in the 1840s. With the coming of cinematography, the camera's capacity to capture the "real" was its initial selling point and, although the cinema was soon captured for fiction, coverage of news events, *actualities* (as the French termed them), continued. Films of travel—"travelogues" (from 1908) or "*documentaires romancés*"—and the first **ethnographic film** appeared (1911), as did scientific movies both popular (*Cheese Mites*, 1903, Charles Urban) and scholarly (*Mechanics of the Brain*, 1926, Vesvolod Pudovkin's footage shot in Pavlov's lab). Governments were quick to see film's value as propaganda (Urban's *Battle of the Somme*, 1916); so were charities (Save the Children's *Russian Famine*, 1921). European artists, such as the painter Fernand Léger, experimented with the manipulation of images of the everyday often in a non-narrative form (*Ballet mécanique*, 1924). Overall, though, non-fiction film was resistant to the growing sophistication of the fictional cinema's narrative techniques.

"Documentary" came to describe a specific non-fiction cinema that melded the camera's ability to document the world with fiction's compelling narratives, but without so manipulating the original material that its claim on the real would become attenuated. Edward Curtis's *In the Land of the Headhunters* (1914), for instance, combined non-actors (aka "real" people) and authentic settings and costumes (albeit in Edward's established still-photographic style of recreations of the immediate past) with a fictional story that had no relationship with the Kwakiutl culture he was supposedly recording. He saw the work, nevertheless, as "documenting," in some sense or another, Native American reality (Holm and Quimby, 1980).

Robert Flaherty, a prospector filming in the Canadian Arctic, failed in his earliest attempts to move beyond what he described as "a scene of this and a scene of that ... no story" (Christopher, 2005, p. 322); but *Headhunters* showed him how. In 1920–1, with specialized technology (hand-cranked Akeley cameras specially designed for use in the wild), Flaherty filmed a dramatic 20-year-old true Inuit story of survival. He cast a trapper, Allakarialuk, renamed for the film "Nanook," as the hero of his reconstruction of this tale. Leaving Curtis's fictional storytelling behind, Flaherty's breakthrough was to realize that footage of "real" people in real (even reconstructed "real") situations could be edited into an exciting narrative, essentially through **intertitles**. The film, which Flaherty not only shot but also, with the help of the Inuit, developed in the Arctic, was *Nanook of the North*. It is, conventionally, considered as the first documentary and it was an amazing commercial success. A brief vogue for dramatized features "of the travelogue type" followed (e.g. *Grass: A Nation's Battle for Life*, 1926, shot in Persia by Ernest Schoedsack and Merian Cooper).

In post-revolutionary Russia, Dziga Vertov's (aka Denis Kaufman's) *Kinoglaz: Zhizn' vrasplokh* ("Kino Eye: Life Caught Unaware," 1924) was, he claimed, "the world's first attempt to create a film-object without the participation of actors, artists, directors; without using a studio, sets, costumes. All members of the cast continue to do what they usually do in life" (Vertov, 1984, p. 34). But not straightforwardly so: for example, to illustrate as vividly as possible how much effort is required to make a loaf of bread, Vertov edited film of the process running backward, starting with the loaf and finishing with the wheat being harvested. His "rhythm of the city" film, *Chelovek s kino-apparatom* ("The Man with the Movie Camera," 1929), added to a montage of city scenes—as in, for example, *Berlin: Die Sinfonie der Großstadt* ["Berlin: Symphony of a City," 1929], made by avant-garde abstract film pioneers Walter Ruttman and Hans Richter—footage of his film's own production process including shots of the cameraman and the editor at work. Less challenging in form but also of lasting importance was *Padenie dinastii Romanovykh* ("The Fall of the Romanov Dynasty," 1927), Esfir Shub's brilliantly re-edited pioneering compilation of the fallen Czar's home movies and newsreel footage.

After the initial attraction of full-length documentaries, the range of possibilities for documentary expression narrowed, as did further explorations of the documentary idea. Already by 1926, Famous Players Lasky, having commissioned Flaherty's second film *Moana: A Tale of the South Seas*, had hesitated to release it; but, after all, *Nanook* itself had been sponsored by a fur company. Documentarists could look for funding outside of the box office.

The term "documentary" was now coming into general use. John Grierson, in a New York newspaper review of *Moana*, had written of the film's "documentary value." Grierson, who was Scottish, upon his return to the United Kingdom, established a publicly funded production unit dedicated to molding films of witnessed—or of reconstructed (i.e. pre-witnessed)—everyday events into satisfying, and instructive, narratives. Grierson's activities established in the United Kingdom a documentary movement making short films for a variety of organizations from the post office (e.g. *Nightmail*, 1936, Harry Watt and Basil Wright) to the energy utility companies (e.g. *Housing Problems*, 1935, Edgar Anstey and Arthur Elton).

The vocabulary of the documentary was being firmly established—observed footage, voice-over commentary, explanatory graphics, added sound effects and music. Synchronous—direct—sound, though, challenged the filmmakers' capacity to avoid reconstruction. Nevertheless, it was essayed, first in the Soviet Union where Shub used interviews in *KShE* ("Komsomal: Pioneer of Electrification," 1932) as did Vertov in *Tri Prisni ni Lenin* ("Three Songs of Lenin") two years later. The first interviews in English were in *Housing Problems*. On the whole, documentarists were uncomfortable with sync dialogue scenes. Even if based on prior witness, sync shooting produced often embarrassed performances by the non-actors involved.

The British work was well received by cinéphiles worldwide, but it failed to find a mass audience. Although it was perceived as being radical in its politics, it was attacked at the time for running away from "social meaning" (Rotha, 1973, p. 30). To its left (in a decade noted for its political polarization), a small group of independent oppositional filmmakers, organized primarily into the Workers Film and Photo League, produced a politically engaged, if often technically inept, body of newsreel and documentary work.

This pattern was to be repeated in the later 1930s in the United States where Pare Lorentz, funded by Rooseveltian New Deal agencies, made five films, most notably *The Plow That Broke the Plains* (1936) and *The River* (1938). Critical opinion sees the final sequences of these films outlining New Deal solutions to the Great Depression as embarrassing add-ons to otherwise poetically exceptional works; but they are the logical outcome of Lorentz's editorial position. Lorentz's crew on *Plow*, Ralph Steiner, Leo Hurwitz, and Paul Strand, were not happy at what they saw as, indeed, an avoidance of "social meaning." They turned to the left, to the American Film and Photo League and its successor organizations.

Sponsors, however supposedly "enlightened" (i.e. non-interfering), always nevertheless obtained the film they paid for. The Nazis got *Triumph des Willens* ("Triumph of the Will," 1935, Leni Riefenstahl), a lengthy paean of praise to dehumanizing fascism, while the radical government in Mexico, for example, hired Paul Strand to make *Redes* ("The Wave," 1936) on the plight of poor exploited fishermen. (Reifenstahl is also responsible for the feature-length sports documentary, the equally triumphalist two-part *Olympia*, 1938, being the first of these.)

Emblematic of the close connection of sponsorship and movie was the career of Joris Ivens. His early poetic films, for example *Regen* ("Rain," 1926), funded by film club enthusiasts, rapidly gave way to commercial sponsorship, for example *Symphonie industrielle* ("Industrial Symphony"—aka "Philips-Radio," 1931), from which he was just as quick to turn away. *Misère au Borinage* ("Misery in the Borinage," 1933), the recreation of a bitter strike in the Belgian coalfield, was again a film club production (Ivens, 1969, n. 88, p. 216). Fifty-five years of nomadic filmmaking all over the world followed, but, like almost all documentarists before the coming of television, Ivens never found substantial, steady, and unencumbered funding.

Given the sponsorship tradition, though, it was easy for the documentary to fit into World War II propaganda efforts. In Britain, government-funded feature-length documentaries reappeared in the cinemas, often dealing with the same subjects as fictional films and doing so more effectively. *Fires Were Started*

(1943), for example, used real firemen to create a picture of their life during the first London Blitz and was more successful than a fictional feature film on the same topic (*The Bells Go Down*, 1943, Basil Dearden). *Fires* was made by Humphrey Jennings, whose small oeuvre contains the most complex documentaries of the era, in terms of their elaborate associative montage and layered sound tracks (e.g. *Diary for Timothy*, 1944).

In the United States, major Hollywood directors turned their hands to documentary (e.g. Frank Capra's *Why We Fight* series, 1942–5; or John Huston's *Battle of San Pietro*, 1945). Overall, the documentary emerged from the conflict with its value well established. In the post-war years, Griersonians were, for example, to establish government film units all over the British Commonwealth along the lines of the National Film Board of Canada, which Grierson himself had created in 1938. Despite this, official production in general, never welcomed by the film industries of the democracies, was cut back.

For smaller nations, which could otherwise not support a feature film industry, documentary allowed for a measure of local activity; in the Netherlands, for example. Such shorts became a staple of art-house programming (e.g. Bert Haanstra's commentary-less study of glass-blowers, *Glas* ["Glass," 1958]. Nowhere, though, was documentary production secure. In France, a group of documentarists moved to prevent the introduction of the double-feature, which would have excluded their work from the cinemas. They preserved the continental European poetic tradition of impressionistic studies, for example George Franju's picture of a slaughter-house, *Le Sang des bêtes* ("The Blood of Beasts"), or Alain Resnais's haunting evocation of the Holocaust, *Nuit et brouillard* ("Night and Fog"), both 1955. Otherwise, apart from Disney's anthropomorphic nature films, the occasional bizarre collection of exotic human excesses (*Mondo Carne*, 1962, Gualtiero Jacopetti) or endurance (*Conquest of Everest*, 1952, George Lowe), and the quadrennial Olympics movie (joined by the world soccer cup feature from 1974 onward), documentary more or less disappeared from the cinema.

The naïve assumption of enlightened commercial sponsorship proved illusory. "Free Cinema" was created in Britain by the next generation to combat the seriousness of the Griersonian oeuvre, with topics such as a teenage dance (*Momma Don't Allow*, 1955, Karel Reisz and Tony Richardson); but the sponsorship trap could not be avoided. All the trucks in *Every Day Except Christmas*, Lindsay Anderson's 1957 study of Covent Garden (then London's fruit and vegetable market), were Fords—except for one old jalopy: Ford Motor Company paid for the film. By the 1960s, this generation, British and French, was abandoning the documentary for fiction.

Television, though, was already mounting a rescue. Although a mass audience still proved elusive, documentaries became a touchstone of the medium's commitment to "quality" public service. Only a little of this directly reflected Jennings' stylistic complexity: Denis Mitchell's *Morning in the Streets*, 1959, for example, is a perfect throwback. On the whole, television was to develop other aspects of the tradition more thoroughly.

Following Shub's lead, really for the first time, the historical compilation documentary, beginning with NBC's *Victory at Sea* (1956, Henry Salomon and others), became a staple. The nature documentary, too, found a welcome on the small screen. Television has also been engaged for decades in producing supposedly definitive authored series on a variety of topics such as Kenneth Clark's *Civilisation* (1969) or Jacob Bronowski's *The Ascent of Man* (1973) both for the BBC; or Carl Sagan's *Cosmos* (1980) for US public television.

The main strand of documentary on the small screen, however, has been long-form news-features in branded slots. *CBS Reports* was to run for more than three decades after 1959 and in its archive are some of American television's finest moments: *Hunger in America* (1968), for example, or *The Selling of the Pentagon* (1971). As public service requirements were removed by broadcasting deregulation in the 1980s such series disappeared from all the US terrestrial networks; but elsewhere, even with declining audience numbers, the news documentary remains established as a mark of public service.

If sponsorship was removed as a problem by television, reconstruction was not. Indeed, the emerging emphasis on documentary as a species of, essentially, television journalism exacerbated the problem. Reconstruction and journalism do not mix; but it was the next generation of North American documentarists themselves who, frustrated at being unable, because of inappropriate technology, to fulfill Vertov's instruction to "show us life," led the charge against reconstruction. Using handheld 16-mm equipment they developed **Direct Cinema**, an observational approach that minimized the interventions of the filmmaker.

The Direct Cinema group (primarily Richard Leacock, D. A. Pennebaker, Al and David Maysles, Robert Drew) began by revisiting Grierson's agenda of social concerns from politics (*Primary*, 1960); to race relations (*The Children Are Watching*, 1960); to foreign affairs (*Yankee No!*, 1960); and capital punishment (*The Chair*, 1962). Direct Cinema also extended the range of documentary subjects with the "rockumentary" (*Lonely Boy*, 1962, Wolf Koenig and Roman Kroitor; *Don't Look Back*, 1963, D. A. Pennebaker) and facilitated, for the first time in documentary's history, invasions of private intimacies (e.g. *A Married Couple*, 1969, Alan King; *An American Family*, 1973, Sue and Alan Raymond).

Rules, a *dogme* (a set of practices that had to be followed), emerged: no interviews, commentary, artificial lights, or added sound. That these injunctions were not always obeyed did not prevent exaggerated claims of evidential purity being made. Frederick Wiseman said of Direct Cinema: "you have to make up your own mind about what is going on. You are not being spoon-fed or told what to think about this or that" (Halberstadt, 1976, p. 301). Nevertheless, whatever the lengths gone to during shooting to avoid mediation, manipulation in the editing room was essential to create absorbing narratives—the essence of documentary since Flaherty. Direct Cinema practitioners dismissed all previous reconstructed work but were soon themselves attacked. Most telling was the ease with which their supposed authenticity could be faked in "mockumentaries" (e.g. *David Holzman's Diary*, 1967, Jim McBride).

The French approach to the new equipment (which they, with the New York group and the National Film Board of Canada, had developed) was to combat such cynicism by integrating images of as much of the production process as possible into the documentary itself. In the year of *Primary*, Jean Rouch, an anthropologist frustrated by the limitations of **ethnographic film**, released *Chronique d'un été* ("Chronicle of a Summer") with Edgar Morin. It too used the new lightweight 16-mm equipment to explore, in a series of encounters arranged by the filmmakers, the *mentalité*—the mind-set—of the French. Unlike the North Americans, Rouch was not seeking to avoid intervention. On the contrary, his **Cinema Vérité** approach depended on it. He was searching for a way to use film to document the inner lives of ordinary people, whether in Paris or in Africa. The climax of *Chronique* finds all the participants of the film sitting in a viewing room after watching a rough-cut of the picture, discussing the truthfulness of their portraits. However, Morin's final on-camera comment—"we are in hot water"—indicated that Cinema Vérité was no more able to avoid the authenticity, or any other, problem, than was Direct Cinema.

Documentary remained in "hot water." For the public, whenever authenticity was questioned, it was always a matter of the documentarists' individual failures, not (as was equally or more often the case) the impossibility of representing unmediated reality, that was at fault. Public opinion completely bought Direct Cinema's authenticity rhetoric and, indeed, extended its *dogme*. Eventually, even departures in the final assembly of a film from the order in which the sequences were actually shot, not part of the original set of rules, were deemed to compromise "documentary value." Older standard procedures, such as cross-cutting reverse angles taken at different times, were all deemed to be unacceptable. Unannounced reconstruction was definitely forbidden. This was despite the fact that Direct Cinema's *dogme* had been diluted by television into "vérité," a style that promiscuously mixed all the older interventionist techniques with Direct Cinema's non-interventionist observationalism. The public, in effect, was holding documentarists to their own claim of authenticity, turning it into something of a millstone.

Paradoxically, this public insistence on "truth" began to emerge as French film theory was declaring that, in the words of Christian Metz, "every film is a fiction film" (1981, p. 47). Postmodernist thinking was ever more quizzical about the authenticity of the image. In the face of this, some (e.g. Carroll, 1996a, pp. 283ff) strenuously reasserted documentary's claim on the real while others proposed more sophisticated explanations of the documentary's "difference that made a difference" (Nichols, 1991, p. 7). These arguments were largely unsatisfactory since all depended, in the final analysis, on the image's "referential integrity" (Hill, 2007, p. 139), which can never be guaranteed—especially in the emerging age of digital image manipulation. More than that, Morin's "hot water" also had an ethical dimension. The exploitation of the documentary subject had not figured in professional discourse and had barely surfaced in academic debate, but it became a central concern for documentary studies as the new millennium began. Anglophone documentarists, though, remained largely unconcerned with issues of theory or ethics. Instead, by the mid-1980s, they were chafing at the restrictions Direct Cinema imposed upon them.

Films recovering techniques eschewed during the quarter century of Direct Cinema's dominance began to appear: Errol Morris deliberately used 35 mm and **film noir** production values in a miscarriage of justice documentary (*Thin Blue Line*, 1988). Space was found for previously excluded feminist or ethnic voices, often seeking new aesthetic forms to express their concerns as in Michelle Citzron's *Daughter Rite* (1980) or Marlon Rigg's *Tongues Untied* (1990). Others more autobiographically explored their own personal histories (e.g. *Sherman's March: A Mediation to the Possibility of Romantic Love in the South During an Era of Nuclear Weapons Proliferation*, 1986, Ross McElwee). Radical **ethnographic film** gave voice to First Peoples with anti-colonialist ethnographers acting as their advocates. In Canada, the Film Board handed the new video cameras to the public in the "Challenge for Change"/"*Pour une société nouvelle*" program (1969). By 1991, the BBC was enabling the public to make their own videos for *Video Diaries*. As the millennium drew to a close, with the arrival of new media platforms, the documentarist as artist, journalist, or advocate was on occasion excluded altogether. Instead there was "viewer content" produced by the audience itself.

Meanwhile, the politically engaged retrieved a 1930s tradition of committed works (e.g. *Night Cleaners*, 1975, Berwick Street Collective; or *Seeing Red*, 1983, Julia Reichert and James Klein). Michael Moore adopted a satiric tone, seen for example in the anti-war *The Atomic Cafe* (1982, Jayne Loader and Kevin and Pierce Rafferty), for *Roger and Me* (1987), an attack on deindustrialization in the United States. This had an unexpected popular theatrical success, which, reinforced by the attention paid to documentary at the Sundance Film Festival, caused a small but persistent revival of cinema distribution for a few feature documentaries. Humor had never been part of Grierson's repertoire but others, notably Mark Lewis, also made it central; his *Cane Toads* (1987) not only documented an ecological disaster, it did so hilariously and unforgettably.

Outside documentary's Anglophone heartlands, the impressionistic European tradition was continued by, for example, Chris Marker (e.g. his meditation on memory, *Sans Soleil/Sunless*, 1983) or Werner Hertzog in his unexpectedly poetic study of the first Gulf War, *Lektionen in Fensternis* ("Lessons of Darkness," 1991). The collapse of Soviet communism led to a flowering of documentary in Eastern Europe, often more in pre- than post-Direct Cinema modes, for example *Belovi* ("The Belovs," 1993, Victor Kossakovsky). Elsewhere, in other parts of Europe previously not given to documentary production (e.g. Austria or Finland), in Latin America, or, more recently, in the Middle East, documentary production traditions were being established.

Even television was affected. Journalistic "vérité" series were threatened by developments. For example, docusoap, which usually cross-cut short scenes of institutional life across several episodes in soap opera fashion, enjoyed a

popularity never before achieved by the small screen documentary. With colorful and often socially effective "real" characters, they also avoided the victim-
hood which had become a mark of the mainstream documentary subject.
Docudrama (or drama documentary), where prior witness in the form of
detailed memoir or actual transcript was used to re-create, with professional
actors, an account of an event, also became a persistent presence in the sched-
ules. Even animated illustrations of prior witnessed events were offered as
documentary: Paul Ferlinger's astonishing cartoon of his privileged childhood
as the son of a senior Czech communist, *Drawn from Memory* (1995), was a
most substantial pioneering effort. In the United Kingdom, a revived interest in
the 1930s and 1940s led to the use of poetic commentaries including the development of personalized songs for the subjects of documentaries to sing on
camera—a species of "docu-musical"; for example, *Feltham Sings* (2002, Brian
Hill, with lyrics by Simon Armitage) involved young offenders in prison.

Such vibrant proliferation suggests that the original vision of the documentary has become too limiting. It heralds a post-Griersonian era. The camera's
ability to show us life remains—whatever the theoretical difficulties of defining
documentary, the ethical dilemmas raised, or, even, the threat to authenticity
implicit in digital image manipulation. Grierson's implicit assumption that the
image contains its own guarantee of authenticity must, though, now be abandoned. Instead, it must be up to the audience to find "documentary value" by
determining whether documentary's structuring (or narrativizing) of recorded
aspects of observation is consonant with its everyday experience of the (non-
intertextual) real.

FURTHER READING

Bruzzi, Stella (2006) *New Documentary*, New York: Routledge.
A comprehensive overview of current documentary practice and challenges.

Chanan, Michael (2007) *The Politics of Documentary*, London: British Film Institute.
Something of an alternative history embracing more than the usual English-speaking heartlands as well as the development of oppositional traditions.

Ellis, Jack and McLane, Betsy (2005) *A New History of Documentary Film*, New York:
Continuum.
The most up-to-date restatement of the received history of the (mainly English-speaking)
documentary.

Nichols, Bill (2001) *Introduction to Documentary*, Bloomington, IN: Indiana University
Press.
An authorative introduction to the complexities of the moral, political, aesthetic, and techno-
logical issues that documentary film raises.

Winston, Brian (2008) *Claiming the Real II*, London: British Film Institute.
An argument (via surveys of comprehensive history and theory) that the documentary now
stands at the beginning of a new phase.

8

ANIMATION

NORMAN M. KLEIN

In order to fully appreciate the unique properties of animation, first we must understand the concept of "the moving picture." A moving picture does not simply require light projection. It may be the viewer who is moving instead. Let us imagine the viewer walking across a room. As a result, painted images on the wall become "animated." They jump to life, twitch like a horse. If the room were inside the palace of Ti (152?), while the viewer walks toward a fixed position, a wall of Titans seems to be struck by lightning. This moving picture was achieved through accelerated and distorted perspective. In yet another kind of moving picture, this room could be at an amusement park in 1900, filled with trick mirrors. Or it may contain sculpture that appears to move, to shape shift as you approach, due to parallax (typical of the Baroque). Or the statue may turn from flesh to stone as you approach (as in the work of Bernini). (See **animation as moving picture**.)

In the western "moving-picture" tradition that leads to cinema, animation emerged first out of late medieval carnival, essentially in the sixteenth century. From carnival, we get clowns, harlequins, many slapstick gags, and death defying illusions. Carnival has also turned into a collective, standing in for many events shared in public—ludic (playful) celebrations. Along with dozens of other holidays (e.g. Feast of Fools, All Saints Day), the four days of carnival were filled with short plays performed by the locals, like "street" theater. They were usually comic allegories, often modeled on the World Upside Down (reversals of gravity, of class and gender roles, death coming to life).

By the Renaissance, many of these carnival events had been transferred into theater (e.g. Commedia Dell'Arte). Shakespeare's *Midsummer Night's Dream* reenacts one of these local carnival farces, then includes a metamorphosis, Bottom's Dream. Thus, a narrative language—a poetics of the moving picture—gathered around animation. Included in this poetics are the World Upside Down, metamorphosis, tricks with perspective (anamorphosis, trompe l'oeil), and ironic shipwreck effects (Rabelais' *Gargantua*, Shakespeare's *The Tempest*). It was a visual grammar that suggested movement before and after. That grammar easily found its way into print illustration: metamorphic faces, called physiognomies; early comic strips; magic emblem books; Callot's *Disasters of War* engravings; eighteenth-century British caricature (Hogarth, Gillray, Rowlandson); and Goya's lithographs.

In the nineteenth century, printed comic strips and sequential illustrated stories expanded this tradition into mass publishing, into books similar to novels as moving pictures. Among the masters of animated novelistic imagery, Toepffer is often cited first, along with Grandville, Gustave Doré, and Edward Lear. In the illustrated novel after 1840, up to 500 wood engravings (vignettes) operated as a parallel moving picture, with water appearing to leak between the pages; or dramatic moments sharing page after page of the text, like choreography, or like a visual orchestral score—both as caricature and melodrama—often with poses and staging very much like cinema before the fact.

By the nineteenth century, many toys ran in sequence, in cycles. They circulated on wheels, on drums, and on spinning devices (not unlike spinning wheels, spinning jennies, early industrial machinery). Their playful spinning operated like clock-like toys (c. 1500–1780; or like a steamboat or a woolen factory. The most famous of these were Plateau's phenakistoscope (1831) and Horner's zoetrope (1834), early prototypes in the evolution of the spinning movie projector; much as the movie screens for magic lanterns were converted into cinema after 1895. These specialized in metamorphosis and inversions, upside-down substitution—devices about persistence-of-vision.

Finally, puppet theater and circuses continued to evolve as moving picture. They were theatrical moving pictures miniaturized. Puppets refer back to carnival/"antic" forms of the moving picture, to spiraling, ironic madness, to gags, and to the world upside down. Antics were clowns who performed buffoonery, ghoulishly funny moments. Zanni (a character in Renaissance Commedia)—or zanies—were buffoons who capered. Thus, clowns are animated corpses who "caper," bring lovable anarchy into the world.

Puppets were enchanted substances, plaster and cloth sculptures that come to life ("enchanted" was essentially a synonym for animation). Puppets inverted substance: the organic and inorganic changed places, went in reverse.

The strings of the puppet were made to be seen. Puppets do not require the willing suspension of disbelief. They are closer to suspended animation. In puppetry, a deadly blow to the head is often comical. Why? Handmade puppets dance easily between life and death.

Animation is a cheerful dance of death. The one exception, of course, is animated horror—in gothic theatrical effects from the early eighteenth century onward, in revenge melodramas, in All Saints Day events. Fright nights are as old as carnival.

The animated dance of death is evident in how Robertson described his Phantasmagoria **magic-lantern** shows in the 1790s, in London. Robertson updated the Baroque moving picture—often about jumps between life and death—to the uncertainties of the French Revolution; and to the "new science" that we now identify as the Enlightenment. Robertson's projections darted unnaturally on the wall, substituted life with death, like an animated séance.

Throughout the nineteenth century, various showmen advanced what Robertson and other optical inventors had begun. This continued almost to the dawn of cinema, for example, at Emile Reynaud's very popular Théâtre Optique in Paris (1892–1900), essentially puppet plays that were rear projected as "luminous" pantomime.

The magician on stage animates by shape shifting. The hand—and the body—moves faster than the eye. In Paris, the magician Jean Eugène Robert-Houdin inspired the boy Georges Méliès. Fifteen years later, in 1888, Méliès bought Houdin's theater, converted it into a vaudeville that specialized in magic-lantern shows; then, after 1895, shifted to trick filmmaking. Similarly, in New York, Ehrich Weiss, magician cardsharp, changed his name to Harry Houdini, escape artist, whose "death-defying" stunts were animated in real time.

Houdini's Manhattan and Méliès' Paris—and cinematographer Robert W. Paul's London—take us next to cinema before 1910 in the West, after the invention of the motion picture in 1892–5. The classic figures were, of course, Georges Méliès, Emil Cohl, and Winsor McCay. That is, Méliès' trick film and Cohl's early cartoon shorts—both in Paris, where animated film was essentially pioneered; and then, animation in New York after 1908, beginning with McCay's cartoon adaptations of his comic strip, Little Nemo.

These films leaned heavily on the visual codes dominant from 1895 to 1910—on print culture blended into popular theater. They resembled little vaudevilles, often filled brief slots at a music hall. Or they were miniaturized vaudevilles on penny arcade reels; or at nickelodeon theaters; or as novelties copying dime-museum magic; or magic-lantern lectures.

Animated vaudeville films, often distributed by Pathé, Gaumont, and Vitascope, came in two varieties, for the most part: special effects mixed with live action (trick films); or paper-cut, entirely hand-drawn cartoons. Many animation studios, particularly Vitagraph (1897–1925), began by producing specifically for vaudeville. One of the owners of Vitagraph, J. Stuart Blackton, specialized in "enchanted drawings," or "lightning hand," a music hall specialty. Vitagraph filmed his vaudeville act. Dressed in tails in front of an audience, Blackton drew portraits quickly on a chalk board, then erased and redrew them, as metamorphosis.

Similarly through Vitagraph, Winsor McCay turned his Gertie the Dinosaur cartoon into vaudeville—a spoof of magic-lantern lectures, in particular. On stage, McCay pretended to talk to his movie creation, as if Gertie were a dog act or a ventriloquist act; or a lecture on natural science, or a creature from Conan Doyle's novel The Lost World. In the final gag of his performance, McCay seemed to jump into the film itself. Leaving on Gertie's back (like a circus act), McCay waved to the audience; and shrank into the distance, while Gertie rode him away.

One might just as easily call this a swan song for animated vaudeville. By 1912, longer forms of live-action drama emerged, from Italy and, of course, from Biograph in New York. That pushed animated shorts increasingly into a more auxiliary role. After 1915, live-action feature films dominate the motion-picture industry entirely, with cartoon shorts sold increasingly as filler before the main show. In the 1920s, many vaudeville theaters were converted into "presentation houses," with live performance before the movie—or with cartoons.

Then, after 1915, new patents transformed animation further. Most of all, they changed how the animated story was **composited**. That is, the layers of space could be stacked onto a surface that could be shot by a camera. Before 1915, animators composited entirely with paper, a cut and slash system not unlike pop-up books at the time. After 1915, they increasingly painted on clear plastic celluloid (cels) instead, except for the water-color paper background. Cels allowed for up to five composited layers, five **depths of field** for movement in space. Cels also changed how the animation business was conducted, moving toward an artisanal version of the assembly line, layer by layer, step by step, much the way movie studios evolved after 1915.

In the United States, cels animation developed mostly in New York, where the American animation industry was centered, for the most part, until 1920. By 1916, John Bray pioneered what evolved into a kind of assembly line for cels animation. His continuing character was Colonel Heeza Liar (modeled on Theodore Roosevelt). Then, in 1920, Vitagraph, now owned by newspaper mogul William Randolph Hearst, hired Bray to produce cartoons adapted from Hearst newspaper comic strips, like George Herriman's Krazy Kat.

By 1923, dozens of animation studios competed in New York, but two dominated: the first owned by Pat Sullivan (but operated entirely by Otto Messmer); the second Fleischer Studios, run by brothers Max and Dave Fleischer. Messmer's Felix the Cat cartoons achieved the largest worldwide audience by far, as many as 750 million viewers. Felix's body type and gags were, by far, the most copied in the industry. At the same time, the Fleischers ran the largest studio in New York, for their Out of the Inkwell cartoons, with over 100 employees.

Clearly, animation houses remained essentially handicraft companies, rarely exceeding 50 employees. However, production methods pointed toward industrial ways of managing time. The shift toward step-by-step assembly grew more apparent each year. Light tables, cameras, and the cel were standardized. Animators' roles were increasingly specialized. By the mid-1920s, a team of five could produce a 7-minute cartoon within about 5 weeks. By 1928, at the end of the silent era, the basic jobs were as follows: first, the director; then the master animator who designed the characters and the extremes within the action; next, the in-betweeners, who literally filled in the frames between; also, the layout artist for backgrounds; and the ink and painters, who copied the drawings onto cels for the camera. (See **animation techniques**.)

Of course, after 1928, with the coming of sound, Walt Disney added even more specialized roles for production: story departments, systems for reviewing pencil tests, for storyboards, interpretive design; and for voice and music, and technicolor. After 1931, in particular—and most of all, in color—Disney developed a new lifelike cinematic grammar for the cartoon, away from the vaudeville and print style of the 1920s and toward a more atmospheric layout. The cycles for movement required more volume, gravity, lifelike rhythm.

Much of this research and development was paid for by enormous business tie-ins for the Disney characters. While rentals for cartoons remained very low, no other animation studio earned even a fraction of what Disney did through licensing. Even Mickey Mouse cartoons, even in technicolor, remained the cheap opening to the double bill, a clever vaudeville in light while the reels were being changed. Finally, in 1938, Disney's studio delivered its competitive answer, its first feature-length color cartoon, *Snow White*, the box office leader for that year. By 1940, Disney payroll increased to over a thousand. Its physical plant grew 20-fold, at a new location in Burbank.

Disney budgets remained many times larger than other animation studios, until World War II shifted production toward animation for the military. But even in the 1940s, only Jack Hanna and Joseph Barbera at MGM could devote as much time for the production of their Tom and Jerry cartoons. Sound after 1928 had severely enhanced costs. The cartoon industry had turned into a vassal of Hollywood. By 1940, every major live-action studio essentially owned its own animation division. The Fleischer Studio had lost its independence and was financed exclusively through Paramount. Then in 1942, the Fleischer brothers lost their studio altogether, which Paramount rebranded as Famous cartoons.

Warner Brothers entirely financed Looney Tunes and Merrie Melodies, from Leon Schlesinger's studio, nicknamed Termite Terrace, in Los Angeles. Walter Lantz ran the animation division for Universal; Bill Terry (infamous for his cheapness) for Columbia. And many smaller animation houses barely survived in the shadow of Hollywood distribution:

Ub Iwerks (1930–6, mostly through MGM). Though the films were uneven and made a flatter use of space and gesture (for five years, only in two-strip color), Iwerks occasionally produced brilliantly inventive allegories, e.g. *Balloon Land* (1935);

Van Beuren Studios at RKO made awkward animated films, but some were wonderfully bizarre, e.g. *The Sunshine Makers* (1935).

The cartoon master works from Disney overwhelmed the competition. Here's a very brief list of some of the most admired, simply from 1934 to 1938: *Three Little Pigs* (1934); *The Band Concert* (1935); *Moose Hunters* (1937); *Clock Cleaners* (1937); *The Old Mill* (1937); and *Brave Little Tailor* (1938). Clearly, Disney set the standard, and innovated the essential tools, for continuity of movement and for how to composite space (e.g. stretch and squash, anticipation).

At the same time, the rich alternatives from Warners after 1937, and from Fleischer in 1931–4, are just as indelible today. Fleischer's Betty Boop and Popeye cartoons expanded the vaudeville moving picture into Swiftian antic caricature, by expanding the possibilities of metamorphosis and choreography. After 1970, the rediscovery of Fleischer graphics and movement inspired a new generation of animators, ranging from Hayao Miyazaki to Sally Cruikshank, and more. In 1980, when I held a fiftieth anniversary tribute to Betty Boop, with her originator Grim Natwick, hundreds of people poured into CalArts. Video artist Ed Emshwiller and others paid tribute to the Fleischer heritage: Betty Boop as Snow White, Grampy as magician. Superman's chrome-blue New York clearly influenced Tim Burton's Batman films, as well as Japanese anime versions of

Neo Tokyo. After 1982, Fleischer animation also became a tonic for animated music videos and was often cited as the birth of the form.

Warners chase cartoons may have left an even larger arc in world cinema, as avatars for action films, for a tightrope style of rapid-fire editing. Tex Avery utterly re-invented the chase, in work at Warners/Schlesinger from 1937 to 1942. He converted Disney action sequences, as in *The Hare and the Tortoise*, into hyperbolic parallel worlds. The viewer literally entered the cartoon, as if through a revolving door. The movie theater itself, even the edges beyond the movie screen, could be tossed into the action. One could argue very easily that every director of action in animation has memorized the velocity of Warners chase cartoons, reviewed many of the key films frame by frame.

Tex Avery's original team (unit) included Bob Clampett, Chuck Jones, and Frank Tashlin, who all became unique masters of the form: Clampett almost liquid in his chases; Jones brilliantly self-reflexive in his gags; and Tashlin taking the chase directly into live-action feature filmmaking. Even the Warners veteran joined the chase: Friz Freleng engineering disaster cartoons, the master of pyramidal gags (a style that he learned while at Disney in 1928–30).

After Avery left for MGM in 1942, the chase continued to evolve at Warners. In hundreds of sparkling variations—modernity responding to the moment—of course, these chases meant war. The grammar of the chase sped up during World War II, then turned its action sequences into cerebral, ironic absurdism in cartoons after 1948, entered the suburban, consumer madness of the 1950s.

A brief sampling of some influential chase-cartoon masterpieces:

Warners: *A Wild Hare* (1940, Avery); *Tortoise Beats Hare* (1941, Avery); *Porky in Wackyland* (1938, Clampett); *Draftee Daffy* (1945, Clampett); *Book Revue* (1946, Clampett); *Rabbit of Seville* (1950, Jones); *Rabbit Seasoning* (1952, Jones); *Duck Amuck* (1953, Jones).

MGM: *Puss Gets the Boot* (1940, Hanna and Barbera); *The Zoot Cat* (1944, Hanna and Barbera); *Red Hot Riding Hood* (1943, Avery); *Dumb-Hounded* (1943, Avery); *King-Size Canary* (1947, Avery); *Bad Luck Blackie* (1949, Avery); *Magical Maestro* (1952, Avery).

Lantz: *Pantry Panic* (1941, Lantz).

After 1950, however, the cartoon industry was increasingly under assault. Financial support was steadily melting, because the Hollywood studio system was in decline. Thus, Avery himself made a number of chase TV commercials (Raid aerosol gags; Frito Bandito). As the studios shrank, the tradition of the animated moving picture reasserted itself. The animation industry, led by Disney, turned toward its roots in architecture, public spectacle, and crossover media.

Disneyland would seem to be all those three. Its opening in 1955 marked the beginning of a land rush. Themed architecture—animation back to its Baroque roots—rapidly colonized many new American suburbs; in stages, from 1955 to 1990. And as an overlapping trend, many inner-city slums made a comeback from 1980 onward, but essentially as suburbanized urban villages, almost as movie-set recreations. Thus, there are suburban and urban forms of animated architecture.

A flourish of scripted, illusionistic spaces appeared, historically in synch with the years after the national freeway system was approved for construction; also as GI Bill suburban tracts were constructed (particularly after the Korean War). From 1955 to 2000, animated architecture "moved" to theme parks, casinos, fast food restaurants, airports, and shopping malls—and finally into private pleasures at home, into the digital era. But first, we shift our attention across the Atlantic.

By the mid-1950s, and for 30 years afterward, the culture of the Cold War—increasingly a shared culture worldwide—brought many European animators into worldwide attention: masters from Czechoslovakia, Russia, France, Britain, Yugoslavia, and Italy, including breathtaking eccentric animated films by Lotte Reiniger (cutout stop motion), or by Alexandre Alexeieff and Claire Parker (pin-screen animation).

Their inspiration came from an utterly different media culture than in the United States. As a result, their films rarely develop continuing characters; their product was not generally paid for by studio systems, at least not systems like Hollywood (though the Soviet Union had a huge centralized animation studio, Soyuzmultfilm, where Disney was much admired); and Italian animators, like Bruno Bozzetto, often worked on TV commercials, much the way that Americans did. Nonetheless, animators in Europe—and in Canada—concentrated on very different aspects in the tradition of the moving picture than animators in the United States. European animation was far more involved in mixed media, puppetry, painting, and collage.

But that is a fascinating list, because each of these categories was also directly linked to fine-arts modernism (see **modernism and animation**). Clearly, European animators filtered the history of the moving picture through the studio arts, through modernism, not through vaudeville, circuses, mass culture in quite the same way as Americans. That modernist direction was certainly true in Germany during the 1920s, where former Dadaists like Viking Eggeling and Hans Richter, and modernist painters like Oskar Fischinger, turned into pioneer animators. However, Fischinger, for example, also worked on cigarette commercials for mainstream movie theaters. So we must ask what we mean by modernism and consumerism in Europe. In fact, in the 1920s, European fine-arts modernism (e.g. Cubism, Expressionism) shifted from studio avant-gardism to mass culture across many fields—in graphic design, in photo montage, in theater, in film editing and art direction, even advertising.

In the United States, modern art enters directly into industrial product design, less into cinema. American products for mass production clearly adopt modern art language much faster in the United States than in Europe: American Fordism, Taylorism, time management, the assembly line, modernist electrical appliances for the kitchen. By contrast, in 1920s Germany, Bauhaus prototypes were famous in the fine arts, but were not mass produced until the 1950s; they were not immediately as marketable as Ford automobiles, or the American Coldspot refrigerator (1928).

The exception to this rule in Europe was cinema. Expressionist art (essentially avant-gardist) entered cinema produced at UFA Studios in Berlin by 1919; and UFA rivaled Hollywood in scale during the 1920s. The avant-garde indeed partnered much more easily within mainstream cinema in Europe, particularly in Germany, Denmark, Sweden, France, and the Soviet Union. As science-fiction buffs know, experimental animation was featured in the German "block-buster" *Metropolis* (1926), and advanced Constructivism in the Soviet designer utopian fantasy *Aelita* (1924). Compare that with Willis O'Brien's stop-motion creatures in *The Lost World* (1925), stunning and popular (they inspired the boy Bob Clampett to become an animator, he told me). But Willis O'Brien emerged from very different sources than Vladeslav Starevich, for example, who was the master inventor of Eastern European stop-motion fantasy animation (particularly from 1911 to 1936), and whose work was then reinterpreted as **Surrealism** by Polish and Czech animators in the 1960s, including the young Jan Svankmajer.

Experimental animation in Europe was quite different narratively from American studios as well. Its narratives were less about vaudeville gags, more about print. Its "characters" were more often abstract shape, non-objective space. The animation cycles clearly resembled the implied movement in modern abstract painting. They were the moving picture as spiritual abstraction, journeys into spirochetic environments, symphonic absence as presence. In *Ballet méca-nique* (1924), former Dadaist Man Ray combined with former Cubist painter Fernand Léger to deliver a headlong collage on the presence of the moving picture, including a fractured Chaplin.

Oskar Fischinger, certainly the central figure in the birth of graphic animation, finally even influenced Disney's *Fantasia* (1940). In the 1970s, his work was deeply studied by animators at Cal Arts who went on to design *Star Wars* (1977). Yet, Fischinger remained the patron saint for abstract animators. After 1965, his influence was just as deep upon computer animators like John Whitney. In the 1990s, the primitive shapes essential for computer graphics programs like Soft Image were much easier to teach to animators after showing them Fischinger's encyclopedic mastery of layered infinite space.

Other masters of graphic animation include Walter Ruttmann, Harry Smith (United States), the magnificent Norman McLaren (Scotsman who spends his career in Canada, reinvents the roles for modernism in handmade animated film), and Len Lye (United Kingdom). But the language of abstraction in animation has been used often in live action. Abstract animation is a drawing that can be a template for any figure that moves on a screen—an abstract spot or a duck hyperbola-ting through a flattened background; or by 1977, an alien warship going into hyperspace.

By the mid-1950s, abstract animation had reshaped even how character animation was designed in Hollywood cartoons, particularly its layout. The leader in this transition was clearly the United Productions of America (UPA), whose liberal allegories relied on very still poses and figure-ground ambiguities: for example, *Gerald McBoing Boing* (1951, Robert [Bobe] Cannon), *A Unicorn in the Garden* (1953, Bill Hurtz). But the same permissions also reached Warners animators, like Chuck Jones (e.g. chase cartoons, *Zoom and Bored*, 1957, and *Dot and the Line*, 1965; particularly his favorite layout artist, Maurice Noble); and inspired Disney animator Ward Kimball (*Toot, Whistle, Plunk and Boom*, 1953).

At the same time, graphic animation inspired highly personal, handmade films, particularly when optical printers were profoundly improved in the 1960s, allowing much more layered compositing, collaging. This can be seen very much in the films with special effects by Ray Harryhausen (particularly from *Jason and the Argonauts*, 1963, to *Clash of the Titans*, 1981), but also the collage, mixed media films of Karel Zeman (e.g. *The Fabulous World of Jules Verne*, 1957; *Baron Munchausen*, 1962); the cutout masterworks of Jan Lenica (e.g. *Labyrinth*, 1963; *A*, 1965) and of David Anderson (e.g. *Dreamland Express*, 1982; *Deadsy*, 1990); and in Canada, the brilliant paint on glass films of Carolyn Leaf (e.g. *The Street*, 1991) and Wendy Tilby (e.g. *Strings*, 1991).

But after 1960, abstract animation blends just as easily into emerging industries: into assembly-line television production, with Hanna-Barbera; into computer graphics by John Whitney and Larry Cuba (the wireframe as diagrammatic volume); into early abstract video games, like *Space War* (1961); even into slot machine design (when pinball technology is transferred to slots by Bally after 1964, much more animated signage, more animated wheels).

Graphic animation was then absorbed into consumer marketing on a scale that grew phenomenally after 1960. For generations, it has been essential in the design of interfaces and Web sites for home computers; for movie titles since the work of Saul Bass (e.g. Hitchcock's *North by Northwest*, 1958); or industrial films that simulate/animate the electronic microscope, like Eames' *Powers of Ten*, 1977—the same year that *Star Wars* premiered, which in turn sparked the new video arcades (animation) industry. And finally, the same graphics is now widely available and present in millions of sites on YouTube, Facebook, and Flickr. Animation becomes a carnivalesque moving picture all over again.

Indeed, the moving picture is a moving target. Animation has been increasingly applied to military simulation and weapons systems, beginning with the company Evans and Sutherland in 1969 (Dave Evans and Ivan Sutherland).

Animated movie space has become essential for major Hollywood films since 1982, or even 1977. The era of cinemascope (early 1950s) led to conversions across the movie-exhibiting world in the 1960s. Then, after 1977–82, movies appear to literally invade (animate) the space occupied by the viewer much more, in two ways:

1 They are more immersive: they sensurround the movie theater itself. They appear to stretch, or wrap the movie around the seats.
2 They are 3D: they are designed to shrink the screen image, by plunging the action into the viewing area itself.

Both ways tend to erase the foreground. They essentially push/animate the filmic space beyond the "fourth wall" of dramatic film, toward the illusion that the viewer actually has been transported into the space of the movie itself. This utterly parallels what takes place in themed architecture, from theme parks after Disneyland to casinos (particularly after 1989), to shopping malls after 1984, even city streets themselves since 1990. In each process, the viewer is animated by illusionistic tricks similar to moving pictures centuries ago. But the story fits into our globalist fantasies: animation pretends to empower the consumer by adding an epic that seems to enhance privacy (perhaps at the expense of intimacy).

By the 1980s, there is already a reaction in animated film to the invasive, immersive, and desensitized side of **globalism**. An intimate stop-motion style becomes very popular, as in films by the Brothers Quay, notably *Street of Crocodiles* (1986). Here the space is miniaturized, handmade—very tactile (haptic), like a puppet's world.

This style borrows powerfully from Eastern European puppet animation (e.g. Jan Svankmajer, Jiri Trnka) as well as collage animation since the 1960s (Zeman). It is both surrealist, expressionist—modernist—as well as centuries old, from the carnival and from the Baroque. The films of Tim Burton clearly play with both sides of this equation: they are highly immersive; yet obsessively play with the handmade qualities of the puppet film.

From the late 1980s on, the ironic, uncanny delight of stop motion about the expressionist body still appears often in music videos, also in the film/installations of Matthew Barney, and the cyber music videos of Chris Cunningham; and needless to say, in hundreds of horror slasher films. And certainly in the revival of the chase cartoon and of Ealing comedy by Nick Park (Wallace and Gromit films, from Aardman Animations).

Tim Burton's films also employ stop-motion puppetry, more whimsically, and combined with gigantic, immersive effects. Similarly, the films of Terry Gilliam are filled with grand Hollywood immersion, but rely on the graphic animation, in his case the brittle collage style of the late 1960s, as in the films of George Dunning (United Kingdom and Canada).

Of course, 1990s Disney character animation makes a comeback, when combined with music-video techniques, in features like *Aladdin* (1992) and *Beauty and the Beast* (1991). This comeback also leans heavily on Warners chase-cartoon rhythms, and the self-reflexive ironies of stop-motion graphic animation (even Japanese animation in the ballroom scene of *Beauty and the Beast*).

The moving picture remains, by definition, a *hybrid* mode of storytelling. That is its genius as a medium. One can see this hybrid remerging yet again in the string of remarkable computer animated features by Pixar, run by John

Lasseter, who is now attempting to reinvent Disney suburban nostalgia into family melodramas with an edge more like Japanese anime, or more specifically the dramatic masterpieces by Hayao Miyazaki (e.g. *Castle in the Sky*, 1986).

The 1970s and 1980s neo-Tokyo punk style of Japanese anime continues to merge with western animation. Indeed, the moving picture will now animate the sides of buildings—giant video screens—and the front of cell phones. Five hundred years of adaptation continue.

FURTHER READING (A VERY SELECTIVE BIBLIOGRAPHY ON ANIMATION IN THE WEST)

Bendazzi, Giannalberto (1995) *Cartoons: One Hundred Years of Cinema Animation*, Bloomington, IN: Indiana University Press.
A world survey that features many of the Eastern and Western European masters as well.

Furniss, Maureen (2008) *Art in Motion: Animation Aesthetics*, London: John Libbey and Company.
A practitioner's historical and aesthetic survey.

Gehman, Chris and Reinecke, Steve (2005) *The Sharpest Point: Animation at the End of Cinema*, Toronto: YYZ Books.
An anthology about the expanded future for animation in our media-saturated economy.

Johnston, Ollie and Thomas, Frank (1995) *The Illusion of Life: Disney Animation*, Los Angeles, CA: Disney Books.
The ultimate memoir and practicum about Disney techniques, by two of the greatest Disney animators.

Klein, Norman M. (1993) *Seven Minutes: The Life and Death of the American Animated Cartoon*, London: Verso Books.
A defense of American animated storytelling as "controlled anarchy."

Maltin, Leonard (1980) *Of Mice and Magic: A History of American Animated Cartoons*, New York: New American Library.
A classic survey of the greatest and the lesser American animation studios.

Moritz, William (2004) *Optical Poetry: The Life and Work of Oskar Fischinger*, Bloomington, IN: Indiana University Press.
A defense of abstraction as animated sublime, based on a lifetime of study and friendship with Fischinger.

Wells, Paul (1998) *Understanding Animation*, London: Routledge.
Solid review of animation literature, to 1998.

9

FILMING "DIFFERENCE"

DAVID DESSER

In the 1950s, Japanese cinema achieved a number of successes at prestigious international film festivals, the American Academy Awards, and in Art-house distribution in the United States and Europe. An examination of the critical response to these films, especially in the *New York Times*—a gatekeeper for Art-house cinema distribution in the United States—reveals that the films were perceived as highly unusual and vastly different, not only from mainstream Hollywood cinema, but also from the **Art films** that were then making a splash at film festivals and Art theaters. This difference was attributed to the varying culture of Japan. This reception based on cultural difference was a deliberate strategy deployed by Japanese distributors who determined that the appeal of these films in the West based on this aspect could be exploited for festival success and **Art-house distribution**. Thus they sent out films of a similar nature, holding back films that were determined to be either "too Japanese" or not Japanese enough. In other words, certain films were deemed to have a cultural dimension that would prove alienating to non-Japanese audiences, while other films might very well be too similar to Western products to garner the kind of attention that the initial prize winners had received. Such a strategy of distributing films based on similar notions of cultural difference would not always work; while other examples reveal that the reception of films, for instance from the African cinema, would be dependent on similar ideas of the specificity of cultural production. An examination of the aesthetic features that helped differentiate Japanese cinema from Euro-American cinema—mainstream and Art cinema, both—will demonstrate how cultural specificity can be deployed to create cinematic works that are both different and accessible.

Though *Rashomon* (Akira Kurosawa, 1951) was not the first Japanese film to be screened for non-Japanese audiences in the West (a handful of Japanese films were shown in New York City in the middle–late 1930s, while the Venice Film Festival was receptive to Japanese cinema in the era of the Axis powers of the 1930s as well), it is largely true that it "opened up" the Japanese cinema to Occidental audiences. The timing was right, for *Rashomon* captured the imagination of the Venice Film Festival audience as well as audiences thereafter on the basis of its participation in the overall break with Hollywood cinema that came to be known as the "Art" film. *Rashomon*—and a handful of Japanese films to follow—could trade on the Art-cinema label while at the same time distinguishing itself from both Hollywood and the European Art film on which it piggy-backed to fame. The sterling reception at Venice, where it won the

Golden Lion, followed by universally good reviews as well as an Academy Award for Best Foreign Language film, inspired its distributor, Daiei, to send other films to European festivals, especially Venice and Cannes. Believing that there was something in particular about *Rashomon* that appealed to Western audiences, the studio sent other films which it deemed to have a corresponding nature, films which did indeed meet with similar acclaim: *Ugetsu* ("Ugetsu monogatari," Kenji Mizoguchi, 1953) netted a Silver Lion at Venice (in a year that saw so many quality productions the jury felt it could award no single "Golden Lion" and instead gave a handful of Silver), while *Gate of Hell* (Jigokumon) took the Grand Prize at Cannes the following year along with another Best Foreign Language Oscar for Japan. In the year following *Rashomon*, Daiei had also sent Mizoguchi's *The Life of Oharu* (Saikaku ichidai onna) to Venice and would the year after *Ugetsu* send the same director's *Sansho the Bailiff* (Sansho dayu); two years after that Mizoguchi would again be a presence at Venice with *Princess Yang Kwei Fei* (Yokihi). It was clear to Daiei and to other Japanese producers and distributors interested in festival acclaim and Art-house distribution that the positive reception of these films was based largely or in large measure on their "difference."

A large ad in the *New York Times* at the time of the film's release is exemplary of how the distribution and exhibition of *Rashomon* traded on the Venice Film Festival award, positive reviews, and the highlighting of difference. Running on December 28, 1951, the ad loudly proclaimed "Best Film of the Year! 1951 Venice Film Festival." Excerpted quotes from critics follow thereon, remarks which clearly indicate that "difference" is the selling point. A quote from the *New York Herald Tribune* calls the film "a striking cinema novelty." The critic from the *New York World-Telegram & Sun* indicates that the film is "strangely fascinating . . ." The *New York Daily News* is unequivocal that "*Roshomon* [sic] is unique cinema." The ad itself begins with a lengthy excerpt from the *Times*'s own review by famed critic Bosley Crowther. The film had been chosen to reopen the rebuilt and refurbished Little Carnegie Theater which had since the 1920s shown prestigious foreign films (the term "Art Cinema" was not in common use in the pre-World War II period). Crowther calls *Rashomon* a "doubly rewarding experience," both for the film itself and the "attractive and comfortable surroundings" of the reopened venue. For the venerable critic, *Rashomon* will prove rewarding for those "who seek out unusual films . . ." He claims that the film is indeed of such an unusual quality as to be "an artistic achievement of such distinct and exotic character it is difficult to estimate it alongside conventional story films." Words and phrases, then, like "novelty," "strangely fascinating," "unique," "unusual," and, perhaps most tellingly, "exotic," indicate that, even in the midst of Italian, French, and British films garnering festival awards and Art-house distribution, *Rashomon* stands out for its difference.

Based on its success at Venice, Mizoguchi's *Ugetsu* found distribution in the United States and other Western nations. Bosley Crowther first reviewed the film for the September 8, 1954 edition of the *Times* when it opened at Manhattan's Plaza Theater (another Art-house venue in mid-town). He seems rather unfavorable toward the film, or at least ambivalent about it. He wants to make it clear that the film will not be especially comprehensible for American audiences, that it will be "hard for even the most attentive patron to grasp as it goes along." This is a matter of both theme and style, he claims. Yet, since the theme turns out to be, at least for him, that "social ambition and greed" are harmful, surely that is hardly difficult for any audience to grasp. Thus it must be that Crowther has hit upon what will be the most salient level at which Japanese films will accentuate their difference: cinematic treatment. He himself comes to appreciate it eventually for its "eerie charm" and its fable-like qualities. Eventually, he concludes, one will find out "what's cooking" and thereby "get flavor from this weird, exotic stew." He goes on to describe the film as containing "demoniac shapes and sounds, hypnotic wailing of voices and some beautiful images." His claim that "Terror is caught in monstrous faces and wildly contorted human forms" seems to indicate that the film's style was indeed somewhat incomprehensible, or highly suggestive, since there are in fact no monstrous faces and contorted human forms, nor any "demoniac shapes" for that matter. But beautiful images and "gorgeous pictorial harmonies" there surely are, and these are what create for Crowther the exoticism of the film.

The cinematic difference represented by *Rashomon* and *Ugetsu* led Crowther to write a follow-up piece which appeared on September 12 of that year. Under the sub-heading "Japanese Films Full of Beauty and Mystery," Crowther pens both an appreciation for the latest in Japanese cinema and an ironic commentary on the lack of their commercial impact. He begins by dryly noting that Japanese films are unlikely to equal TV as competition for Hollywood films in the US film market. Notice here that he is not claiming that Japanese cinema could replace television for the mass audience, but rather that American movie audiences are in no danger of abandoning Hollywood films. He goes on to say that he means no disrespect to *Rashomon* or *Ugetsu*, the films under discussion. Rather,

It is simply that Japanese movies, such as the beautiful *Rashomon* . . . and *Ugetsu* . . . are so different in their concepts and structures from the general characteristics of American films that the average patron of pictures is sure to find them as baffling as their speech.

Yet, Crowther is not positing that the average viewer is incapable of comprehension; rather, that these films are indeed different, that they invite confusion, for the difference, he claims, is owed to the fact that they are products of the varying culture from which these pictures derive. The films feature

symbolisms, innuendoes and subtle moods quite unlike the factual expressions that are native to American thinking and films. The mind and the emotions are excited by devices of **aesthetic** form, fantasy and suggestion, which are much more delicate than the devices that we're accustomed to.

The rest of the piece goes on to demonstrate how, for him, the films are the products of the cultural difference he has identified. *Rashomon*, for instance, is "steeped in a cultural climate so misty and rarefied that an awareness of what was happening in the picture was not at all easy to perceive. . . . And the same is true of *Ugetsu*." He continues to insist that the latter is filled with "weird, restless imagistic action . . . strange, dreamy episodes of love in the exquisite house of the princess; vague, melancholy interludes. . . . Be set for something exotic . . ."

Finally, in reviewing *Gate of Hell* on December 14, 1954, Crowther again invokes difference, here strangeness, to capture the film: "Out of Japan has come another weird and exquisite film." The secret, he claims, to its "stern formality, dignity, self-discipline and sublime esthetic harmonies" lies with the fact that "the very essence of ancient Japanese culture" has been "rendered a tangible stimulant in this film." He goes on to note that the use of color in his **composition**s and texture "is on a level comparable to the best in Japanese art." Writing five days later in the *Times*, Crowther continues to rhapsodize over *Gate of Hell*, calling it a "weird, exotic, tragic film in color so artful and exquisite that it fairly overwhelms the unaccustomed eye." He goes on to acclaim its pictorial compositions and use of **color** as being virtually incomparable to anything he has seen on a movie screen.

Let us stress, then, that in describing these Japanese films that marked the entry of that nation's cinema onto the world's movie screens, Crowther must always invoke the concept of the "exotic." His critical instincts and acumen are clearly sound in his recognition that Japanese culture is at the root of the thematic and, especially, pictorial treatment on view in these films, even if it has been rendered in rather essentialist and even **Orientalist** terms (the "aesthetics" of Japan vs. the "factual" of the United States). And terms like "weird" and "exquisite" similarly invoke a landscape, so to speak, of cinematic difference based on cultural tendencies that are both different and delicate. The difference represented by Italian **Neorealism** and the French **New Wave**, or by the more obviously personal concerns on view in Art-film directors of the 1950s like Ingmar Bergman and Federico Fellini, was never tagged with the sort of bemused bewilderment or effusive praise for its cultural specificities that the Japanese cinema was said to manifest. Terms like "mysterious," "weird," and, above all, "exotic" were never applied. Instead, for Neorealism we find terms like "natural" and "real" (*New York Times*, December 13, 1949); for Fellini's allegorical story of a traveling strongman and the simpleton woman who accompanies him that is *La Strada*, the strengths of Neorealism are invoked—the closest we come to "exotic" in the review is "picturesque" (*New York Times*, July 22, 1956). Bergman's *The Seventh Seal*, another allegory, this one far from the Neo-Realist aesthetic, is similarly met without recourse to terms like mysterious and exotic. Though the film is "initially mystifying," it turns out to be "a piercing and powerful contemplation of the passage of man upon this earth." It is a "tough" but "rewarding" screen experience (*New York Times*, October 14, 1958). In other words, though the films are at some variance with Hollywood's usual fare—allegorical, tough, natural, and real—there is no perceived need to invoke cultural difference by the way of explanation.

"Difference" may have many meanings in the cinematic context, but often explicit in Crowther's recognition of the difference represented by Japanese cinema is the normative quality of Hollywood. He understands the way *Rashomon* veers from the conventional story film and how audiences accustomed to Hollywood's "American" way of thinking may be confused or baffled by it and *Ugetsu*. The excitement generated by these films in Europe may indicate that Hollywood's normative function was operable there as well; and indeed it was. Hollywood's dominance of global movie screens—a process that began after the devastation of World War I and continued thereafter, coming to primacy once again during World War II—had created a situation where Hollywood film style had taken on a normative quality; that any cinematic practice thereafter had to be seen in context of the American model. Film styles, movements, and trends had always to take into account what came to be called the **Classical Hollywood cinema** (see Bordwell *et al.*, 1985, for a discussion of this style).

There arose many different notions of difference throughout cinema history. We find this beginning in the post-World War I period, ranging from the various experimental movements that characterize **German Expressionism**, **Soviet Montage**, and the French **avant-garde**, especially Dada and **Surrealism**. These film movements either built on aspects of the emerging Classical style, emphasizing either the artistry of **mise-en-scène** (in the case of German cinema) or the powers of editing (in the case of the Soviet films), or else rejected much of the American representational strategies and intentions—the non-narrative cinema of Dada and Surrealism or the less naturalistic style of **French Impressionism**. In the post-World War II era, the Art-cinema differentiated itself from Classical Hollywood with relatively small shifts in storytelling and thematic concerns represented by Italian Neorealism (a simplification of Hollywood's style in order to tell stories of far more ordinary people and events); to the prizing of a certain sense of **reflexivity** and self-consciousness about Classical cinema on the part of the French New Wave; and to more radical experiments in various avant-garde practices (many building on 1920s Impressionism and Surrealism, for instance). In the years since the entry of Japanese cinema onto global screens, many cinematic movements attempted to foreground difference—ideological, stylistic, or cultural. The success that greeted movements such as German Expressionism, Soviet Montage, Italian Neorealism, and the French New Wave (and the later entry of other cinemas, such as post-revolution Iranian or **post-colonial** Francophone African cinema) should not disguise the fact that trading on "difference" as a marker and thus gaining a degree of critical or commercial acclaim is no guarantor of success. This may be illustrated by the case of a failed attempt to try and capitalize on the perceived exoticism of the Japanese cinema of the 1950s.

If, as is often claimed, timing is everything, then the ability of the Japanese cinema to deliver the cultural capital of aesthetic difference was partly a product of the new openness of the 1950s, a kind of free-for-all in the postwar world of changing values and ideas. Under the influence and inspiration of the Japanese films that had found acclaim at Venice, Cannes, and the Academy Awards, the Hong Kong-based Shaw Brothers Studio attempted a similar entry onto the world's film screens, especially targeting the European Art-film community via the festival route and attempting wide American Art-house distribution through screenings in New York City, relying on the gatekeeper function of the *New York Times* to try and let these films through, so to speak. It didn't work. Counting on director Li Han-hsiang to be the Kenji Mizoguchi of Mandarin-language Hong Kong cinema, Shaws sent his costume dramas *Yang Kwei Fei* (Mizoguchi's film of that title is based on a Chinese story) and *Empress Wu Tse-tien* to Cannes in 1962 and 1963, respectively, to no particular acclaim. Li's *The Love Eterne*, which had garnered a number of technical awards at the Asian Film Festival of 1963 (but went on to unprecedented box-office success in Hong Kong and Taiwan), similarly captured a technical award at Cannes, but none of the more prestigious prizes at the influential festival. Its reception in New York in 1965, however, was disastrous, with the *Times* claiming that "It runs on and on—it seems forever." The seemingly endless presentation of this 2-hour film was, indeed, attributed to cultural difference and specificity: the film

> is conveyed in a style of narration that roughly approximates the slow and formal conventions of the Chinese theater. That is to say, it is delivered in a succession of elegantly staged scenes in which the dialogue is generally exchanged in reedy, screechy sing-song voices and the acting is done, for the most part, in highly postured pantomime.
>
> (January 16, 1965)

This is the same critic who raved about *Rashomon* and *Gate of Hell* a decade earlier. This time, although Mr. Crowther does find the settings and costumes to be "exquisite" and the leading players "fascinating," he is, as we have just seen, underwhelmed.

Other costume films, many also in the Huangmei-diao opera style, which feature women in the male roles along with other theatrical conventions, like *The Last Woman of Shang* (released in late 1964), *Empress Wu Tse-tien*, *The Grand Substitution*, and *Lady General Hua Mulan* (screened throughout 1965), were received with reviews ranging from hostile ("absolutely artless as far as cinema communication is concerned") to rather cool ("From the strictly Occidental viewpoint [*The Grand Substitution*] is no worse than others in the current cavalcade of imports from the . . . Shaw Brothers in Hong Kong"). It is debatable, and perhaps doubtful, if such films as these would have netted the kind of kudos received by the likes of *Rashomon*, *Ugetsu*, and *Gate of Hell* had they been released a decade earlier. One could fairly argue that both the cinematic artistry and cultural specificity of these films make them unlikely ever to appeal beyond the Chinese audience. Yet, regardless of these, perhaps debatable, issues, the question of timing comes into play, for by the 1960s the Art film had become much more stylistically transgressive and thematically challenging, yet also more codified into something like a coherent genre, through the works of the Italian Michelangelo Antonioni and the films of the French New Wave, especially those of Jean-Luc Godard. The Hong Kong films of this period were simply too far afield from either mainstream Hollywood films or the Art cinema to find a place on global screens at the time.

Returning to the Japanese cinema of the 1950s, Daiei Studios, along with other Japanese producers and distributors, began a deliberate pattern of the production of "films for export" that were to be seen as particularly, but not too specifically, Japanese. The appeal to the exotic required a balancing act: certain films made for the domestic market of the 1950s were deemed "too Japanese" in the sense of containing themes, styles, or motifs that distributors thought would simply be too foreign. Alternately, the Japanese evinced little interest in sending forth films that were fairly in keeping with Hollywood style and American themes. Initially, the strategy was to employ the long-lived form of the *jidai-geki* (literally, period play) to emphasize the historical specificities of the Japanese experience and to employ certain elements of Japanese traditional aesthetics, namely pictorialism, theatricality, **long take**s, flat framing, and either rich contrasts for black and white cinematography or muted color palettes in their Eastmancolor productions. Thus *Rashomon* and *Gate of Hell* are both set in the twelfth century at a time when internal strife is bringing about the end of the glories of the Kyoto court period; *Ugetsu* is set during a later period of civil war and internal strife. (Though little is made of this at the time of their release, the war-time settings of the films are meant to comment on the recently concluded World War II, at least for the domestic audience.) All three films rely on those qualities of Japanese cinema that derive from certain of their traditional aesthetics. The rich black and white cinematography of *Rashomon* and *Ugetsu* (both were photographed by cinematographer Kazuo Miyagawa) recalls the style of *sumi-e* (black ink applied with a brush to white paper). The use of landscape in both films—the forest in *Rashomon*, the lake in *Ugetsu*—is a typical subject for ink paintings. The quality of the color for *Gate of Hell* is typical of that found on folding screens (*byobu*) or narrative picture scrolls (*emakimono*). It is surely no accident that *Gate of Hell* begins with images of a narrative picture scroll—an art form typical of the period in which the film is set and on which the film bases its pictorial characteristics. There was, however, nothing at all natural, so to speak, in the films produced for export. They required the deliberate and self-conscious invocation of tradition. This meant a highlighting of what had already largely passed; some might even say what was never really pure or purely Japanese in the first place. It was the ability, then, to create a kind of tradition, a usable past in Van Wyck Brooks' famous dictum, that enabled these films to derive from selective elements of Japanese tradition a visual style and appeal that could distinguish them from other Art-house films of the period; that could define them as distinctly and distinctively Japanese.

Yet, not all *jidai-geki* were deemed appropriate for festival play or Art-house distribution. Indeed only a handful of period films were released to the West out of the hundreds made starting in 1952 and continuing throughout the rest of the decade. Certainly, many, perhaps most, were hardly of festival-level quality, meant simply to appeal to the domestic market hungry for films that dealt in passing with Japanese culture, tradition, and history or were simply diverting entertainments. Popular films featuring women who played male roles and which featured a good deal of singing (much like the Chinese films of the 1960s which made only a minimal or negative impact overseas) found no overseas venues (and remain little known today outside of Japan). Though their style certainly bears some traces of traditional aesthetics, for the most part they do not manifest the overt invocations of the traditional that may be called exotic, mysterious, or exquisite. So in some sense they were both too Japanese and not Japanese enough.

By the same token, about half of the films made in Japan in the 1950s were not period films at all, but rather *gendai-mono* (literally, modern stories) set in the contemporary era and in modern, urban locales. Most of these were no doubt deemed too reminiscent of mainstream Hollywood cinema. And indeed there is little to distinguish them visually and stylistically from the Hollywood films of the era. Their themes were specific (although often universal nevertheless) and derive from the particular circumstances of Japan at the time, but they could not trade on the distant past nor on obviously traditional aesthetics. The case of film director Yasujiro Ozu is exemplary as regards the twin notions of too Japanese and not Japanese enough and the way in which the notion of cinematic difference came once again to the fore to define the filmmaker who may now fairly be said to stand as the paradigm of cinematic cultural specificity in its difference.

In the 1950s, when Kurosawa and Mizoguchi were gaining international respect and influence, the most respected of Japan's directors at home was Ozu. He has garnered more prestigious awards in Japan than any other director in Japanese film history. Yet, when it came to submitting Japanese films to European film festivals and for US Art-house distribution, Ozu's work was conspicuous by its absence. The typical historical accounting for this lacuna is that in official distribution channels the feeling was that Ozu represented a sensibility and approach that was too Japanese. On the one hand, his films were not Japanese enough, at least insofar as appeals to the exoticism of the Japanese past were concerned, for they are resolutely contemporary in their settings and urban in their locales. On the other hand, his films were deemed too Japanese in the sensibilities on view and the treatment of his favored topic, that of ordinary Japanese leading ordinary lives. Ozu's films are characterized by elliptical and episodic narration along with a lack of overt incident and emotionalism in the plots. This is accompanied by a shooting style that relies on low camera placement, little camera movement (working toward virtually none beginning with his films of the middle 1950s), and slow, measured pacing (many critics mistake his films as possessing long takes; such is not the case, but the leisurely pacing of the films, with many takes of a similar length, and the lack of camera movement, make the films feel slower than Hollywood films of the time). Finally with the rejection of eye-line matches and other editing conventions of Classical Hollywood cinema, Ozu's films seemed simply too specialized, too Japanese for either Art-house audiences or Western mainstream appeal. Toward the end of his life (Ozu died in 1963), his films began to play specialized festivals devoted to showcasing Japanese cinema or to be released in a handful of theaters in large cities in the United States and Europe. At this time, critics acclaimed his films not for their specialized appeal, but for their universality. Ozu's sensibility, far from being too Japanese, was seen as delicate in his ability to capture the precise emotions of ordinary lives as they are lived everywhere and anywhere. By the early 1970s, Ozu had come to be seen as a filmmaker who transcended his Japanese roots.

Under the impetus of academic film criticism, Ozu again came to be seen as specifically Japanese, and his cinema, more than others of his countrymen, was held up as the very paradigm of cinematic difference in its variance from Classical Hollywood. This was the approach taken by the influential neo-formalist film critic Noel Burch, who saw in Ozu's cinema a rejection of Hollywood's "invisible" style. He attributed Ozu's style to Japanese aesthetics, thus making Ozu particularly Japanese in his approach. While subsequent writings have taken Burch to task in certain ways (for his cultural essentialism or lack of grounding in Japanese history and language) or rejected many of his premises, nevertheless Ozu remains the Japanese director most favored by serious film critics and scholars precisely for the difference his cinema represents—a difference that arises, if not out of the essence of Japanese culture, then out of possibilities that may be highlighted to create such differences. In other words, hardly the most Japanese of all directors, or too Japanese for non-Japanese audiences, Ozu could create out of a combination of traditional Japanese painting, theater, and narrative modes something that emanates uniquely out of Japan without recourse to claims that it represents all of Japan or Japanese culture.

The influence of Ozu on world cinema is demonstrable and so, too, is the cinema of Mizoguchi; whereas the impact of Kurosawa is incalculable. Clearly, then, cultural difference does not necessarily translate into cultural opacity or to a specificity so great as to render future borrowings across cultures impossible. The case of African cinema, however, reveals a situation in which difference attributable to cultural specificity is prized and in which filmmakers can specifically highlight those differences to attract notice, yet their films still remain the province of the specialist and have relatively little impact on international cinema. One could wonder why it has been that African cinema, overall, remains the realm of the specialist and why non-African filmmakers have little adapted some of the aesthetic features of African cinema (with some significant exceptions in African-American filmmaking). Still, there is no denying that African cinema was received as the product(s) of cultural specificity and that filmmakers and distributors attempted to trade on difference in order to create a space for African cinema outside of Africa.

111

Writing in the *New York Times* on November 11, 1990, film scholar and critic Berenice Reynaud noted the emergence of African cinema in the United States over the previous few years. African films were screened, she observes, at the Cannes Film Festival and the New York Film Festival. We may note, for instance, that *Yeleen* (Souleymane Cissé, 1987) won a Jury prize at Cannes. Reynaud quotes Caryn James on the film *Tilai* (Idrissa Ouedraogo, 1989) who claims that the director is "both distinctly African and brilliantly universal." A look at James's original review (September 24, 1990) indicates that some of what might be distinctly African revolves around the employment of a "minimal narrative line [and] stark yet gracefully composed images." Reynaud's essay goes on to quote both film directors and scholars in an effort to explain the cultural particularities out of which the film grows. While relying on outside experts is a nice contrast to Bosley Crowther's sweeping generalization regarding Japanese art and culture, the invocation of such experts to explain the context and culture of the films indicates a great deal about their perceived foreignness. Reynaud quotes Manthia Diawara, for instance, who claims that "These films [from West Africa] forge a new cinematic language, a new way of looking at people who, instead of being exotic characters, become human, and beautiful." This "new cinematic language" is, Diawara asserts, a function of the culture out of which it is forged: the films return "to an African knowledge of the pre-colonial time, analyzing its culture, its myths, its religions." The need for information, for context, has been a commonality in both reviews and academic discussion of African cinema. Here is Vincent Canby's take on Ousmane Sembene's *Ceddo* in the *New York Times* (February 17, 1987):

> Ceddo is a folk tale presented as the kind of pageant you might see made famous by history and now surrounded by souvenir stands. It's not cheap or gaudy, but it's an intensely solemn, slightly awkward procession of handsomely costumed scenes designed to pass on a lot of information as quickly and efficiently as possible.

This is to say that the film itself, according to Canby, provides the kind of information needed by outsiders, information that requires, in this case, a certain style and approach. However, it does lead, for Canby, to the "picturesque."

At this point, one should acknowledge the difficulty of encapsulating all of African cinema under a single heading. Certainly, to begin with, one should distinguish between North African and sub-Saharan African cinema. The films produced in places like Algeria, Tunisia, and Morocco have their own particularities, far different than their sub-Saharan neighbors. As for the latter, it has certainly been the nations of Francophone Africa that have put African cinema on the global map. Films produced in Senegal, Burkina Faso, and Mali have created a semi-linked canon of films whose cultural dimensions have created the sense of new styles and approaches to the cinema. Academic critics who wish to characterize the cultural specificity of African cinema tend to focus on these films, especially because of the emergence of Sembene as a recognized and recognizable auteur. Sembene's own invocation of the African griot (a storyteller or singer who is the repository of history and tradition) supports claims for the particular significance of orality in African cinema. Knowledge of the griot's functioning in tribal traditions is important, then, for an appreciation of other African films, such as *Guimba the Tyrant* (1995) by the Malian director Cheick Oumar Sissoko.

The narrative patterns of sub-Saharan African cinema under the influence of the griot is also felt to give these films what might be called an "anthropological" sense of time, where the sense of the simultaneity of the past and the present is palpable. One also sees, therefore, the deployment of local mythology and folk culture. The reliance on slow, even pacing and long shots which place people in their environments (especially films that rely on village settings) may also be seen as a consequence of the oral tradition of African ways of passing on knowledge. Of course, the neo-colonial situation is not ignored in these cinemas, so one must always be conscious of the language deployed, which is to say, whether a film utilizes French or one of the indigenous languages (such as Wolof or Bambara, for instance). Even the use of music may be said to be of significance, with critics noting the frequent use of traditional African instruments on the soundtrack of Sembene's films. Such differences, then, are both notable and important for a full appreciation of the films. Yet, the most successful African film ever released onto international movie screens came from White South Africa which, though it dealt with the native experience (in a certain way), was hardly either typical or representative of the festival and Art-house African cinema.

The Gods Must be Crazy (Jamie Uys, 1980) is the only African film ever to have wide distribution and significant box-office returns in the United States. Reviews of the film played up its comic aspects while also occasionally having recourse to aspects of exoticism or other codes of difference. Thus *Variety* (January 1, 1981) found that the film's main attractions were its "widescreen visuals of unusual locations, and the sheer educational value of its narration." Other reviews were far more positive, with most playing up the fact that the film was a slapstick comedy that poked fun at white society and its technological and other foibles. It is ironic, in a certain way at least, that the most popular film ever made in and about Africa was made by a white director about the Black experience; a film, moreover, that is in every way recuperable by Hollywood film style and genre. **Post-colonial** critics find the film to be horribly racist as it regenerates some of the Imperialist and Colonialist discourse about the "primitivism" of the noble and simple native. Trying, then, to make a film that uses African locales, actors, and aspects of contemporary African life, Uys produced a film that was a tremendous international hit yet lacked any real specificity of Africa's traditions, aesthetics, and rich cultural heritage. Apparently, Black African cinema was always a bit too different to appeal to either mainstream or Art-house tastes.

FURTHER READING

Barlet, Olivier (2000) *African Cinemas: Decolonizing the Gaze*, trans. Chris Turner, London: Zed Books.
Useful survey of African cinemas (English and Francophone) from a variety of angles, including the post-colonial situation, the various narrative and formal devices employed, and the impact of funding and distribution issues.

Bordwell, David, Staiger, Janet, and Thompson, Kristin (1985) *The Classical Hollywood Cinema: Film Style and Mode of Production to 1960*, New York: Columbia University Press.
Now-standard, extremely influential account of the major features of Hollywood film style in the Classical period with intensive formal analysis and historical documentation.

Burch, Noel (1979) *To the Distant Observer: Form and Meaning in the Japanese Cinema*, Berkeley, CA: University of California Press.
Highly influential attempt to read Japanese cinema as a product of the radical elements of its traditional culture as compared to Western representational aesthetics. Both a history and a theory of Japanese cinema that helped bring semiological, Marxist, and neo-formalist theory to bear not only on Japanese cinema but also into film studies more generally.

Desser, David (ed.) (1997) *Ozu's "Tokyo Story"* (Cambridge Film Handbooks Series), New York: Cambridge University Press.
Essay collection devoted to critical analysis of Ozu's film from a variety of historical, critical, and theoretical perspectives.

Ehrlich, Linda and Desser, David (1994, 2008) *Cinematic Landscapes: Observations on the Visual Arts and Cinema in China and Japan*, Austin, TX: University of Texas Press.
A collection of essays discussing the impact of the visual arts on the cinemas of China and Japan dealing especially with issues of mise-en-scène, framing, camera work, color, and thematic patterns.

Mhando, Martin (2000) "Approaches to African Cinema Study," http://archive.sensesofcin ema.com/contents/00/8/african.html
Excellent encapsulation of the important issues and approaches to dealing with the range of African filmmaking that pays particular attention to questions of cinematic difference as a function of cultural specificity with some attention paid to reception as well.

Richie, Donald (2005) *A Hundred Years of Japanese Film*, Tokyo: Kodansha.
Good overview of the history of Japanese cinema with particular attention to major directors, film genres, and movements.

10

MAKING HISTORY THROUGH MEDIA

MARCIA LANDY

Cinema, television, and the Internet are major sources for access to historical knowledge. Nonetheless, numerous instances of media's appropriations of history are controversial because historians, social critics, and film scholars have debated over what constitutes an "accurate" version of past events. It is my contention that, from the **silent cinema** to the present, media have contributed to an expanded understanding of history. This essay does not claim that written and visual histories are identical, but it maintains that visual and aural technologies "contribute to historical thinking" (Rosenstone, 2006, p. 12). This essay examines how the media have made use of the past through identifying various forms and styles for making visual history and will focus particularly on relations between war and cinema. The films discussed include national epics, World War II documentaries and feature films, postwar counter-epic and anti-war films, heritage and anti-heritage treatments of the past, philosophic explorations in film of **history and memory**, particularly **postcolonial** treatments of history, and contemporary versions of history through filming of the Vietnam and Iraq Wars.

NATIONAL EPICS IN SILENT FILMS

Influential films of the silent era that used historical events are customarily regarded as entertaining spectacles rather than texts that offer knowledge through their distinctive uses of the past. *Cabiria* (1914) and *The Birth of a Nation* (1915) helped to establish conventions and codes for the creation of popular commercial history. These films

> invented traditions . . . to establish for a modern community a continuity with a suitable historical past . . . By tracing its origins back into the past, a nation could validate its claims to power, property, and international prestige. (Wyke, 1997, pp. 14–15)

Directed by Giovanni Pastrone, *Cabiria* constructs an **intertextual** display of images drawn from classical art, *The Aeneid*, architecture, sculpture, folklore, and heroic figures, and at the same time alludes to contemporary events (e.g. Italy's colonial aspirations in Libya from 1911 to 1912). The episodes include pagan rituals, human sacrifice, extravagant war machines, scenes of captivity, combat, chase, and rescue, the suicide of a queen, and the triumph of a Roman aristocrat and his slave, to unite the glories of the past with the present Italian nation. The film thus offers a double history—of the creation of Italian nationalism in the twentieth century through cinematic presentations of Italy's ancient past—striking visual production of spectacles of war, natural disasters, an exotic but doomed Carthaginian world, and a regenerated Roman past aligned to the Italian present of the film's making (Dalle Vacche, 1992, p. 29).

The Birth of a Nation is a foretaste of Hollywood's partiality for historical films. Like *Cabiria*, it is a composite of numerous images drawn from the cultural archive: still photographs of the President, daguerreotypes of the Civil War, tableau scenes of Lincoln's assassination at Ford's theater, combat scenes along with a threatened rape, and a melodramatic iconography invoking regional, ethnic, and racial types. While generating protest about historical inaccuracies and racism, the film nonetheless offered a popularly accepted view of the Civil War and Reconstruction, portraying a divided nation redeemed from political and military strife, the containment of the Black population under the aegis of the State, and the reconstitution of the threatened family. This film's storytelling allows access to a national past, enlivens it, and identifies it with the folklore of popular beliefs that remains unchanged to the present, revealing that "American cinema shoots and constantly reshoots a single fundamental film: the birth of a nation-civilisation" that offers "a strong and ethical conception of universal history" (Deleuze, 1986, pp. 148, 151). As such, the film merits consideration as a mode of history making that has held sway in the history of American culture and politics from a position of dominance.

THE NATIONAL EPIC WITH THE COMING OF SOUND

The advent of sound on film gradually introduced new and more "realistic" elements into historical films. The primary actors now had voices: their dialogue could draw more fully than **intertitles** on speeches recorded in the historical archive; theatrical gestures while still grandiose were subordinated to the necessity of personalizing the actor's performance and of heightening the drama. The actor's words and intonation orchestral music, and song drawn from operatic, patriotic, and folk music introduced greater emotional identification with the drama of nation formation. The requirement of dramatizing war was aided by synchronous sounds of thunderous marching legions, clashing weapons, and groans of the dying to reinforce the military spectacle.

The biographical film (biopic), a popular form in the 1930s sound film, celebrated prominent national personages, portraying these individuals as overcoming threats to the life of the nation and to their personal identity. War is vital to many of these "epic" scenarios that dramatize and resolve the precarious character of nation formation. Their heroic protagonists are identified with patriotic oratory, orchestral and popular music, and national monuments—antique edifices, sculptures, and paintings—while choreographed crowd scenes visualized the consent and adulation of the masses.

Made during the heyday of the Fascist regime, the historical ambitions of *Scipio Africanus* (1937) involve the military victory of Rome over African Carthage and the rise of the Roman Empire. Scenes of war and politics are staged in a grandiose style to dramatize the victory of the forces of order over "Oriental barbarism." The combat between the Romans and Carthaginians is filmed with large casts and thundering herds of elephants presided over by the commanding figure of Scipio, who, spurred on by the masses, confronts and overcomes the African enemy to attain military, economic, and political unity. The history is finally not of the Carthaginian War but of Fascist military aspirations in the late 1930s. The film's monumental quality, extreme stylization, and choreography of the leader and of the masses present a visual portrait of coercive power and ambition. Its returns at the box office are evidence that the film was received neither as entertainment nor as effective propaganda, thus offering insights into the aspirations and failures of Fascist culture.

One of the most popular historical films of the twentieth century, *Gone with the Wind*, is a mixture of cinematic forms: epic reenactment of the Civil War and Reconstruction, costume drama, romance, melodrama, slave narrative, and war film. Its popularity resides in part in its spectacle, brilliant Technicolor, use of stars, and melodramatic scenario. For many, the film, adapted from Margaret Mitchell's novel, is a nostalgic myth, glorifying the Old South rather than a historical treatment of the Civil War and its aftermath. In defense of the film as critical history, J. E. Smyth finds that its contribution resides in the portrait of its female protagonist who challenges racial mythology. In a scene that portrays Scarlett, "not [as] only poor white but black as she limps toward the slave garden," emerging as an embodiment of defiance: "Here, in this allegory of the course of southern history (defeat, purge, recovery, revenge), the filmmakers recast the iconic image of southern rebellion as a biracial woman" (Smyth, 2006, p. 160). This image of a biracial feminine figure runs counter to Southern mythology through its visual treatment.

WORLD WAR II, REALISM, AND THE NATIONAL ARCHIVE

Along with radio programming and newsreels, the British cinema during World War II sought to "produce images that would create a sense of national collectivity" (Street, 1997, p. 50). A large number of wartime fiction films proffered portraits of the bonding and sacrifices of men in combat (e.g. *In Which We Serve*, 1942) and the mobilizing of women on the home front who, in addition to maintaining the family, were conscripted into essential war production (e.g. *Millions Like Us*, 1943). Combining fiction and documentary footage, these films are a historical archive of wartime cultural and social images and situations that highlight the myths and realities of war and its impact on conceptions of national identity. Their claims to history are their dramatic enactments of the immediate dangers confronted by ordinary people in exceptional situations, and, as such, "these wartime films are something more than empty propaganda, the characters

117

wrestle with difficult moral and physical problems and when they win through, it is at some cost" (Murphy, 2001, p. 71).

Documentaries such as *London Can Take It* (1940) and *Fires Were Started* (1943) undertook filming the bombing of London and its impact on the populace. They were shot on location and in the studio, and utilized non-actors (Richards, 2000, pp. 26–36). According to Jeffrey Richards, the general picture of the populace was "based on direct observation of how Londoners behaved" (p. 26) during the bombings. The films conform to views of documentary cinema as offering a "direct" encounter with scenes of danger, common people facing hardship and disaster, not only on the battlefront but on the home front. Akin to fiction films of World War II, the verbal and visual rhetoric convey urgency but also the endurance and self-discipline of the populace.

These wartime films were a harbinger of a changing cinematic language exemplified by Italian **Neorealism**, which focused on the everyday rather than the monumental, the ordinary person, metropolitan life, and contemporary events, and used colloquial rather than standard national language. This filmmaking challenged conventional realism and reigning cinematic clichés, substituting problems for resolutions, becoming a cinema of thought. Neorealism brought into existence cinematic forms that were to alter conceptions of the national past.

CRITICAL HISTORY AND NATION FORMATION

A dominant filmmaker identified with Neorealism is Luchino Visconti whose *La terra trema* (1948) was filmed on location with non-professional actors and portrayed the exploitation of Sicilian fishermen and their families. Later in his filmmaking career, Visconti turned more directly to rethinking **national cinema** and its cinematic past. Although his later films abandon elements of style and content associated with Neorealism, they retain Neorealism's critical bent. *The Leopard* (1963), adapted from Giuseppe di Lampedusa's novel, embodies a critique of dominant clichés of history-telling: heroic conceptions of character, representations of social class formations and national identity, and the historical film's anachronistic treatment of the past in relation to the present and future. *The Leopard* constitutes a reflection on history to rethink cinema's uses of the past.

The tradition and style of the national epic often rely on themes like threats to historical continuity and conflicts over power and leadership, and construct scenarios of romance and marriage that end in reconciliation or disaster and involve war. The fusion of an aristocratic and a bourgeois family, presumably a private affair apart from the public arena of power, had consequences for the history of the nation. In its search for "authenticity," *The Leopard* draws on the theater, opera, music, dance, sculpture, painting, and official history of the Risorgimento (the "rising" of Italy as a nation in the nineteenth century), providing a spectacle of the princely world through copies of actual paintings, the elegant fabrics of the actors' costumes, panoramic shots of the Sicilian landscape, antique church architecture, mural paintings, statuary, and excerpts from Bellini's opera *La Sonnambula*.

In *The Leopard* the union of an aristocrat and a nouveau riche woman is the political and economic instrument for thwarting a revolution that would threaten upper-class privilege. The Prince of Salina's (Burt Lancaster) plans depend on bringing the struggle for national unity into line with his own and his family's self-interest, even if this means having to bring members of a lower class into his previously closed circle. Unlike conventional historical films, romance is revealed to be a tool of political expediency. Military conflict, often portrayed as establishing the new Italian nation, differs from epics of nation founding. The battle scene in *The Leopard* comes early in the film, not as a glorious military victory, but as a scene of carnage.

The final segment takes place at a ball with the upper classes gathered to celebrate their victory over the radical Garibaldians. These episodes, viewed largely from the Prince's detached position, visualize the artifice, mannerisms, and material splendor of a world passing into the hands of the new landowners now aligned to the aristocracy and anticipate the coming of Fascism. The ball is the most operatic scene of the film, illuminating how life has become a spectacle that reinforces the rejuvenation of the old order. Through dramatizing the decadence, betrayals, and machinations of this world, the film undermines the spectacle identified with many historical films that celebrate national unity.

WAR AND CINEMA: A COUNTER-HISTORY OF WORLD WAR I

Stanley Kubrick's *Paths of Glory* (1957) is a counter-historical film in opposition to conventional cinema histories of war intrinsic to national cinemas. Set in World War I, the film's cinematic history is derived from official records, national folklore, photography, paintings, and other films, portraying a sordid war fought for the maintenance of national honor, power, and privilege. Kubrick's film visualizes the history not through heroic action, military spectacle, or patriotic rhetoric, but through anti-melodramatic and anti-sentimental treatment of character, architecture, and combat. The chateau that houses the officers invokes the aristocratic heritage of French civilization with its imposing edifice, ornate interiors filled with historical artifacts, paintings, and furniture. In stark contrast, the common soldiers live in narrow muddy trenches and dark, claustrophobic barracks, and fight in battle scenes of mass murder.

Through General Mireau (George Macready), the spectator is introduced to an opportunist in his clichéd, "Hello, soldier. Ready to kill more Germans?" His rigid movements through the trenches reveal his contempt for the common soldiers and his obsession with national honor. His careerism and indifference to life are revealed in his indicting his soldiers for cowardice and treason for what he (and his fellow officers) knew to be a hopeless military operation. By contrast, General Broulard (Adolphe Menjou), an urbane, genial, and seasoned veteran of war and statecraft, is attuned to political expediency; his character is best suited to the rules of the game of statecraft in the upper class: to avoid embarrassment and get the work done.

Colonel Dax (Kirk Douglas) seems to be "a voice of reason . . . but he is not" (Kolker, 2000, p. 112). He too is part of an unrelenting mechanistic class system and is subject to military rules and the orders of his superiors. Dax is the film's instrument for highlighting the inexorable nature of militarism and the naïveté of those who think that war has a human or moral side. In any conventional cinematic history of war, his idealistic efforts on behalf of the men wrongfully charged with treason would have succeeded, but their court martial is a parody of justice, challenging those who think that an appeal to law can mitigate the rules of the war game. The common soldiers are treated as animals, confined to a barn to await their slaughter, struggling vainly to preserve their lives. Kubrick's portrait of militarism relies on an exploration of realpolitik (the practical politics of power), communicated visually rather than polemically, to undermine sentimental treatments of a national heritage bereft of the honor it espouses.

THE HERITAGE FILM: MASTERPIECE HISTORY

"Heritage" was a lucrative and popular source of historical images in the 1980s and 1990s. *Chariots of Fire* (1981), *A Passage to India* (1984), *Maurice* (1987), and *Howard's End* (1992) are adaptations of earlier novels or plays (usually masterpieces) that focus on national identity via the heritage industry (government sponsored and private enterprise creation of museums, architectural restorations, and tourism), the upper classes, and spectacular images of wealth, power, and social mobility. The pictorialist style capitalizes on the tradition of historical films, biopics, and costume dramas through costuming, décor, and architecture derived from painting and location shooting of the great houses.

A Passage to India, directed by David Lean, an adaptation of an E. M. Forster novel, embodies the qualities of heritage filmmaking. Set in India during the British rule known as the Raj, the film offers images of the troubled relations between British rulers and Indian subjects, on the desire of two British women to meet Indians despite the segregationist practices of the Raj. The film is legitimized by authorial signatures, both Forster's and Lean's, and by "quality" production values. The viewer is presented with exotic images of the Indian landscape: the Bombay Gateway, the Marabar Caves, the Temple at Khajuraho, and numerous images of sea and sky with a lesser focus on the Indian world of Chandrapore. The spectacle of imperial power is conveyed through government buildings, the Club, the residence of Mrs. Moore and Adela Quested, and the courtroom.

Lean's film does not suppress but reinterprets political conflict in sexual terms; it links imperialism to the hysterical fantasies of a young woman with limited sexual experience, aroused by India, and who finds no outlet for her sexuality in her relationship with her fiancé. Forster laid the groundwork for merging the white woman's fantasies about the "Orient" with desire for the Indian Other, a transgression against cultural taboos on miscegenation. Adela's

(Judy David) diagnosed "illness" is complicated by her naïveté about sexuality. Her character exposes prevailing racist fantasies in relation to Dr. Aziz (Victor Banerjee) and how representations of the "other" are central to the management of a colonized culture. While *A Passage to India* includes a component critical of British heritage through focus on gendered and sexual identity, its spectacular visual display dampens critical reflections on the film's historical perspective and reinforces a nostalgic conception of colonial India.

COUNTER-HERITAGE: A POLITICS OF HISTORY

Derek Jarman's *Edward II* (1991), based on Christopher Marlowe's play, is a daring assault on heritage filmmaking and longstanding conceptions of British national identity and sexuality. A self-conscious exploration of historical representation, it appeared during the last year of Margaret Thatcher's long siege of British politics, when, as Peter Wollen has written, "Thatcherism succeeded paradoxically in politicizing filmmakers" (Wollen, 1993, p. 49). In *Edward II*, as in Jarman's *The Last of England* (1987), power and sexuality are inseparable. Homosexuality becomes central for understanding past and present exercises of coercive and violent power. The political unrest and violence are initiated with the coronation of King Edward II, who insists upon the return of his exiled lover, Piers Gaveston. The queen, enraged over Edward's "unnatural" relationship, plots with Lord Mortimer the Younger to overthrow the king. The conspiracy results in the grisly deaths of Gaveston and the king, Mortimer's death, and the defeat of the rebels. Order is restored with the coronation of Edward's son, now Edward III. Instead of the visual pleasures to be derived from great architectural landmarks, lavish period costumes, and stylized camera work, *Edward II* (a production by independent company Working Title) took an avant-garde direction to "challenge, or 'make strange' . . . perceptions about past and present" (Hill, 1999, p. 155).

The sets are minimalist, featuring dark corridors and dungeons, a pool of water in which Edward gazes on his reflection or thrashes about in his rage, and a throne without the trappings of a throne room, which bring a violent and sexually repressive past to bear on the present (Hill, 1999, p. 156). Sandy Powell's costuming functions to undermine the displays associated with historical dramas. Jarman compared Tilda Swinton's role as Queen Isabella to Joan Crawford's as chairman of the board of Pepsi Cola, clothed as she is in sumptuous gowns and jewelry, reinforcing an image of deadly femininity, another striking example of the film's appropriating costume to probe sexual antagonisms and their relation to power. The contemporary attire of the rest of the cast includes Edward in pajamas, duffle coat, and suits, OutRage demonstrators in T-shirts and jeans, and the military dress of Mortimer and his cohorts. The film vividly orchestrates and inverts historical images of the British state, past and present, providing a material, physical view of the body politic and a deeply personal and affective meditation on death—Jarman's impending death from AIDS and the deaths of victims of state power. The cinematic image unmasks the ceremonial trappings of national history to expose its heritage of violent spectacle, venturing onto and unsettling the critical terrain of written history on the Renaissance and theater.

HISTORY AND MEMORY ON FILM: A PHILOSOPHICAL PERSPECTIVE

Friedrich Nietzsche, reflecting on historical thinking, writes, "it is possible to live almost without memory . . . but it is altogether impossible to *live* at all without forgetting" (Nietzsche, 1991, p. 62). Historical knowledge depends on forgetting that which obstructs thinking and remembering what is "salutary and fruitful for the future" (Nietzsche, 1991, p. 67). Rethinking the past in relation to the present via the cinema has preoccupied such filmmakers as Alain Resnais (*Hiroshima, mon amour*, 1959), Hans Jürgen Syberberg (*Hitler: A Film from Germany*, 1977), and Jean-Luc Godard (*Prénom Carmen*, 1983, and *Histoire(s) du cinema*, 1988). Their films are philosophic explorations of the cinematic image that seek to comprehend connections between **history and memory** in the shifting terrain of history making, and its reception.

Initially, *Hiroshima, mon amour* was to be a documentary, but Resnais did not want to repeat the style of *Night and Fog* (1955), a film providing, in visual images and soundtrack, a meditation on the Holocaust: "*Hiroshima* turned out to be a film about the impossibility of making a documentary . . ." (Kreidl, 1978, p. 64). Marguerite Duras's script invokes the horror of the Hiroshima catastrophe but is not a documentary. Resnais told Duras, "a film on the atomic bomb itself just couldn't be made, [but] what would be pleasing would be doing a love story . . . in which the atomic agony would not be absent" (Armes, 1968, p. 66).

Through the Hiroshima museum and scenes of survivors in a hospital, the film introduces images of the burned and maimed victims and other visions of destruction to validate the "truth" of the event, but does not rest on these horrendous images and landmarks. It uses them to investigate different responses to seeing and remembering and connects the "atomic agony" to memories of the war in Europe. The film blends the wartime past with the characters' (and viewers') present time, but each of the two characters has "his or her own memory, which is foreign to the other. There is no longer anything at all in common" (Deleuze, 1989, p. 117). Though the present in *Hiroshima, mon amour* covers only 24 hours, it involves different circuits of time that overlap and span over a decade.

These various circuits of time—past, present, and future, personal and collective—are treated through the brief love affair of a Japanese man and a French woman that takes place in Hiroshima. The characters' lives entwine with the Japanese and European theaters of the war. Their different memories collide and threaten to annihilate any possibility of shared memory. The film does not reconcile the two characters by placing them in the same time in the present and with the same memories, but invites the viewer "to understand the past across mutually contradicting positions" (Rodowick, 1997, p. 96).

POSTCOLONIAL HISTORY

Postcolonial thought has focused on the reinvention of history through memory. In such films as *Ceddo* (1977) and *The Camp at Thiaroye* (1987), the filmmaker Sembène Ousmane draws heavily on the Senegalese past and fragments of memory to create cinematic forms and an African pedagogy that involves unlearning the lessons of European colonial history through unearthing and retelling forgotten narratives. Sembène's films are not melodramas, biopics, or monumental epics exalting exceptional individuals; they are storytelling identified with **Third Cinema**, involving different moments of the forgotten African, specifically Senegalese, past.

Ceddo is set in the seventeenth century and draws on folklore, myth, and actual events to portray "the infiltration of Islam both by sword and by politics" (Pfaff, 1984, p. 167), since the focus on Western imperialism has submerged the role of Islam in Senegalese culture. Through the figure of the Princess Dior, *Ceddo* becomes an epic, a reminder of a heroic past overcome by foreign (Islamic) invasions. The film draws on different moments of Senegal's past: the eras of Senegalese royalty, French colonization, and the slave trade, as well as different spoken languages (Wolof, Diola, Arabic, and French) and Islamic, Catholic, and Senegalese religious rituals and practices important to an understanding of Senegal's present and future cultural and social life. Through storytelling the film makes accessible to examination a body of "inherited knowledge." This inherited unwritten knowledge becomes shared through Sembène, the "griot" (the traditional storyteller), who uses cinema to pass on knowledge of the past.

The Camp at Thiaroye is Sembène's version of popular history, a cinematic memorial to African men whose participation in World War II had rarely been told from an African perspective. *Le camp* uses the return of African soldiers from Europe as the point of departure for reexamining the history of fascism and its connections to Western imperialism and colonialism that have been more often associated with Europe. Sembène's film challenges this narrative through focusing on the African "memory" of fascism and involvement in World War II in Europe, dramatizing the ways in which coercion on the part of the French and consent on the part of the African colonials functioned to maintain European colonial power. The men's return home and their incarceration in a "repatriation" camp (similar to a concentration camp) reproduce the same exploitation characteristic of their life in Africa and in Europe. The French repression is massive, involving verbal and physical violence and economic exploitation: the French refuse to pay the men as contracted for their service, keep them incarcerated, and annihilate them at the climax of the film as French tanks destroy them and the camp.

Sembène has said that film is "the memory of history which we keep alive" (Gadjigo *et al.*, 1993, p. 85), an invitation to "destroy myths from the inside" (Deleuze, 1989, p. 222). Through an examination of the different cultural and class backgrounds of the French and Africans, *Le camp* calls attention to the forms of knowledge on which the characters' actions are based. All are implicated in this drama of differences: Sergeant Diatta, a Europeanized African, is multi-lingual, reads French poetry, and is a lover of classical music, having more in common with the liberal French Captain Raymond than with his African comrades; they share belief in the language of reason and justice, though neither understands the language of political power and violence. The other Africans speak a polyglot language known as "Francite," a mix of French and African dialects that parallels their inability to find a language to understand the French. The majority of French officers are rabid anti-communists, racists, and haters of intellectuals who justify duplicity and violence in the name of law and order. Finally, there is Pays, the silent one, a survivor of the Nazi camp at Buchenwald, who, unable to verbalize, can see the coming massacre; he attempts through gesture to warn the men but is misunderstood and ignored. Sembène's postcolonial treatment of history reveals the tragic consequences for the Africans who become betrayers and betrayed.

HISTORY IN THE MAKING: THE VIETNAM AND IRAQ WARS

From the end of World War II, television increasingly became a major source of popular history with such programs as *The 20th Century* and *Civilization*, dedicated to specific national and international events, especially to the history of war and revolution: the US Civil War, the Russian Revolution, the two world wars, the Korean War (after 1975), and the Vietnam War. Films on the Vietnam War continue to be prominent in the media. As film historians have noted, films on that war did not appear until after it had ended. Furthermore, "like Vietnam films, virtually all war memoirs preconceive war in Hollywood terms and continue to mediate the combat in these terms" (Doherty, 1991, p. 255). Oliver Stone's *Platoon* (1986) was distinguished by the military credentials of its veteran director and acclaimed for its realism.

By contrast, Kubrick's *Full Metal Jacket* (1989) is a mix of military indoctrination and scenes of combat that focuses on US Marine Corps rituals for turning young men into sublimated killing machines (or suicidal castrati). The film draws on Hollywood conventions and clichés derived from cartoons and comic books, regarding them as intrinsic to the theatrics of combat—characters' names, jargon, expletives, gestures, and ditties. The soldiers who survive are automata, descendants of Disneyland and *A Clockwork Orange* "hooligans." The landscape is one in which "the human is foregrounded and observed against, rather than from within, the space he inhabits" (Kolker, 2000, p. 190).

Contrasting films on the Vietnam War to recent films on the Iraq War, Michael Wood finds that the Vietnam films focused primarily on damage inflicted on Americans in combat, while recent films on the Iraq War dramatize damage done to the American nation by "an unfinished war . . . both far away and inserted into every realm of domestic life," and "perturbed feelings, a mood that has nowhere to go" (Wood, 2008, p. 23). While Wood does not comment on significant technological changes in constructing the history of the Iraq War, the use of mixed media and the introduction of digital media (camcorders, telecameras, and computer technology) play a significant role in altering portrayals of war in relation to battlefront and home front.

In *Redacted* (2007), director Brian De Palma brought his skills in the techniques of horror to examination of the current war in Iraq. Relentlessly, the film portrays the monstrousness of the young soldiers' situation, showing how they give vent to brutality, resulting in the murder of a family and the rape of a teenage girl. Private Salazar uses his video camera as an opportunity to gain entry into a film school, enlisting his mates, Flake, Rush, and Barton, in recording on tape the rape and murder. The videotape becomes the instrument that invites the audience to entertain questions concerning the dehumanization of the young men and the role of recording these events unanchored in ethical considerations.

While the film focuses largely on the combat zone, it brings the war home through a "coming home" party (also filmed with a video camera), offering a disturbing parallel between the war front and home. When asked to provide "war stories" for his fiancée, friends, and family, Barton describes the atrocities that are "burned into his brain." The horror resides in the refusal of his "audience" to listen to him. His anguished account culminates in a freeze frame of Barton and his fiancée staring like zombies into the camera. The film ends with documentary footage of mutilated bodies of dead Iraqi men, women, and children with their faces "blacked out," the "redaction" exposing the violence perpetrated on the human body by an indifferent officialdom that even robs victims of identification.

The Valley of Elah (2007) similarly invokes media, in this case, cell phone technology as a recording device. The murder of a returnee from Iraq and the determination of his father, Hank Deerfield (Tommy Lee Jones), to identify the perpetrator of the crime becomes the basis for a reexamination through media (including computer screens) of this war. The reiterated recording of a brutal hit and run death of a young Iraqi (in Iraq) is linked to the death of Deerfield's son in the United States, and these two events become an allegory of the war in Iraq and at home. The father's study of the digital footage becomes a strategy for reflecting on images transmitted through media about the war and its impact on the nation.

Mock documentary video footage plays a significant role in *Stop-Loss* (2008): it "records" an encounter at a checkpoint during which American soldiers, under their leader Sergeant Brandon King (Ryan Philippe), are led into an ambush and confront Iraqi snipers in a deadly battle. The soldiers become involved in ruthlessly killing civilians as several of King's men are killed and one is blinded and severely wounded. In addition to the mock video footage, the film uses newsreels from Aljazeera and from a French documentary team. Similar to the video footage, the film is shot with fast cutting, low-key lighting, graininess, and subdued color to achieve a rough documentary style and the effect of immediacy. The TV, newsreel, and other video footage serve as the basis for exploring combat and its traumatic effects on the combatants and their community at home. The film's uses of media are part of the archive of this new war. The highlighting of visual technologies in *Redacted*, *The Valley of Elah*, and *Stop-Loss* invites the spectator to investigate and participate (as in interactive media) in the process of making history.

SUMMARY

The films selected for discussion hardly exhaust the possibilities for understanding "cinematic uses of the past," since it has now become critical practice to rethink the past and present role of cinema in relation to the proliferation of new media, involving the Internet, video games, animation, and their effects. Our understanding of these instruments of communication must be grounded in an awareness of the conditions of production, the role of publicity, the predilections of authors and their designs on audiences, the expression of varied styles, and a study of media reception by scholars. Analysis of media forms has begun to replace weak interpretation and strong judgments about what we mean by history, but we also need to expand and refine our knowledge concerning relations between history and memory so as to better engage with how media creates history, and whether and how this matters.

FURTHER READING

Chopra-Gant, Michael (2008) *Cinema and History: The Telling of Stories*, London: Wallflower.
A succinct analysis of different treatments of the historical film.

Higson, Andrew (2003) *English Heritage. English Cinema: Costume Drama since 1980*, Oxford: Oxford University Press.
Important cultural and stylistic analysis of heritage film production.

Hjort, Mette and Mackenzie, Scott (eds.) (2000) *Cinema and Nation*, London: Routledge.
A collection of essays on film production and changing conceptions of national identity.

Hughes-Warrington, Marnie (2007) *History Goes to the Movies: Studying History on Film*, London: Routledge.
Extremely useful guide to historical and methodological issues for the study of history in film.

Landsberg, Alison (2004) *Prosthetic Memory: The Transformation of American Memory in the Age of Mass Culture*, New York: Columbia University Press.
An examination of changing conceptions in the study of history in media.

Landy, Marcia (1996) *Cinematic Uses of the Past*, Minneapolis, MN: University of Minnesota Press.
An examination of the political and aesthetic dimensions of the various forms of history-making in cinema.

11

INSCRIBING THE HISTORICAL

Film texts in context

ROSEMARIE SCULLION

In recent years, film studies scholars have begun to consider the ways in which historical processes shape the meanings films generate and the contexts in which they are received. This move extends the scope of historical criticism well beyond studies that chart the rise of the film medium or trace the development of film technologies and the evolution of various national industries. New critical approaches that attend to the historical dimensions of the film text represent a departure from the forms of inquiry that held sway in film studies for decades. These methods borrowed insights from linguistics, philosophy, psychoanalysis, and other schools of modern thought, allowing film scholars to shed new theoretical light on how films produce meaning and engage spectators. In adopting these approaches, critics tended to view films under study as autonomous art objects possessing their own syntax and formal structures, a stance that minimized the importance of external forces constituting a cinematic work's social, cultural, and political frames of reference. It is the primacy assigned to such specificities of context that defines the historicist interpretive method. For film studies, a focus on particularities of time and place allows scholars to bring into sharp critical relief the complexities involved not only in representing the past on the screen, but also in accounting for the place film texts and film culture in general occupy in the processes of historical change that shape modern society.

There are numerous ways in which films can express historicity. The first and most obvious form is found in films that engage the past by making historical events, circumstances, and characters the subject of the film narrative. That history may constitute the backdrop of the story recounted, or occupy the center of narrative focus. Such films tend to adopt realist conventions that purport to represent faithfully a history whose meanings are fixed and verifiable. Yet, attention must be paid to the way historical films deploy rhetoric and formulate social, cultural, and political discourses that are themselves open to analysis. In this case, historicist critique entails not simply the study of the historical truth a film represents and a judgment concerning its objectivity and veracity, but also involves an examination of the discourses the film enunciates, that is, the things that can be said with respect to the history in question that are recognized and *understood* to be true by the audiences that view them. These enunciations can take on any number of forms including discourses on race, gender, sexuality, class, and various institutions of power, utterances that formulate the film's meanings in political and ideological as well as specifically historical terms.

Historicist analysis is not limited to the study of films that place historical events and actors at the center of the narrative. Films can display their historicity by capturing and conveying the sensibility of a particular age. Created in conditions that are, consciously or unconsciously, shaped by their own historical moment, the work of interpreting such films involves describing dominant conditions and apprehending the prevailing mind-set of the era while also examining how films engage that particular setting. Dudley Andrew's *Mists of Regret: Culture and Sensibility in Classic French Film* (1995) is a prime example of this kind of critical historicizing. Andrew carefully situates the French film style known as Poetic Realism in the context of the strife-ridden 1930s, showing how the bleak atmosphere and sense of foreboding that inhabits the Poetic Realist landscape express the feeling of impending doom that pervaded French society on the eve of World War II. The portrayal of life in France's popular and working class milieux that one finds in Jean Renoir's *The Human Beast* (1938) and Marcel Carné's *Misty Wharf* (1938) forms social representations that enunciate commonly held beliefs concerning the societal ills that plague lower class existence. However, these films also present images and intrigues in which characters are seen struggling against these conditions, striving to assert their humanity in circumstances in which powerful social forces are arrayed against them. This portrait of class injustice, one that is shared by these and other Poetic Realist films, simultaneously activates the discourse on working class inferiority while also defying it by countering the widely held notion that the poor and marginalized are flawed beings who merit their sorry lot in life. This counter-discourse introduced into the social sphere meanings and images that in significant ways cast the lower orders as victims of the predation of their class superiors and at a moment in time when the rigid hierarchization of French society and justifications for maintaining it were being thrown into radical question.

In the case of Poetic Realism, it is largely class codes and the particular way in which they are bound up with a cinematic display of French masculinity in crisis that defines much of the signifying terrain in Poetic Realist filmmaking. The identification and interpretation of these class and gender discourses owe much to the development of critical paradigms influenced, for instance, by **Marxist** and **feminist** thought, which, in concert with other forms of contemporary critique, have heightened consciousness of the wholesale absence of important social categories (women, the popular classes, the colonized, and other subjugated identities) in conventional historiography which typically highlights the great deeds of male elites. Recent decades have witnessed a proliferation of similarly inclusionary methods of historical investigation in which the scope of inquiry has widened to include an ever-expanding field of social, cultural, and political objects and entities that were once written out of history but whose appearance in historical writing is now texturing and greatly enriching our understanding of the past and its relationship to our present circumstances.

In my discussion here I will consider an aspect of history particular to the film industry that is also defined by absence, namely the government censorship of films that were forcibly removed from the public sphere or in some cases, as I will show, were never allowed even to be made in the first place. In France, the focus of my discussion here, censorship has a long and storied past, offering a compelling example of the power with which films are invested and the threat the medium is thought to represent, particularly at moments of national crisis and upheaval. To study this phenomenon requires a consideration of the precise institutional and legal form censorship has taken, an account of historical changes that took place in the censorship regime over time, and a turn to primary texts, including journalistic and biographical writing that bears witness to its operations and their broader societal effects. I am particularly interested in looking at the censorship that struck a number of French films in the two decades following World War II, a period in which democratic rule was restored to France, but in which filmmakers continued to bear the repressive brunt of government censorship of the sort that had so seriously constrained the film industry during the four years of Nazi occupation between 1940 and 1944. In examining the precise context in which filmmakers were obliged to maneuver in this period, an important dimension of film history emerges, one that exceeds the limits of individual film texts but that also illustrates how forces entirely external to the film medium can shape a work's broader historical significance.

The political censorship I will examine here was pursued by the French government agency known as the Commission de contrôle des films cinématographiques (Film Oversight Board). My interest is in the two decades that followed World War II, an era that was fraught with **Cold War** tensions and the internal and external strifes stirred by multiple wars of decolonization. The Commission de contrôle became actively involved in these struggles and its actions call for an analytical approach that considers what transpires when film texts, particularly ones that fail to conform to the dominant discourses of their time, interface with societal forces intent on containing their disruptive effects. The Commission de contrôle, established in July 1945, supplanted a provisional body operating under the aegis of the French military that determined which films could reach the viewing public after the Allied invasion of Normandy and during the last turbulent year of the war. The censorship board instituted in 1945 drew its title and organizational structure from prewar governmental entities that, in the name of ensuring public order and morality, had also exerted control over the French film industry. Anxious to limit exposure to what it deemed subversive subject matter, it was these earlier commissions that prevented the French public from viewing such interwar classics as Sergei Eisenstein's *The Battleship Potemkin* (1925) and Jean Vigo's *Zero for Conduct* (1933). They also introduced the system of dual visas that required one release authorization for domestic exhibition of films and another enabling their foreign export. After war was declared in September 1939, officials of the Third Republic also declared a number of films from this period, including Marcel Carné's *Misty Wharf*, too "demoralizing" for public viewing in France. Dozens of other films were stripped of their export visas, a measure that sought to prevent the use of

France's own film production in enemy propaganda campaigns. As a result of this interdiction, renowned films such as Marcel Carné's *Hôtel du Nord* (1938) as well as Jean Renoir's *Grande Illusion* (1937) and *The Rules of the Game* (1939) were summarily withdrawn from the international market (Douin, 1998, pp. 189–91).

When the postwar Commission de contrôle was established in 1945, film-makers had every reason to hope that the passing of the extraordinary circumstances that prevailed during the tension-laden interwar period and the traumatic war years would bring forth new freedoms of cinematic expression. Between 1945 and 1950, the Commission constituted at the moment of France's liberation did in fact relax strictures somewhat by granting members of the film profession a number of seats equal to those occupied by the seven individuals who represented various branches of the French State, including the Ministries of Defense, Information, Interior, Foreign Affairs, the Colonies, National Education, and Public Health. This parity lasted until 1950 when a move that numerically weakened the influence of the film industry ended in protest and the resignation *en masse* of its representatives, opening a political vacuum that gave the government unfettered control over the board's decision-making. Although parity between government and industry representatives was restored in 1952, struggles continued over the constitution of a body that, in principle, held absolute authority over all fiction and documentary films made in France. In exercising its powers, the board had a range of restrictive measures at its disposal. The July 1945 decree, in conjunction with a more stringent order issued in 1961, allowed the board to restrict access to films deemed unsuitable for certain age groups, to issue warnings concerning content, to demand modifications and cuts, to ban films entirely, and to withhold the permit required for their foreign export. The measure that produced perhaps the greatest chilling effect was, however, the once optional, but, beginning in 1961, newly required, provision that all film projects obtain an "avis préalable" or prior opinion whereby the board evaluated a film's chances of passing muster once it was submitted for final review. As Philippe Maarek observes, this latter requirement amounted to a form of economic censorship since financiers were unlikely to continue investing in a film that had received an unfavorable prior assessment from the board (1982, pp. 53–4). In deploying these measures, the board had two major, though woefully ill-defined, objectives: the maintenance of public order and the protection of the nation's internal moral order. It was the former criteria that figured in the political censorship that struck a number of films in the two decades that followed World War II (Maarek, 1982, pp. 59–60).

The first of the directors I will highlight here who ran seriously afoul of France's film regulatory regime is René Vautier. For decades this activist filmmaker defied its decrees and in 1973 waged a hunger strike opposing all political censorship of films, an undertaking that helped pressure the French government into abandoning its interventionist ways. Vautier's first run-in with film censorship occurred in 1949–50 during the making of *Afrique '50* ("Africa 1950"), a work that prominent film critic Georges Sadoul has hailed as France's first militant anti-colonialist film. In his 1998 memoir titled *Caméra citoyenne* ("Citizen Camera"), Vautier relates in vivid detail the circumstances that led to the one-year prison sentence he received for making *Afrique '50*, a 17-minute documentary that boldly denounced France's pillaging of human and material resources in the heyday of its colonial rule in West Africa (1998, pp. 29–47). The vigilance with which the government sought to restrict knowledge of its operations in Africa is evident in the special statute that barred any filming in French colonies that was not overseen by a representative of the French government, a provision Vautier flouted and which led to his arrest order, to repeated government attempts to seize the footage he filmed in Africa, and finally to his one-year prison sentence. Vautier was tried under a 1934 statute introduced by then-Minister of the Colonies Pierre Laval that subjected to criminal prosecution any individual who failed to submit a film's complete scenario to the Commission de contrôle prior to filming in any of the colonies or who undertook shooting a film without being accompanied by a colonial official whose presence ensured that filmmakers recorded only pre-approved subject matter. In 1998, Vautier again denounced these measures, explaining that he was not inclined to obey a decree whose author, Pierre Laval, had been executed in 1945 for his own criminal deeds as a collaborator during the Nazi occupation of France during World War II (Vautier, 1998, pp. 31–2).

Vautier's film was originally commissioned by the Ligue de L'Enseignement (The Teaching League), an educational organization seeking to familiarize students in metropolitan France with life in far-flung regions of the country's vast colonial empire. Upon arrival in Africa, however, Vautier was stunned by the disparity between the glittering image of French colonialism that reigned in the *metropole* and the naked hyper-exploitation of indigenous peoples that Vautier and his fellow travelers were able to observe on the ground. Vautier resolved to capture these sordid conditions and to return home with a film that would shatter the myth of colonization as a beneficent civilizing enterprise. Unable to contain his contempt for the spectacle of suffering that surrounded him, Vautier quickly found himself tangling with local officials intent on obliging him to respect the rules of the game that governed filmmaking in the colonies. Vautier's refusal to submit to these dictates instantly turned him into a fugitive from the law and sent him scurrying across a number of Africa's colonial borders with the offending footage in tow, and resolving to collect more along the way.

What was it about Vautier's project that French authorities, both in the colonies and, later, in the *metropole*, found so menacing? The short documentary, which Vautier succeeded in completing upon returning to France, even while on the run, offered but a glimpse of the abject status millions of Africans held in their day-to-day existence under French colonial rule. Marshalling statistics that quantified the plundering of African resources, Vautier launched what would come to be seen as French cinema's first salvo against the country's imperial status quo. The film opens unsuspectingly enough with images of African children romping as they gather around the filmmaker to welcome him and his crew to a presumably typical village in French West Africa. The visitors are greeted with intense curiosity. The only other white people likely to have entered the village prior to this were, we learn, colonial administrators who appeared on the scene either to collect taxes or to seek military recruits. Evoking the hustle and bustle of life in a village in Mali located on the banks of the Niger River, the opening sequences show mothers preparing food and caring for their children, traditional weavers at work, huts under construction, boats being carved out of tree trunks, and fishermen casting their nets, all images of the traditional African everyday that would have met the expectations of the organism that had commissioned Vautier's services. In short order, however, the charm of this "picturesque" foray into village life in the colonies gives way to a very different reality where Africa's indigenous peoples are seen enduring "great poverty" and suffering deplorable working conditions dictated by the mammoth French colonial companies that ruled their existence. Boat builders are so poor that they cannot afford nails and make do without; food is scarce, schools are inexistent, and doctors are nowhere in sight. Vautier's narrator queries his viewer, a subject with whom he strives to establish a complicit camaraderie, asking: "Surprised to see a village without a school or a doctor? In Africa, schools are opened when large colonial companies need accountants and doctors are sent in only when they risk a labor shortage."

Despite its grinding poverty, this particular village is relatively blessed. It has thus far escaped the cruel colonial fate of other African communities Vautier encountered in his travels. For instance, the village of Palaka, located in the northern Ivory Coast, recently had the misfortune of being visited by the tax collector. With actual testimonial footage at the ready, Vautier's narrator explains:

The village chief wasn't able to pay the 3,700 francs in taxes that were owed. On February 27, 1949 at 5:00 a.m. the troops came, they surrounded the village, they shot, they burned, they killed! Here Sikali Wattare, the village chief, was suffocated by smoke and shot in the neck with a French bullet. Here, a seven-month child was killed, a French bullet shot its head off. Here, there's blood on the wall, a pregnant woman came to die, two French bullets in the stomach. On this African soil, four cadavers, three men and a woman assassinated in our name, in the name of the French people.

Why resort to such draconian measures? Onerous taxes and their brutal imposition are an effective means not only of filling French government coffers, but also of forcing those who cannot afford them to go to work for the large colonial companies who pay paltry wages. African labor is so devalued that the colonial companies can forgo investment in expensive labor-saving equipment, the hallmark of modern technological advancement. The only signs of such progress are large dams, built by African workers, that generate electricity and direct it to households of white settlers craving the conveniences of modernity. Throughout the colonies, Africans perform backbreaking labor harvesting riches that are loaded onto cargo ships headed for distant lands. Vautier's narrator acknowledges: "[This] is not the official image of colonization." Those the filmmaker offers his viewers demonstrate conclusively that "colonization, here as elsewhere, is the reign of vultures." Any resistance indigenous peoples mount to the wholesale pillaging of Africa is met with ferocious repression, leaving communities with "burned-out huts, massacred inhabitants, and slaughtered livestock rotting in the sun." To stifle rebellion, the colonial administration "commits crimes in the name of France and in the name of civilization . . . responding to Africans as it has to Madagascans and the Vietnamese, with force, beatings, prison, and guns." Small wonder that Vautier's aim of documenting these wretched conditions entailed one intimidating encounter after another with the repressive powers of the French State.

Outraged by moves to criminalize his project, which, to his mind, involved the simple act of filming "things as they were" (Vautier, 1998, p. 33), Vautier adopted a course of action dictated by his conscientious objection to what he considered the crime of colonialism and did not shrink before the legal consequences it entailed. Upon returning to France, Vautier withstood numerous attempts to seize the footage he had filmed in Africa. Having lost two-thirds of it to police seizure, he made do with the remainder he salvaged and completed a film that, though entirely banned, did succeed in reaching wide audiences whose gathering constituted yet other illegal acts. Vautier was, however, ultimately rewarded for his troubles when *Afrique '50* earned the distinction of being the first 16-mm film to receive the Louis Lumière prize for best short film. He no doubt found even greater satisfaction in the subsequent actions of the French government itself. In the early 1990s, it purchased the rights to exhibit *Afrique '50* in its network of embassies throughout Africa, declaring: "It is politically important today to show African countries that an anti-colonialist sentiment existed in France in the immediate aftermath of the war" (quoted in Vautier, 1998, p. 34). To Vautier, this gesture of belated recognition proved only that the political censorship of film, against which he had struggled for decades, was nothing if not short-sighted.

However myopic the measures the French government took against Vautier in the early 1950s, they were a sign of things to come for French filmmaking relating to matters of empire. With one colonial war raging in Indochina and another eight-year conflict about to erupt in Algeria, the Commission was eager to quash any critical discourses relating to the colonies. Other filmmakers who broached the topic would also find themselves facing the rigors of the law. In 1955 in Marseille, Paul Carpita, another young dissident, saw his *Rendez-vous des quais* ("Rendez-vous on the Docks") torn from its reels by local police who, acting on the orders of the Commission de contrôle in Paris, seized the film as it was about to be shown to a hometown audience. A fiction film memorializing a bitter labor dispute involving thousands of Marseille dockworkers who had also engaged in open protest of the war in Indochina, Carpita's *Rendez-vous des quais* was spirited away to a vault in Paris where it remained under wraps for decades. In 1955, Louis Daquin crossed the censors by adapting Guy de Maupassant's nineteenth-century tale *Bel Ami* in cinematic terms that referenced too closely the colonial conditions in North Africa at the outset of the Algerian War. In 1960, New Wave luminary Jean-Luc Godard stirred the Commission's ire when he represented the pursuits of Bruno Forestier in *Le Petit Soldat* ("The Little Soldier"), resulting in the film's prohibition. Forestier is an intelligence operative who finds himself entangled in the political intrigues of the various warring parties during the Algerian conflict. In one particularly disturbing scene, Forestier is seen being subjected to "la baignoire" (the bathtub), a form of torture known today as "waterboarding." Although the perpetrators in this scene are agents of the Algerian liberation movement, the FLN (Front de la Libération nationale), censors in Paris found the deeply unsettling representation of this interrogation method intolerable, no doubt because it was one of many such methods known to be used by French military forces in their counter-insurgency campaign in Algeria.

The strife engendered by the Algerian conflict also had an effect on the censorship of films whose subject matter involved societies located half-way around the globe, or so commentators in the French press surmised in September 1963 when the ban on Chris Marker's 1960 film *Cuba Si!* was finally lifted by the Minister of Information Alain Peyrefitte. His predecessor, Louis Terrenoire, had banished the film from French screens and blocked its foreign export in July 1961, declaring that Marker's account of the Cuba Revolution of 1959 "did not qualify as a documentary film since it constituted an apology for Castro's regime." "Certainly," Terrenoire continued,

> what is recalled and reported about the previous (Batista) regime conforms to historical truth, but . . . all films [purveying] ideological propaganda cannot receive [the Commission's] authorization if only because of the risks this kind of production carries for public order.
>
> (Quoted in Anonymous, 1963b)

The threat to public order that stood in 1961 when Marker sought release of his film concerned the actions of the French colonist terror organization known as the OAS (The Organization of the Secret Army) which was carrying out operations on the home front in opposition to Charles de Gaulle's efforts to end the war in Algeria. In an incisive essay published in *France Nouvelle* in which he speculated about the real reasons Marker's film had been banned two years prior, Albert Cervoni (1963) echoes other critics who understood that the war in Algeria factored into the threat to public order that Marker's *Cuba Si!* was thought to represent:

> At a moment when Cuba occupied center stage in current political affairs, in a period in which the war in Algeria [and] the O.A.S. presented urgent problems whose gravity was becoming more and more apparent to the French public, [the Commission de contrôle] put under lock and key a

work in which it was a question of a people's right to self-determination, and [that dealt with] democracy, fascism, agrarian reform and revolution. With the crisis of last year emerging (i.e. the Cuban Missile Crisis of October 1962), and with a public that couldn't help but be interested in an island over which one of the most serious threats of world war since 1945 erupted, censors continued to play their extinguishing role.

The ban on Marker's film, which documented developments in Cuba immediately following the Revolution of 1959, was also seen by a number of observers who decried its interdiction as the product of American diplomatic pressure. This was apparent in the press commentary in which the film's release in 1963 was interpreted as a sign of momentary "vacheries" or soured relations between France and the United States, which was thought to impose its will routinely on European allies during the Cold War (see Anonymous, 1963a). Marker's film had underscored the extent of American commercial and political involvement in Cuba prior to the Revolution and, as its title indicates, it was exclamatory in its approval of Castro's moves to rid the Cuban economy of its colonial legacy and its neo-colonial influences. But as Cervoni notes, although Marker clearly displayed his sympathies for the Cuban Revolution, his film was also a source of valuable information on the state of affairs on a Caribbean island that in the early 1960s had suddenly taken on great geopolitical importance. After sketching a somber portrait of Batista's violent rule and of the foreign and oligarchical interests he served, Marker sought to showcase the Revolution's achievements, including efforts to eliminate Cuba's high illiteracy rates, to undertake much-needed land reform, and to supply the population with the decent housing that was sorely lacking on the eve of the Revolution. In often lyrical tones, Marker's film revels in the rhythms of the change taking place in Cuba, a radical transformation in social conditions that even a local priest views favorably:

We are now in the process of resolving Cuba's serious social problems: the problem of housing, of unemployment, of health [services] in the country-side, of education. And it is being done without harming the dignity of the human person, infringing somewhat on the habits of joyful living and debauchery that existed in this country. But this is wise and beneficial. . . . [T]he benefits of the revolution [are] infinitely closer to true social Christianity than the system we had before.

If such a figure of tradition found merit in Castro's reforms, shouldn't the French public have the opportunity to see Marker make the case for the Revolution's legitimacy? At least initially, the Commission's response to such a query would have been an emphatic "NO!" The press commentary that appeared following *Cuba Si!*'s 1963 release readily reveals just how resistant the public was becoming to what was increasingly seen as the autocratic actions of the Commission de contrôle and the Gaullist government that empowered it. Even

Le Figaro Littéraire (Anonymous, 1963c), a conservative publication, carried comments by a film critic who praised Marker's achievement and denounced the board's earlier refusal to accord it a release visa. Declaring that the public was being infantilized by government censorship, he goes on to assert that the French people are perfectly capable of deciding for themselves whether a film is propagating dangerous ideology, the justification Louis Terrenoire had initially given for banning *Cuba Si!* in 1961.

> A people such as ours is old enough to be informed and to judge for itself what exceeds the limits of strict information in the documentary films it is presented. Fidel Castro deserves to be heard when he speaks. At any rate, the perhaps exaggerated optimism with which Chris Marker tells us about and shows us the Revolution is no reason to oppose it with the extreme pessimism of a counter-propaganda, in the service of which considerable means of persuasion were deployed. A people that struggles for its independence and for justice is always right.

In this rhetorical frame, the "people" in question here can easily be understood to refer to the Cuba populace that was striving to free itself, Marker informs us, from 500 years of oppression, but also to the French public that is here encouraged to seek freedom from censorship of the sort that struck Marker's and numerous other films in this period. In any case, the irate press commentary surrounding *Cuba Si!* testifies to a growing frustration with the ways in which government censors manipulated public opinion and did so by masking its authoritarian ways. Again, it is Albert Cervoni who identified the tactics the government used to curtail public consideration of such important matters as "democracy, fascism, . . . and revolution":

> And here you have the film coming out, and it is being released without major mutilation. What should we conclude: that [government] power is liberal? Or rather that it hides its arbitrariness under the guise of liberalism, a false liberalism. Holding up the film's release for so long, [the censors] know that they are seriously compromising the film's career, that the information it provides cannot be exactly the same with a two-year delay and while new concerns have imposed themselves on public opinion.

To counter such delay tactics, Cervoni urges his readers to turn out in great numbers to view Marker's film, not only as a means of resisting the wily ways of state power but also to "better understand what Cuba can mean for a French person who is won over [to the idea of] the universal necessity of liberation."

The critical reviews cited above provide a sense of the impact these films had on contemporary audiences once they were finally released, but they also show how journalistic venues functioned as one of the only sectors of the public sphere in which objections to government censorship could be raised. How would the public know that a banned film even existed if it had not been reported and discussed in the contemporary press? These reviews clearly indicate that measures taken by the Commission de contrôle were seen as arbitrary at best and dictatorial at worst, raising the specter of authoritarian rule and conjuring the memory of France's own undemocratic past under the collaborationist Vichy regime and the Nazi Occupation. In much the same manner as the films that were banned, the press provided a site of resistance to the illiberal tendencies that unquestionably asserted themselves in politics and in culture in this period. Together, the films that were censored and the press that raised its voice in protest troubled the nation's conscience in this turbulent period, writing a counter-history that sheds light on the darker autocratic side of the democratic renewal that France's Fourth and Fifth Republics so eagerly sought in the aftermath of World War II.

The films I have discussed here are embedded in a particularly fraught moment of French history and are bound to a political context that makes the stories surrounding these films especially compelling. Yet whether the historical setting in which films are situated and studied is of the momentous or everyday sort, I hope to have shown here that there is considerable knowledge to be gained from analyzing films with historicist concerns in mind. The questions raised in historicist critique can be asked of all films and answered by exploring the specific circumstances that inscribe these works in precisely defined relations of time and place. Historicizing the interpretation of film texts offers the possibility not only of recovering meanings that are apt to be lost when a film's past is overlooked; it also illuminates a work's enduring social significance and allows us to appreciate how the unfolding past shapes the conditions of our cultural present.

FURTHER READING

Andrew, Dudley (1995) *Mists of Regret: Culture and Sensibility in Classic French Film*, Princeton, NJ: Princeton University Press.
Andrew approaches French classical cinema, and, in particular, its poetic realist expression, by examining the points of contact and interaction between high art and popular culture in France of the 1930s. Andrew focuses attention on the specific historical and cultural conditions in which the poetic realist aesthetic developed, showing how its emergence depended not only on the particularities of the French film industry and the talents of its directors and other film personnel, but also on the symbiotic relationship the cinema developed with other artistic and cultural spheres and with the atmosphere of contestation that characterized the Popular Front era in France.

Ferro, Marc (1988) *History and Cinema*, Detroit, MI: Wayne State University Press.
Drawing from a full range of national film histories from different historical periods (Soviet, French, American, German), Ferro shows that films are both a source and agent of history. As a source of history, they tell us much about the beliefs, attitudes, and conditions that shaped societies in the past. As an agent of history, films act upon societies and produce effects that can alter public attitudes toward pressing issues of their day. Film can also restore historical memory of important aspects of the past that have been ignored by professional historians.

Guynn, William (2006) *Writing History in Film*, New York and London: Routledge.
Guynn adopts a multi-disciplinary approach to studying the historical film, developing a theoretical framework that enables a critical evaluation of the validity of cinematic interpretations and representations of the past. Drawing on the insights offered by the philosophy of history, rhetoric, narratology, and film semiotics, Guynn problematizes the distinction between history and fiction and between fiction and nonfiction. Through a selection of case studies, he illustrates how the films he analyzes both articulate discourses of historical representation and function as sites where a society's collective memory is formed.

Rosenstone, Robert (1998) *Visions of the Past: The Challenge of Film to Our Idea of History*, Cambridge, MA: Harvard University Press.
Rosenstone challenges the conventional view that historical films provide an inferior understanding of the past compared to that produced by professional historians. He finds value in the historical film and argues that, particularly in its postmodern forms, it calls attention to the limitations of conventional written history, creating a visual space in which new conceptions of history and a new cultural relationship to the historical past can emerge.

Sorlin, Pierre (1980) *The Film in History: Staging the Past*, Totowa, NJ: Barnes and Noble Books.
Sorlin provides definitions and strategies for studying the historical film, focusing attention on film production relating to the French Revolution, the Italian Risorgimento, the American Civil War, and the Russian Revolution. Sorlin argues that all historical films are fictional, but they nonetheless participate in creating a culturally shared sense of the past, while also evoking the contemporary moment in which they are created.

Part II

A CRITICAL DICTIONARY: HISTORY,
THEORY, TECHNIQUE

CRITICAL DICTIONARY

Words in **bold** that occur within an entry refer to other entries in the critical dictionary.

ADAPTATION The adaptation of literary and theatrical works as well as popular forms like the comic book has been pervasive throughout film history, beginning with the Lumière Brothers' *L'Arroseur arrosé* (1895). Dudley Andrew estimates that more than half of all commercial films are based on previous texts (in Naremore, 2000, p. 29). Some borrowings from literature aim at adapting classics of high art—Laurence Olivier's *Henry the Fifth* (1945)—popular renditions aim at a more general audience—MGM's literary adaptations of the 1930s—and some reveal a dynamic exchange between cultures—Akira Kurosawa's adaptation of *Macbeth*, or Luchino Visconti's appropriation of an American thriller in his naturalistic *Ossessione* (1942). Obviously, adaptation varies enormously according to historical and cultural circumstances.

The driving force of adaptation has often been more economic than inspirational. In the early years of the twentieth century, filmmakers were in constant need of new subjects and sought to bring broad audiences into the movie theaters by reproducing scenes from successful plays (see **theater**). They also attracted a more bourgeois public by adapting prestigious nineteenth-century novels and developing a style that corresponded to the "realism" of their sources. In the period of **Classical Hollywood** filmmaking, studios often bought successful novels or plays from the New York stage, which they transformed, under the watchful gaze of the film industry's self-censorship board (see **Hays Office**) and civic organizations, into "wholesome entertainment" appropriate for their mass audience (often to the distress of the novelist or playwright who saw his or her work bowdlerized). National cinemas have relied on their literary heritages, often with a greater "faithfulness" to the spirit of the original: for example, the silent Swedish cinema's adaptations of works by Selma Lagerlöf or the frequent literary borrowings in the Japanese genre of the *jidai-geki* (period films). Other tendencies have taken an anti-bourgeois stance against high literature: in 1954 François Truffaut attacked the French Tradition of Quality because, he contended, Quality film relied too heavily on literary texts and diminished the role of the creative director, the only authentic **auteur**. French **New Wave** filmmakers did not, however, eschew adaptation but preferred to find their sources in popular literature (e.g. the hard-boiled detective novel). **Modernist** filmmakers have often conceived of adaptation as an interpretation of the literary source (as in New German filmmaker R. W. Fassbinder's reworkings of classic and modernist novels, *Effi Briest* and *Alexanderplatz*, both of 1974).

How do theoreticians conceive of the process of adaptation: the transformation of a verbal text into an audiovisual one? Is it a translation in which the adapter creates equivalencies between one system of signs and another? What difference does it make that written narratives begin with signification (words, phrases, paragraphs, chapters with their readily available meanings) and attempt to give the impression of perception, whereas film begins with perception (of images and sounds) and works toward signification? What are the principles on which conversions from one medium to the other take place? Should the filmed version attempt to reproduce the **style** and form of the "original"? Already in 1948, André Bazin argued that "faithfulness to form . . . is illusory: what matters is the *equivalence in meaning of the forms*," and these equivalencies have less to do with style than with "characters or their environment" (in Naremore, 2000, p. 20).

Contemporary criticism tends to treat film adaptation as a form of **intertextuality**: the notion that all texts refer to previous texts and are thus involved in an endless process of textual recycling. Sergei Eisenstein famously wrote that "it was none other than [Charles] Dickens who gave [D. W.] Griffith the idea of parallel action." Indeed, Robert B. Ray observes that popular storytelling is particularly open to migration from medium to medium in which a novel may become

a film, a film may become a Broadway musical or a TV series, or the other way around. But intertextual borrowings are also characteristic of modernist text (e.g. all the film and video work of Jean-Luc Godard). The theoretical tendencies of **postmodernism** and deconstruction have largely overturned the hierarchy of forms in which the literary source (the "original") was deemed superior to the derivative film (the "copy"). Bazin observed already in 1948 that we were looking forward to a time when "the unity of the work of art, if not the very notion of the author himself, will be destroyed" (in Naremore, 2000, p. 26). [WG]

Further reading

Naremore, James (ed.) (2000) *Film Adaptation*, New Brunswick, NJ: Rutgers University Press.

AESTHETICS Aesthetics is the branch of philosophy that is concerned with beauty in art, and film aesthetics includes any critical practice concerned with film as a form of art. Since the experience of beauty is generally acknowledged to be a subjective effect or quality rather than objective and measurable, film aesthetics usually involves explaining the specific effectiveness of a film by demonstrating how various film techniques work together to create the unified effect of the film as a whole. This procedure can be mainly inductive, moving from the analysis of details to the big picture of how a film works, or it can be deductive and depend on theories of what, in general, makes films effective or beautiful, for example the manifestation of a director's style or *mise-en-scène* (**auteurism**), the use of formal strategies (**formalism or neo-formalism**), and the mobilization of the spectator's belief in the reality of the image (**realism**). Though in contemporary film scholarship aesthetics is often combined or blended with other approaches, an aesthetic approach can generally be identified by the priority it gives to the internal coherence and uniqueness of a given film as text/object over the external connections which the film has with its contexts (**semiological, ideological, cultural,** historical, etc.). [PY]

See Chapter 3.

Further reading

Bordwell, David (2008) *Poetics of Cinema,* New York: Routledge.
Perez, Gilberto (1998) *The Material Ghost: Films and Their Medium,* Baltimore, MD: Johns Hopkins University Press.

ANALYTICAL EDITING The classical pattern for shooting a continuous scene in which an establishing shot (or master shot) is followed by closer views of actors and activities in the scene. For a fuller definition and description, see Chapter 4 (pp. 57–58). See also **Classical Hollywood Cinema** and **continuity editing**. [WG]

ANIMATION AS MOVING PICTURE Animation must be understood as much older than cinema itself. Any picture that moves—whether it's the viewer moving in relation to what he or she is seeing, or light moving on the screen—can be identified with animation. Thus, special effects in Baroque architecture, the gag in medieval carnival, and the history of puppet all suggest moving pictures that are animated.

As a narrative language, the moving picture tends to be multimedia, is often about controlled anarchy more than drama, and often relies on gags using direct address (characters looking straight at the viewer). As a result, animated film, an essential manifestation of the moving picture, is often self-reflexive (see **reflexivity**), as, for example, when animated characters use the frame of the film as a prop.

Animation studies tends, therefore, to be deeply connected to the archaeology of cinema: the study of the period before the "invention" of the motion picture in 1895 known as pre-cinema. During the early stages of a new medium, animation techniques are often "rediscovered": for example, trick films in **early cinema** (composited by Georges Méliès and Emile Cohl); in early television, the popularity of cartoons from Fleischer and Warners; in early TV commercials, for example at DePati-Freleng and the Leo Burnett Agency, the creation of animated characters like Charlie the Tuna; or Frito Bandito and Raid Kills Them Dead, by Tex Avery for Foote, Cone and Belding; and of course, in the history of computer graphics and video game design. Animators from CalArts helped lay out the early special effects for *Star Wars* (1976). Often, when new forms of moving picture require new forms of story—as in early music videos—the flexible structure of animation is explored more heavily. Animation has also been widely used in amusement park design, and in imagineering at theme parks, from the 1880s onward. [NMK]

See Chapter 8.

ANIMATION TECHNIQUES These include the following: *compositing* (the construction of visual space through stacking layers in depth, whether with paper or celluloid); *stop motion* (shooting a film frame by frame in order to animate drawings or models); *metamorphosis* (the transformation of one image into another through techniques of drawing rather than editing); and *stretch and squash* (drawing successive frames of animated characters in rapid motion so that their bodies seem to expand as they begin to move and contract as they come to rest). Most of these techniques evolved out of the crucial fact in all animated films: that it first develops its continuity of movement on paper. Even today, before being transferred to film, these papers are often flipped, like flip books, or converted into pencil tests (sequences of rough drawings recorded on film or videotape), before the lines are simplified. Sometimes, this paper also has cutouts, or even textured media, like finger painting, or washes of color, or watercolor background. At other times, instead of flat paper, the continuity is three dimensional, like clay sculpture or puppetry.

The original mode of animation (or moving picture) is then transferred frame by frame to film. If the original is more sculptural, then it will be transferred as stop motion. Sometimes the original can be filmed as live action, like a puppet play, then pixilated (sped up); or composited through mattes or optical printing. Today, of course, the final step is digital, onto computer programs.

Animation rarely loses its origins as paper or as sculpture. It is fundamentally self-reflexive, because viewers are always aware of the production process, and multimedia, because animated film always bears the trace of its first-stage medium. Animation layout—spatial design—composites as multimedia as well. Indeed, animated space reveals its layering much more than live-action film. Thus, animation is simultaneous media as simultaneous time. This means simultaneity—or compositing—of different spaces at the same time, and different moments (but not in the sense of the movie set). Animation may be staged in miniature, as may live action; but animation will often exaggerate the miniature, not "hide" it inside filmic space, as a hidden effect. Animation story requires this multimedia irony.

Its cycles of movement reveal the handmade, the other-than-filmic. Thus, animation is essentially cycles of movement from non-cinematic media to cinema, within layers of compositing (compositing of space, of time). Animation techniques, therefore, expose what live action is designed to hide: their repetitive cycles, even holding poses to mentally take us back to illustration. Its simultaneities are much closer to illustration than live action; however, animators have long since learned to deliver an imaginary (live action) camera, as in imaginary **crosscutting**, imaginary **reverse-angle shots**, and so on.

All animation techniques reinforce the illusion of movement, but also the artifice of the handmade. So when master animators Frank Thomas and Ollie Johnston describe character animation as "the illusion of life," this should not be understood merely as **verisimilitude**. Even in Disney "full" animation, as it was called from the mid-1930s onward, the illusion was fundamentally caricature more than live action. But the technique of stretch and squash was developed to keep the volumes of the figures constant.

At Fleischer Studios in the 1930s, extremes of movement ignored stretch and squash, but cycles of movement and character poses often used *roto-scoping*, a technique by means of which images are literally projected up from underneath the light table so that the animator can directly imitate the illusion of live-action film.

These animation techniques maintain the delicate balance between the hand-made and "realistic" cycles of movement. But in recent decades, with computer graphics in particular—and new media for animation like computer games and motion capture and IMAX 3D—the balance has been confused again. New techniques are being developed to restore that anxious, ironic, caricatural transfer from one medium to the next, at large studios like Pixar, and in experimental computer graphics around the world. In the past, no more than five cels could be contained within a frame. Now the number of layers is virtually—indeed virtually—endless, which can sometimes lead to a velvety, plastic (texture-mapped) blank quality, what some have called "polishing the jelly bean." However, through digital animation and special effects, much more ironic **deep focus** techniques are possible (e.g. beyond even the work of Bob Clampett in the 1940s). At the same time, in the mixing of media—the basis of animation—the cuts between layers became more difficult to sustain, and more difficult for the viewer to see. As a result, animators returned much more to stop motion in the mid-1980s, inspired by Jan Svankmajer, who particularly inspired the Brothers Quay. Today, computer-generated techniques refer much more to video editing and cinematic memory, use motion capture much more, and photography. The computer paste-up and infinitely layered results, like the videos of Chris Cunningham, for example, are reminding us of a fundamental historical change in visual codes today—that video has long since absorbed many older media. And yet, the tactile, the haptic, and the meta-morphic—the sensuality of pre-video and the analogue—may be more desirable than ever. Animators are still trained generally on paper and sculpture first, to let the techniques remain caricatural and multimedia. Computer animators often return to building architectural objects, to ancient maps, and to installations in real space, as if to remind themselves of the spark that gives the animated cycle life. As Cunningham's videos show, the human body is increasingly a multi-media object itself, an ironic animated subject. [NMK]

See Chapter 8.

APPARATUS The notion of the cinematic apparatus can be defined as a configuration of technological, psychological, and cultural–ideological conditions for the moving image experience. The cinema theater, for example, is an apparatus consisting of elements like the auditorium with its rows of seats, the screen, projectors and their light beams, the presence of other spectators, and so on. As a material-mental viewing machine the apparatus imposes predetermined conditions upon the viewer. For early psychoanalytically oriented apparatus theory, there was no way of avoiding or countering their effects; they constituted a mental strait jacket that conditioned the identity formation of the spectator, for example the spectator's position as passive and regressive consumer and voyeur (see de Lauretis and Heath, 1980). Nowadays it is more commonly suggested that the cinematic experience is based on negotiation between the givens of the viewing situation (including, of course, the moving images themselves), and the viewer who uses learned and inherited codes to reach his or her stance (Sturken and Cartwright, 2001, Chapter 2). The apparata in other media are obviously different and require analysis based on their specific configurations. [EH]

See Chapter 1.

ART CINEMA The phrase Art cinema is generally used to refer to films whose aesthetic ambition and self-conscious cinephile audience distinguish them from the mainstream of popular film-making. As a historical phenomenon, Art cinema is associated with the rise of global **cinephilia** after World War

II, when the activities of institutions such as film festivals, film journals, and repertory film theaters functioned to produce an international audience for films with aesthetic ambition, often **modernist** in form and valued for the unique style of their **auteurs**. Though the Art cinema is sometimes thought to have reached its peak of achievement in Europe during the 1960s, it has continued to thrive up to the present and is currently produced in locations beyond Europe (Asia, Latin America, North America, Africa, Australia). It is now often financed by international co-production arrangements that reflect the dispersed nature of its target audience. An Art film today will typically have a modest theatrical release in metropolitan centers around the world and reach a much larger audience on DVD. [PY]

See Chapter 3.

Further reading

Bordwell, David (2008) "The Art Cinema as a Mode of Film Practice," in *Poetics of Cinema*, New York: Routledge.
Kovács, András Bálint (2007) *Screening Modernism: European Art Cinema 1950–1980*, Chicago: University of Chicago Press.

ART CINEMA DISTRIBUTION As Barbara Wilinsky notes,

The years after World War II, in which Art cinema developed, were important for the United States film industry. Film attendance declined, and United States courts, in the *Paramount* decision, ordered the film studios to separate from their theater chains. (2001, p. 2)

Under new social formations, such as the move to the suburbs, movie-going habits for mainstream audiences had changed. These conditions created a space for the introduction of new kinds of movies into US theaters. Prominent among these was the Art cinema. Yet, this cinema required new forms of distribution into new kinds of exhibition circuits. During the **Classical** era, the Hollywood studios had a virtual stranglehold on exhibition and only the occasional foreign film would play and usually in only a small handful of theaters. With the divestiture of exhibition from production, individual movie theaters were able to be more selective in their choice of films, and with changes in movie-going habits urban theaters, especially, were in need of films to show. Art films could appeal to these new audiences and movie theaters met this demand with these new kinds of movies. In addition, as Wilinsky notes, the theaters positioned themselves as "Art houses" and offered not only new films, mostly from overseas, but also a new atmosphere in the theater itself (pp. 5–6). Yet, the mechanisms by which these newly christened Art houses would book films also required a new form of distribution that not only could deliver films, but also deliver films that would carry the kind of prestige or interest that mainstream cinema could once rely on via the star system, for instance. In other words, which films from overseas should merit distribution and how to "sell" them became an important issue in the exhibition of Art films.

Given that Art cinema could not rely on stars or studios, or even genre, as a selling point, perhaps the most important manner in which films could attract attention for distribution was via the film festival. Prize-winning films could certainly then trade on the presumed prestige that would accrue with an award. In the immediate post-war era the Venice Film Festival (founded in 1932) proved most important for the introduction of Italian, French, and Japanese cinema. In the early 1950s the Cannes Film Festival (founded in 1946) also emerged as an important venue for the screening of artistic films. By the late 1950s, Cannes had replaced Venice as the premier festival, but Venice retains an important position, as does the Berlin International Film Festival (founded in 1951). Such prizes as the Golden or Silver Lion (Venice), the Palme d'Or (Cannes), or the Golden Bear (Berlin) are important mechanisms both for distributors to discover potential films for export and for the marketing of those films.

Another mechanism for the distribution of Art films was the gatekeeper function of New York City and the all-important review in the *New York Times*. If a review in the *Times* could make or break a Broadway show, so, too, could reviews in the paper call further attention to an Art film for possible wider distribution or squash any hopes for play beyond the Big Apple. Art films were mostly confined to smaller venues in larger cities, with most films playing in only a handful of theaters across the United States, at least until the advent of the multiplex when individual screens in many such venues might be reserved for Art, independent, or documentary films. [DD]

147

Further reading

Wilinsky, Barbara (2001) *Sure Seaters: The Emergence of Art House Cinema*, Minneapolis, MN: University of Minnesota Press.

AUDIENCE STUDIES Initially, film studies concentrated on the film text or narrative, distinguishing itself from mass communication studies, whose traditional focus was on quantifying the effects of the media text. For the film scholar, meaning was encoded in the material offered the spectator, who in turn decoded what he or she saw according to the same rules that produced the film text in the first place. However, scholars such as David Morley, working primarily on television, argued that audiences have a significant degree of agency in determining the meanings of a text. Research by Morley and others associated with the British School of Cultural Studies encouraged film scholars to look more closely at film audiences and the various ways in which they make meanings out of the film experience. Significant to these developments is reception theory, associated with scholars such as Janet Staiger, who analyzed how audiences' relations to a film, as an event, are shaped at a given moment, producing a range of possible interpretations, which deposit sediment and accrue over time (1992). [HR]

Further reading

Everett, Anna (2001) *Returning the Gaze: A Genealogy of Black Criticism, 1909–1949*, Durham, NC: Duke University Press.
Maltby, Richard, Stokes, Melvyn, and Allen, Robert Clyde (2007) *Going to the Movies: Hollywood and the Social Experience of Cinema*, Exeter, UK: University of Exeter Press.
Staiger, Janet (1992) *Interpreting Films: Studies in the Historical Reception of American Cinema*, Princeton, NJ: Princeton University Press.
Stokes, Melvyn and Maltby, Richard (1999) *Identifying Hollywood Audiences*, London: British Film Institute.

AUTEUR Now part of the basic vocabulary of English-language film criticism and scholarship, the term auteur first gained prominence during the 1950s when it was used by French critics writing in film journals such as *Cahiers du cinéma* to identify a film's director as the main creative artist, the *author*, responsible for the totality of its aesthetic achievement. The *politique des auteurs* ("polemic about authors") that originated with *Cahiers* critics such as François Truffaut and Jean-Luc Godard was based in the argument that because only the director had control over the multitude of techniques at work in any film (directing the actors, set and lighting design, cinematography, sound design, editing, etc.) only he or she was in a position to coordinate and use those techniques to aesthetic effect. An auteur's distinctive use of film techniques, often identified with the term **mise-en-scène**, was treated as a stylistic "signature" that could be identified across a body of films that otherwise differed in terms of their genres and subject matter. This style-based definition of film authorship allowed critics to recognize the aesthetic importance of filmmakers working within commercial film industries such as Hollywood (see **style**).

Though it is still in wide use today, the concept of the auteur has had a complicated history since the 1950s. The original French version was taken up by critics around the world and found its most forceful American exponent in Andrew Sarris, who created an elaborate ranking system for directors. But both Sarris and the first generation of *Cahiers* critics were criticized for having a Romantic conception of the individual artist and for creating a personality cult around certain directors that mystified and obscured the more complex ways in which films are actually produced and function in culture and society. During the 1960s and 1970s scholars working in traditions of structuralism, **Marxism**, and **psychoanalysis** critiqued the auteur approach for being implicated in ideological discourses that supported inequitable social conditions (e.g. white heterosexual bourgeois patriarchy), while the historical and **cultural studies** approaches that have been prominent since the 1980s have emphasized the extent to which films reflect their immediate contexts of production and reception as much as or more than the personal world-view of their director. [PY]

See Chapter 3.

Further reading

Hillier, Jim (ed.) (1985) *Cahiers du cinéma: The 1950s: Neo-Realism, Hollywood, New Wave,* Cambridge, MA: Harvard University Press.

Sarris, Andrew (1968) *The American Cinema: Directors and Directions, 1929–1968,* New York: Dutton.

Wexman, Virginia Wright (ed.) (2003) *Film and Authorship,* New Brunswick, NJ: Rutgers University Press.

AVANT-GARDE/EXPERIMENTAL FILM Cutting-edge, oppositional filmmaking that defies mainstream production values and conventional forms of realist narration. This type of filmmaking generally involves small-scale, low-budget productions in which an individual or small group of people perform all of the production tasks and work with materials specific to the film medium to produce a distinctively cinematic visual experience that often features abstract forms and jarring juxtapositions of film images. Well-known avant-garde and experimental filmmakers include Maya Deren, Stan Brakhage, and Jean-Luc Godard. [RS]

See Chapter 6.

Further reading

Dixon, Wheeler Winston and Foster, Gwendolyn Audrey (eds.) (2002) *Experimental Cinema: The Film Reader,* London: Routledge.

Rees, A. L. (1999) *A History of Experimental Film and Video,* London: British Film Institute.

Sitney, P. Adams (2002) *Visionary Film: The American Avant-Garde, 1943–2000,* Oxford: Oxford University Press.

B STUDIOS The period between the **Great Depression** and the 1950s, during which audiences were attracted to theaters by the screening of double features consisting of an "A" movie followed by a "B" movie, also saw the emergence of small independent studios known as "B Studios" (also called "Poverty Row"). Chief among them were companies such as Mascot, Tiffany, Monogram, and Republic Pictures Corporation, which specialized in the production of low-cost "B" pictures classified as such according to the size of their budget, lack of major stars, running time (as low as 50 minutes), and place in the double bill. Films called Programmers could play either half of the double bill. Major studios, unlike B Studios, produced Superspecials and Specials ("A" features) as well as Programmers, but also made "B" features, movies with no stars, low budgets, and shorter running times, for which they charged flat fees rather than a percentage of the box office, often dedicating specialized units such as the Pine Thomas unit at Paramount to their production. Some "B" features achieved cult status and were considered paragons of **Classical Hollywood Cinema**––such as RKO's low-budget horror films produced by Val Lewton in the 1940s, which included *Cat People* (1942), *I Walked with a Zombie* (1942), and *The Leopard Man* (1943), or Republic's "B" Westerns, exceptionally with top-ranking stars such as Gene Autry and Roy Rogers. [HR]

See Chapter 2.

Further reading

Schaefer, Eric (1999) *Bold! Daring! Shocking! True!: A History of Exploitation Films, 1919–1959*, Durham, NC: Duke University Press.

BLOCK BOOKING Common from the 1930s through the 1940s, block booking was the practice by the major studios of selling multiple films to a theater as a package, forcing exhibitors to accept the studio's **"B" movies** and shorts in order to gain access to their big-budget pictures with A-list stars. Because block booking that often entailed "blind sighting"—the purchase of movies unseen—was judged a monopoly practice that stifled competition from independent producers and distributors, the practice was outlawed by a Supreme Court decision in 1948, known as the *Paramount* decree, initiating the demise of the **studio system**. [HR]

See also **production/distribution/ exhibition** *and* **Classical Hollywood Cinema**.

CAMERA ANGLES Technicians define camera angles in terms of a norm: the eye-level position of the standing adult (although the camera is typically placed somewhere lower than the sightline of an average adult). Thus, when angles deviate from this norm, we talk about *low angles* that look up at the subject and *high angles* that look down on it. Angles often have an expressive (**connotative**) function: most conventionally, a low angle lends power or menace to the human figure; a high angle suggests weakness. Extreme high and low angles are unusual and strike us as self-consciously expressive. *Canted* framings are askew, out-of-level shots that often suggest instability. Significantly out-of-norm angles are associated with experimental filmmaking—German Expressionism, the Soviet montage movement, American avant-garde films of the 1960s—and the work of individual *auteurs*, for example Swedish filmmaker Alf Sjöberg. However, Hollywood **film noir** also often uses out-of-norm angles to suggest characters' situations or psychological states or to evoke an atmosphere of danger or dread. Even in today's commercial production, the use of angles such as canted framings is not uncommon in expressing altered states of mind. [WG]

CAMERA MOVEMENTS Camera movement includes several different techniques that shift the camera's position and with it what the spectator sees on the screen. For a description of the *tracking shot*, the *dolly*, the *pan* and the *tilt*, the *crane shot*, the *handheld camera*, and the *Steadicam*, see Chapter 4 (p. 54). [WG]

CAMERA OBSCURA The principle behind the camera obscura was already known in classical antiquity and ancient China: when rays of light traverse a hole (often provided with a lens) into a dark chamber or box, a view of the scenery outside is projected inside in inverted form (it can be reversed by a mirror, etc.). This principle seems to have been first used practically to observe eclipses of the sun in the Middle Ages. Since the Renaissance, camera obscuras were used as artists' tools, scientific demonstration devices, and popular pastime. The camera obscura is still mainly known as the predecessor of the photographic camera, yet its cultural roles, discursive presence as a cultural metaphor, and the range of its applications have been much wider.

While smaller portable camera obscuras (wooden boxes or dismountable contraptions in the form of a tent) were used by artists as aids to sketch scenes, permanent room-sized camera obscuras, housed in little cabins and often built in picturesque locations like seasides, hilltops, parks, and towers, were used for collective viewing. The scenery from the outside was "transmitted" by means of a lens and an angled mirror from the top of the cabin onto a horizontal table in the center of the darkened chamber. Visitors observed moving scenery, which was framed by the edges of the table and thus detached from its "natural" soundscape. They pointed at details with their fingers, occasionally touching the image and admiring leaves moving and birds flying by in silent motion. Approaching enemy could also be put under surveillance in a similar way, pointing to the military uses of the camera obscura.

The fact that the views in the camera obscura are in motion is often forgotten. The principle of transmitting a live image in real time and presenting it on a dedicated surface anticipated broadcast television. The camera obscura also has affinities with today's interactive touch-screen interfaces (like that of the iPhone) manipulated with fingertips. Erkki Huhtamo has considered the camera obscura as an early device used in "touch practice." [EH]

See Chapter 1.

Further reading

Hammond, John (1981) *The Camera Obscura: A Chronicle*, Bristol: Adam Hilger.

CANON A canon is any group of artworks (e.g. pieces of literature, paintings, films) that consensus has identified as being of special and/or lasting importance, usually on the grounds that each of the artworks represents a unique landmark of aesthetic achievement. Film canons are created in a variety of ways, through polls of filmmakers, critics, and scholars that rank the best films of the year, best films of all time, and so on, through the recognition of awards given at film festivals and annual competitions such as the Academy Awards, and through the implicit consensus represented in the syllabi of academic Film Studies courses and film history textbooks. Today the films *Battleship Potemkin* (1925), *Citizen Kane* (1941), and *The Seven Samurai* (1957) are all considered part of "the canon of world cinema" because they have consistently had a presence in the various domains where films are assessed and a consensus about their ranking is established. That said, the canon of world cinema and other subordinate canons are always in flux as critical values evolve. In the climate of **postmodernism**, the very idea of a canon is suspect, as it is seen to wrongly imply that a particular historically and culturally specific set of aesthetic values is somehow universally valid. Critics and scholars can argue that existing canons have built-in biases that, for example, favor European **art cinema** over popular Hindi films (i.e. Bollywood). Though such critiques have effectively served to deflate the permanence and universal authority of film canons, they nonetheless continue to be created and debated. [PY]

Further reading

Sarris, Andrew (1968) *The American Cinema: Directors and Directions, 1929–1968*, New York: Dutton.
Wollen, Peter (2002) 'The Canon', in *Paris Hollywood: Writings on Film*, New York: Verso.

CENSORSHIP An imposition of authority that limits or forbids access to speech, writing, or cultural and artistic production on the grounds that it poses a threat to the community in which it would circulate. Censorship is most often exercised by governmental entities in the name of public order and morality. It can also be pursued by groups and individuals who seek to impede the dissemination of materials they deem in some way objectionable. In times of heightened repression, individuals can also succumb to self-censorship, recoiling before the possibility of creating works of art or expressing thought they believe or know will be subject to censorship. [RS]

See Chapter 11 and entries on the **Hays Office** and **Socialist Realism**.

CHARACTER Characters are the (usually) human entities whose actions constitute the film's story. At least since the early classical period (*c.* 1917), the character in film has taken the form of the psychological and moral being characteristic of Western literature and theater (as opposed to the broad social types characteristic of **early cinema**). Characterization is the process by means of which the audience establishes the identity of the character in response to the clues the film provides: the character's physical appearance, gestures, actions, speech, the settings in which he or she appears, and the comparisons the audience makes between one character and others. Characters may also be defined in relation to character types: for example, the femme fatale of **film noir**.

Characterization in cinema is conditioned by the specificity of the medium. Because of their richly detailed image and soundtracks, films tend to observe characters from the outside (called external focalization in narrative theory), giving indirect access to the internal experience of character through techniques such as psychological editing (see **motivation**). Only occasionally do films give direct access to the inner workings of the character's mind (internal focalization), for example through interior monologue in voice-over or **subjective shots** that "distort" the image or subjective elements of the soundtrack that evoke the character's emotions or thought processes.

With the exception of animation, the fictional character in film is embodied in an actor (in contrast to the novel where the reader produces mental images of the character). The fiction film presents a specific kind of fusion of actor and character that is, many critics contend, quite distinct from theater. A theatrical character may be played by numbers of actors (the many interpretations of Hamlet), whereas in film a character is normally played by a single actor who is closely identified with the role and the role with him. (Audiences in the studio era recognized the consistency of the Jimmy Cagney gangster, despite the evolution of the character through Cagney's career.) Major exceptions are to be found in the remake, the repeated adaptations of literary sources, or the film series (the several incarnations of James Bond that have engendered critical comparisons). The film actor also brings to the character the history of the roles he or she has played in the past (e.g. a Bette Davis character). (See **film acting** and **star system**.) Some theoreticians contend that the film spectator's close **identification** with characters is conditioned by the fact that characters are present through images and reproduced speech but are absent as real being, in contrast to theater where the actors are physically present. [WG]

See Chapter 4.

CINEMA VÉRITÉ was introduced by ethnographer Jean Rouch in a conscious echo of the Soviet 1920s term *kinopravda*. Cinema Vérité utilizes handheld, sync sound equipment (initially 16-mm film) and available light, to penetrate beneath the surface (as did Dziga Vertov's "kino-eye"). In the later 1950s, Rouch had become increasingly frustrated by the limitations of **ethnographic film** and was experimenting in trying to document his subjects' inner lives, for example *Moi, un noir* ("I'm Black," 1958). This project called for **synchronous sound** but, as he found in *La Pyramide humaine* ("The Human Pyramid," 1959), where he brought black and white pupils in an African high school together, 35-mm sync equipment killed spontaneity. In Paris in 1960 he was able to take advantage of the first silent-running (self-blimped) 16-mm "Éclair" camera and a portable audio tape recorder to film the encounters he and co-director Edgar Morin arranged for *Chronique d'un été* (*Chronicle of Summer*) (1960). To ensure that audiences understood their role, Rouch and

Morin also filmed their own involvement—exactly as Vertov had done in *Man with a Movie Camera* (1929). This reflexivity became the mark of Cinema Vérité in contrast to **Direct Cinema**'s directly contrary intention of self-effacement. Especially in the English-speaking world, it was not much emulated, but Rouch's interventionism is one source of **reality television**. [BW]

See Chapter 7.

Further reading

Hockings, Paul (ed.) (1975) *Principles of Visual Anthropology*, The Hague: Mouton.

CINEPHILIA ("love of cinema") is a term used to designate a desire for films that is to some extent self-conscious and driven by and productive of a formal or informal education in film history. Cinephilia can be broad-based and have "the art of the cinema in general" as its object or more narrow and focused on specific aspects of the cinema (e.g. Italian Westerns, the films of the Bollywood star Amitabh Bachchan), but in either case it is defined by the cinephile's desire to see the films he or she loves and learn as much as possible about them. In what we might call its myth of origins, cinephilia arose during the 1950s and 1960s due to factors that allowed for a comprehensive education in film history (cinémathèques, film clubs and repertory theaters, the screening of classic films on television, etc.) and generated excitement regarding contemporary production (as expressed in **film journals**, the concept of the **auteur**, film festivals, etc.). Though

there has been debate as to whether cinephilia has retained its vitality and cultural significance since the 1960s, the opportunities for gaining a formal and informal education in film history (via VHS and DVD technology, specialized cable television channels, Film Studies programs, etc.) and the number of cinephiles taking advantage of those opportunities are undoubtedly much greater today. [PY]

Further reading

Keathley, Christian (2006) *Cinephilia and History, or the Wind in the Trees*, Bloomington, IN: Indiana University Press.

CLASSICAL HOLLYWOOD CINEMA Classical Hollywood Cinema refers to a visual style and mode of production used in the American film industry that flourished between the 1910s and the 1960s, with the years between 1930 and 1948 considered to be the Golden Age of Hollywood.

Classical Hollywood Cinema favored a seamless visual style based on **continuity editing** designed to achieve a "natural" effect in which the viewer does not notice when cuts are made or when the camera moves. Narrative fluidity was achieved through the use of a distinctive visual syntax that depended upon certain strategies: the practice of moving from a wide, or establishing, shot to a medium shot, and then to close-ups of characters, known as "coverage"; the 180-degree rule of "not crossing the line" (see Chapter 4); the use of a **reverse-angle** or shot/reverse shot sequence for dialogue; and the use of three-point **lighting**, to soften and idealize the characters, and maximize their beauty.

The plots of this cinema characteristically involve an economical narrative organized according to a three-act structure, in which a cause-and-effect chain of action, triggered by a central character's personality, desires, and choices, moves toward resolution and **closure**. Particular actors, producers, directors, writers, stunt men, craftspersons, and technicians regularly participated in the same creative team, resulting in a consistent film **style** and **mise-en-scène**, identified with a particular studio. Universal, for example, in the 1930s was known for its horror films characterized by expressionist lighting and composition (see **German Expressionism**) created by its teams of recent European refugees fleeing fascism.

Most Hollywood pictures of the classical period were highly formulaic, repeatedly recycling the conventions of a select number of popular **genres**: westerns, gangster films, musicals, melodramas, and screwball comedies. Despite the predominance of these formulas, many masterpieces were produced by the studio system, such as *Casablanca* (1942), *Citizen Kane* (1941), *It Happened One Night* (1934), *King Kong* (1933), *Red River* (1948), and *Top Hat* (1935). The year 1939 alone saw the appearance of such classics as *Gone with the Wind*, *The Wizard of Oz*, *Stagecoach*, *Wuthering Heights*, *Mr. Smith Goes to Washington*, and *Only Angels Have Wings*.

"The Big Five" major studios (Warner Brothers, 20th Century Fox, RKO or Radio-Keith-Orpheum, Paramount, MGM or Metro-Goldwyn-Mayer), and to a lesser degree the "Little Three" or minor studios (Universal, Columbia, and United Artists), dominated film production during this period. Each studio had its own stars, whose images and personae it sought to promote both on-screen and off-screen, leading to the creation of a **star system**. Stars contracted to MGM through the 1930s, for example, included Clark Gable, Lionel Barrymore, Jean Harlow, Norma Shearer, Greta Garbo, Jeannette MacDonald, Nelson Eddy, Spencer Tracy, Judy Garland, and Gene Kelly, while stars contracted to Warner Brothers included Edward G. Robinson, James Cagney, Bette Davis, Joan Blondell, Barbara Stanwyck, Olivia de Havilland, and Errol Flynn.

The eight studios used **vertical integration** (to varying degrees) to control all aspects of the film's **production, distribution, and exhibition**. Between them, they owned a vast network of first-run theaters in major cities and effectively operated as an oligopoly, controlling the entire market. Between 1930 and the 1950s, the eight studios were able to secure 95 percent of all film rentals and close to 70 percent of all box-office receipts. The monopolistic practices of the studios were resented and resisted by independent producers, and in 1948 a Supreme Court ruling, known as the *Paramount* decree, in the case of the United States versus Paramount, forced the studios to give up their theaters in an act known as "divorcement" and "divestiture." (See *United States* v. *20th Century Fox*, 882 F.2d 656 [2d Cir. 1989], cert. den. 110 S. Ct. 722 [1990].) The effects of this decision, combined with the rise of television in the 1950s, contributed to the decline of Classical Hollywood Cinema, which, from the 1970s, was replaced by New Hollywood. [HR]

See Chapter 2.

Further reading

Balio, Tino (1993) *Grand Design: Hollywood as a Modern Business Enterprise, 1930–1939*, New York: Scribner.
Bordwell, David, Staiger, Janet, and Thompson, Kristin (1985) *The Classical Hollywood Cinema: Film Style and Mode of Production to 1960*, New York: Columbia University Press.
Schatz, Thomas (1997) *Boom and Bust: The American Cinema in the 1940s*, New York: Scribner.

CLOSURE The degree to which the complications of a film's plot are unraveled and brought to resolution (denouement). The classical Hollywood film provides the model of systematic closure in which the destiny of all the major characters is revealed in a manner that satisfies audience expectations (with a predilection for the happy ending). More *open* structures include episodic narratives made up of loosely connected events or narratives with open endings in which the basic situation of the characters is not fully resolved or characters are caught in a cycle of events that seems to have no beginning or end. Openness is a characteristic of **modernist** filmmaking. Political modernists in particular reject closure because the events and situations they represent on film have to be resolved in the real social world, not in the closed imaginary world of fiction. [WG]

Further reading

Bordwell, David, Staiger, Janet and Thompson, Kristin (1985) *The Classical Hollywood Cinema: Film Style and Mode of Production to 1960*, New York: Columbia University Press, pp. 12–23.

COGNITIVE THEORY Neo-formalist scholars such as David Bordwell (1989) and Kristin Thompson (1988), whose goal was to describe film as an aesthetic system, claimed a scientific basis for their project by invoking cognitive theory, a dimension of psychology that seeks to understand how the brain processes information, emphasizing the functions of memory, judgment, and reasoning. Offered as a challenge and a scientific alternative to cine-psychoanalysis and other "interpretive" (as opposed to descriptive) scholarship, cognitivism was promoted by philosophers like Noël Carroll, who heralded it as producing objective analyses of films (as opposed to the presumably murky, subjective musings of **ideological** or **feminist** criticism) and a scientific analysis of the spectator's activity of viewing (as opposed to the hapless "passivity" of the spectator trapped in the unconscious states and positions of Freudian or **apparatus** theory). Bordwell and Thompson's *Film Art: An Introduction*, first published in 1979 and re-edited many times since, became one of the most widely read introductory textbooks in cinema studies without, however, permanently displacing such interpretive methodologies as **psychoanalysis**, **Marxism**, **feminism**, and **semiology** as significant approaches in film scholarship. [HR]

Further reading

Bordwell, David (1989) *Making Meaning: Inference and Rhetoric in the Interpretation of Cinema*, Cambridge, MA: Harvard University Press.

Bordwell, David and Carroll, Noël (1996) *Post-Theory: Reconstructing Film Studies*, Madison, WI: University of Wisconsin Press.

COLD WAR In diplomatic parlance, a cold war is a conflict between two parties in which struggles are waged without resulting in direct military engagement. From the end of the **Second World War** to the early 1990s, the United States and the Soviet Union, the two postwar superpowers, faced off in a continual contest that pitted the capitalist democracies of the West against Communist regimes belonging to the Warsaw Pact. The Soviet Union led this alliance, which included East Germany, Poland, Czechoslovakia, Bulgaria, Hungary, Romania, and Albania in its membership. The most menacing aspect of this struggle between East and West in this period was the nuclear arms race that at key moments, most notably the Cuban Missile Crisis of October 1962, was believed to threaten the survival of the planet. This threat of annihilation and the prospect of mutually assured destruction kept the conflict between the United States and the Soviet Union from erupting into open hostilities, though proxy wars were waged in this period, particularly in Korea (1950–3) and Viet Nam (1946–75) where, along with China and Cuba, Communist insurgencies developed following the Second World War. In addition to their areas of dominance in Europe, both the United States and the Soviet Union staked out spheres of political, military, and economic influence in Africa, Asia, and Latin America where the United States sought to arrest the spread of communism to countries emerging from colonial rule. The Cold War ended in 1991 when the Soviet Union collapsed and Communist regimes throughout Central and Eastern Europe also fell. [RS]

See the following for further information on the impact of the Cold War on the cinema: **HUAC** for a discussion of the anticommunist witch hunts in the Hollywood cinema during the Cold War; **Socialist Realism** for a discussion of the cultural politics of the Soviet block and its extension into China after Mao's revolution; and **Third World Cinema** for a discussion of the "third path" to political liberation.

Further reading

McMahon, Robert (2003) *The Cold War: A Very Short Introduction*, Oxford: Oxford University Press.

Westad, O. A. (2007) *The Global Cold War: Third World Interventions and the Making of Our Times*, Cambridge: Cambridge University Press.

COLOR Color is perhaps the least studied of all the basic expressive elements of the medium. Most historical discussion of color emphasizes the development of technologies that mark off broad periods of color reproduction.

1   In very early cinema, workers, most often women, hand-painted films frame-by-frame in an assembly line process. Such painting achieved graphic pictorial effects, most famously in the fantasy films of Georges Méliès.

2 Tinting is a technique by means of which the film stock is dyed a single color, which appears in the lighter areas of the image. A popular technique in the silent features of the late 1910s and 1920s, tinting achieved conventional effects: a blue wash indicated night time, warm yellows characterized electrically lit interiors, red color was used for fire scenes. Toning was used to color the dark spectrum of the image. Tinting and toning could be combined to create more complex effects.

3 Subsequent experimentation with color was based on two photographic techniques. *Additive* processes projected the black-and-white film through two- or three-colored filters—red, blue, green—where their superimposition created often subtle color effects. In the 1920s, Technicolor's early two-strip additive process, for example, projected images through red and green filters. *Subtractive* processes—the basis of modern color cinematography—produce colored film stock through three superimposed layers, each of which "subtracts" one of the primary colors from its spectrum. Technicolor's three-strip subtractive process, with its splashy color effects, dominated the market between 1935 and 1960. With the development of the Eastmancolor subtractive process around 1955, color became more nuanced and cheaper to produce, and color film asserted its dominance over black-and-white in the 1960s.

From the aesthetic point of view, film criticism has not developed a theory of color or a general approach to discussing color on a par with other basic elements of filmmaking. One reason for this lack is that colors have no established meanings—they are fundamentally polysemic—and their **connotations** vary historically, culturally, and indeed idiosyncratically in the art of certain **auteurs**. The audience's understanding of the use of certain colors is rarely as universal as its understanding of the meaning produced by a lighting system, for example. Moreover, color in film has often been described as having the status of an *attribute*, not an autonomous element of composition or expression. In Jean Mitry's view (2000), for example, color is a subsidiary element that *adds to* the dramatic and psychological meanings of the film and must be motivated by them. Color can reinforce, for example, the "dramatic tension" between the "lush green of the prairies" and the "unrelieved desolation" of the rocky location of the final confrontation in Budd Boetticher's *Seven Men from Now*, 1956 (p. 226). He argues, moreover, that the rigid symbolization of color—red equals blood, or passion, or anger—is naïve and self-conscious, as is most use of expressionistic color intended to suggest the internal subjectivity of a character.

Modernist filmmakers like Jean-Luc Godard and Michelangelo Antonioni, on the other hand, are less interested in color for its "realism" and its discretion than for its expressive, even expressionistic, qualities. Their work tends to foreground elements of color. Godard's use of the distancing effect of color filters at the opening of *Contempt* (1963), or the strong chromatic contrasts in *Weekend* (1967), or his self-consciously painterly composition in *Passion* (1982), stimulate the spectator's critical functions and his or her awareness of chromatic effects.

Most conceptions of color in film take an art historical approach in which film's use of color is likened to that of painting. Film critics and theoreticians—Rudolf Arnheim, André Bazin, or Eric Rohmer—advocate for the painterly potential of film. The study of expressive color is not, however, limited to modernist filmmaking. In mainstream film, color can also be studied in relation to certain periods of a **genre**—the "excessive" quality of color in 1950s **melodrama**—and in relation to its role in the narrative system of "colorists" like Alfred Hitchcock. [WG]

Further reading

Dalle Vacche, Angela and Price, Brian (eds.) (1992) *Color, the Film Reader*, New York: Routledge.
Mitry, Jean (2000) *The Aesthetics and Psychology of the Cinema*, Bloomington, IN: Indiana University Press.

COMPOSITION A term inherited from the fine arts, composition refers to the organization of the space of the image, which the filmmaker achieves through **mise-en-scène** and **framing**. Thus, one can describe an image in terms of its linear composition, the play of light and shadow, the use of color, set design, the blocking of actors and their movement within the frame, among others. Audience awareness of pictorial composition often depends on the length of the take—a long take allowing more time to observe the image. Composition may also become apparent through the juxtaposition of elements from shot to shot—contrasting

lines of movement from one shot to the next in Sergei Eisenstein's work, for example. Based on an analogy with music, the soundtrack can also be considered a work of composition in which the elements of dialogue, noise, and music are organized to produce specific effects. (See **sound**.) [WG]

CONTINUITY/CONTINUITY EDITING Continuity in film can be understood at two levels. First, there is the continuity produced by projecting the series of individual frames at a speed (since the advent of sound) of 24 frames per second. The discontinuous succession of frames becomes for the spectator an uninterrupted flow of images in movement.

Second, continuity editing refers to the relationship between shots in a sequence that is maintained through the system of **matches**. Because matched cuts maintain the spectator's orientation to the space of the scene, they are less aware of the cut (the effect often called "invisible editing") and focus on the sense of clear dramatic development. The shooting script is the first stage in establishing the continuity of a film because it sets out on paper the succession of camera positions and the articulation between them. A more elaborate shooting script may include *storyboards*: usually relatively crude sketches, or sometimes photographs, of the shots accompanied by descriptions that may give elements of sound, shifts in blocking of actors, camera movements, and so on. Storyboards are crucial in animation.

It should be remembered that many historians view continuity editing as emblematic of the classical Hollywood style and therefore part and parcel of the international hegemony of the American cinema. Oppositional cinemas—political, **experimental**, **nationalist**, and **modernist**—have often conceived of their resistance to Hollywood in terms of dismantling basic codes of continuity. Experimental and modernist film practices, for example, have often emphasized the discontinuity between shots that breaks the spectator's sense of **transparent** flow and stimulates a more active relationship between spectator and text. (See **avant-garde/experimental film**, **New Waves/New Cinemas**, and **Soviet Montage Movement**.) [WG]

See Chapter 4.

Further reading

Bordwell, David and Thompson, Kristin (2008) *Film Art: An Introduction*, New York: McGraw-Hill.
Reisz, Karel and Millar, Gavin (1953–68) *The Technique of Film Editing*, London and New York: Focal Press.

CROSSCUTTING (INTERCUTTING) An alternation of shots represents two or more separate aspects of the action that are occurring more or less simultaneously and can be described by the pattern a/b/a/b. Chase sequences that alternate the pursuer and the pursued establish a spatial relationship between the two parties (we see, for example, the pursuer entering a space that was previously crossed by the pursued) and a time relationship that can be described as "meanwhile." Crosscutting patterns can become quite complex and involve three or more aspects of an action. The classic example is the last-minute rescue. In Griffith's

Biograph films (1908–13) a typical situation involves three spaces: a) the interior of a building where a young woman becomes aware that b) outside the building there are miscreants attempting to break in; and c) in a third, more distant space the male protagonist learns of the danger and begins the ride to the rescue. A pattern of alternation between a, b, and c develops: each repetition increases the danger of the woman in a, as the miscreants in b pursue their break-in, and brings closer the moment of salvation, when the male protagonist arrives on the scene. An increasingly rapid alternation between aspects of the action is a form of rhythmic editing, intended to increase tension in the spectator. Historically, crosscutting is often considered the first form of cinematic editing and a fundamental break with theatrical representation. In classical filmmaking, it has been especially prevalent in certain genres (the gangster film, the Western, the thriller). [WG]

CULTURAL STUDIES A branch of historical study that focuses on a society's cultural production. Objects of study may include the history of artistic expression, such as the literature, painting, music, and architecture of a particular age. In recent decades, cultural historians have begun to consider what French historians have called the "history of mentalities," an area of investigation that focuses on the belief structures and habits of thought that shaped life in past societies, including spiritual attitudes, collective rituals, symbolic practices, and other cultural forms that defined community values as they were shared in everyday life. These new cultural historical methods have opened vistas on to the past that provide access to the experience of traditionally marginalized groups including women, the popular classes, heretics, children, and a host of other identities whose voices have until recently been ignored and lost to history. These new approaches to the study of cultural history, many of which question theoretically what it means to represent societies and cultures of the past, provide useful analytical models for approaching films that either represent history on the screen or that pose questions concerning the historical moment and the culture context in which a particular film was produced. [RS]

See Chapters 10 and 11.

Further reading

Bonnell, Victoria and Hunt, Lynn (1999) *Beyond the Cultural Turn: New Directions in the Study of Society and Culture*, Berkeley, CA: University of California Press.

Ginzburg, Carlo (1992) *The Cheese and the Worms: The Cosmos of a Sixteenth-Century Miller*, Baltimore, MD: Johns Hopkins University Press.

Hunt, Lynn (ed.) (1989) *The New Cultural History*, Berkeley, CA: University of California Press.

DECOUPAGE In terms of film production, découpage refers to the process of breaking down the film into significant pieces. The film script divides the film's action into a series of sequences or scenes; the shooting script further divides the sequences into individual shots and serves as a basis for organizing the work of the director and technicians. The

work of découpage is further refined in editing, in which the shots receive their final definition. Critics have found the term useful because it allows us to describe the process of structuring a film from its broad outlines to its finest detail. [WG]

See Chapter 4.

DEDRAMATIZATION The rejection of the classical narrative film's emphasis on tightly scripted dramatic action in favor of less plot-driven narratives. Dedramatization creates moments called *temps morts* (dead time) in which the suspension of action allows for the observation of character, daily life, specific environments, and social milieus. Dedramatization emerged as a tendency in the period following the **Second World War** and is most often associated with Italian **Neorealism**, which called on cinema to give a more accurate representation of the social experience of ordinary people. Roberto Rossellini radicalized the notion through a set of principles of film practice: the rejection of the script or any sort of **découpage** of the film prior to shooting; the recognition of the significance of location and its effect on characters; the importance of improvisation for both actors and the director; the rejection of the self-consciously expressive qualities resulting from the film's artistic construction; and a slow pacing that reflects the filmmaker's wait for the emergence of the real. Examples of Rossellini's approach can be found in his early films like *Rome, Open City* (1946) or *Paisàn* (1947) or in the series of films he made with Ingrid Bergman, such as *Stromboli* (1949) or *Voyage in Italy* (1953).

Dedramatization is a prominent feature in the work of many **modernist** filmmakers, for example Michelangelo Antonioni, Andrei Tarkovsky, and Abbas Kiarostami. Influential French filmmaker Robert Bresson produced a theory of cinema and a body of work that are both coherent and rigorous in their rejection of everything dramatic in cinema. To make a film is to wait for an unanticipated encounter with the real that has nothing to do with theatrical structure and actors ("No actors. No direction of actors . . . No staging"). Bresson begins with the concept of the human *model*, whose inner life may be glimpsed in the photographic fragments of his disjunctive style. [WG]

Further reading

Bresson, Robert (1986) *Notes on the Cinematographer*, trans. Jonathan Griffin, London: Quartet.
Rossellini, Roberto (1992) *My Method: Writings and Interviews*, ed. Adriano Aprà, New York: Marsilio.

DEEP FOCUS CINEMATOGRAPHY The technique of deep focus cinematography allows a filmmaker to keep several planes of the image, that is, the foreground, middle ground, and background, in focus at the same time. This technique is usually achieved by using wide-angle **lenses** that have a greater **depth of field** (the distance between planes the lens is capable of keeping in sharp focus) than normal or telephoto lenses. In practice, the use of deep focus has consequences for other aspects of film style; by allowing the action or multiple actions to be staged in several planes, it tends to eliminate the need for editing and produces the

long take. When combined with camera movements that reframe the action in accordance with narrative and/or aesthetic concerns, it becomes possible to capture a long scene in a single shot, a technique often referred to as the **sequence shot**. The aesthetic possibilities of this technique were pioneered by the French director Jean Renoir during the 1930s, given a comprehensive demonstration in *Citizen Kane* (Orson Welles, 1941), and celebrated by the French critic André Bazin for creating a more active and realistic mode of spectatorship. The technique is used most often and extensively by directors working in the art cinema. [PY]

Further reading

Bazin, André (1967) "The Evolution of the Language of Cinema," in *What Is Cinema?*, vol. 1, trans. Hugh Gray, Berkeley, CA: University of California Press.
Bordwell, David (1997) *On the History of Film Style*, Cambridge, MA: Harvard University Press, pp. 46–82.
Bordwell, David (2005) *Figures Traced in Light: On Cinematic Staging*, Chapters 3 and 4, Berkeley, CA: University of California Press.

DENOTATION/CONNOTATION Denotation refers to the literal meaning (of a word or an image) before the reader or spectator discerns the affective or symbolic attributes of what the word or the image represents. In film theory, denotation has been associated with the analogy between objects in the world and the visual (and aural) representations that allow us to recognize and identify them. The image of a horse corresponds by analogy to a horse in the space of our normal vision.

Denotation works on other levels. For example, we make judgments about distance and depth in the two dimensional space of the screen by analogy with our perception of real space, measuring the size of an object (e.g. an approaching car) as an indicator of its distance from the camera. Denotation also encompasses editing patterns. For example, **crosscutting** is a way of denoting the relationship between two or more related aspects of an action.

Denotation as the first level of meaning is, of course, an abstraction. It assumes that "pure" representation can be isolated from the subjective activity of reading or watching a film. In fact, all representations work simultaneously on the denotative and connotative levels. Connotation refers to the emotional or symbolic meanings we attribute to objects we perceive in the image or on the soundtrack. We can't see a horse on screen without seeing it through our personal "lens" or through the "lens" of our cultural experience. Representations of human characters in film solicit in the spectator very subtle and complex affective judgments. Critics often analyze the work of connotation inherent in the technical choices a filmmaker makes: to shoot from a low rather than normal **camera angle**, for example, or to use low-key **lighting** to bring out the atmospheric character of a place, can be seen as subjective techniques that confer connotative meaning. [WG]

Further reading

Barthes, Roland (1977) "Rhetoric of the Image," in *Image–Music–Text*, trans. Stephen Heath, New York: Hill and Wang.

Metz, Christian (1990) "Problems of Denotation in the Fiction Film," in *Film Language: A Semiotics of the Cinema*, Chicago: University of Chicago Press.

DEPTH OF FIELD Refers to the area of the image that is perceived as being in focus. Depth of field is a measure of the optical field that is calculated in terms of distance from the camera. The area of focus is centered around a primary plane (most often bringing into relief the actors and actions that are the *narrative* focus at any given moment); it begins at a minimal point near the camera and extends to a maximal point in depth beyond the primary area of focus. **Lenses** have considerable impact on the perceived depth of field: wide angle lenses "exaggerate" the depth of field, whereas telephoto lenses "collapse" the planes in depth. Great depth of field results in deep focus images that relate different planes of the image and bring out the actors' relationship to their environment (see **deep focus cinematography**). Shallow focus, which gives sharpness of detail to a single plane, tends to isolate actors from the setting in which they act and often requires refocusing to keep the narrative center of the image in sharp focus. Rack focus is a technique for adjusting the depth of field within a single shot, bringing different planes of the image into focus in order to emphasize their importance.

The use of depth of field has varied enormously in film history. Images in early cinema are noteworthy for their great depth of field, beginning with the actualities of the Lumière Brothers. Many filmmakers used great depth of field to stage actions in depth: relating foreground and background actions for dramatic purposes. The work of Louis Feuillade and D. W. Griffith includes fine examples of this kind of staging. Great depth of field in the silent era was accompanied by high contrasts between dark and light. Panchromatic film stock, which had the advantage of rendering a subtler gradation of grays, came into general use beginning in 1926; because it was less light sensitive, deep focus was difficult to achieve and was generally abandoned. The creation of more sensitive panchromatic film and more intense studio lighting made possible the reemergence of deep focus cinematography in *Citizen Kane* (1941), considered an aesthetic revolution that had considerable impact on films of the late 1940s and 1950s. Since the 1980s, however, the tendency to use closer shots and more rapid cutting has severely reduced the use of deep focus cinematography in commercial cinema. [WG]

Further reading

Bazin, André (1967) "The Evolution of the Language of Cinema," in *What Is Cinema?*, vol. 1, trans. Hugh Gray, Berkeley, CA: University of California Press.

Bordwell, David (1997) *On the History of Film Style*, Cambridge, MA: Harvard University Press, pp. 46–82.

Mitry, Jean (1999) *The Aesthetics and Psychology of the Cinema*, Bloomington, IN: Indiana University Press, pp. 168–229.

DIASPORA FILMMAKING The ancient Greek word diaspora (a scattering) first referred to Jews expelled from Palestine and living in exile from their homeland; it was later applied to the massive displacement of people by the African slave trade and subsequently to "widescale dispersal and migration movements that were emblematic of the 20th century" (Braziel and Mannur, 2003, pp. 1–22). Migrations are often coerced, as in the case of the Jews and African slaves, but also may be "voluntary," particularly in the case of peoples emigrating in search of work or those fleeing political oppression. Diasporas of the twentieth century included European and Asian migrations to the United States in the early part of the century; the flight from fascism and Nazi deportations of the 1930s and 1940s; and the massive movement of refugees in the postwar period. In the second half of the century, diaspora refers in particular to migrations of formerly colonized peoples seeking economic well-being, often in the countries of their colonizers: Indian and Pakistani immigrants in the United Kingdom, North and sub-Saharan Africans in France, Indonesians in the Netherlands, among others. Postcolonial migrations continue to characterize diasporas of the twenty-first century, but other economic migrations have also arisen: for example, the free movement of labor within the "borderless" European Union, particularly from Eastern to Western Europe. The United States, where immigration—legal and illegal—has been a constant feature of economic and social life, continues to experience large-scale movements of populations, most notably Latin Americans through the south-western border states. Population movements like these frequently stir up discussions of national borders and national identity, often led by anti-immigrant reactionaries (like Nativist movements in the United States or the National Front in France).

The culture of diasporic communities hinges on its more or less hybrid character: immigrant groups maintain, in varying degrees, their identity in relation to the host culture, either because they intend to return home or feel the need to preserve their heritage (the culture of "nostalgia") or because the host culture resists their integration. Most diasporic cultural forms express this experience of marginality.

Diasporas have been frequently represented in film, often by socially conscious filmmakers: early twentieth-century immigration in Charlie Chaplin's *The Immigrant* (1917); the deportations of the Holocaust in Claude Lanzmann's *Shoah* (1985); movement of labor in Luchino Visconti's *Rocco and His Brothers* (1960); and flight from political oppression in Elia Kazan's *America America* (1963). **Postcolonial** migrations have been the subject of an enormous number of films and an emerging field of research. The following are some of the major diasporic cinemas: the beur cinema about second generation North Africans in France; films by sub-Saharan filmmakers who have lived in Europe and made diaspora a major theme of their films; and films about the Turkish immigrant experience in Germany or Indian and Pakistani communities in the United Kingdom. In a quite different context, Israeli and Palestinian filmmakers explore the consequences of the successive waves of Jewish refugees returning to Palestine and the problems of cultural conflict and national identity. Historically a nearly mythic destination for immigrants, the immigrant groups in the United States have produced, or have been the subject of,

myriad films about the diasporic experience: Italian and Jewish immigration in the early twentieth century, the "hyphenated" experience of the Asian-American and African-American communities, "border films" about Latin American immigrants to the United States, among others. [WG]

Further reading

Braziel, Jana Evans and Mannur, Anita (2003) *Theorizing Diaspora*, London: Blackwell.
Hall, Stuart (1994) "Cultural Identity and Diaspora," in Patrick Williams and Laura Chrisman (eds.) *Colonial Discourse and Post-Colonial Theory: A Reader*, New York: Columbia University Press.
Nacify, Hamid (2001) *An Accented Cinema: Exilic and Diasporic Filmmaking*, Princeton, NJ: Princeton University Press.

DIEGESIS Film criticism employs the term diegesis to refer to the fictional world of the story: what the film represents to us, or, rather, what we collaborate in representing in response to the information the film communicates to us. To use French theoretician Christian Metz's definition, the diegesis is the whole work of **denotation**: the story that develops in fictional space and time, the characters, settings, and events. Although linked to fiction, the concept of diegesis is equally applicable to documentaries or historical films as they also produce credible representations of past or contemporary events. The terms *extradiegetic* or *nondiegetic* refer to elements that are not part of the world represented by the film but stand outside and often comment upon what is happening in the narrative. The film score (defined as **music** whose source cannot be located inside the story-world) is extradiegetic, as is the **voice-over** commentary. [WG]

DIGITAL SOUND Since the birth of cinema, the dominant form of sound recording has been analogue sound. Whether it is **sound-on-disk**, **sound-on-film**, or **magnetic sound**, each technology was based on the direct conversion of sound vibrations into mechanical, optical, or electrical vibrations. However, with the advent of digital recording in the 1970s, it became possible to convert sound waves into electronic data that could be reproduced. All analogue recording media are subject to some forms of unwanted noise (record scratches, optical edit pops, tape hiss), yet, ideally, digital sound was a method of recording sounds and reproducing them without the addition of noise. The analogue-to-digital conversion involves the sampling of a sound source at a given bit size and storing the information as electronic data. By playing the data back through a digital-to-analogue filter, the sound is reproduced without any added noise. If the sampling rate and bit size are high enough, the sound is virtually identical to the original.

The use of digital sound in cinema first came via the use of portable digital production recorders (DATs) and the introduction of digital recording and mixing in **postproduction**. The use of digital sound recording and editing saved some time and labor in production and postproduction, and it simplified the storage and transfer of recorded information. By the 1990s,

most work in postproduction was done digitally with the use of either nonlinear editing platforms like Avid or digital sound mixing programs like ProTools. It wasn't until 1992, however, that digital sound started to be used in the theatrical release of films with the introduction of Dolby Digital. Dolby Laboratories introduced Dolby Digital with the release of *Batman Returns* by encoding five channels of sound information with low frequency enhancement (often referred to as 5.1 sound) onto a 35-mm filmstrip. The sound material is compressed using a digital codec to allow for all five channels to fit into one data stream. Upon playback, the digital sound is uncompressed and rechanneled to the appropriate theater speakers. A year later the DTS Corporation introduced a digital sound system with a slightly higher sound quality for *Jurassic Park*. Their DTS sound works by having the digital sound information compressed onto a CD that is played in interlock with the film projector (ironically, a variation on how the very first Vitaphone sound system worked). That same month, the Sony Corporation introduced a third digital sound system, SDDS, which like Dolby Digital encodes its data on the 35-mm film. Although all three systems were initially in competition, today nearly all prints are released with Dolby Digital, DTS, and SDDS soundtracks available. [JB]

See Chapter 5.

Further reading

Holman, Tomlinson (2007) *Surround Sound: Up and Running*, 2nd edn., Burlington, MA: Focal Press.

Sergi, Gianluca (2005) *The Dolby Era: Film Sound in Contemporary Hollywood*, Manchester, UK: Manchester University Press.

DIRECT CINEMA (popularly, "fly-on-the-wall"documentary)Documentaries shot handheld (initially on portable 16-mm film equipment) using (ideally) only available light and sound. Commentary and interviews were also to be avoided. Throughout the 1950s frustration with the necessity of reconstruction caused by sync—direct—sound shooting increased until the search for more mobile equipment that would allow for available-light handheld **synchronous sound** shooting became central. (Because of war-time combat footage, the handheld camera, lacking the preternatural steadiness of studio mounts, had become a mark of authenticity.) By 1960 the technology (see **documentary film: technology**) was to hand and Direct Cinema was to dominate Anglophone documentary production for the next three decades, its "rules" (or *dogme*) becoming, in the public mind, the essential marks of documentary authenticity. This dominance, however, moved the documentary more firmly than its pioneers had intended toward the journalistic. It curtailed both older documentary methods and inhibited the introduction of new ones. [BW]

See Chapter 7.

Further reading

Saunders, Dave (2007) *Direct Cinema: Observational Documentary and the Politics of the Sixties*, London: Wallflower.

DISCOURSE In linguistics, discourse refers to speech events, sets of statements that extend beyond the sentence, such as ordinary conversations, panel discussions, television news, or poetry readings. Such speech supposes a community of speakers and listeners (a discourse community) who share a common language in which linguistic forms (such as grammar) and the meanings produced when people speak are subject to codes and conventions.

Film theory of the early 1970s was influenced in significant ways by the concept of discourse formulated by French linguist Emile Benveniste, who posited that human subjectivity is formed in language through the use of personal pronouns such as "I" and "you": the speaker and the listener who are engaged in a dialogic exchange. For Benveniste, the term *discourse* refers to enunciations that clearly mark the presence of both a speaker and listener either through the use of personal pronouns or through indicators such as "here" and "now" that situate linguistic exchanges in time and space. A *story*, by contrast, is an apparently impersonal mode of enunciation in which events or circumstances are recounted without any discernible speaker producing the account: stories appear to tell themselves.

While the film medium does not allow for interpersonal exchanges of the sort Benveniste describes (like television, it is a "one way" medium in which the viewer has no way to respond), film theorists have productively adopted his story/discourse distinction in analyzing the ways in which films produce signification. Classical film narratives, for instance, appear to generate stories effortlessly because they typically do not present identifiable speakers or narrators who stand out as the source of the message formulated. The aesthetic of **transparence** refers to the classical film's effacement of the work of production: in viewing a film, we are not immediately aware of the contributions of the collective team of filmmakers—director, cinematographer, lighting technicians, and so on. However, closer examination reveals that films are acts of communication. The processes of production—script writing, mise-en-scène, shooting, editing—imply that an entity—Etienne Souriau called it "the Great Image Maker"—is responsible for producing the film's message, even if this Image Maker cannot be located in a single identifiable "speaker." [RS and WG]

Further reading

Benveniste, Emile (1971) *Problems in General Linguistics*, Coral Gables, FL: University of Miami Press.
Silverman, Kaja (1983) *The Subject of Semiotics*, New York: Oxford University Press.

DISCOURSE THEORY In the field of critical theory, the term discourse refers to the statements and practices generated in precise social contexts. Discourses—the discourse of historians, legal discourse, the discourse of art exhibition—are governed by rules and therefore in some way involve the exercise of power. In *The Archaeology of Knowledge* and *The Discourse on Language*, philosopher Michel Foucault argued that discourse involves historical processes and is formulated in institutional settings in which power relations define what can or cannot be said, who is allowed to speak, how authority is established and deployed, and how the statements made are recognized to be true. Historical discourse, for example, is the product of the professionalization of historical writing, which at the end of the nineteenth century established the university, with its laws and hierarchies, as the arbiter of historical truth. Discourses generated within institutional settings create their objects of knowledge that are then acted upon as if they were objectively real, rather than being the product of discursive formations. In this dynamic, social structures are not made up of autonomous individuals who act freely. Instead, institutions constitute speaking subjects through whom they then wield authority and power.

Foucault's notion of *genealogy*—the active investigation of social discourses in order to uncover their lineage and their hidden structures—is an important methodology for film historians. It counters the model proposed by classical **Marxism**, in which the economic infrastructure determines the cultural superstructure—a determinist model that has mainly been applied to the study of the economic history of film industries. The notion of discursive practices provides a more flexible approach in which power is not conceived only in terms of economics and labor relations but in its many institutional forms. For example, one can examine from this perspective both the industrial production system constituted in the Hollywood studio era, which is in fact a complex system of discourses, or the classical documentary of the 1930s and 1940s that relied on government or private financing and whose critical discourses comply with (or attempt to resist) the laws of patronage. As a medium of social communication, cinema produces numerous social, cultural, and political discourses that can be identified and examined for the forms of power and kinds of knowledge they purvey. [RS]

Further reading

Foucault, Michel (1982) *The Archaeology of Knowledge and the Discourse on Language*, New York: Pantheon.

DOCU-DRAMA (aka DRAMA DOCUMENTARY) uses prior witnessed events, at its purest in the form of actual transcripts, as the basis of a script, cast with professional actors playing the original participants. The documentary value of the result turns on the detail of the source. Given the dramatic traditions of the West (where past events, as in Shakespeare's histories, have long furnished plots) something more accurate than generalized references to actual events is needed. In 1970, Leslie Woodhead used the prison diaries of a dissident Soviet general to document life in the Gulag, *The Man Who Wouldn't Keep Quiet*. Robert Kennedy's memoir of the Cuban Missile Crisis was the basis of a "made-for-TV" feature, *The Missiles of October* (1974, Anthony Page, with William Devane as President John F. Kennedy). Drama documentaries have maintained an intermittent but constant presence in television programming. Retrospectively, the

term has been applied to documentaries from Flaherty to Jennings because of their reconstructional elements, but the crucial difference is that drama documentary uses professional actors, which the older documentaries never did. Currently, using the best available scientific evidence, "conditional documentaries" on events which are yet to happen have been produced: *Smallpox* (2002, Daniel Percival) documented the consequences of a biological weapon terrorist attack with the tag-line, "It's all true. It just hasn't happened yet." [BW]

Further reading

Paget, Derek (1998) *No Other Way to Tell It: Dramadoc/Docudrama on Television*, Manchester, UK: Manchester University Press.

DOCUMENTARY FILM: DEFINITION Documentary refers to a specific approach to the utilization of **nonfiction** image capture which balances the camera's capacity to record reality against the structuring of such material into narratives or logical arguments. It has been variously defined: "the creative treatment of actuality" (John Grierson, 1933); "all methods of recording on celluloid any aspect of reality interpreted either by factual shooting or by sincere and justifiable reconstruction, so as to appeal either to reason or emotion, for the purpose of stimulating the desire for, and the widening of human knowledge and understanding, and of truthfully posing problems and their solutions in the spheres of economics, culture and human relations" (World Union of Documentary Filmmakers, 1948); "aspects of the observer's perception of what happened in the presence of the camera" (Richard

Leacock, 1974). All these definitions can be glossed as: the structuring (or narrativizing) of recorded aspects of observation. [BW]

See Chapter 7.

Further reading

Ellis, Jack and McLane, Betsy A. (2005) *A New History of Documentary Film*, New York: Continuum.

Nichols, Bill (2001) *Introduction to Documentary*, Bloomington, IN: Indiana University Press.

Winston, Brian (2008) *Claiming the Real II: Documentary: Grierson and Beyond*, London: British Film Institute.

DOCUMENTARY FILM: TECHNOLOGY
Documentary film has always been of marginal economic importance to the film industry and has therefore tended to adopt and adapt mainstream film technology. A rare exception to this was the introduction in 1915 of the Akeley, a rugged hand-cranked camera specially designed for location shooting. Despite the coming of sound, silent footage could still be shot on comparatively small, nonblimped (i.e. noisy) 35-mm tripod-mounted cameras and audio added later. Sync, on the other hand, required full-sized studio cameras, even larger optical sound recorders, and, on location, massive generators, and was therefore limited until the professional utilization of 16-mm post-World War II.

Primarily driven by the needs of television newsfilm, 16-mm's development in the 1950s finally caused documentarists to adopt what had been previously seen as an amateur gauge. (Although introduced in 1923, it had been largely ignored even after Kodak marketed a 16-mm sound system in 1938.) TV news had adopted single system 16-mm cameras (with sound recorded on a narrow magnetic strip on the celluloid replacing one set of sprockets). Attendant technologies— portable battery-powered lights and editing machines with separate paths for celluloid and sprocketed audio-tape, "fast" film stocks (capable of working in low light levels)—were also developed in response to broadcast news's requirements throughout the later 1950s. Documentary's contribution was to push for ergonomically designed self-blimped (i.e. silent running) cameras, which could be easily handheld (e.g. the French "Éclair" and the German "Arriflex BL"), to be operated with separate battery-driven ¼ inch audio tape recorders (e.g. the Swiss "Nagra")—the so-called "separate-magnetic" or "sep-mag" system. The Steinbeck editing table for this was developed by German television, and sophisticated, that is, wireless, methods of keeping the cameras running synchronously with the tape recorders were introduced in the early 1960s in the United States.

Lightweight video cameras were initially developed for surveillance purposes and only slowly replaced film equipment. The first experimental video documentaries were shot on Sony "Portapaks," introduced in 1969. The comparatively slow pace of uptake was not only a consequence of video's initial poor quality but also its lack of a full range of editing and postproduction capabilities. For example, prior to the widespread introduction of computer-based editing systems, what was gained in the flexibility of effects on the visual track was lost on the audio side. Digital image capture and computer-based editing are now documentary production norms although 16-mm film and even 35-mm are still not unknown. [BW]

See Chapter 7.

Further reading

Winston, Brian (1996) *Technologies of Seeing: Photography, Cinematography and Television*, London: British Film Institute.

EARLY CINEMA has replaced the term "primitive cinema," now considered pejorative, to designate the period from 1895 to 1917. In most traditional accounts, early cinema is a period of stammering (the cinema didn't know what to say or how to say it) but also of a slow advance (with frequent backsliding) toward its mission: to tell stories using the techniques that belong specifically to cinema. From this perspective, cinema has a "natural language," which was discovered when filmmakers understood that the basic unit of filmmaking is the shot, not the scene, and that fragmentary views, taken from different camera positions, could be edited together to form a narrative continuity.

In the late 1970s, film historians began to question this teleological perspective and sought to show that early cinema adopted other approaches to filmmaking that could not be dismissed as a lack of mastery. Increased access to film archives and systematic research led film historians to more concrete and extensive analyses of the films and therefore to a more accurate picture of developments in the period. They also reevaluated the period in theoretical terms, emphasizing the notion of difference. The early cinema is radically opposed in its basic structures to dominant narrative cinema (Noel Burch); its modes could be considered "pre-classical" in relation to the structures of the classic narrative film (David Bordwell, Janet Staiger, and Kristin Thompson, 1985); early films, often composed of a single shot, *displayed* images rather than told stories (André Gaudreault's notion of *monstration*, 1988); early cinema involved an "aggressive mode of address" of the audience, a demand for attention (Tom Gunning's "cinema of attractions," 1990). [WG]

Further reading

Elsaesser, Thomas (ed.) (1990) *Early Cinema: Space Frame Narrative*, London: British Film Institute.
Gunning, Tom (1998) "Early American Film," in *The Oxford Guide to Film Studies*, Oxford and New York: Oxford University Press.

EDITING is the most important aspect of **postproduction**, overseen by the editor and often a team of specialists who trim and fit the shots together to produce the finished form of the film's image track. For a discussion of the practice of editing see Chapter 4 (pp. 55–60); see also **continuity editing** and **matches**. Integral to postproduction is sound mixing, supervised by the sound editor, which articulates the relationship between elements of the soundtrack and between the sound and image track. See

postproduction sound and **postsynchronous sound**. [WG]

ETHNOGRAPHIC FILM No academic discipline has been more assiduous in its use of film as a research tool than has cultural anthropology. The first film of fieldwork (*Torres Straight Expedition*, Alfred Haddon) dates from 1911. Nevertheless, far from demonstrating the scientific viability of cinematography, ethnographic filmmaking has actually illustrated its limitations as evidence; it has always been a controversial enterprise. Apart from the conservatism of the anthropological establishment, the popularity of documentaries (from the earliest *documentaires romancés* through *Nanook*, 1922, to *Mondo Carne*, 1962, and its like) was seen as debasing serious visual anthropology. Even ethnographic film made by anthropologists themselves was problematic. For one thing they often used professional filmmakers insensitive to ethnographic concerns; for another they needed the films to help raise funds with the public, which required the distortions inherent in narrativizing.

Frank Boaz, on the other hand, in 1930 filmed fragments of native American dances with the participants wearing their usual European clothes. This field-note style of "record footage" was to come more to the fore with the utilization of 16mm (e.g. Margaret Mead and Gregory Bateson's series on *Character Formation in Different Cultures*, 1936–8). "Record footage" has persisted, for example Richard Sorenson's Papuan series with titles such as *South Fore: Children IV: Waisa Village, Eastern Highlands, East New Guinea, December 16, 1963.*

Despite this, visual anthropologists generally tended toward more complete narrativized films (e.g. *The Hunters*, 1958, John Marshall; *Dead Birds*, 1963, Robert Gardner). Film, moreover, remained surprisingly ambiguous as scientific evidence. Jean Rouch's study of a Western African cult's ritual practice in *Les Maîtres fous* ("The Mad Masters," 1957) was seen, when screened publicly, as racist—to his extreme distress. Sync sound did not help. For example, Timothy Asch's *The Ax Fight* (1975) replays uncut record footage of an incident in a Yanomamö village (plus four different edits and a voice-over diagram) to describe what was going on, but this thorough procedure still leaves many possible alternative explanations open.

Film's inherent flaws as evidence coupled with a rising sensitivity to anthropology's insoluble connections to European colonialism led to Jean Rouch's attempts to penetrate surface realities more deeply, eventually creating **Cinema Vérité**. Not only that, by the 1970s the cultural limitations of the technology itself as a product of the West were becoming apparent. David McDougal, for instance, noted how inappropriate the camera was to filming "low intensity activity" because it privileged close-ups of the individual; color film, moreover, was designed to photograph Caucasian skin tones. Led by Australian First Peoples, a turn was made to allow ethnographic subjects to make their own films, initially with the aid of Western anthropologists (*Two Laws*, 1972, the Borroloola People and Caroline Strachan and Alessandro Cavadini). [BW]

See Chapter 7.

Further reading

Hockings, Paul (ed.) (1975) *Principles of Visual Anthropology*, The Hague: Mouton.

FASCISM An extreme right political ideology that emerged in Europe in the aftermath of World War I, largely in reaction to the ascendancy of Marxist ideology and the 1917 Communist Revolution in Russia. Itself a modern mass movement, fascism spurned the Marxist claim that class struggle is the motor force of history, positing instead mystical notions of national, and, in the case of German Nazism, racial, unity and purity as society's founding organizing principle. Seeking to subordinate the interests of the individual to those of the totalitarian state, fascist regimes embrace single-party rule in which all-powerful, authoritarian leaders govern by fiat, while also demanding and often winning the fealty of the masses. Characteristics of fascist rule typically include the outlawing of opposition political parties and trade unions, the eradication of civil liberties, aggressive nationalism and expansionist militarism, genocidal racial and ethnic cleansing policies, strains of populist thought that co-exist with accommodation of economic elites, and promotion of traditional gender and sexual ideologies that favor masculine domination. Examples of fascist regimes include Germany under Adolf Hitler (1933–45) and Italy under Benito Mussolini (1922–43).

In Nazi Germany, the film industry became a direct instrument of the fascist state, with its operations overseen by Joseph Goebbels and the Ministry of Propaganda. The marshalling of film industry resources for propagandistic ends is evident in such renowned works as Leni Riefenstahl's *Triumph of the Will*, a highly stylized filmic record of the 1934 Nazi Party gathering at Nuremburg, and *Olympia*, a documentary on the 1936 Berlin Olympics where Hitler showcased fascist ideals and ambitions. The German film industry also generated such notorious works of Nazi anti-Semitic propaganda as Veit Harlan's *The Jew Süss* (1940), a film that garnered wide audiences in Germany and other Nazi-occupied countries during World War II. In Italy, Mussolini also invested substantially in the Italian film industry by creating an institute for training film personnel and by building Cinecittà, one of the most expansive cinema production sites in the world. [RS]

See **Second World War**.

Further reading

Paxton, Robert (2004) *The Anatomy of Fascism*, New York: Knopf.
Ricci, Steven (2008) *Cinema and Fascism: Italian Film and Society, 1922–1943*, Berkeley, CA: University of California Press.
Schulte-Sasse, Linda (1996) *Entertaining the Third Reich: Illusions of Wholeness in Nazi Cinema*, Durham, NC: Duke University Press.

FEMINISM A corpus of thought in which the subordinate status of women in patriarchal society has been critiqued and politically contested. Various expressions of feminist thought affirm that, rather than existing as a fact of nature, women's subordinate status is a social construction and the product of unequal power relations under patriarchical systems that establish male authority and dominance in public and private life. Feminism takes the form of political activism advocating women's equality before the law, in the domestic and reproductive spheres, in the workplace, and perhaps most importantly in the culture at large. It has also become a thriving field of scholarly inquiry and theorization in a wide range of academic disciplines, including an important area of Film Studies developed by leading film scholars such as Laura Mulvey, Claire Johnston, Kaja Silverman, Mary Ann Doane, and Teresa de Lauretis. A central concern of feminist film criticism is defining the position women occupy as objects of visual pleasure in conventional filmmaking and understanding the construction of sexual difference in film narratives and in the dynamics of film spectatorship. [RS]

Further reading

Carson, E., Dittmar, L., and Welsch, J. (eds.) (1994) *Multiple Voices in Feminist Film Criticism*, Minneapolis, MN: University of Minnesota Press.
Kaplan, E. Ann (ed.) (2000) *Feminism and Film*, Oxford: Oxford University Press.

FICTION The representation of a sequence of actions that the filmmaker offers and the spectator takes as imaginary. Fictional narratives create a "contract" with the spectator, which is often signaled by what French theorist Jean-Marie Schaeffer (1999) calls *paratextual* markers. For example, when you pick up a book whose subtitle is "a novel" or

when you are watching a film in which actors are playing characters, you implicitly acknowledge that the actions represented are taking place in an imagined world and have no direct impact on real experience. Many theorists, in particular John Searle (1975) and Gérard Genette (1991), contend that fiction can be defined by the relationship it maintains between the work's author and its narrator. In fiction, whether filmic or literary, the author who constructs the narrative is not the same as the narrator who tells the story. The author does not ask the reader or spectator to believe that what the narrator is telling is true. Since the author makes no truth claim, he or she is not socially responsible for what the narrator tells and cannot be brought up on charges for representations made in a novel or film, or criticized by historians for the work's historical inaccuracies. Fictional narratives are different from what are called pragmatic discourses in which the speaker (or writer or filmmaker) communicates with a listener (reader or spectator) with the intent to persuade, influence, inform, or otherwise have an impact on actions or situations in the real world. [WG]

See also **nonfiction**.

Further reading

Chatman, Seymour (1978) *Story and Discourse: Narrative Structure in Fiction and Film*, Ithaca, NY: Cornell University Press.
Guynn, William (2006) *Writing History in Film*, London: Routledge.

FILM ACTING Through rehearsal and often individual script analysis, a film actor finds the facial expressions, gestures, movements, and vocal choices to convey a character's temperament, social situation, shifting feelings, and evolving relationships with other characters. As with other aspects of cinema, performances differ between films of different genres, time periods, and production regimes. As a result, just as there are various editing styles and conventions for sound design, films feature a range of acting styles. For instance, exaggerated facial expressions and light, flicking vocal inflections are part of the overall style and meaning of Marx Brothers' comedies, yet they would be incongruous in the Terminator films, which require actors to use strong, direct gestures and vocal expressions that are pressed out of their tightly bound bodies. In films from different eras and **aesthetic** contexts, one also finds differences in the way performance details are combined with other filmic elements. For example, in *Singin' in the Rain* (1952) and many other studio-era musicals, framing and editing become quite secondary to performances, especially during show-stopping numbers, while in **modernist** films such as *Weekend* (1967), camera movement can be dominant, as when the camera tracks along the line of cars, trucks, and carts stuck in traffic in the French countryside.

While working professionals recognize that screen actors draw on the same kind of training and preparation employed by stage actors, audiences still have many misconceptions about film acting. One is that **framing** and **editing** "do" the acting in film; another is that film actors "play" themselves in films. These ideas go back to the early twentieth century, when **theater** was the established art form and critics sustained the status quo by equating stage performances with "true" acting and screen performances with captured "natural" behavior. However, the demands of working out of sequence, surrounded by distractions, and sometimes without rehearsal or a scene partner actually require film actors to rely on training, experience, and more individual preparation than that required for stage productions. Moreover, while mistakes can be edited and editors/directors can select the takes that convey the scene's meaning and significance, editing and framing choices are consistently made so that audiences are able to see and focus on the minute details of actors' carefully crafted expressive behavior. In the absence of the connotatively rich gestures and expressions that actors contribute, there is no performance to frame or edit.

The misconception that film acting is not "true" acting can be cleared up in part by the work of the Prague School (1926–48). These theorists recognized that actors in everyday life are distinct from **characters** in story worlds *and* that actors are distinct from performance details, which are gestures and expressions that can be identified and interpreted. They proposed that both film and theater audiences respond to and base their interpretations on performance details, not the actor. In the 1970s, Michael Kirby's influential essay on acting and not-acting also identified acting, not with presence, but with discernible actions, colored by the **connotations** suggested by the spatial and temporal qualitative aspects of gestures and expressions. Recent studies on mirror neurons have confirmed the Prague theorists' insight that recognizable human actions form the basis of audiences' dramatic inferences and emotional responses.

Confusions about screen performance can also be remedied by recognizing that audience responses to all aspects of a film, including the moment by moment changes in actors' facial expressions, small physical gestures, vocal intonations, and movements in space, are affected by various factors. To some degree, interpretations of performances in an individual film are colored and even predetermined by factors outside the film itself. For example, Stephen Heath's 1981 essay, "Body, Voice," outlines ways that our reactions to film performances are influenced by extra-textual associations activated by **star** images and references to cultural types. Yet, Heath also echoes the Prague School's recognition that gestures and expressions are the core of performance, for he proposes that audience interpretations are affected by what he calls filmic "intensities," which are distinct from actors, as well as the agents and characters in the story world. These "intensities," which are evocative in themselves, are cinematic elements, observably present in films.

In sum, then, performance details in film acquire dramatic significance the same way they do on stage: through their relationship to other formal elements in the production, the dramatic facts established by previous scenes, and audiences' extra-textual associations. Filmic gestures and expressions also convey meaning the way lighting,

framing, and editing choices do: through their relationship to other cinematic choices and audience associations. Thus, what is often overlooked is that, while audiences encounter acting choices in relation to other cinematic elements, they also experience and interpret nonperformance elements through their conjunction with acting choices. Reckoning with this two-way interaction, one can see that screen acting is a full-fledged component of film, no more and no less important than framing, editing, lighting, sound design, and other cinematic elements. [CB]

Further reading

Baron, Cynthia and Carnicke, Sharon Marie (2008) *Reframing Screen Performance*, Ann Arbor, MI: University of Michigan Press.

Tomlinson, Doug (ed.) (1994) *Actors on Acting for the Screen: Roles and Collaborations*, New York: Garland.

Wojcik, Pamela Robertson (ed.) (2004) *Movie Acting: The Film Reader*, New York: Routledge.

FILM ARCHIVES, CINEMATHEQUES, AND THE PRESERVATION MOVEMENT A film archive is an institution devoted to the collection and preservation of films and film-related materials (e.g. film criticism and scholarship; scripts, promotional materials, production documents, etc.). Since films were not always recognized as a valuable part of the historical or cultural heritage, the original motive for the creation of film archives—the preservation of film prints—initially had to be pursued in the face of considerable indifference. Since the 1930s film archives have been created and supported by national governments (the Cinémathèque française, the British Film Institute, the National Film Board of Canada, the National Film Archive of India), by industrial concerns and private individuals and groups (George Eastman House, Anthology Film Archives), and by universities (Harvard Film Archive, UCLA Film and Television Archive). A cinematheque is an archive that also functions as an exhibition venue. The most famous of these is the Cinémathèque française in Paris, legendary because of its founder Henri Langlois's heroic efforts to save its collection from destruction by the Nazis during World War II and because of the role its screenings had in educating the generation of **cinephiles** who became the directors of the French New Wave. If the historical and cultural heritage of film is now secure, it is due to the work of Langlois and other pioneering film archivists, a work that continues and is coordinated by organizations such as the International Federation of Film Archivists (FIAF). [PY]

Further reading

Roud, Richard (1983) *A Passion for Films: Henri Langlois and the Cinémathèque Française*, New York: Viking Press.

FILM JOURNALS are magazines devoted to film criticism and journalism, and which often feature interviews with directors, actors, and other creative professionals involved with filmmaking. Located somewhere between trade publications such as *Variety* that target a professional audience working in the film industry and mass-audience publications

devoted to the lifestyles of movie stars and other celebrities (such as *People* or *Premiere*), film journals are aimed at the segment of the general public interested in the art and history of the cinema. From the 1970s onward, film journals have also been where much academic film scholarship is published. The critical debates in film journals have often been influential in shaping both the general public's understanding of film and the dominant tendencies of academic film studies. For example, debates over the aesthetic potentials of the silent cinema in European film journals during the 1920s, the principles of **Neorealism** in *Cinema* (Italy) during the 1940s, the **auteur** theory in the *Cahiers du cinéma* (France) during the 1950s, and the ideological effects of cinematic form in *Screen* (Britain) during the 1970s and 1980s have all had a lasting impact on the way in which films are understood. [PY]

Further reading

Hillier, Jim (ed.) (1985) *Cahiers du cinéma: The 1950s: Neo-Realism, Hollywood, New Wave*, Cambridge, MA: Harvard University Press.

Hillier, Jim (ed.) (1986) *Cahiers du cinéma 1960–1968: New Wave, New Cinema, Reevaluating Hollywood*, Cambridge, MA: Harvard University Press.

FILM LANGUAGE Is film a language? This enduring question has an interesting history. Let's look at three major responses.

1   In the 1920s Soviet avant-garde filmmaker and theoretician Sergei Eisenstein asserted that film could indeed become a language. The

American cinema in the period between 1908 and 1917 had developed a model of filmmaking based on a succession of relatively short shots linked together into sequences through the techniques of continuity editing. It was tempting then to draw an analogy between the sequence of words that constitute a sentence in spoken or written language and the sequence of shots that constitute, it could be argued, a filmic equivalent of verbal statements. In contrast to the Hollywood model that constructed an apparently coherent narrative world (see **diegesis**), Eisenstein hypothesized a film language in which the shot was conceived as a *fragment*, cut out of the real world and arranged in sequence with other fragmentary shots. According to this concept, the fragment has no meaning of its own—it is a unit of discourse—and as such participates in creating meaning through its relationship with other fragments, in the manner of verbal signs. This interaction between shots, which Eisenstein characterized as textual conflict not narrative continuity, formed the basis of filmic discourse. Conflict was expressed in terms of contrasts of lighting, movement within the frame, volume, shot scale, and so forth. In its most abstract form, Eisenstein's theory contended that images, extracted and separated from the photographed world, could become purely conceptual through *intellectual montage*, and he experimented with such intellectual effects, particularly in his film *October* (1928).

2   In the early 1950s French critic André Bazin wrote a very brief history of film language that stood in absolute opposition to the conception put forward by Eisenstein. In "The Evolution of the Language of Cinema" Bazin distinguished two fundamental types of filmmakers: "those who put their faith in the image and those who put their faith in reality" (1967). In the first category, the filmmaker's art is distinguished by the artifices he or she employs: on the one hand the "plastic" manipulation of the image, as in the **mise-en-scène** characteristic of **German Expressionism**, and, on the other, Soviet-style montage that created meanings that did not belong to the images themselves. Bazin saw in Eisenstein's work not a film language but a stilted rhetoric that interposed itself between the spectator and the reality the image provides.

For Bazin an authentic film language is based on respect for reality: the spatial integrity of the scene and the duration of events. Montage is in fact "forbidden" whenever it imposes a univocal meaning on reality. Reality is by nature ambiguous, and the image, which reproduces the world in a mechanical fashion (by means of the lens, light-sensitive film stock, etc.), dispenses with human intervention (and distortion). The filmmaker's task, then, is to allow reality to speak in its own language. In film history, Bazin valorizes what he sees as a common approach to filmmaking exemplified in the films of major figures like Robert Flaherty, Erich von Stroheim, and F. W. Murnau in the silent period, and in the sound era Jean Renoir, Orson Welles, and William Wyler. **Deep focus cinematography** and the long take are the privileged "language" of this approach because they render in the image some of the ambiguity of the real.

3   In the 1960s and early 70s, the question of film language was subjected to a radical reevaluation on the basis of two parallel fields of study developed in the late nineteenth and early twentieth centuries: **semiotics** (developed by American philosopher Charles Sanders Peirce) and **semiology** (founded by Swiss linguist Ferdinand de Saussure). For Saussure, the sign is comprised of two elements: the signifier is the "present," perceptible part of the sign (the phonemes we hear); the signified is the "absent" part of the sign (the images or concepts the phonemes evoke in the mind). Saussure argued that the relationship between the signifier and the signified is entirely *arbitrary*. There is no motivated relationship, for example, between the phonic sequence h-o-r-se and the image/concept the sounds produce in the brain.

Using linguistic theory developed by semiology, Christian Metz demonstrated, in contradistinction to Eisenstein, that film does not operate like verbal language. The shot, far from being analogous to a word, resembles a complete statement: a close-up of a revolver is the equivalent of (at least) "here is a revolver." Moreover, film and verbal language are separated by the different materiality of their signifiers: language is made up of arbitrary signs (phonemes) that refer to concepts in a symbolic manner; film is made up of images and sounds that "reproduce" reality in great phenomenological detail. Unlike the arbitrary relationship between signifier and signified in Saussure's theory of the linguistic sign, the patterns of light, shadow, and color recorded on film and projected on the screen (the filmic signifier) have an existential relationship with the objects and actions in reality we recognize in the images on the screen (the film's signified). Linguists call this kind of relationship between signifier and signified *motivated*.

And yet, Metz argues, film is a kind of speech (a *langage* in Saussure's terminology) based in a system of codes that take the place of the grammar of language. Metz undertook to show the existence of cinematic codes in developing his Grand Syntagmatique in which he constructs a typology of segments (what he calls syntagmas) that can be discerned in the classical film (see **sequences**).

Metz also observed that film language lacks one of the essential features of verbal language: the dialogic exchange in which the speaker who says "I" and refers to the listener as "you" can trade places with the listener who in turn becomes the speaker who says "I." The film communicates with the audience but doesn't allow the audience to respond. Moreover, film language is highly *impersonal*: images seem to come into being of their own accord, while the signs of the narrator's presence—what Metz calls *marks of enunciation*—are largely covert. They are, in general, perceptible "against a background of norms and codes": the striking use of angles, very long takes, flattened perspectives, and asynchronous relationships between sound and image, for example, may stand out against the norms of practice in a given period and make us aware of a narrating voice. [WG]

Further reading

Bazin, André (1967) *What Is Cinema?*, vol. 1, trans. Hugh Gray, Berkeley, CA: University of California Press.

Eisenstein, Sergei (1991) "Sergei Eisenstein: Selected Works," in Richard Taylor and Michael Glenny (eds.) *Towards a Theory of Montage*, vol. 2, trans. Richard Taylor, London: British Film Institute.

Metz, Christian (1990) *Film Language: A Semiotics of the Cinema*, Chicago: University of Chicago Press.

Silverman, Kaja (1983) *The Subject of Semiotics*, New York: Oxford University Press.

FILM NOIR Is noir a genre, a movement, a style? This is one of the most ticklish problems that film criticism has faced. The term emerged in France in the postwar period as critics saw the "dark" American films that had been refused circulation during the Occupation, including such early noir as *The Maltese Falcon* (1941), *Double Indemnity* (1944), and *Mildred Pierce* (1945). The term "film noir" appeared in French journals in 1946 and derives from the *série noire*, a series of crime novels published by Gallimard. Noir referred to an international phenomenon but referenced in particular the writing of "hard-boiled" crime novelists such as Raymond Chandler, Dashiell Hammett, and James M. Cain. In the first book on the topic, Raymond Borde and Etienne Chaumeton (1955/2002) saw in noir a synthesis of genres, such as gangster, detective, horror, and social problem films, a mixture of social realism and nightmare that "produces a psychological and moral disorientation, an inversion of capitalist and puritan values, as if it were pushing the American system toward revolutionary destruction" (Naremore, 1998, p. 22).

The critics associated with the French **New Wave** gave **auteur** status to many directors of noir films, partially because the films could be distinguished by their visual and narrative styles rather than thematic content. Critics in the United States—Raymond Durgnat, Paul Schrader, and others—provided further studies of noir motifs. Film noirs take place in the seedier districts of urban America (Los Angeles in particular) that evoke feelings of paranoia and claustrophobia. These desperate spaces are inhabited by morally ambiguous figures: no-account drifters, gangsters, corrupt politicians, and private eyes, whose verbal exchanges are pithy and cynical. Noir plots of entrapment often involve femmes fatales, whose power and dangerous sexuality challenge the male order (E. Ann Kaplan, 1983). The noir narrational style has been associated with a prolonged **flashback** structure and the narrative voice-over by a character, both epitomized in Billy Wilder's *Double Indemnity*. Noir's **mise-en-scène** (J. A. Place and L. S. Peterson, 1974) exploits low-key **lighting**, the menacing shadows of night-for-night shooting, unbalanced and disturbing compositions, extreme or canted angles, and tight framing.

The noir period has traditionally been defined as extending from *The Maltese Falcon* (1941) to *Touch of Evil* (1958) and reflects, according to

Colin McArthur (1972), the cultural malaise and foreboding of the aftermath of the **Great Depression** and the **Second World War**. Critics have seen, for example, the impact of the nuclear menace of the **Cold War** in Robert Aldrich's *Kiss Me Deadly* (1955). Many historians contend that émigré directors, writers, actors, cinematographers, composers, and technicians fleeing Hitler—this large expatriot community was dubbed "Weimar on the Pacific"—brought to Hollywood a dark vision of the world and the expressionist style of German films of the silent and early sound eras. This style was visible notably in elements of mise-en-scène such as low-key lighting and expressive sets and settings, often framed from out-of-norm angles, that suggested the internal lives and predicaments of characters. Noir filmmakers, however, preferred on-location shooting to the flagrantly artificial studio sets of the Expressionist era. (For a sample of such films see Fritz Lang's *Scarlet Street*, 1945, and *The Big Heat*, 1953; Robert Siodmak's *The Killers*, 1946; Otto Preminger's *Laura*, 1944; and Billy Wilder's *Sunset Boulevard*, 1950.)

However, the defining features of noir are so uncertain that it is difficult to identify a stable corpus of films. Do we include, for example, Raoul Walsh's Western *Pursued* (1947), which is lit in the noir style and has some of noir's fatalism and Freudianism? Moreover, it is possible to see noir as a genre extending well beyond the 1950s (and beyond the American cinema). French New Wave filmmakers paid homage in their films to the conventions of noir (e.g. François Truffaut's *Shoot the Piano Player*, 1960). Akira Kurosawa's *The Bad Sleep Well* (1960) and *High and Low* (1963) reveal the Japanese director's love of noir narratives and settings. Polish director Roman Polanski made the noirish political film *Chinatown* in 1974. Noir (now in color!) seems to reappear in Hollywood in the 1980s in such films as Lawrence Kasdan's *Body Heat* (1981) or Michael Mann's *Manhunter* (1986). "Neo-noir" makes a strong showing in the 1990s with films like Stephen Frears's *The Grifters* (1990), Abel Ferrara's *Bad Lieutenant* (1992), and remakes like Martin Scorsese's *Cape Fear* (1991). [WG]

Further reading

Kaplan, E. Ann (ed.) (1983) *Women in Film Noir*, New York: Methuen.
McArthur, Colin (1972) *Underworld USA*, London: BFI/Secker and Warburg.
Naremore, James (1998) *More than Night: Film Noir in Its Context*, Berkeley, CA: University of California Press.

FIRST WORLD WAR was critical to the fate of European cinemas. Until 1912, French films (from production companies Pathé frères and Gaumont) and Italian films (after 1905) were the most widely distributed in the world. The American film industry in this period, by contrast, concentrated on domestic distribution although it had begun to compete with European products by setting up centers abroad (e.g. in London) for its film distribution. The outbreak of the war and the social and economic conditions it imposed were devastating for the formerly dominant French and Italian industries. Film production was curtailed; circulation of films across borders was stemmed; and the conscription of personnel for the armed service and the transfer of raw film stock to munitions further weakened the industry. While some film producers in Sweden and Russia were able to continue their level of production, France and Italy were compelled to significantly reduce their output.

By 1916, Hollywood, by then a fully developed film industry with designs on the international markets, was poised to fill the breach and very quickly became the major purveyor of films to the world. Because of expanded markets, American films were highly profitable, enriching the studios' production budgets and therefore the production values of their films. American dominance, which was in large part a result of the First World War, persisted and has been one of the major forces shaping film history to the present moment.

The German film industry had a quite different fate. Prior to the war, German production was weak compared to the French, Italian, and American industries. However, after the war broke out, Germany banned foreign film imports (except from Sweden and Denmark) and, by military order, merged German production, distribution, and exhibition companies. Thus the UFA (Universum Film Aktiengesellschaft) was formed in 1917 and the UFA studio, the largest in Europe, was built, preparing for the rich period of production in the 1920s. [ML and WG]

FLASHBACK/FLASH-FORWARD (see **narrative order**)

FORMALISM AND NEOFORMALISM Formalism is an approach to film **aesthetics** that assumes that the effects of

cinematic art are primarily derived from the ways in which film images are visually composed and edited, rather than from the spectator's engagement with their representational content (i.e. the characters, stories, and worlds they present to us). In the standard narratives of classical (i.e. aesthetics-based) film theory, formalism is typically opposed to realist film theories based in the unique potentials of the photographic image. In a historical sense, formalist film theory originated and had its most fertile development during the silent period, when theorists such as Hugo Munsterberg, Rudolph Arnheim, and Béla Balázs argued that the cinema's ability to combine rhythmic effects and visual compositions through editing made it a "pure," that is, non-representational, art, analogous to instrumental music. Though his theory had different sources and aims, the ideas of the Russian theorist-filmmaker Sergei Eisenstein also focused on the formal qualities and effects of images and editing.

Neoformalist film theory, associated most closely with the work and influence of the film scholars David Bordwell and Kristin Thompson, originated in the work of Russian literary theorists such as Victor Shklovsky, Boris Eichenbaum, and Roman Jackobson during the 1920s and 1930s. Neoformalist analysis emphasizes the role and importance of specific "devices," formal mechanisms governing the immediate cognitive interaction—the film-created play of memory, expectations, novelty, and so on—between the spectator and the film, and is often implicitly or explicitly opposed to approaches which emphasize the role of extra-cinematic contexts (i.e. culture and history) in determining the experience of a film through interpretation. [PY]

See Chapter 3.

Further reading

Balázs, Béla (1972) *Theory of the Film: Character and Growth of a New Art*, New York: Arno Press.

Bordwell, David (2008) *Poetics of Cinema*, New York: Routledge.

Thompson, Kristin (1988) *Breaking the Glass Armor: Neoformalist Film Analysis*, Princeton, NJ: Princeton University Press.

FRAMING Choosing the camera set-up—its distance from the subject to be filmed and the angle it adopts—is the act of framing the image. The choice is significant on several levels. For a discussion of the framing and the way it constructs filmic space, see Chapter 4 (pp. 52–53). [WG]

FRENCH IMPRESSIONISM: *PHOTOGÉNIE* Variously described as a tendency or a movement in the French cinema of the silent era, Impressionism grouped together most of the filmmakers of the "first avant-garde" of the 1920s. Louis Delluc, perhaps cinema's first theoretician, founded in 1920 the first *ciné-club* (an association of enthusiasts of alternative films) that would champion the projection of films outside commercial distribution and created the influential journal *Cinéa*.

A basic assumption shared by Impressionist filmmakers was that the filmic image should not simply produce a copy of the real world but should transfigure it through techniques that belong specifically to the film medium. Theoretician and film-maker Jean Epstein developed this idea through his concept of *photogénie*. The term photogenic acquires a meaning much stronger than the ordinary sense of a person or object whose image is enhanced by photography. Rather, *photogénie* suggests a transmutation that is unexpected, poetic, uncanny. Thus, the motion picture camera produces images of a transmuted world in which the spectator's sensory and psychological experience is intensified.

The fundamental intent of Impressionist films was to suggest the internal state and emotions of characters: dreams, fantasies, memories, and subjective points of view. It shared this objective with **German Expressionist** film. However, instead of relying on elements of mise-en-scène—expressionist sets, acting, lighting all shot in studio—Impressionism exploited the resources of the camera and editing that possess, its advocates argued, the transformative power of the cinematic art. These included optical devices like prolonged superimpositions, out-of-focus images, accelerated and slow-motion cinematography, and masking and split screens that change the shape of the frame. Impressionist films were also characterized by unusual techniques of shooting: framing that isolates a character or object from its context, "non-normative" angles, shooting with filters or through gauze, shooting into distorting mirrors—techniques that all suggest the subjective point of view of a character. Editing was also exploited for emotional effect, beginning with the work of Abel Gance, whose *La Roue* (1923), with its fast-paced rhythmic montage, had considerable impact on the Impressionist movement. Impressionist **mise-en-scène** was noteworthy for its advocacy of a naturalistic acting style and its preference for shooting on location. It made extensive use of lighting for striking effects. For examples of Impressionist films, see Marcel L'Herbier's *L'Inhumaine* ("The Inhuman Woman," 1924), Jean Epstein's *L'Auberge Rouge* ("The Red Inn," 1923) and *La Chute de la maison Usher* ("The Fall of the House of Usher," 1928), Germaine Dulac's *La Souriante Madame Beudet* ("The Smiling Madame Beudet," 1923), and Abel Gance's *Napoléon* (1927). The experimental film in the 1920s had little distribution outside the ciné-club movement, and many Impressionist filmmakers made a living directing quite conventional films for the commercial film industry. [WG]

Further reading

Abel, Richard (1984) *French Cinema: The First Wave, 1915–1929*, Princeton, NJ: Princeton University Press.

FUTURISM An **avant-garde** movement that spurred innovation in a number of artistic arenas including literature, painting, photography, sculpture, cinema, and architecture. Inspired by F. T. Marinetti, whose declaration titled "Founding and Manifesto of Futurism" appeared in 1909 in the French newspaper *Le Figaro*, Futurism celebrated the dynamism of the machine age and reveled in the unconventionality and newness of industrial urban life. Declaring their antipathy for all things

traditional, Futurists venerated speed and the violence of movement it entailed, vowing, as Marinetti's Manifesto declared, "to sing the love of danger, the habit of energy and fearlessness." The Futurists showed a fascination for new technologies such as the car and the airplane, laboring in their art to bring a still tradition-bound Italy, kicking and screaming if necessary, into the modern age. Their worship of modernity led Futurists to laud the destructive force of war and what they saw as its "hygienic" or cleansing powers; this embrace of war nestled ideologically with the affinities Futurists would later develop for Mussolini's fascist vision of Italy's national regeneration. [RS]

Further reading

Perloff, Marjorie (2003) *The Futurist Moment: Avant-Garde, Avant Guerre and the Language of Rupture*, Chicago: University of Chicago Press.

GAG In a broad sense, a gag is any device used to create comic effects on film. Sight gags, which depend only on the visual effect of an on-screen event (i.e. not verbal language), are featured in many of the earliest films in cinema history (such as those of the Lumière brothers and Georges Méliès). Sight gags were central to the slapstick comedy of Mack Sennett and were given what many consider their most refined treatment in the work of the silent comedian-filmmakers Charles Chaplin and Buster Keaton. As theorized by the Czech playwright and critic Vaclav Havel, a gag is a device whose comic effect derives from the coincidence of two contradictory ways of understanding an event on-screen. When for example in *The Gold Rush* (1925) Charlie Chaplin's Tramp character eats a boot as if it were a Thanksgiving turkey, the humor derives from the fact that the spectator's perception of this event is simultaneously poised between two interpretations of a single object (i.e. boot as boot, boot as turkey). Drawing on the ideas of Russian formalism, Havel argues that such humorous coincidences function to defamiliarize and freshen our perceptual reflexes. In addition to sight gags, there are many similar devices for creating comic effects in film: verbal gags can be created by using puns and other techniques, and gags can also be created by events that illuminate the contradictions in characters. In one form or another, gags are the basic unit of all film comedy. [PY]

Further reading

Carroll, Noël (1996) "Notes on the Sight Gag," in *Theorizing the Moving Image*, New York: Cambridge University Press.
Havel, Vaclav (1984) "The Anatomy of the Gag," in *Modern Drama XXIII.1*, Toronto, ON: University of Toronto Press.

GENRE Cinematic genre may be defined as "a collection of shared rules that allows the filmmaker to use established communicative formulas and the viewer to organize his own systems of expectations" (Francesco Casetti, 1999, p. 271). Westerns, for example, were set on the American Western frontier during the second half of the nineteenth century. Stories followed a clear pattern of conflict and resolution revolving around stock characters such as the rancher, the gun slinger, the good wife, the drunken Indian, and the prostitute with a heart of gold, treating common themes such as the conflict between nature and civilization, with good (civilization) inevitably triumphing over evil (nature). A Western that fails to meet its audience's expectations in terms of plot, setting, **iconography**, character, and world-view risks disappointment and hostility; however, as audience's experiences and tastes have evolved over time so has the genre.

While the notion of genre can be conceptualized according to a number of different models, the model that is currently dominant is the semantic-syntactic model inspired by the work of Rick Altman (1989), which defines genre in terms of the relationship between its semantic elements (attitudes, characters, settings, enunciative strategies, etc.) and its syntactic traits (organizing principles and narrative strategies, such as alternation, confrontation, parallelism, etc.). For example, though *Oklahoma* (1955) mobilizes the characters, setting, and iconography of the Western, it is a musical in terms of the story itself and how it is told, which includes forms of singing and dancing not acceptable in a Western.

The nature of genres is not absolute and fixed, but extremely fluid and susceptible to change. The Western in its long history has undergone a number of transformations. Today spectators accept and even demand a gun slinger who is sympathetic as in the case of Russell Crowe's interpretation of Ben Wade in the recent remake of *3:10 to*

Yuma (2007), which comments ironically on the masculine ideals that animated the 1957 version of the film, while still remaining a clear example of the Western genre. Among the most popular genres are the Western, the gangster film, the romantic comedy, the action film, the musical, the biopic, the disaster film, the martial arts film, and the road movie, many of which originate in **Classical Hollywood Cinema**. [HR]

See Chapter 2.

Further reading

Grant, Barry Keith (2007) *Film Genre: From Iconography to Ideology*, London: Wallflower.
Moine, Raphaëlle (2008) *Cinema Genre*, Malden, MA: Blackwell.
Neale, Stephen (2000) *Genre and Hollywood*, London: Routledge.

GERMAN EXPRESSIONISM The film movement German Expressionism was part of a much broader tendency within German art and culture that began before World War I. *The Cabinet of Dr. Caligari* (Robert Wiene, 1919) is generally considered the film that launched the movement, which reached its peak during the middle of the 1920s and began to decline by the end of the decade. In terms of its visual **style**, German Expressionism is defined by several characteristic features, all designed to express the extreme emotional and mental states of characters (e.g. claustrophobia, paranoia): the use of sets constructed and painted in abstract, geometrical forms, low-key **lighting**, and superimpositions and other special effects. In the hands of its two most celebrated directors, F. W. Murnau

and Fritz Lang, the style also incorporated elaborate **camera movements** and **long takes**. In terms of its representational content, Expressionism often focused on narratives of insanity, the supernatural, and mythology; considering both the form and content of Expressionism in relation to contemporary German society, the philosopher and cultural critic Siegfried Kracauer saw it as symptomatic of the rise of Nazism. Though German Expressionism came to an end as a distinct movement by the early 1930s, its stylistic influence on subsequent filmmaking has been profound; apart from the direct impact on American film through the migration of German filmmakers to Hollywood, and its pronounced influence on the horror genre, its unique array of techniques are now simply considered part of the expressive resources of cinema in general. For examples of Expressionist films, see Paul Wegener and Carl Boese's *Der Golem* ("The Golem," 1920); Fritz Lang's *Dr. Mabuse, der Spieler* ("Dr. Mabuse, the Gambler," 1922), *Siegfried* (1924), and *Metropolis* (1927); and F. W. Murnau's *Nosferatu* (1922) and *Faust* (1926). [PY]

Further reading

Eisner, Lotte (2008) *The Haunted Screen: Expressionism in the German Cinema and the Influence of Max Reinhardt*, Berkeley, CA: University of California Press.
Kracauer, Siegfried (1947) *From Caligari to Hitler: A Psychological Study of the German Film*, London: D. Dobson.

GLOBALIZATION A term that describes the flow of capital, commodities, labor, and technology across national borders, creating greater interconnectedness among human societies and cultures. In recent decades, these processes have accelerated and extended their geographic reach, largely as a result of government-negotiated free-trade agreements that have reduced or eliminated barriers designed to protect domestic production and trade against foreign competition. Proponents argue that all parties benefit from globalization while critics charge that it has advanced the interests of large multinational corporations benefiting from the spread of free-market principles that have ill served local economies, workers, and the environment. Globalization has entailed the worldwide dissemination of American culture, a development that is particularly evident in the success Hollywood cinema has had in penetrating foreign markets and dominating international film distribution networks. The integration of the world economy has, however, also brought other national cinemas to global prominence, including Chinese, Hong Kong, Indian, and other non-Western film industries emerging in the developing world that have been aided by transnational financing and production practices. [RS]

Further reading

Ezra, Elizabeth and Rowden, Terry (eds.) (2006) *Transnational Cinema: The Film Reader*, New York: Routledge.
Lechner, Frank J. and Boli, John (eds.) (2008) *The Globalization Reader*, Malden, MA: Blackwell.
Naficy, H. (2001) *An Accented Cinema: Exilic and Diasporic Filmmaking*, Princeton, NJ: Princeton University Press.

GREAT DEPRESSION The Great Depression was a worldwide economic downturn, starting with the stock market crash on October 29, 1929, known as Black Tuesday, and lasting for a decade. It had a major effect on the film industry, causing lay-offs, salary cuts in the studios, and the closing of theaters. Movie attendance and industry profits did not recover to their 1929 high until World War II; however, in the years following 1933, the industry was no longer in crisis. Despite having less income, lured by such marketing strategies as double features and giveaway programs of free cutlery and dishes, Americans continued to attend films, motivated by a desire to escape temporarily from the dreariness of reality into a fantasy world of social elegance and general opulence, a wish to have values restored and moral codes re-validated, and a yearning to believe that life could be sound once again.

Pre-code films such as the Warner Brothers gangster films, including *Little Caesar* (1930) and *Public Enemy* (1931), offered a new mythical hero, whose disappointment in the American dream echoed that of Depression audiences. The systematic adoption of sound encouraged the development of demotic voices that identified the gangster as a member of a recently immigrated ethnic group. Under pressure from the **Hays Office**, other popular genres, such as screwball comedies like *It Happened One Night* (1934) or musicals such as *Curly Top* (1935) featuring the ever cheerful child-star Shirley Temple, emphasized distraction and entertainment. [HR]

Further reading

Bergman, Andrew (1971) *We're in the Money: Depression America and Its Films*, New York: Harper and Row.

HAYS OFFICE (MPPDA) The Hays Office (1922–45) was the regulatory body established by the major film companies (the Motion Pictures Producers and Distributors Association or MPPDA) with a view to preempting federal intervention into the industry. It is primarily known (though this was not its only function) for administering a set of **censorship** guidelines governing the production of motion pictures in the United States. The office was headed by Will H. Hays (1879–1954), who compiled a list of subjects deemed inappropriate and a moral system, based on Roman Catholic theology, that movies should promote (known as the Hays Code).

Hired by MPPDA in 1922 as a result of the sustained public criticism of the movie industry's perceived contribution to moral and social decay as well as to the threat of censorship at the state level, Hays had little success in enforcing the Code that he established until American Catholics began a crusade against Hollywood in 1933. The Catholic Legion of Decency produced a list of banned films, which were then boycotted and picketed by its members. In response, an even more stringent Code was formulated and administered under the direction of Joseph Breen.

In order to respond to the more stringent requirements, with each film requiring a Production Code Administration (PCA) certificate before it could be released, **genres** evolved. The gangster formula with films like *G-Men* (1935) shifted from the rise and fall of a gangster-protagonist to a focus on law-enforcement. Fallen-women films like Jean Harlow's *Red Headed Woman* (1932) were replaced with tamer, and wackier, screwball comedies, such as *The Awful Truth* (1937). From 1934, the PCA was instrumental in enforcing this Production Code, which, under pressure from changing public standards and the influx of foreign films, was replaced by the MPAA rating system in 1968. [HR]

Further reading

Bernstein, Matthew (1999) *Controlling Hollywood: Censorship and Regulation in the Studio Era*, New Brunswick, NJ: Rutgers University Press.

Moley, Raymond (1945) *The Hays Office*, Indianapolis, IN: Bobbs-Merrill.

HISTORY AND MEMORY are terms that have been critical in film studies, cultural studies, and the disciplinary study of history in recent years. A number of historians, most notably Hayden White and Robert Rosenstone, have argued that film deserves to be considered as a medium capable of producing authentic history on film. This position does not merely refer to the genre of the historical film but extends to mainstream innovative dramas, biographical film, and documentaries. The impetus to rethinking the role of history on film (and in literature) has emerged from several quarters: **feminism**, studies of the Holocaust, reassessments of popular culture, numerous writings on **postcolonialism**, among others. What these approaches share is a mistrust of dominant forms of history making from above that do not take into account the narratives of people involved in historical events whose voices have not been heard. In particular the emphasis on "popular memory" has been associated with **"Third World"** writings of the 1960s and 1970s. Popular memory designates a mode of narration that is sensitive to the silences of formerly colonized peoples who have been spoken for by historians and anthropologists but who have not had the opportunity to narrate their relations to the past. Popular memory seeks to recreate the past by turning to the resources of oral narrative, folklore, and personal and social recollections in the interest of "decolonizing the mind." Since the **Second World War**, international cinema has produced a large number of texts that focus on the role of memory exemplified by the films of Alain Resnais, especially *Night and Fog* (1955) and *Hiroshima, mon amour* (1959), Claude Lanzmann's *Shoah* (1985), Ousmane Sembène's *Emitai* (1971), *Ceddo* (1977), and *Le Camp de Thiaroye* (1988), or more recently in the work of Rithy Panh on the Cambodian genocide in *S-21* (2003). [ML]

See Chapters 10 and 11.

HORIZONTAL/VERTICAL INTEGRATION Horizontal integration occurs when one firm in the same industry and in the same stage of production is taken over or merged with another firm—as in the case in which the owner of MGM, Kirk Kerkorian, acquired United Artists in 1981, creating MGM/UA Entertainment Co. Vertical integration occurs when companies involved in the production of different products are united through a hierarchy with a common owner. For example, in 1924 Marcus Lowe created MGM by purchasing Metro Pictures, Goldwyn Pictures, and Louis B. Mayer Pictures, with the purpose of providing films for his Lowe's Theaters chain. By the 1930s, the American cinema industry had become dominated by eight studios, which were vertically integrated in terms of the production, distribution, and exhibition of films. The extent of this integration was ended by the *Paramount* decree of 1948, which required distributors to divest their theater assets. [HR]

See Chapter 2 and **studio system**.

HUAC The House Un-American Activities Committee was a committee first formed in the United States House of Representatives in 1934 with the charge of investigating the propagandistic activities of agents of German Nazism working in the United States. In 1938, the committee began investigating Communist influences in the American theater, a prelude to its 1947 probe focusing on the Hollywood film industry and its alleged Communist sympathies. Ten members of the Hollywood community who were called to testify before the HUAC refused to bow to its demands for information on the grounds that the questioning to which they were subjected infringed upon their First Amendment right to free speech. The so-called "Hollywood Ten" found themselves facing harsh penalties, including prison sentences and blacklisting that ended many of their careers, a fate shared by other Hollywood talent during the 1950s and early 1960s when **Cold War** tensions ran highest. Hundreds of individuals, including directors, screenwriters, actors, and composers, were placed on the Hollywood blacklist, which targeted such well-known figures as Dalton Trumbo, Lillian Hellman, Charlie Chaplin, Hanns Eisler, Paul Robeson, Lee Grant, Zero Mostel, and Dashiell Hammett, who authored the book *The Maltese Falcon*. [RS]

Further reading

Ceplair, Larry and Englund, Steven (2003) *The Inquisition in Hollywood: Politics in the Film Community, 1930–1960*, Champaign, IL: University of Illinois Press.
Gladchuk, John (2007) *Hollywood and Anticommunism: HUAC and the Evolution of the Red Menace, 1935–1950*, New York: Routledge.

ICONOGRAPHY Iconography refers to the study of motifs in the visual arts, for example symbolic motifs in the history of Christian art or classical motifs in European art. Iconographical motifs are generally viewed as recurrent and conventional but open to variation. In film **genres**, iconography applies to many elements of **mise-en-scène**: the way characters dress (the flashy gangster), the settings in which they act (the closed space of the home in the family melodrama), the "tools of the trade" (the horse, the gun in the holster in the Western), the lighting (the night-for-night shooting in the classic **film noir**). Iconographic motifs usually have a strong symbolic character. They may remain relatively consistent over time (as in the Western) or may evolve substantially (as in the gangster film). **Auteur** criticism, on the other hand, focuses on the individual filmmaker and approaches iconography from a quite different perspective: the filmmaker's appropriation of genre

imagery to express a personal vision; or the filmmaker's idiosyncratic use of visual motifs in films outside or against genre (e.g. iconography in the films of David Lynch or Theo Angelopoulos). [WG]

Further reading

Grant, Barry Keith (2007) *Film Genre: From Iconography to Ideology*, London: Wallflower.

IDENTIFICATION is a term that film theorists adopted from Freudian psychoanalysis and which describes the relationship between the spectator and characters, particularly heroic characters, in film or theater. The spectator's special pleasure consists in "inhabiting" a role, putting himself or herself in the place of the character so as to experience situations and emotions not normally available in daily life. Identification with a character implies a playful sort of illusionism: in the interest of a vicarious pleasure, spectators pretend to believe in the events and characters that are in reality only spectacle; at the same time, they pretend to deny themselves (that is, the fact that they are simply spectators and that their real existence has nothing to do with the fictional world evoked in the play or film).

While embracing these notions, film theorists see identification in film operating on two other levels. First, spectators identify with the fictional world of the film by accepting to construct that world in their minds. They do so in response to the complex and fragmentary representations in image and sound the film provides. However, before identifying with the fictional world, spectators identify with what theorists have called the *cinemato-graphic apparatus*: the darkened auditorium, the projector, the screen with its play of light and shadow. The audience sits with the projector behind their backs, their gaze assimilated to the cone of light projected onto the screen. This identification refers back to others, notably: the camera whose look the projector reconstitutes and the look of the "filmmaker" (French theorist Etienne Souriau's idea of the Great Image Maker) who stages the image (and sound).

Theories of identification have been important to **psychoanalytic** approaches to film, particularly in the 1970s, when the work of French psychoanalytic theorist Jacques Lacan was influential. **Semiologist** Christian Metz, for example, has compared the spectator's "regime of consciousness" in the movie theater to that of dream and fantasy. Others have developed the comparison between the spectator's relation to the screen and the *mirror phase* in child development according to which infants of 6 to 18 months perceive themselves in the mirror and anticipate, on the basis of reflected images, the unity of their bodies (see **imaginary**). Moreover, psychoanalytic theories of identification have been the basis for research on women and film (see **feminism**). [WG]

Further reading

Laplanche, J. and Pontalis, J.-B. (1973) *The Language of Psycho-Analysis*, trans. Donald Nicholson-Smith, New York: W. W. Norton & Company.

Metz, Christian (1981) *The Imaginary Signifier: Psychoanalysis and the Cinema*, Bloomington, IN: Indiana University Press.

IDEOLOGY In **Marxist** thought, ideology refers to the political, cultural, and symbolic processes that make class domination appear to be a natural phenomenon rather than the product of complex belief systems that justify the privilege and power of certain socio-economic groups. These beliefs are inculcated, often unconsciously, through the operations of various social institutions and cultural forms that allow elites to wield authority and advance their interests without directly coercing those who are subjected to their rule. In his influential work *Ideology and Ideological State Apparatuses*, French philosopher Louis Althusser argued that a host of institutions (churches, schools, the family, political parties, the media, and the arts) are involved in the work of legitimating social inequality, constituting an ideological apparatus that makes the hierarchical status quo seem to be an immutable reality. Since the early 1970s, film scholars, most notably those contributing to the British journal *Screen*, have engaged in the analysis and critique of class and other forms of ideology that are purveyed in films and film culture. [RS]

Further reading

Althusser, Louis (2001) "Ideology and Ideological State Apparatuses," in *Lenin and Philosophy and Other Essays*, New York: Monthly Review Press.
Comolli, Jean-Luc and Narboni, Paul (1971) "Cinema/Ideology/Criticism," in Leo

Braudy and Marshall Cohen (eds.) (2004) *Film Theory and Criticism*, Oxford: Oxford University Press.

Rosen, Philip (ed.) (1986) *Narrative, Apparatus, Ideology: A Film Theory Reader*, New York: Columbia University Press.

IMAGINARY In the theory elaborated by French psychoanalyst Jacques Lacan, the imaginary refers to the earliest phase in the formation of human identity, a pre-linguistic stage in which the child perceives its being to be inseparable from that of the mother. This illusory sense of plenitude experienced in the imaginary register gradually gives way to relations of difference as the child passes through the "mirror phase," a moment in which it begins to sense its bodily integrity and distinction from the mother through the intermediary of an exterior image. In acquiring language, the child finally accedes to the realm of symbolism and culture, taking his or her place within the social order. In his influential work *The Imaginary Signifier*, film theorist Christian Metz argues that viewing cinematic images unconsciously recalls the delights of the imaginary register and the mirror stage, thereby accounting for the fascination with the image and the satisfaction spectators experience while watching films projected on the silver screen. [RS]

Further reading

Lacan, Jacques (2006) "The Mirror Stage as Formative of the I Function as Revealed in Psychoanalytic Experience," in *Ecrits: The First Complete Edition in English*, New York: Norton.

Lemaire, Anika (1979) *Jacques Lacan*, New York: Routledge & Kegan Paul.

Metz, Christian (1981) *The Imaginary Signifier: Psychoanalysis and the Cinema*, Bloomington, IN: Indiana University Press.

INDIES (AMERICAN INDEPENDENT FILM) A movement of alternative filmmaking that arose in the late 1960s and became particularly important after the waning of the Hollywood Renaissance (see **New Waves/New Cinemas**), the industry's movement away from small and medium budget films, and the consecration of the blockbuster. The Indie aesthetic is a nebulous version of **auteurism** with an emphasis on the filmmaker's need for self-expression and the movement's commitment to alternative "visions" that challenge the rigid conventions and subject matter of big-budget productions. Many independent filmmakers are graduates of film schools where they developed professional expertise, particularly in the tools of the digital age, and acquired a sense of film history.

The emergence of the Indies is associated with the Sundance Film Festival, a showcase for independently produced documentary and fiction films launched in 1985. Sundance became known particularly for its promotion of films by women and ethnic minorities. In 1989 Sundance "discovered" Steven Soderbergh's *sex, lies, and videotape*, which became a big commercial success. By 1990 critics began to describe Sundance as a "feeding frenzy" where agents and executives come to "discover" their own quirky but marketable films. Indies have also had enormous success at the major European film festivals, notably Cannes, and have attracted funding from European producers, for example Canal+. New Line Cinema Corporation and Miramax Films (purchased by Disney in 1993) are the best-known distributors of independent films in the United States. The success of Indies has been supported by a committed fan base (composed particularly of students and educated baby boomers) and lucrative returns from niche video markets. Luminaries of the Indie movement include John Sayles, David Lynch, Susan Seidelman, the Coen brothers, Spike Lee, Jim Jarmusch, and Quentin Tarantino. [WG]

Further reading

Hillier, Jim (ed.) (2001) *American Independent Cinema: A Sight and Sound Reader*, London: British Film Institute.

INTERACTIVE MEDIA refers to applications where a constant, active, and physical interplay between the user and the application forms the basis of the experience. The interaction takes place across a user interface that can consist of various elements, a screen, keyboard, mouse, and so on, but also of software elements accessed via a graphical user interface (GUI). Typical examples of interactive media are computer and video games, where the rapidity of the interaction often plays a crucial role. The Internet is also basically interactive in that the user makes constant decisions and actively negotiates the experience. Interactivity can exist on various levels that have gradually appeared within the media. A simple level is interruption, as manifested in the momentary stopping of the cranking of the Mutoscope (see

peepshows), the switching on and off of the television set, or rewinding a videotape. On another level we may speak about selection between different existing options, as in many multimedia applications. According to Gene Youngblood, the highest level of interactivity would be "creative conversation," where the interaction between the user and the application becomes nearly symbiotic, and both affect each other in the course of the interaction process. Such a possibility is still largely utopian, although applications of artificial intelligence point in this direction. Interactive media could be considered a development of what Erkki Huhtamo has called the tradition of "touch practice" (see Chapter 1). [EH]

See Chapter 1.

INTERTEXTUALITY designates the references one text (a film, a novel, a painting, etc.) makes to other texts that have preceded it. To take an obvious example, a filmed version of *Romeo and Juliet* refers to the play by Shakespeare. Because they are audiovisual texts, films may refer to other arts such as drawing, painting, and photography (e.g. *The Birth of a Nation*, 1915, offers "facsimiles" of photographs of famous Civil War scenes); they may include excerpts from classical music, jazz, or hip hop, as part of the musical score or as music whose source comes from within the story. They may refer to works of theater or literature (plays, novels, short stories), as in the film's adaptation of a novel. Films may also borrow from other films, television, and now the Internet. A film in a particular **genre** refers to characteristics of all the films that belong to the genre (an immense group of texts).

The references to other texts in a film take a number of forms. They may be quotations from another work, for example Brian De Palma's restaging of part of Eisenstein's Odessa Steps Sequence in *The Untouchables* (1987). They may constitute a parody: an imitation of the style and content of other texts for comic effect, for example in Mel Brooks' Western, *Blazing Saddles* (1973). The *remake* is also intertextual and may follow more or less closely the work on which it is based, for example Gus Van Sant's *Psycho* (1998), which attempts to reconstitute Hitchcock's film nearly shot by shot. Intertextuality may take the form of a *collage*, in which filmmakers, particularly experimental filmmakers, "glue" together audio-visual material from various sources: staged shots, found footage, static images of all sorts, sounds excerpted from previous works, and so forth.

It is useful to ask the question about the intentions of intertextual references. Are they intended as homage? Do they serve to reinforce a particular perspective or critically call into question the work alluded to or quoted? Do they establish an aesthetic or social kinship? Or are they part of an elitist game: who is able to catch the references? [ML and WG]

Further reading

Allen, Graham (2000) *Intertextuality*, London: Routledge.
Stam, Robert (1985) *Reflexivity in Film and Literature: From Don Quixote to Jean-Luc Godard*, Ann Arbor, MI: University of Michigan Press.

INTERTITLES In the silent era, written titles, on separate title cards, communicated information that the succession of images could not provide on its own. In very **early cinema**, each shot was often introduced by a title summarizing the action. After 1907, intertitles became longer and more complex as films were increasingly long and complex and were distributed in outlying towns where no lecturer would be present to provide commentary. However, many critics saw intertitles as an interruption of the action, often deleterious to suspense, and recommended discretion in their use. "Purist" filmmakers of the **silent film** era, notably F. W. Murnau, attempted to demonstrate that the art of film could do without verbal language altogether if every visual element were saturated with meaning.

Intertitles persisted nonetheless and performed several functions. (1) They gave the audience narrative information. In introducing an episode, for example, the intertitle could identify the location of a scene or establish a date or time, or the time lapse between the previous episode and the one to come ("a week later"). Intertitles were also used to describe the dramatic situation of the scene or episode to come in a brief synopsis. (2) The intertitle could provide dialogue between characters, as in the classical form of the dialogue card that is inserted into the continuity of a relatively close shot of the speaking character. Dialogue titles could specify characters' thoughts without recourse to theatrical gesturing. They also appear less intrusive to the audience than other intertitles because they are **diegetic** in nature, and not an extradiegetic intervention on the part of the narrator. (3) Intertitles could also provide editorial commentary on the action, for example in the form of the moralizing narrator in D. W. Griffith's portrayal of the wounded South in *The Birth of a Nation* (1915) or the ironic Marxist commentator in Esfir Shub's *The Fall of the Romanov Dynasty* (1927).

Although considerably less frequent, intertitles continued to be used in the sound era, particularly to indicate settings, dates, and times. In **modernist** filmmaking, titles have been used to emphasize the artificial, constructed character of the film and to prevent the easy identification of the spectator with character and action (see **Marxism** and notion of *distanciation*). [WG]

Further reading

Bowser, Eileen (1990) *The Transformation of Cinema: 1907–1915*, Berkeley, CA: University of California Press.

JUMP CUT Two shots taken from the same or approximately same angle and edited together as if they were part of a continuous action when in fact their discontinuity reveals a jump in time. The most ordinary example is the television interview shot continuously from a single angle and in one long take that is subsequently edited to remove unwanted footage: the interviewee appears to "jump" from one pose to another. The jump cut violates the principle of continuity editing (it is a "bad **match**"). However, it may be a purposeful violation of continuity editing. Jean-Luc Godard's *Breathless* (1959) makes significant use of the jump cut for its disruptive effect, and the jump cut became one of the stylistic features of new wave movements of the 1960s. The term is sometimes used to indicate any jarring effect produced by editing. [WG]

See **New Waves/New Cinemas**.

LENSES The transparent optical devices mounted in the camera that refract light so that it converges and forms an image on the light-sensitive surface of the image plane. (In projection, the lens performs the opposite function: light shines through the printed image and is refracted by the projector lens onto the screen.) The focal length of a lens refers to the distance between the center of the lens and the image plane. A "normal lens" for 35mm film has a focal length of 50mm. Such a lens doesn't distort the relationship between the various planes of the image: they appear to be staggered in depth as they are in our perception of real visual space.

Wide-angle lenses have shorter focal lengths and render images that "distort" perception. Orson Welles and Gregg Toland used wide-angle lenses in *Citizen Kane* (1941) to achieve certain visual effects: an enlarged foreground and an exaggerated sense of depth. This results in the visual elongation of actors or objects in the immediate foreground (becoming grotesque in certain shots in *Kane*) and creates the impression of outsized sets and of the precipitous movement of actors from background to foreground or the reverse. The *fish-eye* lens is an extreme wide-angle lens that suggests a warped perception of reality.

Telephoto lenses have long focal lengths (more than 50mm) and produce quite the opposite effect: they bring a distant subject toward the foreground of the shot's visual field and collapse the perception of depth, so that actors or objects in the background of the "real" space being photographed appear on screen as much closer to those in the foreground. If the wide-angle lens broadens and deepens space, the telephoto lens flattens it. In contrast to the effect of the wide-angle lens, movements between foreground and background taken by a telephoto lens appear as exaggeratedly slow. Telephoto lenses have often been used in documentary filmmaking when the action being filmed is distant from the camera or when the filmmaker wants to avoid intervening in an event. Shooting scenes in fiction films with telephoto lenses came into practice in European **modernism** and in the Hollywood Renaissance of the 1960s and 1970s. See, for example, Michelangelo Antonioni's *Red Desert* (1964) or Robert Altman's *The Long Goodbye* (1972).

Zoom lenses have variable focal lengths that allow for shifts between wide angles and longer focal lengths, giving the impression that the camera is moving toward or away from the subject although it remains stationary. The zoom-in increases the focal length (flattening out the background) while the zoom-out produces the reverse effect (increasing the breadth of the foreground and extending the sense of depth). The zoom lens is very useful in documentary filmmaking when the filmmaker needs to adjust his or her view of an action or bring another element of the action into focus. It has also been used in feature films to shift emphasis within a shot—bringing our attention to a detail or pulling back to give a broader context to the action. [WG]

Further reading

Konigsberg, Ira (1997) *The Complete Film Dictionary*, New York: The Penguin Group.

LESBIAN/GAY/QUEER CINEMA "New Queer Cinema" remains one of the most hotly contested subjects in contemporary film criticism and is a particularly slippery cinematic "genre" to define. The phrase was historically coined by New York-based film critic and cultural theorist B. Ruby Rich, in response to the apparent "new wave" of queer films dominating the program at the 1991 Sundance and Toronto Film Festivals, which crucially brought together, for the first time, those widely perceived to be the leading visionaries of the "wave": directors Gregg Araki, Todd Haynes, Derek Jarman, Isaac Julien, Tom Kalin, Jennie Livingston, Christopher Münch, Marlon Riggs, and producer Christine Vachon. But the "phenomenon" wasn't officially cemented into the cultural zeitgeist until after the publication of Rich's *Village Voice* and *Sight & Sound* reflections on the importance of this allegedly unique cinematic movement which, in her words, finally put "queers on the map as legitimate genre subjects" (1992, p. 35).

New Queer Cinema was seen to mark a timely and unprecedented "epistemic shift" in that it proffered a challenging new horizon of politics, identity, and pleasure far beyond the oppressive, suffocating landscape of the "heteronormative." Rich's invocation of the phrase thus attempted to bring some necessary cohesion to what was, in reality, a fairly amorphous series of very different films that had appeared, to much critical acclaim, at the turn of the 1990s. Films which set a precedent, bravely rejecting the at times overly cautious and antiseptic "gay is good" identity politics of earlier "lesbian and gay" efforts, in favor of an aggressive drive toward generic reclamation, narrative subversion, and the re-negotiation of post-AIDS sexualities. They were unapologetic and politically incorrect celebrations of the criminal and the perverse, that aimed to "'take back' materials used by straight cinema—stereotypes, stories, genres—and in an anarchic, subversive spirit, rework them, and thus alter their social and political implications" (Glyn Davis, 2002, p. 26). The closeted and homophobic subtexts of such postwar Hollywood classics as Alfred Hitchcock's *Rope* (1948) and *Strangers on a Train* (1951), or Richard Fleischer's *Compulsion* (1959), for example, were thus laid bare—literally—in new queer films *Poison* (Todd Haynes, 1991) and *Swoon* (Tom Kalin, 1992); an irreverent strategy that sought to take a defiant stance by re-appropriating the mainstream's unrelentingly negative portrayal of "killer queers" and "deadly dykes": "putting the homo back in homicide" (Rich, 1992). And in contrast to the persistent reinforcement of "compulsory heterosexuality" and the rigid binarisms of gender as unquestionable and untraversable norms that characterized the "mainstream"—both straight and gay—New Queer Cinema alternatively sought to "explode taboos" and overturn more established lesbian/gay definitions and representations, in an effort to celebrate the multiplicity of queer sexualities and identities (Harry Benshoff and Sean Griffin, 2006, p. 221).

The much-vaunted films and filmmakers that "officially" led the vanguard of this new independent movement—though never formally organized as such—were primarily exalted Sundance award winners *Paris Is Burning* (Jennie Livingston, 1990), *Poison* (Todd Haynes, 1991) and *Swoon* (Tom Kalin, 1992). Together with Marlon Riggs' *Tongues Untied* (1990), Gus Van Sant's *My Own Private Idaho* (1991), Derek Jarman's *Edward II* (1991), Christopher Münch's *The Hours and Times* (1991), Gregg Araki's *The Living End* (1992), and a number of other lesser cited film and video works by the likes of Sadie Benning, Su Friedrich, John Greyson, Isaac Julien, Pratibha Parmar, and Monika Treut—to name but a few—these films were groundbreaking in their uncompromising commitment to destabilize the familiar, hetero-normatively inclined conventions of cinema. New Queer Cinema implied that the seemingly passé "genre" of lesbian and gay film was undergoing a long overdue yet undeniably progressive "renaissance," heralding an exciting transitional period of renewal which refused in any way to compromise.

The oppressive representational conventions of Hollywood were thus replaced with a uniquely queer visual **aesthetic** and mode of address—that owed much to the formative works of the American Underground and *Avant-Garde*—and at last gave a voice to those who had for so long been silenced and relegated to the margins.

It was the "politics of representation" that dominated most post-Stonewall lesbian and gay studies of film (i.e. after the spontaneous demonstrations in Greenwich Village in 1969 that initiated a new and militant stage of the gay rights movement) and where New Queer Cinema or "queer cinema studies" more broadly marked a fundamental departure. The landmark civil rights movements of the 1960s and 1970s were very much imbued with the need to link the personal with the political, and so those pervasive and reductive stereotypes that had persistently characterized the representation of so-called social "minorities" became the obvious sites for political redress: "the amount of hatred, fear, ridicule, and disgust packed into those images is unmistakable" (Richard Dyer, 1984 [1977], p. 27). Focusing specifically on the persona of the "sissy" that frequented many of the Hollywood comedies of the 1920s and 1930s, and the predatory "butch" lesbians and suicidal "sad young men" to be found in numerous thrillers of the 1950s, as particularly salient examples, Vito Russo's seminal study, *The Celluloid Closet* (1981), details how these stereotypes both reflected and perpetuated the oppression of lesbian and gay people in society: reproducing dominant stereotypes that elided both the reality and diversity of lesbian and gay lives and identities. These were stereotypes that had evolved interdependently with the socio-pathologizing discourses of gender inversion and sexual deviance that typified the homophobic attitudes of the times. They not only operated as narrative shorthand for what the films themselves dared not acknowledge (for fear of attracting the wrath of the arbiters of the production code), but were deployed as a way to legitimize the embedded "heteronormative" ideological frameworks of the films in which they appeared. Stereotypes thus functioned to both reduce and fix "difference," and empower and differentiate the "normal"/heteronormative from the "abnormal"/queer: "mak[ing] fast, firm and separate what is in reality fluid and much closer to the norm than the dominant value system cares to admit" (Dyer, 1993, p. 16).

The knowingly self-referential—or "homo pomo"—constructions of the New Queer Cinema have therefore, in contrast, marked a radical shift in the contemporary lesbian and gay cultural milieu; profoundly changing popular views on society, sexuality, and culture, and more importantly, inspiring new mobilizations of community, representation, and cultural engagement (see Arroyo, 1997, p. 79). Whereas more politically motivated filmmaking in the wake of Stonewall had prioritized the value of projecting a rather selective image of lesbian and gay solidarity, recent queer studies of film have shown, only too effectively, that the roles of spectatorship, subtext, and sensibility can be far more productive in revealing an altogether more complex, or queerer, history of cinema. [RG]

See also **queer theory**.

Further reading

Aaron, Michele (ed.) (2004) *New Queer Cinema: A Critical Reader*, Edinburgh: Edinburgh University Press.
Benshoff, Harry M. and Griffin, Sean (eds.) (2006) *Queer Images: A History of Gay and Lesbian Film in America*, Lanham, MD: Rowman & Littlefield Publishers Inc.
Doty, Alexander (2000) *Flaming Classics: Queering the Film Canon*, New York: Routledge.
Russo, Vito (1981) *The Celluloid Closet*, New York: Harper & Row.

LIGHTING affects the quality of the image we perceive through varying the intensity of illumination and creating patterns of light and dark. In Hollywood in the studio era, the classical formula is called the three-point lighting system and, as the term suggests, consists of three sources of light:

1   The *key light*, placed to the side of the camera, gives the shot its overall illumination, highlighting the body or the face of the actor. The lighting may be *high key* if the key light is bright, as is typical in genres such as the romantic comedy or the musical. *Low-key* lighting means that the key light is turned down in the interest of creating more expressive areas of light and shadow, as in the classic **film noir**.
2   The *fill light* is less bright than the key light, set at an angle from the key, and functions to soften the "hard" shadows created by a bright key, particularly on the actor's face.
3   The *back light* is set behind the actor, opposite the key light, and functions to detach the body and

head of the actor from the background. It is often used to create an "aura" around the head particularly of female stars.

Other types of lighting produce specific effects. *Source lighting* emphasizes particular sources of lighting in a scene: a desk lamp in a darkened room, light filtering through venetian blinds. *High contrast lighting* creates strong patterns of light and shadow (as was the case in much of the silent era). Both source and high contrast lighting were used by Orson Welles in films such as *The Lady from Shanghai* (1947) and *Touch of Evil* (1958). In a completely different spirit, some filmmakers have preferred to shoot in *available light* (i.e. without any artificial lighting extraneous to the location), as documentary filmmakers of the **Direct Cinema** movement did on principle. Many filmmakers of the **New Wave** movements of the 1960s and more recently the Danish *dogme* group have also advocated shooting with available light in the interest of a new, anti-spectacular **realism**. [WG]

See Chapter 4.

Further reading

Alton, John (1995) *Painting with Light*, Berkeley, CA: University of California Press.

LONG TAKE (see **take**, **deep focus cinematography**, and **sequence shot**)

MAGIC LANTERN is the prototypical slide projector and the form from which later projectors, including digital ones, developed. It appeared soon after 1650. Although its origins remain unclear, its appearance had to do with various factors, such as the interest in experimental research in optics by scholars such as Christiaan Huygens (who may have invented it) and currents of "natural magic," particularly prevalent among the Jesuits. It was a way of investigating, explaining, and demonstrating the "wonders" of the God-created universe, without questioning its metaphysical basis. An important part of natural magic was "artificial magic," the use of human-made contraptions to demonstrate various phenomena found in nature.

Ever since their origins in the mid-seventeenth century, lantern slides had been made to move. Animated mechanical lantern slides were already described in handbooks of optics in the early eighteenth century. The tricks included brass levers, rotating rackwork mechanisms, and superimposed sliding glass plates. In the nineteenth century the selection of effects was enriched by chromatropes (abstract kaleidoscopic rackwork slides), moving astronomical diagrams, and other inventions. Even when lantern slides did not contain actual movable elements, they were animated by the projectionist. Pushing a long slide of a wide landscape or many painted figures through the slide stage of the magic lantern could create an impression of a moving procession or sweeping panoramic gaze.

Phantasmagoria was a special form of magic lantern show first introduced in the late eighteenth century. Its two most famous proponents were Étienne-Gaspard Robertson, who opened his "Fantasmagorie" in Paris in 1798, and Paul Philipsthal, who introduced his "Phantasmagoria" in England in 1802 and may have been the original inventor. It remained popular until the 1840s–50s, and appeared even later (although the word was often loosely applied and has recently been used to describe media–cultural phenomena such as video games and horror movies). The origins of Phantasmagoria are related to two determinants: the popularity of necromancy and other esoteric practices, and the need to discover new uses for the magic lantern that had largely lost its novelty value already in the eighteenth century. In the Phantasmagoria the magic lantern was hidden from sight, often mounted on wheels, and pushed and pulled along rails behind a translucent screen. The lantern slides had figures emerging from a black opaque painted background, which created the illusion that the figures were hovering in the air and approaching the audience. Sound effects were used to enhance the effect.

Dissolving views were a type of magic lantern projection that was first introduced in the 1820s–30s (probably in England), and became popular for the rest of the century. Dissolving views originally involved a pair of identical magic lanterns with oil lamps as illuminants, as well as mechanical shutter blades that were used to block or reveal the light beams from the lens tubes. From the 1850s–60s special biunial magic lanterns were used. They had two optical tubes and oxy-hydrogen gas illuminants installed in a single lamphouse. The gas flames could be raised and lowered by means of a "dissolving tap," which made the mechanical

MARXISM

dissolver unnecessary. The aim was to create a continuous "seamless" projection, where lantern slides would imperceptibly dissolve into each other. One scene could turn into another, the day metamorphose into night, figures appear in the sky, and so on. Such effects later became part of film language, although they were normally produced in the postproduction process rather than during the performance. [EH]

See Chapter 1.

Further reading

Robinson, David, Herbert, Stephen, and Crangle, Richard (eds.) (2001) *Encyclopedia of the Magic Lantern*, London: The Magic Lantern Society.

MARXISM is a body of political thought that emerged in the work of Karl Marx (1818–83) and Friedrich Engels (1820–85). Marxism stages a fundamental critique of free-market capitalism, an economic system that presents itself as rational, even "natural," and leads to a harmonious social order. Refuting this ideology, Marx argues that the capitalist economy is a system of exploitation in which the only freedom left to the majority of citizens is to sell their labor, so that the value they produce, minus wages and other "expenses" of production, accrues to the capitalist class. Marx's theory of historical materialism asserts that the history of social transformations is the history of class struggles conceived as *dialectical* (i.e. the notion that change emerges from the conflict between oppositional forces). In the example of modern capitalism, the

emerging class (the proletariat) grows up within the economic and social structures imposed by the dominant class (the bourgeoisie) and ultimately assumes its revolutionary role: to overthrow capitalism and establish a new society where human relationships are transformed and class oppression abolished. Marx argues for a historical view in which human identities and ideas are not natural givens but are products of historical development (e.g. there is no eternal human nature, no feminine essence, etc.).

Classical Marxists contend that the economic base of a society (its modes of production and the social relations they impose) determines the superstructure (the culture produced by that society). Perhaps because of this determinism nineteenth-century Marxism did not produce a separate aesthetics, beyond its support of critical representations of social conditions in the realist novel. Indeed, Marxist determinism presents a problem for cultural critics: if the superstructure is determined by economics, it has limited autonomy and is destined to reflect dominant bourgeois class relations rather than develop revolutionary consciousness. Cultural critics may consequently give into a feeling of inescapable helplessness.

In the early Soviet period, film's importance as a social instrument was recognized and filmmakers openly debated the question of what kind of films the revolutionary movement should produce. Important figures like Sergei Eisenstein, Vsevolod Pudovkin, and Dziga Vertov argued about how best to construct a revolutionary film practice and made films that were intended to controvert the bourgeois romanticism of the American and European fiction film (see **Soviet Montage Movement**). After 1928, this pluralism of approaches was quickly eradicated by Stalin's "politically correct" line on culture, and Soviet filmmaking, under the eye of the state, was reduced to following the aesthetics of **Socialist Realism**. Elsewhere in the world, Marxist filmmaking has been principally associated with revolutionary movements: in Mao's China, filmmaking followed the Socialist Realist path, whereas in Castro's Cuba, filmmakers were more influenced by **Neorealism** and political **modernism** (see also **New Waves/ New Cinemas**).

The Frankfurt School (Institute for Social Research at the University of Frankfurt, established in 1923) undertook a philosophical revision of Marxist thought on culture. The members of this Marxist "think tank" (among them: Theodor Adorno, Walter Benjamin, and Max Horkheimer) argued that the grand narrative of nineteenth-century Marxism stood aloof from the reality of social experience in their contemporary world. They advocated an interventionist response to the specific historical context within which culture is produced. Adorno and Horkheimer contended that the *culture industry* acts on human individuals to give them the illusion of freedom and choice while luring them into acquiescing in their own passivity. They called on critics to intervene through critical analysis of the consumerist culture. In his influential essay, "The Work of Art in the Age of Mechanical Reproduction," Benjamin argues that cultural objects that can be produced in multiple copies (photography and especially film are cited as primary examples) and therefore viewed by a mass audience eradicate the "aura" of art that is based in the art object's singularity and originality. For Benjamin, mechanical reproduction makes mass art possible and ushers art into the sphere of politics.

In his theory of Epic Theater, German playwright Bertolt Brecht advocated, beginning in 1926, a conscious resistance to bourgeois forms of culture by maintaining the audience in a state of critical attention. This *distanciation* (*Verfremdung*) results from the performance of works that constantly point to their own artificiality (this is theater, not reality) and use "defamiliarizing" techniques that destabilize audience expectations. Therefore the audience remains alert and resists identifying with action and character (see **identification**); instead of responding to theater as a cathartic experience (the purging of emotional tensions), the audience is led, through the play's didactic character, to make judgments of a political/ideological nature that encourage revolutionary action. During the 1930s Hungarian philosopher Georg Lukács debated Adorno, Benjamin, and Brecht questioning the value of modernism and reasserting the centrality of critical realism.

In the 1960s Brecht's notion of *distanciation* and Althusser's revision of the Marxist notion of **ideology** were very influential in the political theories developed by **film journals** such as *Framework* in the United Kingdom, *Cineaste* in the United States, and the radicalized *Cahiers du cinéma* group in France. In a manifesto by J.-L. Comolli and J. Narboni entitled "Cinema/ Ideology/Criticism" (1969), the Cahiers' editorial board revived a number of central Marxist ideas: that film criticism should be "scientific," on the model of historical materialism; that film should be understood as a particular product, manufactured in a mass industry and subject to the capitalist economy, and that all films exist necessarily within the dominant ideology. It was, on the one hand, the task of Marxist critics to analyze and categorize films according to the extent of their compliance with or resistance to dominant models. It was the duty of Marxist filmmakers, on the other hand, to produce films that were revolutionary on the level of expression and on the level of the message communicated (e.g. in the political films of Jean-Luc Godard, Jean-Marie Straub and Danièle Huillet, and Glauber Rocha). Ironically, this type of revolutionary cinema in the Soviet Union and Eastern Europe—in the work of filmmakers like Andrei Tarkovsky or Miklós Jancsó— was part of a resistance to repressive bureaucratic Marxism and the aesthetics of Socialist Realism. [WG]

Further reading

Benjamin, Walter, *et al.* (2008) *The Work of Art in the Age of Its Technological Reproducibility, and Other Writings on Media*, Cambridge, MA: Belknap Press of Harvard University Press.
Comolli, Jean-Luc and Narboni, Jean (1971) "Cinema/Ideology/Criticism," in Leo Braudy and Marshall Cohen (eds.) (2004) *Film Theory and Criticism*, Oxford: Oxford University Press, pp. 812–19.
Williams, Raymond (1977) *Marxism and Literature*, Oxford: Oxford University Press.

MATCHES The continuity system that developed as a hallmark of the **Classical Hollywood** style depends on a system of matches whose function is to create a clear narrative flow from one shot to the next within a **sequence**. For a list of the principal types of matches and their definition, see Chapter 4 (pp. 57–58). [WG]

MEDIA ARCHAEOLOGY The term "media archaeology" has come to refer to a particular way of studying media as a historically attuned enterprise. Media archaeologists claim they are "excavating" forgotten media–cultural phenomena that have been left outside the canonized narratives about media culture and history. Histories of suppressed, neglected, and forgotten media have begun to appear, ones that do not point selectively and teleologically to the present cultural situation and currently dominant media as their "perfection," as traditional histories (including cinema history) often do. They have challenged the "rejection of history" by modern media culture and theory alike by pointing out hitherto unnoticed continuities and ruptures. As a consequence, the area considered relevant for media studies has begun to expand both temporally and spatially. The field of research has been extended back by centuries and is also expanding beyond Western media cultures. Some prominent scholars linked to media archaeological approaches (although all of them don't necessarily define themselves as media archaeologists) are Friedrich Kittler, Siegfried Zielinski, Erkki Huhtamo, Jussi Parikka, and Wolfgang Ernst. [EH]

See Chapter 1.

Further reading

Huhtamo, Erkki and Parikka, Jussi (eds.) (forthcoming) *Media Archaeology: Approaches, Applications and Implications*, Berkeley and Los Angeles, CA: University of California Press.

MELODRAMA A mode of representation whose modern form dates from the French Revolution and includes novels, plays, and films. The nineteenth-century melodrama derives from the popular dumb show (movement and gesture without speech) accompanied by music. Melodramatic theater became a kind of postrevolutionary public forum in which new values and sensibilities were expressed in forms legible to all. Peter Brooks (1976) has analyzed the major defining features of melodrama: (a) "excessive, parabolic" stories involving intense human encounters that "strip the façade of manners" to reveal "moments of symbolic confrontation"; (b) the compulsion to tell all, a victory over repression in which "the characters stand on the stage and utter the unspeakable"; (c) the "polarization into moral absolutes" of good and evil; (d) the definition of characters, not as psychologically complex personalities, but as "primary psychic roles" in conflict; (e) the experience of "excruciation" in which characters are tried and asked to "bear the unbearable"; and (f) an emphatic rhetoric of "simple truths" expressed in histrionic performance (melodramatic "exaggeration") and spectacular illusions (fires, floods, etc.).

Early cinema in search of story material "cannibalized" nineteenth-century melodrama in both theatrical and novelistic forms. It has been argued that all dramatic films from the silent cinema are melodramas because they depend on mime and gesture and are accompanied by music. The melodramatic mode early became a permanent presence in most national cinemas, and its protean nature has allowed it to adapt to new historical and cultural conditions and to move across genres. Melodrama persists to the present in both commercial and art cinemas, in **genre** pieces from *Terms of Endearment* (1983) to *Titanic* (1997) or in the work of Spanish **auteur** Pedro Almodóvar, for example, and very substantially in television, particularly daytime programming.

Critical studies of melodrama began in the early 1970s and generated approaches that were often at variance. In an important early study, Thomas Elsaesser (1972) attempted to reevaluate the "despised" genre by giving privileged status to the films' **mise-en-scène**. Thus melodrama could be seen as a form of spectacle in which the semantic content of dialogue (the meanings it produces) is less important than the semantic function of mise-en-scène, whose "excess" may in fact overwhelm the narrative itself. In his view, the family is the site of melodramatic action: characters are constrained by bourgeois codes of behavior and are pushed to the edge of hysteria in the claustrophobic atmosphere of the home. Elsaesser characterized the melodramatic films of certain **auteurs** in the 1950s—Vincente Minelli, Max Ophuls, Otto Preminger, Nicholas Ray, and especially Douglas Sirk—as potentially "subversive" critiques of the conservative values of melodrama (e.g. the need to bring the rebellious woman back into the patriarchal fold at the end of a film). Rick

Altman, among others, also argued that melodramatic excesses stand in opposition to the action-centered narratives and "transparent" style of the **Classic Hollywood film**, indicating a "competing logic, a second voice" (1988).

In the late 1970s two strains of criticism of melodrama emerged, both rejecting what they considered the undue emphasis on mise-en-scène analysis. The sociological/**Marxist** tendency argues that the key to analyzing melodrama comes from an understanding of the function of real social relations under capitalism: the family as the site, not of production but of reproduction, in which women and children live a marginalized existence. The **feminist** tendency foregrounds the structure of patriarchy that places women in contradictions that cannot be resolved in life but only in the "mythical" denouements of fiction. Feminist analysis is complex and has emphasized two approaches: the more formal study of texts and research on the production of films like the "weepies" and their reception by female audiences.

More recently, critics like Linda Williams (2001) have moved away from the description of melodrama as an excessive form that stands in opposition to classical filmmaking. Melodrama is, she argues, "a mode existing across many media" and across genres and should be seen, not as oppositional, but as the dominant mode in American narratives—literary, theatrical, filmic, and televisual—when they are centered on moral problems. Feminist criticism has limited melodrama by restricting it to the study of the woman's film. It is necessary, Williams argues, to return to the root of the melodramatic mode in the tradition of humanist realism. [WG]

Further reading

Brooks, Peter (1976) *The Melodramatic Imagination: Balzac, James and the Mode of Excess*, New Haven, CT: Yale University Press.
Cook, Pam (ed.) (1994) *The Cinema Book*, London: British Film Institute.
Williams, Linda (2001) *Playing the Race Card: Melodramas of Black and White from Uncle Tom to O. J. Simpson*, Princeton, NJ: Princeton University Press.

MISE-EN-CADRE (see also **framing**) The term was first used by Soviet filmmaker Sergei Eisenstein and designated the work of composing a shot. More recently, the term has been taken up by theoretician André Gaudreault (1988) to make a distinction between the activities that belong to **mise-en-scène** and are analogous to theatrical staging and those that signal the intervention of the filmmaker to prepare the individual shots that will become the units of an edited sequence. Mise-en-cadre thus describes the stage in the process of production that follows mise-en-scène: the activity of framing the field to be shot through positioning of the camera in terms of angle and distance. Through mise-en-cadre the filmmaker uses composition to organize the existing visual field to create specific effects. [WG]

See Chapter 4.

MISE-ÈN-SCÈNE A French term that comes from theater and designates the craft of staging a play. Mise-en-scène in film has come to mean all the activities that prepare the actors and the sets for the shooting: rehearsing the actors for their performance in front of the camera, including blocking their movements, organizing the exchange of looks among them, rehearsing dialogue and gesture, and fashioning the actors' appearance through costume and make-up; constructing the set and dressing it; and designing the lighting that illuminates actors, set, and action. Mise-en-scène is the audio-visualization of the narrative. Thus we could say that if the script is the preliminary phase of verbal representations—characters and actions are narrated and described in words—mise-en-scène is the phase of *showing* the events: the characters are embodied in actors and the actors move through the concrete space of the scene. Actors and set become audio-visually concrete phenomena to be filmed.

In the context of 1950s French criticism, mise-en-scène took on a broader meaning. Instead of describing only the staging of the film, mise-en-scène referred to all the artistic operations by means of which the film's **auteur** (its director) created the film in specifically cinematic terms: mise-en-scène in the classical sense, but also framing, editing, and so forth. As a result, the theatrical or literary source and the script with its written dialogue were downplayed as part of film art, on the basis that these "pre-cinematic" elements lie outside the *specificity* of the film medium. François Truffaut famously decried literary cinema in his diatribe against the French Cinema of Quality that presumed to ennoble the cinema through the adaptation of "serious" literary texts and the use of "legitimate" actors from classical theater. **New Wave** critics pursued the

ideal of a filmmaking that "revealed reality": the filmmaker captured the action and gestures of actors in their integrity and in their real contexts. [WG]

See Chapter 4.

Further reading

Bordwell, David (2005) *Figures Traced in Light: On Cinematic Staging*, Berkeley, CA: University of California Press.
Truffaut, François (2000) "A Certain Tendency of the French Cinema," in Joanne Hollows, Peter Hutchings, and Mark Jancovich (eds.) *The Film Studies Reader*, London: Oxford University Press.

MODERNISM AND ANIMATION The tradition of Graphic or Experimental Animation is deeply identified with Modern Art since 1925, beginning most of all with the early abstract films of Viking Eggeling and Oskar Fischinger; but also beginning with work by Hans Richter and Walter Ruttmann in the late 1920s. Afterward, Graphic Animation evolved systems of layout and editing based on abstraction, collage, distancing effects, and color field painting. These systems do not rely on the rules of drama and character in the same way as character animation. But Graphic Animation in no way precludes characters in a story. The movement cycles and character design are simply much more self-referential (see **reflexivity**).

At first, Graphic Animation clearly borrowed from Expressionism, Dadaism, Constructivism, and Surrealism. In the 1920s, many European modernists, like Marcel Duchamp, Man Ray, and Fernand

Léger, also experimented with essentially nonfigurative cinema. Many narrative live-action films of the 1920s, notably Fritz Lang's *Metropolis*, or classics in 1920s **Soviet Montage**, inserted elements of abstract cinema.

By the 1950s, however, Abstract Animation had branched out in many directions beyond European 1920s modernism, drawing on sources that went back centuries—within the history of the Moving Picture (see **animation as moving picture**)—to puppet theater, movable books, graphic design (particularly typography and page layout), woodblock prints, engraving, vaudeville theater, the comic strip; even the shadow puppet in the films of Lotte Reiniger. Also, the impact of consumerism after World War II, in advertising and design, profoundly shifted how Graphic Animation was used, for the branding of products, for TV commercials. This transition was essential to animated shorts produced at UPA in Los Angeles, at the Canadian Film Board (led by Norman McLaren), by independent filmmakers in the United Kingdom, San Francisco, and New York (e.g. Len Lye, Harry Smith), and Czech masters like Jan Trnka.

By 1965, optical printing dominated Graphic Animation; today, computer graphics. But for the system of graphic narrative to be optimized, the history of all media that inspire the Moving Picture must be part of the story itself, as if figures were collage ideograms from mass culture more than characters in drama. Graphic Animation still emphasizes expressionist distortion as point of view, and collage optical effects, but clearly, with computer games so influential,

and computer graphics in general, the global culture has embraced abstraction as story thoroughly—so thoroughly that it is difficult to imagine a digital tool or application today that does not rely on the moving icon or ideogram. Also, graphic animation pioneered the use of abstract, nonfigurative space that is basic to all special-effects design, and computerized cartography. [NMK]

See Chapter 8.

MODERNISM AND POLITICAL MODERNISM
The label "modernist" is applied to a film based on a critical interpretation; it is not a category that governs the production or popular reception of a film, as in, for example, a studio's decision to make, or a spectator's decision to see, a "Western" or an "art movie." The manifestations of modernism in the cinema are as varied as they are in any art, and it is consequently difficult to arrive at a single inclusive definition of the term. For some theorists, the philosopher-critic Walter Benjamin for example, the photographic basis of films gives them a tendency to produce modernist effects. If modernism in the older arts consists of rejecting traditional artistic conventions and embodying the experiences of modern life, then Benjamin would argue that the technology of film makes it inherently modernist in effect: film was *born* modern. Other theorists define modernism in terms of specific formal strategies or an oppositional relation to conventional film styles. Most examples of cinematic modernism display one or more of the following characteristics: self-consciousness

or **reflexivity** with regard to cinematic conventions, which can range from being militant and oppositional (as in political modernism) to being playful and/or reverent (as in much art cinema); a commitment to make the fullest use of the inherent properties of film as a medium (i.e. moving photographic images, recorded sound, rhythmic effects, etc.); a willingness to abandon the representational illusion, that is, the conventions that support a spectator's "transparent" access to a **diegetic** world that represents reality (fictional or documentary); and a focus on the potential for abstract or formalist effects.

Modernism in one form or another has been manifested throughout the history of the cinema and in diverse geographic and cultural locations. Though modernist effects are dispersed across the history of the cinema, they are more pronounced and concentrated in some films, and it is therefore possible to identify a spectrum of three distinct categories of films based on this principle of concentration. At one end of the spectrum lies **avant-garde** or **experimental** film, the audience for which has more in common with the audience for contemporary high art (abstract painting or modern jazz); here the modernist effects are most concentrated, the length of films is not determined by the norms of commercial exhibition, and often all of the characteristics listed above might be applicable to an individual film. At the other end of the spectrum we can locate a degree of modernism in filmmakers working within the mainstream such as Orson Welles or Alfred Hitchcock; the

narrative structure of *Citizen Kane* (1941) or the editing patterns of *Rear Window* (1954) give each film a degree of reflexivity that might justify applying the label "modernist." Between these two polar extremes lie the many manifestations of modernism in the international art cinema— films such as *Breathless* (Jean-Luc Godard, 1960) or *Stalker* (Andrei Tarkovsky, 1979)—where modernist effects are very explicit and pronounced, but where certain aspects of mainstream fictional narrative filmmaking are respected (standard feature-length running times, diegetic and narrative coherence).

Political modernism refers to a specific subgroup of the modernist art cinema that was most prominent during the late 1960s and early 1970s. The broad historical context for political modernism was the **Cold War** (1945–91), when influential countercultures on either side of the divide (intellectuals, artists, university students) actively critiqued the ideologies that enforced oppressive social relations both within their own societies and abroad (racism, class divisions, sexism, totalitarianism, Vietnam, and other proxy wars).

Since the form and content of contemporary mainstream filmmaking was seen to reproduce those oppressive ideologies, political modernist filmmakers such as Jean-Luc Godard (France), Glauber Rocha (Brazil), Miklós Jancsó (Hungary), and Nagisa Oshima (Japan) employed modernist effects aggressively in the belief that film could play a role in the broader political struggle for liberation. For various reasons, the activities and impact of these political countercultures (demonstrations and protests) on filmmaking, popular music, and other artistic activities are thought to have reached their peak in 1968, though they did in fact continue well into the 1970s. [PY]

See Chapter 3.

Further reading

Kovács, András Bálint (2007) *Screening Modernism: European Art Cinema 1950–1980*, Chicago: University of Chicago Press.
Orr, John (1993) *Cinema and Modernity*, Cambridge, MA: Blackwell.
Rodowick, David Norman (1988) *The Crisis of Political Modernism: Criticism and Ideology in Contemporary Film Theory*, Urbana, IL: University of Illinois Press.

Motivation refers to the manner in which a sequence of narrative events is justified. The most common justification is a developing chronological/causal structure, particularly apparent in linear narratives: event A is followed by event B on the chain of discourse; event A is the narrative cause of event B (see **narrative order**). When a sequence of narrated events proceeds according to this logic, there is no need for a narrator to intervene since the events seem to "recount themselves." As Gérard Genette observed (1969), the "cost" (in terms of narrative intervention) is low.

Motivation also refers to character motivation: the complex of reasons, intentions, and impulses that determine a character's action. One of the defining features of the development of cinema as a story-telling medium (1908–15) was its increasing reliance on characters'

psychological motivation as the narrative engine that propels the story forward. Psychological motivation is one of the most frequent reasons for a cut within a scene (e.g. the cut to the reaction shot). This narrative and psychological system of motivation is characteristic of classical filmmaking and contributes to the style referred to as **transparence**.

See Chapter 4.

Further reading

Bordwell, David, Staiger, Janet and Thompson, Kristin (1985) *The Classical Hollywood Cinema: Film Style and Mode of Production to 1960*, New York: Columbia University Press, pp. 12–13.
Gunning, Tom (1994) *D. W. Griffith and the Origins of American Narrative Film*, Urbana, IL: University of Illinois Press, pp. 85–130.

Multilingual versions In the early years of sound film (1929–33), the technology used to record sound on disk or on film did not allow for the easy dubbing of a soundtrack from one language into another. Preparing a film for a foreign language release required re-filming nearly all the scenes with a different cast speaking the dialogue in another language. These multilingual versions were often made simultaneously with the original language version, where each scene would be duplicated in up to two other languages. Therefore each different language version, when edited and completed, was actually a distinct version, often with different running lengths and scenes added or cut from the original. [JB]

See Chapter 5.

Further reading

Ďurovičová, Nataša (1992) "Translating America: The Hollywood Multilinguals 1929–1933," in Rick Altman (ed.) *Sound Theory/Sound Practice*, New York: Routledge.

O'Brien, Charles (2005) *Cinema's Conversion to Sound: Technology and Film Style in France and the U.S.*, Bloomington, IN: Indiana University Press.

Music The discussion of music in film generally presupposes one type of musical accompaniment: a *nondiegetic* score (see **diegesis**). From the very earliest film presentations, music regularly was used to accompany the images. As this practice expanded from simple piano accompaniment in **nickelodeons** to orchestral scores in the late silent period, audiences became accustomed to the idea of hearing music with filmed presentations. During the transition to sound in the late 1920s, this trend continued with score music being pre-recorded for presentation with films. As film sound became more sophisticated with the introduction of dialogue and sound effects, the use of music continued. The musical score would often accompany certain characters in a technique known as *leitmotifs* (or character "theme" music) and generally prompt the reaction of the audience to narrative dramatic events. The music, however, remained predominantly nondiegetic and heard only by the audience, not by the characters in the film.

When the characters are able to hear (or presumed to be able to hear) the music, this is called diegetic source music. The most common example is the visualization of musicians in a film, where the audience understands that the music they are hearing is being produced by an **on-screen** source. Sometimes source music can be **off-screen**, such as the music in a dance sequence where we initially see a band playing and their music continues even though we no longer see the band on screen. Another common form of source music is when music is reproduced by electrical means, such as a diegetic radio or stereo. This is very common in contemporary releases, and a film may have a nondiegetic score as well as diegetic source music, often designed to be released as two separate soundtrack albums. This programming of popular songs as either source or score music by a music supervisor is a rather recent trend in the marketing of film music. [JB]

See Chapter 5.

Further reading

Gorbman, Claudia (1987) *Unheard Melodies: Narrative Film Music*, Bloomington, IN: Indiana University Press.

Smith, Jeff (1998) *The Sounds of Commerce: Marketing Popular Film Music*, New York: Columbia University Press.

Narration (see **narrative**)

Narrative The recounting of a chronological sequence of events, real or imaginary, constituting a narrative whole and recognized as such by its audience. Narrative has a closed structure characterized by a beginning, a middle, and an end (Aristotle). Reality, in contrast, has no narrative structure: it exists as the unstructured flow of experience. In a similar way, one can say that the materials of stored memory or unorganized historical facts deposited in archives take on meaning only when the person who remembers or the historian gives them narrative form.

Narrative may be considered from three points of view.

1 Narrative is a *discourse*: a text that transmits a sequence of events through a specific means of expression. Film, for example, communicates using the moving image, spoken and written language, music, and sound effects. It also has its own expressive structures: editing of images and sounds, different shot scales, sequence structures, and so forth. The novel *Gone with the Wind* and the film of the same name may recount, more or less, the same events, but they are radically different because of their different mediums of expression.

2 Narrative is also the *story*: the narrated world of the film—its events and characters—as viewers construct them in their minds in response to the film's (or novel's) discourse (see **diegesis**).

3 Narrative may be considered from the point of view of the activity that produces it: its *narration*. Every narrative is the product of an act of narration that implies that there is someone telling the story and someone receiving it. The narrator in a film, the agent responsible for organizing the film's discourse, has been described as *impersonal* because narration in film tends to be covert. With seeming effortlessness, the camera produces a richly detailed representation of space and time without the apparent intrusion of a narrating voice. However, we do become aware of a narrating voice when a film chooses stylistic devices that deviate from the norms, for example in most **art films**, but also in the work of self-conscious filmmakers in commercial production, for example Alfred Hitchcock (see **style**). The special character of filmic narration can also in part be explained by distinguishing two separate stages of film production. The first is the stage of *showing* (André Gaudreault's *monstration*, 1988): the **mise-en-scène** and the **framing** that produce the shot. The second corresponds to *telling*: the stage of **editing**, in which the shots are articulated together to form a narrative continuity.

Films may also contain narration by characters, for example a character who introduces a flashback (see **narrative order**). The intervention of these secondary narrators is usually either temporary or intermittent. In the example of the flashback, after the introductory moment in which the secondary narrator narrates in voice-over and his or her subjectivity is emphasized by a close shot of the face, the film returns to the impersonal mode of narration.

In telling a story, narrative operates according to two different sequences in time: the story time (the period of time the story's events cover) and the time of narration (the time it takes to tell the story). A two-hour film, for example, may recount events that last a single day or it may condense the events occurring to a family over more than one generation.

For a discussion of the viewer's participation in the act of narration, see **cognitive theory** and **spectator**. [WG]

Further reading

Bordwell, David (1985) *Narration in the Fiction Film*, Madison, WI: University of Wisconsin Press.
Chatman, Seymour (1978) *Story and Discourse: Narrative Structure in Fiction and Film*, Ithaca, NY: Cornell University Press.
Metz, Christian (1990) *Film Language: A Semiotics of the Cinema*, Chicago: University of Chicago Press.

NARRATIVE ORDER The order in which the actions of the story are presented to the spectator. The order may be a simple linear chronology, or linearity may be inflected with more or less extensive flashbacks or flash-forwards. Linear narratives organize actions in the chronological order of their occurrence in the story. In the progression of sequences A, B, and C, A occurs before B, which occurs before C. Linear order is the most frequent in cinema, particularly dominant in classical filmmaking. Linearity allows the spectator to read the succession of sequences not only as chronological but also as a chain of cause and effect: the police informer hears the gangsters plotting to hijack a shipment of alcohol; he therefore informs the police; and because of this tip, the police organize a trap for the gangsters. Linear order has the advantage of appearing to unfold "**transparently**," that is without the narrator having to intervene to cue a change in the chronology of events.

In the *flashback*, the linear progression of the film's story is interrupted so that an event in the past relative to the narrative present can be related. Very often the flashback functions to clarify some psychological aspect of a character or to shed light on the source of a conflict. Character X's perverse behavior in the present is explained by the abuse he endured as a child. Normally, the flashback in film is signaled by a cue. For example, the character who is remembering an event is shot in close-up with a pensive expression; a dissolve begins that makes the transition to the past event, often accompanied by music or voice-over ("I can still see . . . "), or both. As French theoretician Christian Metz observed, the flashback has no special form that establishes its "pastness," and the spectator entering the movie theater during a flashback has no way of recognizing its temporal character. One of the features of image and sound in film is their quality of presence.

Examples of "flashbacks" in the form of superimpositions on a shot "in the present" are to be found as early as 1908. However, extensive use of flashbacks developed only after 1913 in the American cinema. Complex flashback structures can be found in European films of the early 1920s. Such structures usually involve a frame story: a character who knows the protagonist (or the protagonist himself as an older person) introduces a series of flashbacks concerning the protagonist's trials and tribulations, thus establishing a pattern of alternation between present and past in which the flashbacks dominate. Relatively rare in the American cinema of the 1930s, the flashback structure underwent a remarkable revival with *Citizen Kane*, which began a vogue for narrative complexity in the 1940s and 1950s. Certain **auteurs** have experimented with flashbacks as a form; notable examples include Alain Resnais's

Hiroshima mon amour and Akira Kurosawa's *Rashomon*.

The *flash-forward*, which interposes usually brief shots of future events between actions narrated in the present, is relatively rare, perhaps because it is more difficult to motivate. A psychic character, for example, may introduce the flash-forward as a vision of the future, or the narrator may insert shots that serve as a brief foreshadowing of a future event or as a commentary on the present action. [WG]

See Chapter 4.

Further reading

Chatman, Seymour (1978) *Story and Discourse: Narrative Structure in Fiction and Film*, Ithaca, NY: Cornell University Press.

Metz, Christian (1990) "Notes Toward a Phenomenology of the Narrative," in *Film Language*, Chicago: University of Chicago Press.

NATIONAL CINEMAS The nation has been defined as "an imagined political community," which exists as a "deep, horizontal comradeship" despite social divisions and inequalities (Anderson, 1991, pp. 1–7). Members of the community adhere to nationhood through a sense of belonging, which they do not recognize as a political commitment but experience as an identification close to that of kinship or religion. The nation defines itself by differentiation: it exists within circumscribed borders and sets itself in opposition to other nations in both territorial and ideological terms.

The notion of national cinemas supposes that a set of films made within the territory of a nation by indigenous filmmakers who work within a specific cultural tradition constitutes an expression of national identity. It stems from the nineteenth-century idea that the *genius* of a nation—the salient cultural features that form its essential character and differentiate it from other nations—is expressed through its literature and art. However, culture is not a reflection of nation-ness; it helps construct it, often through a rhetoric that unifies a society that may be rife with social conflict.

National cinemas, like other cultural formations, evolve, inflected by social situations and the historical moment. A national film industry may be distinguished by its mode of production (e.g. the "artisanal" tradition of French filmmaking as opposed to the "industrial" Hollywood model), by social and aesthetic principles (e.g. those of the Italian movement known as **Neorealism**), and by the enumerable cultural codes that permeate it: codes of gesture, posture, or speech, codes of manners, codes of humor, conventional representations of gender or **race**, among others.

Moreover, one can distinguish between films that come from the center of culture and support a conservative myth of the nation, and those that come from the margins and challenge the reigning conception (Hayward, 1993, pp. 1–17). Robert Burgoyne demonstrates how even in the American cinema in the late twentieth century some historical films challenged the "image of social consensus" and reenacted "the narrative of Nation, in terms of stories of ethnic, racial and gender struggles" (1997, p. 6) in the interest of establishing a new civic pluralism.

Historically, national cinemas have been theorized in terms of their resistance to the dominant model of the Hollywood cinema. The emergence of the American cinema, its classical forms of narration, and its economic hegemony established, particularly after the **First World War**, a new relation of forces. The Hollywood film expanded into international markets displacing, among others, the formerly strong national production in European countries like France and Italy. In the 1920s, an era of strong nationalisms, European cinemas created national identities through their economic and aesthetic opposition to Hollywood. **German Expressionism** and **French Impressionist Cinema** are examples of such nationalist cinemas. The rise of **fascism** and the approach of the **Second World War** increased national consciousness and reinvigorated conservative representations of the Nation, particularly in propaganda films. In the Soviet Union, whose filmmakers and theoreticians in the 1920s had attacked Hollywood in the name of class warfare against bourgeois cinema, films were increasingly nationalistic under the strict control and censorship of the Stalinist period (see **Socialist Realism**).

In the aftermath of the Second World War, revolutionary movements defined themselves in national terms. The Cuban revolution, waged against American domination and its puppet government, for example, produced a strong national cinema, as did the cinemas of Eastern Europe in their resistance to domination by the Soviets. Although presumably committed to a common third way, **Third World**

Cinemas were often national in inspiration. In general, the notion of national cinemas has been supported by most traditional histories of film, which organize the discussion of periods of film production in geographical terms, most notably according to national boundaries. [WG]

Further reading

Anderson, Benedict (2006) *Imagined Communities*, London: Verso.
Burgoyne, Robert (1997) *Film Nation: Hollywood Looks at U.S. History*, Minneapolis, MN: University of Minnesota Press.
Hayward, Susan (1993) *French National Cinema*, London: Routledge.

NEOREALISM A movement in Italian cinema that originated during the closing years of the **Second World War** and reached its peak in the early 1950s. It began with critical polemics in the film journal *Cinema* against the artificial "white telephone" movies (a reference to the opulent sets constructed at Mussolini's Cinecittà studios) that dominated Italian production during the 1930s and early 1940s. Critics such as Cesare Zavattini argued that Italian cinema needed to renew itself by drawing on the realist traditions of Italian literature and attempt to represent Italian social conditions with greater authenticity. As the war drew to a close, filmmakers such as Luchino Visconti, Federico Fellini, Roberto Rossellini, and Vittorio De Sica began to make films that addressed contemporary Italian society using a variety of new techniques: location shooting, the use of available light, episodic narratives, nonprofessional actors, improvised scenes, and idiomatic dialogue. Films by Rossellini such as *Rome, Open City* (1945), *Paisa* (1946), and *Germany Year Zero* (1948) directly addressed the war and its aftermath, while others focused on the struggles of socially marginal groups and individuals (*La Terra Trema*, Visconti, 1947; *Bicycle Thieves*, De Sica, 1948). When presented to an international audience via film festivals and the emerging art cinema exhibition network (see **art cinema distribution**), the aesthetic achievement and social significance of Italian Neorealism were immediately recognized, and it began to have an impact on filmmakers around the world ranging from the French New Wave and the Cinema Novo movement in Brazil to individual directors such as Satyajit Ray in India. Due in part to the low-budget, nonstudio-based nature of its aesthetic, Neorealism has continued to be an important and viable model for young filmmakers. [PY]

Further reading

Bazin, André (1971) *What Is Cinema?*, vol. 2, Berkeley, CA: University of California Press.

Marcus, Millicent (1986) *Italian Film in the Light of Neorealism*, Princeton, NJ: Princeton University Press.

NEW WAVES/NEW CINEMAS Since the early 1960s the label of "new wave" or "new cinema" has been applied to a number of movements within national film cultures. In a general sense, such labels are applied when a body of films appears which somehow distinguish themselves—by their **modernist** effects, the pronounced style of their auteur directors, their similar subject matter and cultural influences—from the more conventional and commerce-driven filmmaking that preceded them and continues to surround them. New Waves and New Cinemas are in some cases also defined and given coherence by the professional collaboration between the filmmakers who constitute them. The first and most famous of these movements was the French New Wave, in which a group of critics writing for the French film journal *Cahiers du cinéma* during the 1950s—Jean-Luc Godard, Francois Truffaut, Eric Rohmer, Claude Chabrol, and others—began to make films during the early 1960s. Some other examples are the New Italian cinema of the 1960s (Michelangelo Antonioni, Federico Fellini, Pier Paolo Pasolini), the Czech New Wave of the 1960s (Vera Chytilova, Milos Forman, Jiri Menzel), the New German Cinema of the 1970s (Wim Wenders, Rainer Werner Fassbinder, Werner Herzog), the New Hollywood Cinema of the 1970s (Francis Ford Coppola, Martin Scorsese, Robert Altman), and the New Iranian Cinema of the 1980s and 1990s (Abbas Kiarostami, Mohsen Makmalbaf, Jafar Panahi). New Waves and New Cinemas are often considered to end when their original vitality and coherence is lost and their filmmakers become absorbed by the mainstream art cinema. [PY]

Further reading

Neupert, Richard (2007) *A History of the French New Wave*, Madison, WI: University of Wisconsin Press.

Nowell-Smith, Geoffrey (2008) *Making Waves: New Cinemas of the 1960s*, New York: Continuum.

NICKELODEON Nickelodeon or nickel-Odeon (a *portmanteau* term combining nickel, meaning 5¢-coin, and the Greek word *Odeion*, a roofed-over theater) was the name popularized by Harry Davis and John P. Harris for the small, storefront theater they opened in Pittsburgh, Pennsylvania, in June 1905. Subsequently, the term was adopted more generally, referring to small, neighborhood movie theaters in the early twentieth century. Nickelodeons would characteristically show short films a few minutes long, to a piano accompaniment. Subjects included short narratives, scenics (views of the world from moving trains), "actualities" (precursors of later documentary films), illustrated song slides, local or touring song and dance acts, comedies, melodramas, problem plays, stop action sequences, and sporting events. The rise of the more expensive feature film and the movie palaces that could afford to exhibit it brought an end to the nickelodeon. [HR]

See **early cinema**.

Further reading

Bowers, Q. David (1999) *Nickelodeon Theatres and Their Music*, Blue Ridge Summit, PA: Scarecrow Press.

Musser, Charles (1990) *The Emergence of Cinema: The American Screen to 1907*, New York: Scribner.

NONFICTION (see also **fiction**) Many theoreticians now agree that nonfiction can be distinguished from fiction by the relationship the author (or filmmaker) maintains with the reader (or spectator). In nonfiction, the writer or filmmaker is directly responsible for what he or she says or represents. Nonfiction operates under the constraints of the real: what it represents must correspond to facts in the world. The author is the narrator of events and can be held accountable for misrepresentations by various "authorities": academic historians or anthropologists as judges of historical or ethnographic films, for example. Other cases may be more ambiguous: would it be possible to hold Oliver Stone responsible in a court of law for what some see as inaccuracies or calumnies in his historical fiction?

In relation to the audience, the writer or filmmaker is under the obligation to make clear the nonfictional character of a work. This can be done through what French theoretician Jean-Marie Schaeffer calls *paratextual* markers. In a literary work this may be a simple marker such as "a history" as the subtitle for a work by a historian. In film, a similar marker can appear as an intertitle or as a statement made in voice-over. Or more subtly, we often recognize works of nonfiction by signs inside the film texts themselves: the voice-over in the classic **documentary** or the techniques that belong to **Direct Cinema**. There are of course parodies of nonfiction that imitate nonfictional forms without nonfiction's serious intent ("mockumentaries"). The boundary between fiction and nonfiction is not always clear, and there are films that negotiate, or pretend to negotiate, between fiction and nonfiction. What does it mean when a film indicates it is "based on a true story"? Is a film fictional or nonfictional if it combines interviews with historical witnesses and heavily fictionalized representations of characters and events, as in Warren Beatty's *Reds* (1981)? [WG]

Further reading

Guynn, William (2006) *Writing History in Film*, New York and London: Routledge.

ON-SCREEN/OFF-SCREEN SPACE Because the filmic image appears as if cut out of a broader reality, we are called upon to imagine the filmic space as extending beyond all four edges of the frame, as it does "beyond the set" and into the space behind the camera. In deciding to shoot at certain distances and angles, the filmmaker involves us in the complex play between what is included in the image and what is excluded from it. This play between on-screen and off-screen space—one of the major dramatic resources of film—is cued by several techniques: the entrance and exit of characters, the location of the source of **sound**, point of view series established through the eye-line **match**, analytic editing that gives us fragmentary views of the space of a scene, among others. [WG]

See Chapter 4.

ORIENTALISM Introduced into literary and cultural studies by critic Edward Said (1935–2003) to account for the images and function of "the East" (specifically in his work on North Africa) for nineteenth- and twentieth-century literary and academic critics in Europe and the United States whose work implicitly or explicitly supported Imperialism. For Said visions of Arabs and Islam functioned to create them as "Other" to the Euro-American nations and their Imperialist project. The East, Said claimed, has been consistently characterized as exotic, inscrutable, unknowable, and feminine, against the logical, rational, factual, and masculine West. The concept was later applied to a larger geographic realm which came to encompass Asia more generally.

Adapted into film studies, Orientalism came to define those texts which imaged Asia as inscrutable, exotic, dangerous, and feminine. Associations between Asia and picturesque landscapes, rich color tapestries, and certain "quaint" customs (the harem, geisha) were notable features said to define the Orient for Western consumption. The feminized man and his de-sexualization was another characteristic associated with imaging the Orient as Other to the masculine Western way of being and behaving. Demonizing Arabs and Asians as rapacious and bent on world destruction is also characteristic of Orientalism. Also associated with **psychoanalytic** and **postcolonial** theory. [DD]

See Chapter 9.

Further reading

Bernstein, Matthew and Studlar, Gaylyn (1997) *Visions of the East: Orientalism in Film*, New Brunswick, NJ: Rutgers University Press.
Said, Edward (1978) *Orientalism*, New York: Pantheon Books.

PANORAMAS The Panorama was invented by Robert Barker, an Irish-born painter living in Edinburgh, Scotland. In 1787 he was granted a patent for *An Entire New Contrivance or Apparatus, which I Call La Nature à Coup d'Oeil, for the Purpose of Displaying Views of Nature at large by Oil Painting, Fresco, Water Colours, Crayons, or any other Mode of Painting or Drawing*. Barker's patent described a method of creating and displaying very large paintings. An enormous canvas, depicting a single situation or location, was stretched horizontally along the inner wall of a cylindrical building, so that its ends merged seamlessly. Hiding the upper and lower margins and controlling the light falling on the painting turned it from a representation into a simulation, an illusory environment. The visitors entered the space through a dimly lit corridor, eventually ascending onto an elevated platform erected at the center of the building. While observing the gigantic circular view, they were meant to feel, as Barker put it, "as if really on the very spot."

The *moving panorama* has often been considered a spin-off of the circular panorama, but it is also connected with the long traditions of visual storytelling. Instead of being surrounded by a static wrap-around painting explored by walking around a viewing platform, the audience was *seated* in an auditorium. Unlike circular panoramas that were shown in buildings erected for the purpose, moving panoramas were normally presented in public venues, such as community halls, local opera houses, theaters, or churches that were also used for other purposes. Facing the spectators was a kind of picture. It was either surrounded by a freestanding frame or "cut out" from a drop curtain covering the front of the auditorium. During the presentation, a long roll of paintings was moved horizontally (in a few cases, vertically) across the "picture window" from one vertical roller to another. It was operated by means of a mechanical cranking system hidden behind the scenes. The roll could contain continuous "panoramic" scenes, series of successive views, or combinations of both. The movement was continuous, intermittent, or both. "Special effects," including backlit sequences and moving cut-out figures, were often used. A lecturer stood next to the picture window, explaining the scenery to the audience. The presentation was accompanied by music and sometimes by sound effects as well. Although it was normally the sole attraction, the moving panorama could also form a combination with other items, including live performances, such as musical acts or feats of *legerdemain* (sleight of hand). The duration of the exhibition varied, but by the mid-nineteenth century 90 minutes or more had become common.

Like the circular panorama, the *Diorama* was also a permanent urban attraction, a building functioning as a "viewing machine." Daguerre and Bouton's original Diorama opened its doors in Paris on July 11, 1822 at 4 Rue Sanson. In 1839 it burned down, after which Daguerre retired from the Diorama business (Bouton, however, opened a new Diorama in Paris on his own). A second Diorama was opened in London at Regent's Park on September 29, 1823, and operated there until 1851. The basic structures of the buildings in Paris and London (and some others) were quite similar. The audience was placed in a sloping amphitheater that could be mechanically rotated around its axis. Each program consisted of two gigantic (*c.* 22 × 14 meters) painted canvases that were seen at the end of tunnel-like stage openings. The distance of the paintings from the audience was 13 meters, and the dimensions of the tunnels had been calculated to mask their edges. Thanks to this, the views seemed to extend centrifugally outside of the spectators' fields of vision. After one of the paintings had been observed for about 15 minutes, a bell would ring, and the auditorium would rotate—by means of a crank-operated mechanism underneath—until it faced the other opening. Of the two paintings on show one depicted an exterior and the other an interior. The best-remembered subjects are Daguerre's views of Swiss mountain valleys and interiors of cathedrals and chapels by both Daguerre and Bouton. [EH]

See Chapter 1.

Further reading

Huhtamo, Erkki (2004) "Peristrephic Pleasures on the Origins of the Moving Panorama," in John Fullerton and Jan Olsson (eds.) *Allegories of Communication: Intermedial Concerns from Cinema to the Digital*, Rome: John Libbey, pp. 237–8.
Hyde, Ralph (1988) *Panoramania! The Art and Entertainment of the "All-Embracing" View*, London: Trefoil Publications in Association with Barbican Art.
Oettermann, Stephan (1997) *The Panorama: History of a Mass Medium*, trans. Deborah Lucas Schneider, New York: Zone Books [orig. 1980].

PEEPSHOW (PEEP PRACTICE) Projecting luminous images for an audience by means of a projector, such as a **magic lantern**, was never the only way of consuming moving images. Since the seventeenth century there existed another parallel trajectory that Erkki Huhtamo has called "peep practice." Peepshow boxes were used both in public and private contexts to display images that had been initially hidden from the gaze. One of their origins points to devices created to demonstrate the perspective theories of the Renaissance, like those designed by the fifteenth-century theorist Leon Battista Alberti. Following this line, seventeenth-century Dutch artists like Samuel van Hoogstraten and Carel Fabritius created perspective boxes as demonstrations of their skill: the inside walls of a box were painted in such a manner that a correct perspective view could be seen through a carefully placed peeping hole. Peepshow also became part of the optical repertory of "natural magic," an intellectual current particularly prevalent among the Jesuits in the sixteenth and seventeenth centuries. Mirrors, small objects, and pictures were placed inside the boxes to create miraculous infinite reflection effects (that formally recall works by contemporary artists like Lucas Samaras and Yayoi Kusama).

In the eighteenth century large peepshow boxes were exhibited at fairs and on market squares by itinerant showmen. The views were hidden inside a box, and to access them one had to glue one's eye(s) to an opening provided with a magnifying lens. Illumination was provided by candles or by opening and closing "doors" at the sides of the box. The display of curiosities in such a manner was obviously based on economic calculation. Almost anything could be made attractive by initially disguising it from the gaze and preparing the experience by verbal promises, hints, and suggestions. A coin provided the means to satisfy these artificially created expectations. The showmen attracted viewers by visual impressions of sensational topics such as the wonders of China, famous palaces, battlegrounds, or the devastation caused by the Lisbon earthquake. A veritable industry emerged to produce perspective views (*vues d'optique*) for them. These were produced in great quantities and in a more or less standardized format by several centers—Paris, London, Berlin, Augsburg, and Bassano in Northern Italy. Such views typically depict identifiable geographic locations—cities, palaces, squares, and other public sites. There are also fanciful depictions of foreign lands like China, mythological scenes, and views with topical subject matter: public celebrations with fireworks, city fires, battles, and natural catastrophes, such as the disastrous Lisbon earthquake in 1755.

Peepshows were also used in the homes of the aristocracy already in the eighteenth century. Eventually they turned into toys encountered in the nurseries of the bourgeoisie in the next century. However, the idea of peering into a hole was evoked again and again along the cultural trajectory leading from the eighteenth-century peepshows to nineteenth-century devices like the Megalethoscope (a handsome piece of "optical furniture" for the salon), the stereoscope, and the zoetrope and further to early moving picture viewers

such as the Mutoscope and the Kinora. Devices for domestic use accompanied the popularity of public entertainments from old-style touring peepshows to new forms like the Cosmorama, the Kaiser Panorama, and eventually the Kinetoscope and the Mutoscope.

The Mutoscope, first introduced in 1897, was a novelty peepshow box for viewing "animated photographs." Unlike its motor-driven predecessor, Edison's Kinetoscope, the Mutoscope was hand-cranked and relied on the principle of the flip book. The frames of the moving pictures had been copied onto paper slips attached to a rotating cylinder. The cranking speed could be freely adjusted, and the session interrupted at any point to observe a particularly interesting frame (perhaps a half-naked lady). The "proto-interactive" nature of the Mutoscope was clearly expressed in an advertising booklet in 1897:

In the operation of the Mutoscope, the spectator has the performance entirely under his [*sic*] own control by the turning of the crank. He [*sic*] may make the operation as quick or as slow as fancy dictates. . . and if he [*sic*] so elects, the entertainment can be stopped by him [*sic*] at any point in the series and each separate picture inspected at leisure; thus every step, motion, act or expression can be analyzed, presenting effects at once instructive, interesting, attractive, amusing and startling.

The Mutoscope was more reliable than the Kinetoscope and could be shown in places where electricity was not available. The Kinetoscope soon disappeared from the market, while the Mutoscope became a great success that lasted until the 1950s. [EH]

See Chapter 1.

Further reading

Balzer, Richard (1998) *Peepshows: A Visual History*, New York: Harry N. Abrams.
Hendricks, Gordon (1964) *Beginnings of the Biograph*, New York: The Beginnings of the American Film, pp. 59–65.
Huhtamo, Erkki (2006) "The Pleasures of the Peephole: An Archaeological Exploration of Peep Media," in Eric Kluitenberg (ed.) *Book of Imaginary Media: Excavating the Dream of the Ultimate Communication Medium*, Rotterdam: NAi Publishers.

PLOT POINTS Dramatic events that change the situation of characters and the direction of the plot. Often unanticipated (as in Marion Crane's murder in *Psycho*), a plot point may be a reversal of fortune (the Cary Grant character in *North by Northwest*, mistaken for the imaginary agent Kaplan created by US intelligence, thus becoming an object of pursuit), a moment of recognition in which the true nature of an event is revealed (the realization by characters in *The Birds* that the birds have begun an attack against humans), or a confrontation that brings to a climax the tensions between characters (in *Sabotage* Mrs. Verloc's murderous response to her husband's dismissive remarks about her brother's death, which he caused). Technical manuals on screenwriting often stipulate that the "well-made" film should be structured in three acts and each act punctuated by a major

plot point: the first occurs after the first act (the exposition or set-up); the second occurs after the second act (the "confrontation") and leads to the film's resolution (Field, 2005). [WG]

See Chapter 4.

Further reading

Field, Syd (2005) *Screenplay: The Foundations of Screenwriting*, New York: Delta.

POETIC REALISM A film style shared by a number of French filmmakers that reflected the general malaise gripping French society on the eve of World War II. The directors associated with the Poetic Realist aesthetic include Jacques Feyder (*Pension Mimosas*, 1934), Jean Vigo (*L'Atalante*, 1934), Julien Duvivier (*Pépé le Moko*, 1936), Jean Renoir (particularly *La bête humaine*, 1938), and most notably Marcel Carné. Inspired in part by realist fiction of the nineteenth and early twentieth centuries, Poetic Realist films typically feature working-class heroes struggling in marginal social settings whose bleak atmospherics seem to bear down on the lead characters with implacable, destructive force. Emblematic of Poetic Realist movement are the films directed by Marcel Carné and scripted by poet Jacques Prévert, particularly *Quai des brumes* (1938) and *Le jour se lève* (1939). The films' protagonists are played iconically by Jean Gabin, and the characters move in shadowy, often fog-enveloped surroundings that are the hallmarks of the Poetic Realist aesthetic, characteristics of the form that renowned artists such as set designer Alexandre Trauner and cinematographer Eugen Schüfftan were instrumental in creating. [RS]

Further reading

Andrew, Dudley (1995) *Mists of Regret: Culture and Sensibility in Classic French Film*, Princeton, NJ: Princeton University Press.

POINT OF VIEW A critical term that has at least two different (if related) meanings. First, point of view has long been used in literary criticism to describe the position from which events and characters are presented. Do we follow events from the point of view of an omniscient narrator, who can be anywhere, including in the minds of the characters? Do we follow them from the point of view of a character or characters, as in first-person narration ("I encountered him one day . . .")? Or do we follow events from an external point of view that limits itself to observing characters, behaviors, and situations? In film, direct access to the inner mental processes of characters is infrequent. Although prevalent in the work of certain filmmakers and genres in particular periods, the interior monologue, for example, is relatively rare. Rich in concrete detail, film has been described as observational in relation to external reality and behaviorist in its depiction of **characters** (we interpret characters by means of outward signs of facial and body language, comportment, dialogue, and action). Moreover, film is generally impersonal in its mode of **narration**: events seem to recount themselves and we rarely ask, "Who is telling this story?" In the fiction film, a narrator may intervene in **voice-over**. His or her voice may speak as the film's storyteller or as a character within the fictional world of the film. However, voice-over in fiction films often introduces us to characters and situations and then retreats, allowing the impersonal mode of representation to take control. This is often the case in flashbacks (see **narrative order**) introduced in voice-over.

The second meaning of the term is specifically cinematic and has to do with the position the camera adopts in relation to the action of a shot (the camera's point of view). Very often the viewpoint is "neutral" (a "nobody's shot"); that is, the shot does not identify who is looking. However, the point of view may belong to the film's narrator or to one of its characters. A character's point of view is established by the *eye-line match* and may result in a point of view series that typically alternates shots of the character looking off-screen with shots of what he or she is looking at (see **matches**). Because it puts us in the position of the character (we look with him), the eye-line often reinforces our **identification** with characters. However, point of view does not always imply sympathy with a character or moral approval. We may also identify a shot with the film's narrator in situations in which there are signs of the subjective act of looking but the look is not ascribed to any character (e.g. the expressive tracking-in shots in many Hitchcock films). Finally, we may identify the look with the camera when we are made aware of the camera's presence (e.g. footage from a hidden camera spying on someone's private life, or camera consciousness produced in **documentary** or **ethnographic films**). [WG]

Further reading

Branigan, Edward R. (1984) *Point of View in the Cinema: A Theory of Narration and Subjectivity in Classical Film*, The Hague: Mouton.
Cavell, Stanley (1979) *The World Viewed*, Cambridge, MA: Harvard University Press.
Mitry, Jean (2000) *The Aesthetics and Psychology of the Cinema*, Bloomington, IN: Indiana University Press.

POPULAR FRONT Political coalitions that unite center-left and left political parties in pursuit of electoral and other political gains. Between 1934 and 1939, with the encouragement of Soviet leader Joseph Stalin, Communist, parties throughout the West were urged to ally with Socialist and centrist parties in order to consolidate political power in the face of the mounting threat posed by the extreme right advances made in fascist Italy and Germany. In striving to impede the rise of fascism in other Western countries, Socialists, Communists, and some centralist parties formed political alliances aiming to preserve republican regimes and democratic rule, most notably in France and Spain, where Popular Front coalitions achieved important electoral victories in 1936. The Soviet policy of promoting such coalition-building came to an end in 1939 when the Soviet Union signed a treaty with Nazi Germany known as the Nazi–Soviet Non-Aggression Pact.

Numerous intellectuals and artists joined the anti-fascist struggle that strove to advance social democracy in the 1930s. In France, the populist sensibilities in Marcel Carné's **Poetic Realist** films owe much to their historical moment and to the class consciousness that asserted itself in French social life in this period. Carné worked for a time with a film collective known as Ciné-Liberté, a group that drew much of its creative energy from the widespread social contestation of the day. Famed director Jean Renoir also threw his support behind the French Popular Front movement, making several films, including *The Crime of Monsieur Lange* (1935), *Life Belongs to Us* (1936), and *Grand Illusion* (1937), that highlighted the value of class solidarity and the collectivist ethos that gained strength as the Left rose to power in 1936. When the Popular Front waned and war clouds began to gather on the horizon, Renoir became more concerned with fractures in the national community, a sentiment that accounts for the call he appears to be making in *La Marseillaise* (1938) for unity amongst all sectors of the society, an appeal that turns to sardonic critique in his immediate prewar film *The Rules of the Game* (1939) where both the upper and lower classes are seen engaging in trivial pursuits that Renoir himself likened to "dancing on a volcano." [RS]

Further reading

Alexander, Martin and Graham, Helen (eds.) (1989) *The French and Spanish Popular Fronts: Comparative Perspectives*, Cambridge: Cambridge University Press.
Buchsbaum, J. (1988) *Cinema Engagé: Film in the Popular Front*, Urbana, IL: University of Illinois Press.

Reader, Keith and Vincendeau, Ginette (eds.) (1986) *La Vie Est A Nous: French Cinema and the Popular Front, 1935–1938*, London: British Film Institute.

POSTCOLONIAL STUDIES emerged as a field in the late 1970s. It addresses the legacy of European colonialism, which began in the late fifteenth century with the Columbian "discovery" of the New World and culminated in the early twentieth century with European (and American) economic and political domination over three-quarters of the world's land mass. Movements for national independence for the colonies began in the 1960s and were largely complete by the end of the century. The writings on postcoloniality are identified with such cultural critics as Edward W. Said and Gayatri Chakravorty Spivak and address a range of issues: the importance of rethinking the histories of subjugated cultures; the imperative to deconstruct the history of Western conceptions of the colonized *other*; the rejection of Western *metanarratives* (overarching histories that support the dominance of Western modernism); and the need to develop strategies of interpretation for postcolonial cultures that address questions of race, nationalism, and imperialism. Critical histories of cinema such as those by Robert Stam, Ella Shohat, Manthia Diawara, Philip Rosen, and Mary Ann Doane have illuminated the history of the representation of the colonized and ethnic minorities in film and studied strategies filmmakers have developed for "decolonizing the mind." [ML and WG]

See Chapters 10 and 11.

Further reading

Williams, Patricia and Chrisman, Linda (eds.) (1994) *Colonial Discourse and Postcolonial Theory: A Reader*, New York: Columbia University Press.

POSTMODERNISM As a common sense understanding of the term would suggest, postmodernism is, generally speaking, a term applied to cultural phenomena that come "after" **modernism**, phenomena that appear after modernism in a historical sense and that also differ from it in terms of their formal qualities and cultural functions. As theorized by the French philosopher Jean-François Lyotard, postmodernism occurs when the ideological power of various "master narratives"— modernism in the arts, the ideals of the nation-state, and progress in the realm of political history—no longer has any purchase on the imagination and beliefs of the public: in the most general sense, postmodernism is, then, the cultural effect of skepticism toward the master narratives of modernity. The clearest and most influential formulations of how this effect is manifested in the cinema are found in the work of the American cultural critic Fredric Jameson. Jameson argues that postmodernism is the result of a heightened sense of historicism on the part of the public. The specific idioms of modernism, the techniques it uses, appear "dated" to the public; the postmodern sensibility views all cultural idioms as dated, as clichés. Postmodern film culture caters to this sensibility by presenting the spectator with films that recycle the idioms of the past, pastiches that feed both our nostalgia for the past and/or our ironic distance from it. Thus films like *Chinatown* (Roman Polanski, 1974), *Body Heat* (Lawrence Kasdan, 1981), and *Blade Runner* (Ridley Scott, 1982) all recycle the narrative structures and visual style of the **films noir** of the 1940s. In a general sense, Jameson's formulations can be seen as relevant to many films produced since the mid-1970s. [PY]

Further reading

Corrigan, Timothy (1991) *A Cinema Without Walls: Movies and Culture After Vietnam*, New Brunswick, NJ: Rutgers University Press.

Jameson, Fredric (1991) *Postmodernism, or the Cultural Logic of Late Capitalism*, Durham, NC: Duke University Press.

Sprengler, Christine (2009) *Screening Nostalgia: Populuxe Props and Technicolor Aesthetics in Contemporary American Film*, New York: Berghahn Books.

POSTPRODUCTION SOUND The process of preparing sound for motion pictures occurs in two phases: the recording of sounds during production (see **production sound**) and the editing, re-recording, and creation of sounds in postproduction. Even though a large amount of sound is usually recorded during the shooting of a film, those sounds may or may not be used in the final film. The primary form of production sound is dialogue. Dialogue recorded on location is re-synchronized to the images in postproduction by the dialogue editor. Even though it would seem logical to use the exact production dialogue recordings for each take, often the dialogue editor will choose the best audio takes and edit them to fit the actor's lip movements.

Occasionally, the dialogue editor will actually create dialogue by editing together different words or even parts of words. If the production dialogue recordings are incomplete or inadequate due to excessive background noise, actors are asked to repeat their lines in a looping or automated dialogue replacement (ADR) session. This requires the actor to repeat lines in synchronization with a short passage from the film. Once the lines are synchronized the ADR mixer adjusts the sound quality via filters and added reverberation to match the original production recordings.

In addition to dialogue, occasionally sound effects are recorded live during production. More common, however, is the addition of sound effects in postproduction. This includes the addition of diegetically present sounds (gunfire, car sounds, door slams, etc.) and the creation of ambient backgrounds. Generally, most sound effects are taken from sound effects libraries, although some filmmakers will request the creation of new sound effects for a film. For example, when George Lucas wanted an entirely new experience for the audience with *Star Wars*, he hired Ben Burtt to create new sounds for the film. Burtt spent over a year recording and editing sounds together to create hundreds of new effects and even the languages spoken by the aliens and robots. The person in charge of compiling all of the sound effects in postproduction is the supervising sound editor. When an individual works with the director to craft the sound of a film in both production and postproduction, this is often referred to as sound design.

Although sound editors, supervising sound editors, and sound designers all add sound effects to a film, there is also a highly specialized form of sound effect creation known as Foley. Named after Jack Foley, the innovator of a method for creating live sound effects at Universal Studios, the term "Foley artist" or "Foley walker" was introduced in the 1970s to refer to the process of live sound replacement. The term used by Foley himself was "direct-to-picture," which demonstrates how sound effects artists would perform sounds in postproduction to match the on-screen movement of characters. But in the 1970s the role of the Foley artist began to gain acceptance within the film industry and the live Foleying of sound effects developed as an expedient approach to sound effect creation. Originally, direct-to-picture was used to replace the missing sounds of footsteps and clothing rustles lost due to the lower sensitivity of microphones. Yet, since the process evolved, Foley artists are now called in to perform sounds as an efficient and economical way to add sound effects to films.

The final process of postproduction sound involves assembling all the individual sounds (dialogue, sound effects, and music) into a final mix. This is done with the supervising sound editor and the music editor, and run by the re-recording mixer. The re-recording mixer is responsible not only for ensuring that all the desired sounds are present and balanced in the mix, but also for their spatial dispersion in the multichannel **surround sound** versions. [JB]

See Chapter 5.

Further reading

Ament, Vanessa Theme (2009) *The Foley Grail: The Art of Performing Sound for Film, Games, and Animation*, Burlington, MA: Focal Press.
Yewdall, David Lewis (2007) *The Practical Art of Motion Picture Sound*, 3rd edn., Burlington, MA: Focal Press.

POSTSYNCHRONOUS SOUND Because most **production** sound is recorded separately from the image, it must go through a process of being re-synchronized with the film footage in **postproduction**. This is achieved through the recording of a time code alongside the sound that allows for their precise synchronization with the images. However, sometimes sounds are added in postproduction that also need to be synchronized with the images. The most common form of this is dubbing, where dialogue is translated into another language and the words are synchronized as closely as possible to the characters' lip movements. [JB]

Further reading

Handzo, Stephen (1985) "Appendix: A Narrative Glossary of Film Sound Technology," in Elisabeth Weis and John Belton (eds.) *Film Sound—Theory and Practice*, New York: Columbia University Press.

PRE-CINEMA Concept commonly used to describe technological developments, phenomena, **apparata**, and institutions that preceded the introduction of celluloid film-based moving pictures at the end of the nineteenth century. Some examples of things considered as "pre-cinematic" are **magic lantern** projections, optical persistence of vision devices, and chronophotography. Although still in use, the notion is nowadays often considered problematic (in particular by **media archaeologists**), because it posits a sharp rupture between "pre-cinema" and "cinema" proper, and has a teleological component, treating cinema as the goal and fulfillment of earlier developments. Instead, much recent research has emphasized continuities that link developments considered as "pre-cinematic" with later phenomena. With the emergence of numerous electronic and digital forms of moving pictures, cinema has lost its earlier dominant position in the culture of the moving image. Parallels can be detected, for example, between interactive games and the manipulation of nineteenth-century optical toys, although these should not be treated as directly related. The notion "pre-cinema" should therefore be limited to cases where the discussion explicitly concerns the origins of film and cinema. [EH]

See Chapter 1.

PRODUCTION/DISTRIBUTION/EXHIBITION
As the complexity of both the process and product of filmmaking grew, the industry became compartmentalized into three distinct, but inseparable, entities.

Production The earliest filmmakers could finance themselves. In 1903, the average one-reel film cost between $200 and $500; however, the rising costs of film production in the first three decades of the twentieth century meant that capital needed to be raised from outside sources. The effect of this need to raise finance was to subordinate the filmmaker to the studio, which in turn was answerable to the banks from which the money was advanced, in a system described as vertical integration (see **horizontal/vertical integration**). Since the demise of the **studio system**, two divergent developments affecting film production have occurred: on one hand, the growth of independent producers and small production companies, and, on the other, takeovers and mergers that have seen studios becoming subsidiary corporations of larger enterprises, a phenomenon known as **horizontal integration**. Examples include the takeover of Columbia Pictures by Sony Corporation and the transformation of Warner Bros. into Warner Communications in 1972, followed by its merger with Time Inc., and subsequently its purchase by AOL.

Distribution Film distribution passed through three stages. Initially, production companies sold their prints to exhibitors who would travel around the country presenting shows of their stock. As theaters became established in the early 1900s, however, and the rate at which bills changed increased, middlemen began to buy prints from filmmakers in order to rent them to exhibitors, pricing films according to production costs and popularity. The third phase began when Paramount introduced the practice of **block booking**—the requirement that theaters lease a number of the studio's minor films in order to gain access to its most prestigious titles—a practice soon emulated by other studios. Even though this monopolistic practice of vertical integration was dismantled because of a Supreme Court ruling in 1948, distributors remain an integral part of the film industry.

Exhibition The first theaters were the **nickelodeons**, composed of a simple storefront with a screen, a projector, and chairs, and usually located in working-class neighborhoods.

As cinematic productions gained in sophistication and prestige, exhibitors began building big movie palaces in the hearts of major urban centers to appeal to middle-class audiences, often with extravagant and exotic decor. With the spread of suburbs in the 1950s and early 1960s, drive-in movie venues became popular. The current era has seen the introduction of the multiplex cinema (theaters with two or more screens, showing more than one film), often within the fabric of older movie palaces. New multiplexes are now also common in the malls of suburban shopping areas. Finally, many movies are now watched by individuals in their own home, on DVD or video format. [HR]

See Chapter 2.

Further reading

Acland, Charles R. (2003) *Screen Traffic: Movies, Multiplexes, and Global Culture*, Durham, NC: Duke University Press.

Gomery, Douglas (1992) *Shared Pleasures: A History of Movie Presentation in the United States*, Madison, WI: University of Wisconsin Press.

Hark, Ina Rae (2002) *Exhibition: The Film Reader*, London: Routledge.

PRODUCTION SOUND The process of recording sounds for films at the same time as the images is called production sound. Generally this refers to the recording of dialogue, but it can also include live sound effects or music. In most narrative films, the production sound team is comprised of the boom operator and the sound mixer. The boom operator is responsible for positioning the microphone close to the actors to record their dialogue while being careful not to have the microphone appear in the frame. The sound mixer is responsible for actually recording the dialogue and adjusting the recording levels on the set. Prior to the 1970s both jobs would often be credited in films simply as "sound," though they are distinct from the sound work done in **postproduction**.

Under certain circumstances filmmakers have a preference for using only dialogue and sound effects recorded during production. This is known as *direct sound* and it is prevalent in documentaries as well as certain narrative cinemas. For example, direct sound is far more common in French and Spanish cinema than in Hollywood, and as a result there is often a greater sense of verisimilitude between the sounds and images in direct sound film. However, the preference for direct sound is often just a choice, and several national cinemas, such as the Italian cinema, favor the use of **postsynchronous sound**. Other than the recording of music live on location, most **music** for films is recorded in the studio during postproduction.

Sound effects may also be recorded as part of production sound, but often this is done separately from the dialogue recordings. This makes it easier to edit the dialogue in postproduction because dialogue and sound effects sometimes require very different recording levels. When sound effects are recorded on location this is sometimes called "wild sound." A special kind of production sound is "room tone," which is the background sounds that are always present in a live location (air handling, street sounds, electrical hum, etc.). Recording room tone, or "M.O.S.," allows sound editors to "fill in the blanks" between dialogue takes in post-production. [JB]

See Chapter 5.

Further reading

O'Brien, Charles (2005) *Cinema's Conversion to Sound: Technology and Film Style in France and the U.S.*, Bloomington, IN: Indiana University Press.
Yewdall, David Lewis (2007) *The Practical Art of Motion Picture Sound*, 3rd edn., Burlington, MA: Focal Press.

PSYCHOANALYSIS Both cinema and psychoanalysis (as a theory and a therapeutic practice) are associated with a larger shift in cultural organization marked by a move away from religion and tradition to a secular society based on consumerism and the search for the new. Psychoanalysis was part of a trend that articulated the goals of human life not through altruism and the subordination of the individual will to divine injunctions but through personal fulfillment. No longer were individuals enjoined to struggle against their desires for the sake of a transcendent good, but rather to reconcile these with a need to achieve a resolved, personal individuation. Movie palaces, with their opulent interiors, became a new substitute place of worship for an audience newly preoccupied with material possessions as a means of attaining personal happiness and social standing. Similarly, for many, the spectator's experience of a film served as a substitute, among others, for the religious one. It is perhaps not coincidental, then, that the invention of cinema (1895) coincided with the rise of psychoanalysis, which was marked by the publication of *Studies on Hysteria* (Breuer and Freud, 1966) in which Sigmund Freud (1856–1939) initially developed his theory of the unconscious and the relation of repressed memories to hysterical symptoms and neurosis, which became the foundation for his therapeutic method.

A number of films in the sound era take up psychoanalysis as a topic, with John Huston's *Freud* (1962) and Alfred Hitchcock's *Spellbound* (1945) among the better-known titles. Psychoanalysis also influenced the **Surrealists**, who in turn had an impact on art cinema directors such as Luis Buñuel (1900–83). Similarly **avant-garde** directors such as Maya Deren sought to portray the dream state on film according to the principles of dream analysis set forth by Freud. Scholars such as Krin Gabbard have detailed the complicated relationship between psychiatry (including psychoanalysis) and its representation in film (Gabbard and Gabbard, 1987); however, the most profound effect that psychoanalysis has had on the cinema is in the area of film criticism and theory. Early and sporadic efforts (that continue today) produced material that analyzed the personal pathologies of a given director, as in the monumental biography written by Donald Spoto on Alfred Hitchcock (1983).

More influential in terms of scholarship was the contribution of French theorists influenced by Jacques Lacan and other French Neo-Freudian analysts such as Jean Laplanche. Arguably inaugurated in 1970, in an issue of *Les Cahiers du cinéma* (no. 223), in which film scholars use the tools of psychoanalysis in a discussion of John Ford's *Young Mr. Lincoln* (1939), psychoanalytic approaches to film studies rapidly proliferated, developed by scholars such as Raymond Bellour, Thierry Kuntzel, Jean-Louis Baudry, and Christian Metz, whose work was published in English in 1981 under the title, *The Imaginary Signifier: Psychoanalysis and the Cinema*. Picking up on Freud's ideas, especially as elaborated by Lacan, while seeking to marry psychoanalysis with neo-Marxist theories of **ideology**, Metz argued that a film has many of the features of dream for the cinematic spectator, mesmerized and immobilized in a darkened room before a larger than life screen, which floods the spectator's mind with images from the outside, rather than from the inside as in the dream state. Metz's thesis led to further studies of the symbolic language of cinema, of the spectator as a desiring subject, and on cinema as an institution designed to regulate the desires of its audiences, in which concepts such as oedipalization, scopophilia (the voyeuristic desire to see), fetishism (sexual excitation produced by nongenital objects), and narcissism (love directed at one's own image) play a fundamental role. For several decades, psychoanalytic approaches, often referred to as cine-psychoanalysis, constituted a dominant perspective in cinema studies. The influence of this perspective was felt perhaps most acutely in the area of **feminist** film theory, in which psychoanalysis provided a tool for understanding the production and signification of "woman" as a symbolic category within a specific cultural field that had an ideological function in terms of preserving a patriarchal social structure.

In recent years, psychoanalytic approaches have been variously criticized beginning with neo-formalists such as David Bordwell, who claimed that researchers who rely upon psychoanalytic models tend to find what they seek and that the analysis thus produced constitutes a personal reflection rather than a scholarly excavation. Other scholars have objected to the heteronormativity of psychoanalysis (in which heterosexuality is posited as the norm against which all other sexual identities are measured) as well as its exclusive focus on the contemporary Western European subject and, thus, its implicit ethnocentrism and ahistoricism. In spite of these criticisms, psychoanalysis remains a strong influence in film scholarship, largely because it offers a methodology that attempts to address the problematic of desire, which remains at the heart of the cinematic experience, whether it be in a cineplex, or in front of a home computer. [HR]

Further reading

Bergstrom, Janet (1999) *Endless Night: Cinema and Psychoanalysis, Parallel Histories*, Berkeley, CA: University of California Press.

Kaplan, E. Ann (1990) *Psychoanalysis and Cinema*, New York: Routledge.

Mulvey, Laura (1989) *Visual and Other Pleasures*, Bloomington, IN: University of Indiana Press.

QUEER THEORY The concept was initially suggested by preeminent film scholar Teresa de Lauretis in a landmark edition of the feminist cultural studies journal *Differences* (1991), as a means to counter what she saw as the cultural fiction of compulsory heterosexuality. It proposes an analytical model with the key aim of exposing the instability of dominant "heteronormative" paradigms and practices of gender and sexual identity (Warner, 1993). In particular, queer theory critiques those entrenched gay/straight oppositions that shape and condition social understandings and representations in order to both regulate and sustain specific balances of power, exclusion, and oppression—legitimizing the ("normal") heterosexual over the ("abnormal") queer. So in an extension of earlier writings by Judith Butler (*Gender Trouble, 1990*) and Eve Kosofsky Sedgwick (*Epistemology of the Closet*, 1990), de Lauretis called for the rejection of more established, and apparently limiting, "gay and lesbian" identity politics; and the re-appropriation of this previously derogatory term of abuse (queer) to designate a more inclusive frame within which to incorporate a diverse range of "nonstraight" formations of gender and sexuality that are seemingly "untethered from 'conventional' codes of behavior" (Aaron, 2004, p. 5). Encouraging a radical challenge to the monolithic foundations of a naturalized heterosexual social contract, queer theory reconfigured social identity as a **postmodern** state of

continual flux and indeterminacy, precariously yet productively situated at the point of convergence between political resistance and "deviant" self-invention: "another discursive horizon, another way of thinking the sexual" (de Lauretis, 1991, p. v). In other words, it marked a very real shift in thinking around issues of gender and sexual subjectivity, in an effort to reveal those differences and silences that had long been suppressed within such a hetero-centrically inclined social matrix.

Although there have been a variety of quite divergent theoretical frameworks included under this blanket term, most queer theorists acknowledge the extent to which the texts and communicative strategies of mass culture have both shaped and defined our understandings of gender and sexuality (Doty, 1993). Queer theory's connection to the study of film has, therefore, been evident from the start. As de Lauretis and many of her contemporaries concede, the emergent "queer cinemas" have been quick to respond to the transgressive capacities of film as a means for subversive re-imagining: creating as it does a simulative voyeuristic space for the restaging of an endless array of sexual meanings, pleasures, and interpretive strategies. Moreover, queer filmmakers were not only influenced by these new debates, but were also, in parallel, providing decidedly rich textual material in their films to further sustain their conceptual development. Butler's groundbreaking deconstruction of the totalizing "performative" regimes that govern the naturalization of gender, for example, found particularly fertile "matter" in the troublesome gender-blenders that populated Jennie Livingston's iconic queer documentary *Paris Is Burning* (1990). Whereas even Hollywood, with its long history of censorship and "pretense to heterocentrism," was, as Alexander Doty and Ellis Hanson contend, "one of the queerest institutions ever invented" (Ellis, 1999, p. 7).

Queer studies of film—as opposed to lesbian or gay studies—have hence become particularly effective at revealing those anomalous moments in cinematic texts that not only underline the tenuousness of heteronormative moral and representational registers, but also enable much queerer modes of cinematic (dis)engagement. Films such as Ridley Scott's lesbian wish fulfillment road movie *Thelma and Louise* (1991) or the butt-slapping camp machismo of brother Tony's homoerotic opus *Top Gun* (1986) provided the surprisingly suggestive sites of sexual instability required for more queerly orientated spectators to "read-against-the-grain" of their preferred heterosexist narrative constructions. The label of "queer" was therefore invoked as a means to explain—albeit problematically—those complex linkages of **spectatorship** and textual coding that can't easily be described by, or contained within, conventional understandings and categories of sexuality and/or gender. Accordingly, queer audiences have had to develop more sophisticated critical modes of "negotiative spectatorship," so as to resist mainstream cinema's commonly oppressive and exclusionary economies by re-imagining those "horizons of possibility" (Mayne, 1993, p. 92) that eschew the film's dominant hetero-centric preoccupations. The fragility of accepted notions of cultural

signification that seek to disavow more "alternative" readings of film is thus exposed via this slippery interface between text and reader, and as a consequence proffers an intriguing challenge to their heteronormative preconditions and effects. [RG]

See also **Lesbian/Gay/Queer Cinema**.

Further reading

Butler, Judith (1990) *Gender Trouble: Feminism and the Subversion of Identity*, New York: Routledge.

de Lauretis, Teresa (1991) "Queer Theory: Lesbian and Gay Sexualities," *Differences: A Journal of Feminist Cultural Studies*, 3(2): iii–xviii.

Doty, Alexander (1993) *Making Things Perfectly Queer: Interpreting Mass Culture*, Minneapolis, MN: University of Minnesota Press.

Jagose, Annamarie (1995) *Queer Theory: An Introduction*, New York: New York University Press.

RACIAL REPRESENTATION refers to depictions of racialized or ethnic groups that are distinguished by their own history, culture, and identity. The definitions of such groups are often self-imposed but may also be imposed by others, and they are constantly open to debate. According to Ella Shohat and Robert Stam, "Racial categories are not natural but constructs, not absolutes but relative, situational, even narrative categories, engendered by historical processes of differentiation" (1994, p. 19).

Furthermore, race is distinguished by passive affiliation—the racial group into which one has been born—while ethnicity is distinguished by active affiliation—the racial group with which one aligns oneself (Shohat and Stam, 1994, p. 20). In spite of the difficulties associated with defining race and ethnicity, what can be agreed upon is that, in the American context, these terms refer to the racial diversity that exists in American life and culture and includes the depictions of groups such as African Americans, Hispanics, Native Americans, Asians, and so on, as they appear on the screen. If the struggle these various groups have endured in the cinema industry is similar, their relationship to the industry is unique. As each racial group is distinguished by its own deeply rooted history in the American cinematic experience, I will focus on one such group, African Americans, and how they have been depicted historically in film, in order to exemplify how these various racialized groups have been represented and reconstructed on screen. The historical processes of representation I describe can of course be seen at work in the construction of racial and ethnic identity in all cultures.

Cinematic representations of African Americans can be traced to the infancy of the cinema industry; however, these representations were more often than not provided by white actors appearing in black-face. Yet, as early as 1897 the Edison Film Company released two films that featured "real" blacks in productions such as *The Dancing Darkey Boy* followed by *Colored Troops Disembarking* (1898)—a film that provided footage of black soldiers marching off to the Spanish–American War. These rather short films were followed by longer dramatic productions such as *Uncle Tom's Cabin* (1903), a film based on

Harriet Beecher Stowe's popular novel and one that was so appealing that it was repeatedly remade until 1927. Despite the fact that the mainstream cinema industry included blacks, unfortunately they were caricatured in their representations as was the case with D. W. Griffith's *The Birth of a Nation* (1915)—a film that elicited a storm of protest as well as censorship difficulties because of its representations of blacks. The production depicted blacks as corrupt by showing them stuffing ballot boxes during an election; portrayed them as rapists, as when the white Flora leaps to her death after being pursued by the black Gus; and displayed blacks as incapable politicians who pass frivolous laws while eating fried chicken and drinking liquor during legislative sessions. Griffith's caricatures of blacks as violent, incompetent, laughing stocks, cowards, and so on persisted in later representations.

Yet, even before Griffith's production a generation of black filmmakers had emerged: William Foster of Chicago, for example, produced *The Railroad Porter* (1913), and later Noble and George P. Johnson, associated with the Lincoln Motion Picture Company of Omaha, produced *The Realization of a Negro's Ambition* (1916). Oscar Micheaux, one of the most prolific black filmmakers in cinema history with offices in Chicago and New York, produced *The Homesteader* (1919) to rectify the black screen image. With this production and others Micheaux attempted to provide black characters who had morals, values, ambition, and education, and who strived for higher ideals in life rather than those who conformed to the less wholesome representations popularized by the mainstream cinema industry. More importantly his characters were centered in these films and assumed the role of hero or heroine rather than being exclusively relegated to the role of villain or scoundrel. These black filmmakers represented the beginning of an independent cinema movement designed to challenge the representations that emanated from Hollywood. As ambitious as these efforts might have been, they did not deter Hollywood from producing all-black cast films as was the case with *Hallelujah* (1929) and *Hearts in Dixie* (1929)—a trend that returned in the 1940s with productions such as *Cabin in the Sky* (1943) and *Stormy Weather* (1943). These films co-existed with those released by the independent cinema movement that stood to challenge the parodic constructions popularized by Hollywood productions. Undeterred, the mainstream industry continued to explore the issue of race in productions such as *Imitation of Life* (1934), *Lost Boundaries* (1949), *Pinky* (1949), and *Home of the Brave* (1949), in, however, perfunctory or tendentious a fashion.

As Hollywood seemingly grew more liberal in its representations, so too did the black screen image—an image that frequently reflected the socio-political discourse that prevailed in America's racial politics. By the 1960s some of the first black stars—at least according to Hollywood's standards—were being constructed, but these gains were overshadowed by the more assertive and defiant images that dominated the screen because of the emergence of the Civil Rights Movement—a movement that ushered in an era of black exploitation films such as *Sweet Sweetback's Baadasssss Song* (1971), *Shaft* (1971), and *Super Fly* (1972).

The recognition that blacks were beginning to assume their rightful place in American life and culture resulted in more serious treatments of black life as in the production of *A Soldier's Story* (1984) and *The Color Purple* (1985). This trend continued in subsequent decades as black life could no longer be ignored in all of its complexity and idiosyncrasy. It was realistically or affectively represented in productions such as *Do the Right Thing* (1989), *Daughters of the Dust* (1990), and *Boyz N the Hood* (1991)—directed by Spike Lee, Julie Dash, and John Singleton, who, among others, helped spawn a new generation of African American filmmakers. In a more contemporary period, sometimes described as a postracial era, the cinema industry has witnessed a plethora of black actors—Denzel Washington, Morgan Freeman, and Halle Berry, for example—who have become crossover artists and who assume roles in films not designated as racialized roles. However, even with these gains the racial codings dominant in Hollywood films since the silent era have not entirely disappeared. [CR]

Further reading

Bogle, David (2001) *Toms, Coons, Mulattoes, Mammies, & Bucks: An Interpretive History of Blacks in American Films*, New York: Continuum [orig. 1973].

Shohat, Ella and Stam, Robert (1994) *Unthinking Eurocentrism: Multiculturalism and the Media*, London: Routledge.

Stewart, Jacqueline Najuma (2005) *Migrating to the Movies: Cinema and Black Urban Modernity*, Berkeley and Los Angeles, CA: University of California Press.

REALISM In a general sense, the term "realistic" is applied to a film whenever some aspect of the **diegetic** world it presents—the credible psychology of the characters, the idiomatic specificity of the dialogue, the use of episodic "slice-of-life" narratives, the use of actual locations and available light—corresponds to the spectator's understanding of the real world. The realistic treatment of subject matter is therefore not an objective quality but rather a subjective, culture-dependent effect. A film that seems realistic to one spectator may not seem so to another; though it may seem obvious that *The Grapes of Wrath* (John Ford, 1940) is a more realistic representation of America during the 1930s than *The Wizard of Oz* (Mervyn LeRoy, 1939), some critics might argue that the second film articulates the spirit of the period more accurately than the first. Thus, in a general sense, realism, like its parent term reality, is more or less impossible to define.

There is, however, a more specific sense in which the term realism is used in Film Studies. Realism is the term commonly used to refer to theories that value films whose effects are rooted in the singular credibility of cinematographic images and recorded sound. Though they may have different ideas about the political and aesthetic potential of these effects, Walter Benjamin, Siegfried Kracauer, and André Bazin all base their theories of cinema in the basic technology of mechanical reproduction. Rooted in his argument about photographic ontology, Bazin's aesthetic theory of realism has had perhaps the greatest influence on the discipline of Film Studies. Though best known for arguing that the **sequence shots** in the work of Jean Renoir and Orson Welles replicated the freedom of perceptual engagement that spectators have in real life, Bazin's flexible brand of realism also addresses very different manifestations: Italian **Neorealism**, the work of **auteurs** such as Charles Chaplin, Luis Buñuel, and Robert Bresson, the Western genre, the face of Humphrey Bogart, and so on. In all these varied examples, Bazin argues that the cinematic style is effective because it is built around the spectator's irrational belief that the image has a special connection with the real world and, because the spectator's engagements with the image are in some sense more *active*, more comparable to his or her engagements with real life. [PY]

Further reading

Bazin, André (1967) *What Is Cinema?*, vol. 1, Berkeley, CA: University of California Press.
Kracauer, Siegfried (1997) *Theory of Film: The Redemption of Physical Reality*, Princeton, NJ: Princeton University Press.

REALITY TELEVISION consists of unscripted artificial situations, created by producers, which are filmed according to observational documentary norms. Because the subjects are not professional actors pretending to be fictional personas, in some circumstances "documentary value" can be claimed. At one end of the "Reality TV" spectrum are game shows whose winners are determined by displays of skill or aptitude (e.g. talent contests), and only limited documentary value can be said to be involved. More clearly akin to documentary is programming at the other end of the spectrum, that is, "formatted" or "constructed" documentaries whose content is the result of arrangements made by the production team, somewhat like **Cinema Vérité**'s practice. Only the intention of the producers (titillation as in *Wife Swap*, 2003) distinguishes it from Jean Rouch's experimental exploration of inner lives. Between these two poles stands the "Reality TV game show" where the encounters match those of the formatted documentary but the audience votes a "winner" as in the game shows (e.g. *Big Brother*, first seen in the Netherlands in 1999). [BW]

See Chapter 7.

Further reading

Biressi, Anita and Nunn, Heather (2005) *Reality TV: Realism and Revelation*, London: Wallflower.

REFLEXIVITY In the most general sense, a film manifests the quality of reflexivity whenever it deliberately makes the spectator conscious of its status as a film. If the conventions that govern most fictional narrative filmmaking are designed to absorb the spectators in the reality of the events and **diegetic** world depicted, that is, to make them forget they are watching a movie, reflexivity is manifest in any purposeful element that reminds one that one is watching a

movie. Bad acting can remind the spectator that he/she is watching a movie but does not count as reflexivity because it is not purposeful, but if an actor turns to the camera and asks the spectator a question ("How do you like my acting?") this counts as a reflexive gesture. Reflexivity is closely associated with **modernism** in the cinema and is often a central feature of **avant-garde** or **experimental** cinema. Films that include quotations from other films or that have filmmaking as their subject matter are obviously reflexive (see **intertextuality**), but this quality can also be manifest in more subtle and indirect ways as when, for example, the editing implicates the spectator in the voyeuristic behavior of the James Stewart characters in Alfred Hitchcock's *Rear Window* (1954) and *Vertigo* (1958): we are forced to become conscious of the moral relations involved in film spectatorship itself. [PY]

See Chapter 3.

Further reading

Stam, Robert (1985) *Reflexivity in Film and Literature: From Don Quixote to Jean-Luc Godard*, Ann Arbor, MI: University of Michigan Press.

REVERSE-ANGLE SHOOTING (SHOT/ REVERSE SHOT) refers to a pattern of **continuity editing** frequently used in conversations or stand-offs between characters. It is, in fact, a variant of the point of view series and obeys the 180-degree rule (see Chapter 4). Character A looks off camera in shot 1; in shot 2 we see the person he or she is looking at; in shot 3 we return to character A; and so forth. In reverse-angle series, over-the-shoulder framing is common. Reverse-angle shooting appears in the early 1910s in the American cinema, but also in European cinemas of the 1920s. It becomes a dominant and enduring form in Hollywood with the advent of sound—imposing itself as the norm for shooting conversations. Some directors, even in Hollywood but particularly in modernist movements, rejected the easy psychological effects of shot/reverse shot, and tended instead to keep the camera at a distance from the characters' faces or to shoot characters with their bodies turned away from the camera in order to make their emotional states more ambiguous. (See the work of Michelangelo Antonioni, Miklos Jancsó, or Theo Angelopoulos.) Japanese director Yasujiro Ozu is well known for taking liberties with reverse-angle shooting by allowing much freer camera placement than the 180-degree rule dictates. [WG]

See Chapter 4.

SCALE OF SHOTS The terms for designating the size of shots are predicated on the distance between the camera and the actors being filmed. The *long shot* shows the full bodies of the actors and includes some of the contextual space above and below them; in the *extreme long shot* the actors are quite small in an encompassing environment. The *medium shot* includes a range from the knees-up (also called the American shot from the French term *plan américain* because of its prevalence in the classical Hollywood film) to the waist-up shot. The *close-up* isolates the human face (or an important dramatic object) from its context and varies from the medium close-up (from chest to shoulders up), to the facial close-up, to the extreme close-up (which shows only part of the actor's face). These designations come from technicians' practice and are approximate rather than precise. [WG]

See Chapter 4.

SCREEN PRACTICE A concept launched by Charles Musser to refer to the tradition of projecting luminous images on the screen. Musser used the concept to demonstrate that the idea of projecting moving pictures on a screen was not an original invention of the silent film era. It was based on a long-existing tradition involving **magic lantern** projections that were often commented on by a lecturer ("illustrated lectures" was a term used particularly in the United States). Arguably, one might suggest that shadow theater, Bänkelsang (Moritat), and other modes of visual storytelling such as moving **panorama** shows also qualify as forms of screen practice, although their relationship to cinema may have been less direct and they may not have used a "screen" in the same sense as the magic lantern and cinema projections. Erkki Huhtamo has suggested that, beside screen practice, there were two other practices that he calls "peep practice" and "touch practice." These often interact and merge with each other in the history of moving images. [EH]

See also Chapter 1 and **peepshows**.

SECOND WORLD WAR (1939–45), and the rise of extreme right-wing movements in the 1930s that led to it, was a worldwide conflict that had an enormous impact on national film industries. The war generated an unprecedented outpouring of propaganda in efforts to mobilize mass audiences in support of both the Axis powers and the Allies. All the combatant nations continued to produce escapist fiction, but also features that supported the war efforts and helped maintain public morale. Censorship by the state took on more or less virulent form in the Axis nations.

The Nazi Party ruled Germany beginning in 1933 and exercised control over the film industry, which it gradually nationalized under propaganda director Goebbels. Germany maintained the tradition of escapist fiction at the massive UFA studios (see **German Expressionism**) but the state also directly financed propaganda films—*Staatsauftragsfilme*—which extolled the German past, reviled the Jews, and glorified Hitler and his regime and its ideology (see **fascism**). In flight from the totalitarian and anti-Semitic regime, which set out in 1933 to rid the film industry of all Jews, many German and Austrian filmmakers immigrated to Hollywood (e.g. Fritz Lang, Billy Wilder, Robert Siodmak, and Max Ophuls).

Under fascist Mussolini, who came to power in 1922, Italian film production saw its first major expansion since the 1910s: the construction of the vast Cinecittà studios, rivaling those of the German UFA, and government protectionist policies and controls on distribution and exhibition made possible a flourishing entertainment industry, in particular genre films—especially stylish studio-shot romantic melodramas and comedies known as the white-telephone films. Unlike the Nazis, the Italian fascists never nationalized the film industry. The relative weakness of the regime and the policy of nonintervention in private industry allowed for a more open climate. The state's creation of the film school, the Centro Sperimentale, and the school's journal, *Bianco e nero*, promoted theoretical reflection and encouraged the emergence of a young generation of intellectuals and filmmakers interested in a naturalistic cinema (see **Neorealism**).

In Britain and the United States, documentaries contributed to the war effort. Emerging from the left documentary movement under John Grierson, filmmakers used the classic documentary style for war-time propaganda, and the poetic work of Humphrey Jennings captures the ethos of the determined British in films like *Listen to Britain* (1942) and *Fires Were Started* (1943), and the uncertainties facing the British nation at the close of the war in the innovative *Diary for Timothy* (1945). In a Hollywood mobilized in support of the war effort, Frank Capra produced a series of propaganda documentaries entitled *Why We Fight* (1942–5).

The postwar situation was desperate for war-torn worlds of Europe, the Soviet Union, Japan, and other Far Eastern countries. The United States emerged triumphant and prosperous from the war on every level and in a position to help with postwar reconstruction through the Marshall Plan. Despite the devastation, recovery in

Europe was fairly rapid. However, the Soviet occupation of Eastern Europe and half of Germany established the boundaries of the Iron Curtain countries where the Soviet Union imposed the censorship structures and aesthetics of **Socialist Realism**. The **Cold War** was already developing in the midst of the Second World War, and the North Atlantic Treaty Organization formed in 1948. In Japan the American Occupation under Douglas MacArthur imposed censorship measures and encouraged development of the film industry. The Chinese Revolution of 1949 brought the Communists to power. The war was followed by strong independence movements in the colonized world, supported by the movements known as **Third World Cinema**.

Two events of the war would have a deep and lasting impact on all spheres of culture: the revelation of the Nazi extermination camps and the American atomic devastation at Hiroshima and Nagasaki. One finds reflections of these events in popular culture (some critics see postwar **film noir** as permeated by atomic anxiety). After a period of silence, the art cinema and documentary began to represent the horrors of the camps and Hiroshima (e.g. Alain Resnais's *Night and Fog*, 1955, and *Hiroshima mon amour*, 1959). A new kind of investigative documentary sought out living witnesses to genocide, perpetrators, and victims (e.g. Marcel Ophuls's *The Sorrow and the Pity*, 1969, about collaboration in France during the Occupation, and Claude Lanzmann's monumental *Shoah*, 1985). The Second World War provided and continues to provide material for countless fiction films, most of which tend to eschew historical documentation and erase public memory of events in favor of clichéd representations. [WG]

SEMIOTICS/SEMIOLOGY A field of study that examines how language and other sign systems create meaning. First developed in the late nineteenth and early twentieth centuries by the American philosopher Charles Sanders Pierce and the Swiss linguist Ferdinand de Saussure, the science of signs they proposed, particularly Saussure's, greatly influenced the theoretical paradigms that emerged in a number of disciplines in the mid-twentieth century, including literary and cultural studies, linguistics, sociology, anthropology, psychoanalysis, and film theory. In Saussure's semiology, the sign is comprised of two elements, the signifier (the written or spoken word), and the signified (the idea that word evokes in the mind). Saussure argued that the relationship between the signifier and the signified is entirely arbitrary, that is, it is the product of cultural convention. These signs function within a language system governed by rules that order the production of meaning. Signs only become meaningful in a dynamic of difference in which they distinguish themselves by what they are not, that is, other signs operating in the system. This notion of signs functioning differentially in a closed system that operates according to its own internal rules became a founding concept in the development of Structuralist thought. (For a discussion of film semiotics, see **film language**.) [RS]

Further reading

Metz, Christian (1981) *The Imaginary Signifier: Psychoanalysis and the Cinema*, Bloomington, IN: Indiana University Press.

Metz, Christian (1990) *Film Language: A Semiotics of the Cinema*, Chicago: University of Chicago Press.

Silverman, Kaja (1983) *The Subject of Semiotics*, New York: Oxford University Press.

SEQUENCES, TYPES OF A sequence (*syntagma* or *segment* in the vocabulary of semiology) is generally understood to mean a series of shots that are intended to be read together as an episode of the plot in narrative films. (Note that, in critical practice, "scene" and "sequence" are often used interchangeably. We have opted for retaining the distinction between the two terms, as defined below.)

There have been many attempts to construct a typology of sequences; the most notable is Christian Metz's Large Syntagmatic Category of the Image Track (*Film Language*, 1990), which classifies segments in the classical narrative cinema. Models of sequential ordering have, however, been tested in film analysis and often contested because they are not universally applicable. At best one finds some agreement on sequence structure in the Hollywood films of the classical era between 1914 and 1940. Such models often fail to account for sequence structure in films from other periods and other cultural traditions. Documentary and experimental films pose further problems of segmentation.

It seems reasonable, however, to retain the most common types of sequential construction on the classical model:

1 Sequence shot. (See separate entry.)
2 Elliptical sequence. A series of shots, constituting an episode of the plot in narrative films, skips over presumably unimportant moments. Elliptical sequences are used to condense the time of an event and increase the speed of narration. For example, a 2-minute sequence of shots of a car moving across the screen in changing landscapes may represent a 300-mile trip. Many elliptical sequences condense time less radically, that is, are less discontinuous. The continuity in elliptical sequences is usually assured by **matches** on screen direction or the unity of the space within which the sequence takes place. Thus a woman returning to her apartment may be presented elliptically as a series of excerpts (she meets a neighbor on the stairs, puts down her packages to rest, etc.) as long as she continues to ascend the stairs in the same recognizable locale.
3 Scene. A series of shots that represent a continuous development in time, as in the theatrical scene. Thus we understand the action as having no elliptical breaks, even though this continuity is presented by multiple shots (see **analytical editing**).
4 Cross-cut sequence (parallel editing). An alternation of shots represents two or more separate aspects of the action that are occurring more or less simultaneously and are usually described by the pattern a/b/a/b. (See separate entry: **crosscutting**.)
5 Descriptive sequence. A series of shots that does not represent an action but serves rather to describe the place where an action will take

place. In classical filmmaking, descriptive sequences often occur at the beginning of a film. The first shots of Hitchcock's *Psycho*, for example, give us successive views of Phoenix, Arizona, as the camera swoops closer and closer to the window of a hotel room where the film's action begins.

6   Montage sequence (episodic sequence). Brief scenes that lack development are edited together (often linked by **transitional devices** such as dissolves or swish pans) in order to condense a lengthy action. Welles used montage sequences—what he called "lightning mixes"—in *Citizen Kane* to abridge dramatic developments, for example in the celebrated "breakfast scenes" that describe Kane's disintegrating marriage to his first wife Emily.

7   Associational editing. A sequence of shots that have no apparent relationship in narrative time and space but relate to each other in a symbolic fashion. Most often the shots form a pattern of alternation (a/b/a/b/a/b) that is based in a contrast or comparison. In D. W. Griffith's *A Corner in Wheat* (1909) or in many films of the **Soviet Montage Movement**, the contrast is between the lives of the poor as opposed to the lives of the rich. Sergei Eisenstein's theory of *intellectual montage* proposed a sophisticated kind of associational editing that would give film the flexibility of verbal language (see **film language**). Whence his aspiration to film Karl Marx's *Das Kapital* (1867). [WG]

See Chapter 4.

SEQUENCE SHOT First coined by André Bazin in discussing the work of Orson Welles, the sequence shot is generally understood to be a lengthy shot that includes a coherent unit of narrative action, that is, a scene, in a single unbroken take. Due to the fact that the movement of events and figures during many dramatic scenes would place them outside the range of focus of a fixed camera position, sequence shots often involve **deep focus**, staging in multiple planes, and camera movements that follow the action. This combination of techniques first originated in the work of Jean Renoir during the 1930s, but has since been used often in the international **art cinema**, in the work of filmmakers such as Andrei Tarkovsky, Miklós Jancsó, and Béla Tarr. André Bazin, the most famous proponent of realist film theory, argued that sequence shots provide the spectator with an experience that is more closely analogous to visual experience in real life. [PY]

SILENT CINEMA is a term applied (retrospectively) to the long period of filmmaking from 1895 to the advent of sound in the late 1920s. The term covers extended historical developments, such as **early cinema**, and the emergence and consolidation of the **Classical Hollywood film**; **national cinemas**, embodied, for example, in the Italian spectacle films or the German Autorenfilm based on the work of famous authors; and a great diversity of movements and styles, such as **French Impressionism, German Expressionism**, and the **Soviet Montage Movement**.

The word "silent" is not entirely accurate, since there was almost always sound produced during the projection of a silent film: a live lecturer might give a running commentary on the film, a pianist would select pieces from his repertoire to accompany the action on screen, and certain sound effects might be produced. A musical score, written for full orchestra, was sometimes created for prestige productions like D. W. Griffith's *The Birth of a Nation* (1915). Feature films after 1911, with their longer running times, their multiplicity of shots, more elaborate **mise-en-scène**, and extended storytelling, were increasingly accompanied by more sophisticated sound and music. (See Chapter 5.)

It is nonetheless true that the cinema before 1927 was silent in an important way: it was incapable of furnishing synchronized dialogue, which was the natural medium of expression in theater. Many theorists contend that the lack of the spoken word instigated a search among early filmmakers for substitutes for language and that the silent cinema developed its own modes of expression to compensate for this lack. It is important to retain three major expressive features in silent films. (1) Silent films relied on a system of gestures and mime, which became subtler as filmmakers began to position the camera closer to the actors, but persisted nonetheless until the advent of sound. (2) The silent cinema posited the ideal of expressing everything through the image (and, as a corollary, avoiding the too-frequent recourse to **intertitles**, which provided dialogue or narration but interrupted the flow of images). (3) It developed a system of expressive **editing** that helped make the meaning of the succession of shots evident to the spectator. [ML and WG]

Further reading

Aumont, Jacques, *et al.* (1992) "Film as Audiovisual Representation," in *Aesthetics of Film*, Austin, TX: University of Texas Press.

SOCIALIST REALISM A rigid aesthetic and political doctrine that dominated film production in the Soviet Union during the rule of Joseph Stalin (1927–53) and after. Socialist realism was imposed by Soviet policy under the dictate of hardened bureaucrats. At the sixteenth Party Congress in 1928, Stalin established state control of the arts: "The cinema is the greatest medium of mass agitation. The task is to take it into our hands."

The basic propositions of Socialist Realism include the following: (1) The proletarian revolution needs to produce a new cultural worker whose task is to ally himself with the Communist Party and reflect in art the realities of a socialist society. (2) Art must take on a didactic purpose: to address the masses, to exalt the revolutionary tradition, and to participate in the construction of a new socialist man. (3) Art should therefore produce exemplary narratives and characters that typify Soviet ideals. (4) Socialist art must combat **formalism** (any complex or modernist style), the decadent art of the bourgeoisie of the West, and the bourgeois notion of artistic freedom.

Soviet bureaucrats sought to ferret out formalist tendencies contaminating art in the Soviet Union through the political criticism of filmmakers, which functioned as part of the system of Stalinist purges. The first victims of political attacks were members of the **Soviet Montage School**, Sergei Eisenstein in particular. Filmmakers were forced to acknowledge their errors and recant. The Soviet film industry imposed a program of censorship that controlled production in the interest of political correctness: scripts were subject to repeated review before approval was granted; the shooting of a film could be halted at any time; and a finished film could be denied distribution and shelved indefinitely.

In the wake of World War II and Soviet occupation of Eastern Europe, state control of the arts and censorship were extended to the whole Soviet bloc. Film production was nationalized and Socialist Realism adopted as regimes' official aesthetic. Film schools were established in most East European countries on the model of the VGIK, the highly respected Moscow Film School. A similar process of nationalism and state control of film production took place after the Chinese communist revolution (1949). Chinese filmmakers were obliged to adopt Socialist Realist principles and to take the Soviet production system as a model.

Periods of cultural repression in the communist world were broken at times by periods of relaxed censorship known as thaws. The first began after Stalin's death (1953) when Nikita Khrushchev denounced Stalin's despotic regime at the Twentieth Party Congress (1956) and, without repudiating Socialist Realism, called for a more moderate approach to cultural politics. The thaws allowed a new generation of filmmakers and new national cinemas to emerge beginning in the late 1950s and 1960s. Ironically, these movements originated in the film schools the Stalinist state had established: the VGIK in the Soviet Union, the Lódz school in Poland, the FAMU in Czechoslovakia, and the Budapest Academy in Hungary.

Thus the Soviet bloc produced a new generation of filmmakers who had undergone rigorous training in all aspects of film production and had been exposed to a broad film culture denied the general public. They rejected the doctrine of Socialist Realism, not through a cinema of direct political opposition, but by reclaiming their freedom of expression. (See **New Waves and New Cinemas**.) [WG]

Further reading

Taylor, Richard (1983) "A 'Cinema for Millions': Soviet Socialist Realism and the Problem of Film Comedy," *Journal of Contemporary History*, 18: 439–61.
Taylor, Richard (1986) "Boris Shumyatsky and the Soviet Cinema in the 1930s: Ideology in Mass Entertainment," *Historical Journal of Film, Radio and Television*, 6 (1): 43–64.

SOUND Sound, in its generic definition, refers to the presence of dialogue, music, and/or sound effects in a motion picture. More specifically, it can define how the sound functions in the film in relation to the image. Sound is often described in terms of its acoustic characteristics such as loudness, pitch, and timbre. Loudness is commonly referred to as the volume of a sound, and the range of volumes in a recording is its dynamic range. Pitch is the perceived highness or lowness of a given sound, while timbre is its textural quality. Even though these three terms borrow from musical terminology and can be useful in describing many types of sounds, they cannot explain all the characteristics of how sound functions in cinema. Specifically, a sound occurs in a particular space and takes on spatial characteristics known as reverberation. This is why sounds made in a small room or in a large auditorium are perceived differently.

But perhaps the main way that sound is described in motion pictures is in relation to the image. Sounds can be **on-screen** when a source for the sound is indicated in the image (such as a mouth moving synchronously with dialogue), or **off-screen** if the sound's source is presumed to be outside of the frame line. A more complex relationship between sound and image occurs in the distinction between **diegetic** and *nondiegetic* sounds. Diegetic sounds are those that are present in and realistic to the world of the film. For example, the sounds of waves and crashing surf may be diegetic for a film set on a beach, but they would be heard as nondiegetic if played over images of a desert. However, if the camera were to pan to reveal that the desert was next to an ocean, sounds that were initially perceived as nondiegetic would be understood retrospectively as diegetic and off-screen. Nondiegetic dialogue is usually called **voice-over** because it is presumed to be separate from the diegetic world of the images. Diegetic **music** is usually called source music

whereas nondiegetic music is called score music. [JB]

See Chapter 5.

Further reading

Bordwell, David and Thompson, Kristin (2008) "Sound in the Cinema," in *Film Art: An Introduction*, 8th edn., New York: McGraw-Hill.
Chion, Michel (1994) *Audio-Vision: Sound on Screen*, ed. and trans. Claudia Gorbman, New York: Columbia University Press.

SOUND-ON-DISK/SOUND-ON-FILM (OPTICAL SOUND)/MAGNETIC SOUND Concurrent with the creation of the Orthophonic Victrola, an electrically amplified turntable, engineers at Bell Laboratories developed the Vitaphone sound system that recorded sounds onto a 33 1/3 rpm, 16-inch disk. Each disk allowed for 10 minutes of recording time, which was the time needed to maintain synchronous playback with a 10-minute reel of film. The Vitaphone sound-on-disk system was the first viable sound synchronization technique in commercial cinema when it was introduced by Warner Bros. studios in 1926. It was challenged, however, with the appearance of Fox's Movietone and RKO's Photophone sound-on-film systems in 1927 and 1928, respectively. Each system used light valve technology to record the sound waves as an optical soundtrack of visual wave oscillations on the film alongside the image. These visual oscillations could subsequently be converted back into sound when the print passed over a photo-electric cell. In the case of the Movietone system, the sound was a variable-density recording, whereas the Photophone system used a form of variable-area recording. Although both provided acceptable sound quality, and much greater stability than the Vitaphone disk system, it was decided in 1939 that the variable-area system would become an industry-wide standard for 35-mm film sound.

After the commercialization of magnetic recording by the Ampex Corporation in the late 1940s, magnetic sound reproduction was introduced to cinema in the early 1950s. This first occurred with the 7-track sound system designed for Cinerama presentations. The tracks were recorded on a filmstrip coated with magnetic recording material that was played in interlock with the system's three film projectors. The sixth track was mixed in postproduction as an ambient **surround channel** and the seventh channel functioned as a control track. A year later 20th Century Fox studios debuted their CinemaScope widescreen system that featured four tracks of sound recorded on four magnetic stripes on the edge of the 35-mm film. Neither Cinerama nor CinemaScope included an optical soundtrack so they both required exhibitors to invest in new sound equipment. Although these magnetic sound systems were impressive and included **multichannel sound**, the prints were very expensive and wore out quickly. By the end of the 1950s, most exhibitors had returned to playing monophonic optical prints and stereo optical sound is still included on most commercial prints today along with **digital sound** formats. [JB]

See Chapter 5.

Further reading

Belton, John (1992) "1950s Magnetic Sound: The Frozen Revolution," in Rick Altman (ed.) *Sound Theory, Sound Practice*, New York: Routledge.

Koszarski, Richard (1989) "On the Record: Seeing and Hearing the Vitaphone," in Mary Lea Bandy (ed.) *The Dawn of Sound*, New York: The Museum of Modern Art.

SOVIET MONTAGE MOVEMENT The Soviet Montage Movement developed in the wake of the Russian Revolution of 1917 and reached its peak of development during the 1920s. The aesthetic principles that became prominent in Soviet filmmaking during this period were the product of several distinct factors: the influence of the work of D. W. Griffith, especially regarding the power of editing; traditions of modernism in the traditional high arts, especially the movement known as Russian **Futurism**; and the necessity of producing a type of art appropriate to a Communist society. The famous experiments of the filmmaker and film-school teacher Lev Kuleshov are a crucial part of the movement's "myth of origins"; by editing the same close-up of the actor Mosjoukine together with three different reverse-angle shots (of a plate of soup, a dead woman in a coffin, and a child playing), he discovered that the spectator's impression of the actor's performance seemed to change accordingly (i.e. from a portrayal of hunger, to sorrow, to tender affection). The conclusion that Kuleshov and his students drew from such experiments is that the meaning of events on film is not in the elements of profilmic reality depicted (i.e. Mosjoukine's face or a dead woman) but is rather a function of how those elements are edited together (i.e. Mosjoukine's face + dead woman in a coffin = "sorrow"). From this common starting point the styles and ideas of the major directors of the movement such as Sergei Eisenstein, Vsevolod Pudovkin, Alexander Dovzhenko, and Dziga Vertov developed in different directions. Though to the contemporary spectator their films might seem very similar—they all depend equally on the power of rapid, complex editing and dynamic visual compositions—at the time their differences were often the focus of intense and heated debates. Many of the major directors of the movement exerted an influence on younger filmmakers through their work as teachers, and the writings of Eisenstein, Pudovkin, and Vertov have had a lasting impact on subsequent film theory. Key films of the movement include *Battleship Potemkin* (Eisenstein, 1925), *Mother* (Pudovkin, 1926), *The Man with a Movie Camera* (Vertov, 1929), and *Earth* (Dovzhenko, 1930). [PY]

See Chapter 3.

Further reading

Eisenstein, Sergei (1957) *The Film Form and the Film Sense*, New York: Meridian Books.

Gillespie, David (2000) *Early Soviet Cinema: Innovation, Ideology and Propaganda*, London: Wallflower.

SPECTATOR is a term derived from the Latin verb *specere*, meaning "to look at." Research about the cinematic spectator (or spectator studies) was concerned, however, not with actual audiences, but with the ways in which an ideal spectator was inscribed and positioned within the film text and through the cinematic apparatus (the viewing conditions—dark room, immobilized audience, large screen, flickering lights, etc.—in which the film was shown). Scholars like Jean-Louis Baudry, Raymond Bellour, and Christian Metz, as well as the feminist Laura Mulvey, drew upon **psychoanalysis** to hypothesize the essentially oedipal nature of the cinematic spectator and his pleasures, in particular the voyeuristic mechanisms whereby the spectator identifies with the camera gaze. Feminist film theorists such as Tania Modleski (1988), Mary Ann Doane (1991), and Elizabeth Cowie (1997) countered the notion of a monolithic Oedipalized spectator with analyses that focused on pre-oedipal structures, such as masochism, narcissism, and fantasy. With the waning of psychoanalysis as the dominant theoretical paradigm in Film Studies, as well as the proliferation of new viewing conditions (the VCR, the DVD player, and various digital technologies), spectator studies have moved beyond textual analysis to include other forms of audience studies, such as ethnography. In tandem, an area called *dispositif* studies has emerged that examines the mechanisms whereby new viewing conditions produce new kinds of viewing pleasures. [HR]

Further reading

Campbell, Jan (2005) *Film and Cinema Spectatorship: Melodrama and Mimesis*, Oxford: Polity.

Rosen, Philip (ed.) (1986) *Narrative, Apparatus, Ideology: A Film Theory*

Reader, New York: Columbia University Press.

STAR SYSTEM The star system of Classical Hollywood cinema refers to the method of creating and promoting film stars in order to enhance and exploit their box-office appeal. Characteristically, a studio would discover an emerging actor with talent, and mold a carefully crafted persona for him or her through a number of strategies, including the supply and dissemination of carefully controlled information and the sculpting of his or her physical appearance—as in the case of Lana Turner, who, under the tutelage of the producer–director Mervyn LeRoy, changed her name, dyed her hair blonde, shaved off her eyebrows, and adopted a wholly fictitious personal history. The personae created for stars usually conformed to a type, such as the vamp (first embodied by Theda Bara, born Theodosia Burr Goodman), presented by Fox's publicity department as an Arab siren; the suave lover, as exemplified by Cary Grant (born Arthur Leach); or the seductive blonde, immortalized by Marilyn Monroe (born Norma Jeane Mortenson). Once their persona was established, stars would be typecast in one movie after another.

The elevation of stars to the status of eroticized and fetishized icons was greatly assisted by the cinematic styles and techniques of **Classical Hollywood Cinema**, which insured the star's prominence in almost every scene: the inclusion of the film's protagonist in a majority of the film's shots; the isolation of him or her in the center of the frame to be admired and gazed upon; the use of close-up shots, accompanied by sculpted low-key **lighting** softened with gels and gauzes; and the dressing of the star in glamorous clothing. Such packaging and presentation meant that stars like Mary Pickford and Rudolf Valentino became adored with a fervor unprecedented in the history of entertainment. One consequence of this system was the advent of fan magazines, such as *Motion Picture Story Magazine* and *Photoplay*, which published photos, interviews, behind-the-scenes stories, and movie plot summaries (all carefully controlled by the studio to which the star was contracted) to satisfy the insatiable curiosity generated about stars.

The star system of Classical Hollywood began to decline when stars began to become selective about the roles they were prepared to undertake, and the increasing intrusion of the news media began to erode the mystique and mythologizing that the studios had attempted to manufacture. Stars were unsatisfied with the meager salaries (compared to those earned by top stars today) and quite rightly thought that they could command higher prices; however, they also sought to control their own careers in terms of their choice of roles, to the point of directing and producing films themselves. In post-Paramount Hollywood (see **studio system**), as the power of the studios declined, that of the stars continued to grow—or at least that of certain stars. Stars no longer enjoyed the stability and support that a studio provided to its stable of actors and actresses. Success came quickly—or not at all. New Hollywood was particularly harsh in its treatment of actors and actresses working in supporting roles, for whom the studios had provided a source of reliable employment and the security and time to develop their craft.

Today, a star system persists but it lies largely under the control of talent agencies such as MCA, PR firms, and the stars themselves. The greater access of journalists to the private lives of stars means that the former division between their on-screen and off-screen existences can no longer be maintained, with the result that stars, in spite of their higher salaries and clout within the entertainment world, no longer have the Olympian, larger than life status that they enjoyed under the Hollywood star system. [HR]

See Chapter 2.

Further reading

Fisher, Lucy and Landy, Marsha (2004) *Stars: The Film Reader*, New York: Routledge.
Gledhill, Christine (1991) *Stardom: Industry of Desire*, New York: Routledge.
McDonald, Paul (2000) *The Star System: Hollywood's Production of Popular Identities*, London: Wallflower.

STUDIO SYSTEM The studio system refers to the industrial organization of film production, distribution, and exhibition that characterized **Classical Hollywood**. This was a **vertically integrated** system (see **horizontal/vertical integration**) in which a few studios, called the Majors, controlled the industry, relying on a system of division of labor and standardized production (known as the Classical Hollywood style). As a result of the Paramount Decree of 1948, the studio system was dismantled. Even before the Paramount Decree, the studio system was in decline, with fewer and fewer people attending movie theaters. A number of factors contributed to this decline including middle-class Americans' move from the urban areas to the suburbs, the attendant rise of other leisure activities associated with a suburban lifestyle (including television—but also participant sports, gardening, home renovation, etc.) that competed with cinema-going, and finally the rising cost of motion pictures themselves. While some of the major studios continue to be active in the film industry today, they function largely as financial backers and distributors, with directors, stars, and agents having a much greater decision-making role in terms of individual projects than they did under the studio system. [HR]

See Chapter 2.

Further reading

Anderson, Christopher (1994) *Hollywood TV: The Studio System in the Fifties*, Austin, TX: University of Texas Press.
Balio, Tino (1976) *The American Film Industry*, Madison, WI: University of Wisconsin Press.
Gomery, Douglas (1986) *The Hollywood Studio System*, New York: St. Martin's Press.
Schatz, Thomas (1988) *The Genius of the System: Hollywood Filmmaking in the Studio Era*, New York: Pantheon Books.

STYLE Style refers to the particular expressiveness of a work, of a filmmaker, or of a group of films. Style concerns form rather than content and is based on a notion of difference: how is the style of a certain filmmaker, or the style of a film movement, or the style of a particular film, a departure from the accepted norms of filmmaking in a given cultural and historical context? Thus a style may be personal to a filmmaker, who asserts his or her freedom from conventions and purposely transgresses against certain dominant codes and conventions of filmmaking (see **auteur**). In the style developed by Hong Kong filmmaker Wong Kar Wai with his cinematographer and set designer, for example, the extended shots of places are a departure from the norm of the *establishing shots* in the Hollywood tradition, because they evoke atmosphere and metaphor more than physical space (the notion of *kongjing* in Chinese). Style may also be collective and define the expressive characteristics of a movement: the style of **French Impressionism**, based on the transformative power of the cinematic image, or **Direct Cinema**, whose stylistic features arose from new lightweight cameras and recording technology. It may also refer to periods of filmmaking, even quite lengthy ones, on the model of art history's description of styles such as baroque or classical. Paradoxically, style in this sense describes a historical and cultural period in which a given set of stylistic norms becomes established, even dominant. For example, the Hollywood style, as described by film scholars Bordwell, Staiger, and Thompson (1985), is a set of pervasive stylistic norms that came to dominate production internationally for several decades. One can also describe stylistic influences that are more circumscribed or jump across periods in film

history. For example, the influence of Orson Welles' and Gregg Toland's **deep focus cinematography** on American films of the 1950s, the influence of Italian filmmaker Roberto Rossellini's **dedramatized** style on the emergence of **modern cinema**, or the more contemporary reemergence in American films of stylistic elements of **film noir**. [WG]

Further reading

Bordwell, David (1997) *On the History of Film Style*, Cambridge, MA: Harvard University Press.

SUBJECTIVE SHOTS A shot presents a specific point of view in space and time. Most shots are understood as objective ("nobody's shots"): they are simply given to be seen without the look they imply belonging to anyone in particular. Subjective shots indicate we are seeing (and hearing) from the point of view of either the film's author or narrator or one of the characters. The narrator takes possession of the shot through an expressiveness that calls attention to itself. Experimental films are full of "poetic" techniques—unusual framings and angles, "expressionist" use of light and shadow or color, unusual relationships between image and sound, and so forth—that suggest the "presence" of the film's author. (See **Soviet Montage Movement**, **French Impressionism**, and **German Expressionism**.) However, even in commercial cinema, such practices exist, albeit less frequently. In *Vertigo*, for example, a forward tracking shot expressing impulsive desire propels the camera across the floor of a San Francisco restaurant toward the seductive Kim Novak, but the point of view doesn't belong to the soon-to-be obsessed James Stewart, but to the implied author, "Hitchcock."

More frequently subjective shots belong to a character. In the technique of the eye-line match, for example, a series of shots establish the subjectivity of the look: a first shot of a character looking off-screen is followed by a second shot representing what he or she is looking at in the immediate off-screen space (see **point of view**). In this case, we the audience are sharing the point of view of the character, a technique that tends to increase our identification with the character. Similarly, a panning shot may suggest a character's observation of a scene, or a handheld camera may suggest a character's walking movement. In the silent era in particular, images distorted by camera angle, blurred focus, superimpositions, and so forth were used to suggest a character's dream, fantasy, madness, or altered states of consciousness. [WG]

SURREALISM A term coined by French poet Guillaume Apollinaire and later adopted by the avant-garde intellectuals and artists who gathered around the writer André Breton, a leading figure of the movement. Emerging in France in the 1920s, Surrealism sought to tap the powers of the unconscious mind in order to release mental and artistic life from the strictures of rational thought. The Surrealists favored the use of montage and developed the notion of automatic writing, a creative practice that encourages the free flow of words

and imagery expressed in a state of semi-consciousness. Interpretation of the startlingly incongruent associations and illogical forms generated in this process were thought to yield a higher understanding of the world, one that was truer to life than that revealed in the realist art the Surrealists spurned. The Spanish director Luis Buñuel, who made films in Spain, France, and Mexico, is best known for introducing surrealist concepts and the movement's aesthetic vision in the cinema, most notably in *Un Chien Andalou* (1929), a work in which he collaborated with surrealist painter Salvador Dali, and in *L'âge d'or* (1930). Buñuel's taste for provocation in the latter film, which assailed the ideological and moral constraints of bourgeois society, earned him the wrath of conservative forces in France, where in December 1930 the film was banned, seized by the police, and withheld from release for decades. [RS]

Further reading

Breton, André (1969) *Manifestos of Surrealism*, Ann Arbor, MI: University of Michigan Press.
Durozoi, Gérard (2004) *History of the Surrealist Movement*, Chicago: University of Chicago Press.

SURROUND SOUND/MULTICHANNEL SOUND
With the development of widescreen technologies in the 1950s came the birth of multichannel sound systems. These were technologies for reproducing sounds in a theater from a number of different speaker locations that allowed the placement of sounds across the plane of the image and into the theater. The speakers located along

the sides and back of an auditorium were called surround speakers because of their ability to surround an audience with sound. Although the technology behind multichannel sound in the 1950s was not used regularly in the 1960s, the creation of Dolby Stereo in the 1970s re-initiated an era of surround sound presentations that continues in the multiple **digital sound** systems for theaters and home use. [JB]

See Chapter 5.

Further reading

Holman, Tomlinson (2007) *Surround Sound: Up and Running*, 2nd edn., Burlington, MA: Focal Press.

Sergi, Gianluca (2005) *The Dolby Era: Film Sound in Contemporary Hollywood*, Manchester, UK: Manchester University Press.

SUSPENSE AND SURPRISE Suspense has been associated with certain directors (Alfred Hitchcock, "master of suspense") and certain **genre**s (the thriller), but it is also a basic spectator response to the unfolding of most narratives. In its heightened form, suspense results from the spectator's identification with a character in danger (whether or not the character is the hero). In Hitchcock's *Sabotage* (1936), the spectator follows with increasing anxiety the young, retarded Stevie, who has been asked to deliver a package somewhere in London that is, unbeknownst to him, a time bomb, and who is distracted from his mission by various circumstances. Spectator awareness of the situation and its danger is a crucial element in suspense as

is the spectator's desire for a positive outcome (whence the audience's negative response in *Sabotage* to Stevie's death on a crowded bus). One of the principal features of suspense, then, is the dilation of time: while maintaining its intensity, the film delays the outcome of the action. With surprise, on the other hand, the spectator is unaware of an impending event that will in fact violate what he or she expects to happen. The spectator's experience is one of shock. Although the event is unanticipated, in the well-plotted film it should not appear gratuitous but justified by foreshadowing. Surprise often constitutes a moment of narrative reversal: because of this event the plot takes a significant turn. (The unexpected murder of Sonny Corleone in *The Godfather* changes the balance of power between rival families and therefore the course of the plot.) The interplay between suspense and surprise is often taken as one of the hallmarks of successful plotting. [WG]

See Chapter 4.

Further reading

Truffaut, François (1983) *Hitchcock*, New York: Simon & Schuster.

SYNCHRONOUS SOUND/ASYNCHRONOUS SOUND With the transition to sound in the late 1920s and early 1930s, filmmakers had to consider how they were going to apply sounds to cinema. The obvious model was synchronous sound, which had been the goal of film technicians since the origins of cinema. Most of the first sound films worked toward the technical mastery of synchronizing sound and image, especially the spoken word. Although this was impressive from a technical standpoint, it was often very uninteresting cinematically. Several early sound shorts featured synchronous musical performances and some spoken elements, but with a stationary camera and a theatrical presentation style, these films contrasted sharply with previous film styles.

Due to the refined nature of late silent cinema, many filmmakers found synchronous sound to be redundant and called for the use of asynchronous sound. In particular, a number of **Soviet Montage** directors felt that by using sound in juxtaposition to the images—a technique often known as counterpoint—sound could be used more creatively and cinema could become more forceful as a medium. In theory, sounds themselves could be used as elements of montage with meaning generated in the relationship between one sound element and the next, as well as with the image. Although this came to fruition in some of the early Soviet sound films, such as Dziga Vertov's *Enthusiasm* (1930), most early Soviet sound cinema featured synchronous or semi-synchronous sound. In practice, however, the concept of asynchronous sound can be heard in a number of European films from the transition period.

One of the prime proponents of creative sound and image relations was René Clair. In 1929, Clair praised the use of **off-screen** sounds in MGM's *The Broadway Melody* and, at the same time, Alfred Hitchcock was using off-screen sounds and subjective sounds in *Blackmail*. This prompted Clair to set up creative relationships between sound and image, developing new sound techniques. In his first sound film, *Sous les toits de Paris* (1930), Clair would often shift between sound and image to let one or the other advance the narrative. His main goal was to avoid the redundancy present in many of the early sound films. *Sous les toits de Paris* had both synchronous passages, especially music, but included several scenes where either sound or image is dominant. This technique, while not immediately successful, is still used quite often today, especially when we hear sounds that are not directly synchronized to an **on-screen** source. [JB]

See Chapter 5.

Further reading

Eisenstein, S. M., Pudovkin, V. I., and Alexandrov, G. V. [1927] "A Statement"; Pudovkin, V. I. [1929] "Asynchronism as a Principle of Sound Film"; Clair, René [1929] "The Art of Sound"; all in Elisabeth Weis and John Belton (eds.) (1985) *Film Sound—Theory and Practice*, New York: Columbia University Press.

TAKE In the shooting process, a take refers to the continuous filming of a shot and may be followed by one or more retakes if the first is not successful. The take is distinguished from the shot, which is the unit between two cuts that appears in the finished film. An exception to this distinction is the **long take**, which refers to a shot of long duration as it appears in the film. A *long take* should be distinguished from a *long shot*, which refers to the spatial relationship between the camera and the subject of the shot it records. (See **scale of shots**.) [WG]

THEATER The emergence of film as art has traditionally been cast as a struggle against the theatrical. In this view, innovators, notably D. W. Griffith, invented a new film language in order to rescue the cinema from the slavish imitation of theatrical techniques of representation. As film historians over the past 30 years have shown, the historical relationship between theater and film is much more complex.

First, one has to distinguish between different types of theatricality. In very **early cinema** (1890s–1907), it was popular forms of entertainment—**magic lantern** shows, spectacles of illusionism, vaudeville—that were influential on film. Georges Méliès, for example, who had incorporated magic lantern projections into his spectacles at the Théâtre Robert Oudin in Paris, recognized the illusionist possibilities of motion pictures. He exploited the filmic techniques of stop-action cinematography and superimposition of images to create *spectacles féeriques* (visual fantasies). Vaudeville exhibition of films dominated in the United States until at least 1905, and vaudeville's format—a series of unrelated acts—required short films where narrative development was limited. Moreover, films for the vaudeville circuit were often nontheatrical in form. Actualities—the documentary films pioneered by the Lumière brothers—were very popular on the circuit, and their plein-air shooting explains in part why in short narrative films of the period, like Edwin Porter's *The Great Train Robbery* (1903), there is such a contrast between the theatricality of the interior shots and the more realistic exterior shots with their freer placement of the camera.

In this period, certain conventions of theatrical representation are preserved: the sense of presence of the proscenium, the nonexistent fourth wall that opens the scene to the spectator; the camera's placement, which is both frontal (centered and perpendicular to the set) and relatively distant from the actors (leaving considerable space above their heads); the more or less frontal positions of actors who turn their bodies toward the audience (camera); constructed, light theatrical sets in interiors; and the tendency to preserve the dramatic unit of the scene (see Chapter 4).

The second type of theatricality to influence cinema was the dramatic or "legitimate" theater. This influence is generally understood to arise from the desire to make longer films that could rival the coherent narrative of the stage play and attract a more affluent audience (although there is considerable scholarly debate on the class character of audiences in the different venues of early cinema). Particularly important was the dramatic film's reliance on developed characters and on narrative as a sequence of motivated action (see **narrative order** and **motivation**). Dramatic films, with their closely linked scenes, would replace the earlier cinema's practice of presenting, in fragmented form, peak moments extracted from popular plays.

The dramatic film emerged around 1908 in France with the Film d'Art's production of *L'Assassinat du duc de*

253

Guise. The Film d'Art employed actors from the legitimate theater, established conventions of theatrical performance (close to pantomime), and included verbal narration and dialogue in the form of **intertitles**. It has been argued that the Film d'Art failed because it was ultimately incapable of providing a satisfying equivalent for spoken dialogue. Its ambition was taken up by D. W. Griffith at Biograph at more or less the same time. Griffith, himself an actor and playwright, regularly employed actors from the dramatic stage. However, in this period Griffith worked toward dramatic principles of characterization and narrative coherence through nonverbal means, what Tom Gunning describes as the emergence of the Narrator System (Gunning, 1994). Thus the cinematic treatment of space and time and the art of editing emerge historically as an attempt to rival theatrical representation.

The conversion to sound that began in the mid-1920s brought the return of the theatrical model. Stage plays were adapted to the screen and actors from theater brought their practiced diction. In the early sound era, due to limited-range microphones, the need to enclose the camera in a sound-proof booth, the need to record sound directly with the image, among other recording conditions, many of the acquisitions of the silent film were at least temporarily lost: camera mobility was constrained, actors' blocking was determined by microphone placement, editing, particularly crosscutting, became impossible. The result was a static form of theatrical representation: talking tableaux. Theoretical debates ensued. Manifestos from one side (that of René Clair, Charlie Chaplin, Sergei Eisenstein) attacked "filmed theater" and advocated a return to "pure" cinema, or to a creative, "dialectical" treatment of sound and image; and the other side (Marcel Pagnol) defended the direct adaptation of plays.

Subsequently, the relationship of film to theater has persisted. Plays continued to be adapted to the screen but, in contrast to "canned theater," typically included exterior sequences that would be impossible on stage. In the United States directors and actors have often had dual careers. Orson Welles was wooed to Hollywood as a brilliant theatrical director, and Actors Studio founder Elia Kazan and method actors like Marlon Brando and James Dean had a significant impact on acting styles on screen in the 1950s. In Europe, a certain *cinéma d'auteur* retained strong theatrical qualities in works by filmmakers as different as Max Ophuls, Ingmar Bergman, and Rainer Werner Fassbinder. In a general way, the most persistent heritage film assumes from theater is the tendency to respect the spatial organization established by the proscenium, particularly for scenes shot in interiors: the camera observes from the point of view of the missing fourth wall the actors who turn their bodies toward the camera. [WG]

Further reading

Bazin, André (1967) *What Is Cinema?*, vol. 1, Berkeley, CA: University of California Press.

Kracauer, Siegfried (1960) *Theory of Film: The Redemption of Physical Reality*, Princeton, NJ: Princeton University Press.

THIRD WORLD CINEMA is a concept used to describe emerging political filmmaking in Africa, Asia, and Latin America from the 1960s to the mid-1970s. The Third World distinguishes itself from the first world of the West (particularly the United States and Europe) and the second world of the Soviet Union and the Eastern Bloc countries—the two combatants engaged in the **Cold War**. Third World movements aspired to show a third path, one that would lead to political and economic revolution and human liberation. Third World filmmakers believed they needed to combat Hollywood hegemony in both financial and ideological terms. It was the filmmaker's duty to subvert the model of the **Classical Hollywood Cinema**, to create new forms, and to address the audience of formerly colonized peoples in directly political terms. Film viewing became a political activity: Third World films did not allow their audiences to escape from the tribulations of their lives; on the contrary, the films asked them to confront them. Among the most significant movements in Third World Cinema are Brazil's Cinema Nôvo, the postrevolutionary Cuban cinema, Argentina's "Third Cinema," and sub-Saharan black African cinema, among others. [ML]

Further reading

Barlet, Olivier (2000) *African Cinemas: Decolonizing the Gaze*, trans. Chris Turner, London: Zed Books.
Burton, Julianne (ed.) (1986) *Cinema and Social Change in Latin America: Conversations with Filmmakers*, Austin, TX: University of Texas Press.

TRANSITIONAL DEVICES (FADE, DISSOLVE, WIPE, SWISH PAN) Visual effects that serve as transitions between sequences, or, more rarely, within sequences. They are not images but optical effects that manipulate previously shot footage. Transitional devices are more or less emphatic and self-conscious depending on the extent to which they have come into conventional use. They are analogous to the chapter break in a literary text or a blank space on the page within a chapter separating aspects of the action.

The *fade* is an optical effect that signals a significant break in the action and usually a significant shift in time and place. The fade-in begins with a blank screen onto which the first image of a sequence appears through dissolve as the lighting of the image increases. The fade-out reverses this effect by dissolving out of an image to a blank screen. In the fade-to-black the blank screen is dark; in the fade-to-white, the exposure increases until the image bleaches out. These effects were originally achieved in the camera by gradually opening or closing the aperture. Since the 1920s they have routinely been done in an optical printer.

The *dissolve* is a visual transition between two shots that are superimposed one on the other: the first image seems to disappear as the second takes its place. The effect of appearance/disappearance is created through the increasing exposure of one image and decreasing exposure of the other. In the silent cinema, change in exposure was achieved by manipulating the diaphragm of the camera, but in the sound film of the 1930s and 1940s it was accomplished by means of the optical printer. The process had already been used to link images in **magic lantern** shows, popular in the nineteenth century, and the dissolve appeared very early in film history. The spatial transition inherent in the dissolve normally implies a temporal transition: either the narrative moves elliptically forward, or backward in the case of the dissolve introducing a flashback. The dissolve was a common device in the classic period of filmmaking in the 1930s and 1940s. Thereafter it became less common, perhaps because it had become a trite convention.

The *wipe* takes the form of a line moving across the screen that "wipes away" one image and replaces it with another. The wipe, like the dissolve, usually indicates a shift from one sequence to another. The graphic pattern of the wipe is variable: vertical, diagonal, iris-in or out, a "burst," and so on. It was a common transitional device in the 1930s and 1940s but subsequently became rare, perhaps because it is so emphatic and signals the narrator's intervention in the film. The wipe still appears occasionally as an effect self-consciously borrowed from the classic cinema. It is also used as a transitional device in television for speeches or interviews taken from a single camera setup so that the editor can abridge the material to its salient moments.

In the *swish pan* or *whip pan* the camera pans so rapidly on its axis that the image of the first shot becomes blurred and a second shot, also beginning with a rapid pan, can be edited with it. The swish pan indicates a transition from one sequence to another, suggesting the simultaneity or rapid

succession of events. In *Citizen Kane*, Orson Welles describes the disintegration of Kane's relationship with his wife Emily through a series of brief scenes at the breakfast table, linked with swish pans and overlapping sound, that telescopes the lengthy dissolution into a very brief screen time. [WG]

TRANSPARENCE designates a tendency in film aesthetics that values the access film gives to empirical reality and devalues films that make a display of their art (see **realism**). In transparent films, the techniques of production are not immediately perceptible to the audience: the framing of shots is not jarring, longer takes are preferred to rapid-fire cutting, editing when it occurs is "invisible" (see **editing/continuity editing**), the actors' performances are discreet, and so forth; all this to produce in the spectator an enhanced "illusion" of reality. The notion of transparence underpins the influential work of French critic André Bazin. It came under attack in the 1960s and 1970s when Marxist critics, particularly in France, pointed out the ideological character of transparent filmmaking in which the world would seem to speak about itself without the intervention of human agents. [WG]

VERISIMILITUDE Combines the notions of truth and likeness and is close in meaning to *plausibility*. Aristotle made the distinction between truth (what really happened, the basic content of history) and what could plausibly happen (the basic content of literature of the imagination). Verisimilitude is normative: what the audience in general is willing to accept as conforming to its experience of the world. In film, verisimilitude concerns the credibility of the world the film represents, for example its representation of locations and social contexts, and the clear causality of the plot and motivation of characters. Verisimilitude suggests a comparison the audience makes between its experience of the real world and the world of the film. However, verisimilitude is to a large extent established through narrative codes that the audience identifies as credible through its long exposure to them. This is most apparent in certain genre films—the musical or the science fiction film, for example—which work according to conventions that have little relation to the spectator's experience of reality (see **genre**). [WG]

VOICE-OVER NARRATION The use of the human voice as a narrator for moving images is one of the earliest practices in film sound. Live narration to explain the context of the images or the narrative was common during cinema's first decade and continued as a specialized practice throughout the silent era. In Japan, the role of the narrator was elevated to the level of art through the *benshi,* or the act of narrating a film live. The *benshi* not only described the events occurring on screen, but he also would speak and act out character parts in relation to their actions. In the case of Japanese silent cinema, filmmakers would often create visual narratives using looser elements of continuity, knowing that a *benshi* would fill in the missing details. A similar practice occurred in Québec with the film lecturer known as a *bonimenteur,* in Germany with the *kinoerzähler,* and in Spain with the *explicador.*

With the advent of synchronous sound recording, the role of the live narrator was made obsolete, much to the dismay of these well-established traditions. Narration could be added to cinema as voice-over (sometimes called voice-off), but it differed from live narration due to the absence of the speaking figure. The voice-over narrator is another form of **asynchronism** where the audience is unsure who is speaking or where the voice comes from. While this may have caused some dismay for the first audiences of sound films, the presence of a narrating voice was familiar enough to make voice-over narration very popular in documentaries and newsreels. In narrative cinema, however, the voice-over took on a different function when it was used to let characters narrate their own stories in a form similar to first-person, singular novelistic writing. This technique, borrowed from radio plays, became quite popular in cinema starting in the 1940s. As the use of voice-over became more prevalent it opened up new dramatic possibilities of unstable narrators, contrasts between screen time and narrational time, and even the counterpoint between **narration** and images. [JB]

See Chapter 5.

Further reading

Chion, Michel (1999) *The Voice in Cinema*, ed. and trans. Claudia Gorbman, New York: Columbia University Press.

Kozloff, Sarah (1988) *Invisible Storytellers: Voice-Over Narration in American Fiction Film*, Berkeley, CA: University of California Press.

BIBLIOGRAPHY

Aaron, Michele (ed.) (2004) *New Queer Cinema: A Critical Reader*, Edinburgh: Edinburgh University Press.

Abel, Richard (1984) *French Cinema: The First Wave, 1915–1929*, Princeton, NJ: Princeton University Press.

Acland, Charles R. (2003) *Screen Traffic: Movies, Multiplexes, and Global Culture*, Durham, NC: Duke University Press.

Alexander, Martin and Graham, Helen (eds.) (1989) *The French and Spanish Popular Fronts: Comparative Perspectives*, Cambridge: Cambridge University Press.

Allen, Graham (2000) *Intertextuality*, London: Routledge.

Althusser, Louis (2001) *Lenin and Philosophy and Other Essays*, New York: Monthly Review Press.

Altman, Rick (1988) "Dickens, Griffith and Film Theory," *South Atlantic Quarterly* 88: 2.

Altman, Rick (1989) *The American Film Musical*, Bloomington, IN: Indiana University Press.

Altman, Rick (ed.) (1992) *Sound Theory, Sound Practice*, New York: Routledge.

Altman, Rick (2004) *Silent Film Sound*, New York: Columbia University Press.

Alton, John (1995) *Painting with Light*, Berkeley, CA: University of California Press.

Ament, Vanessa Theme (2009) *The Foley Grail: The Art of Performing Sound for Film, Games, and Animation*, Burlington, MA: Focal Press.

Anderson, Benedict (1991) *Imagined Communities: Reflections on the Origin and Spread of Nationalism*, London: Verso.

Anderson, Benedict (2006) *Imagined Communities*, London: Verso Books.

Anderson, Christopher (1994) *Hollywood TV: The Studio System in the Fifties*, Austin, TX: University of Texas Press.

Andrew, Dudley (1984) *Film in the Aura of Art*, Princeton, NJ: Princeton University Press.

Andrew, Dudley (1995) *Mists of Regret: Culture and Sensibility in Classic French Film*, Princeton, NJ: Princeton University Press.

Anonymous (1963a) "Cuba Si!," *Le Canard Enchaîné*, September 12.

Anonymous (1963b) "Symphonie pour un peuple libre," *L'Humanité*, September 14.

Anonymous (1963c) "Cuba Si!," *Le Figaro Littéraire*, September 28.

Armes, Roy (1968) *The Cinema of Alain Resnais*, London: Zwemmer.

Arroyo, José (1997) "Film Studies," in A. Medhurst and S. R. Munt (eds.) *Lesbian and Gay Studies: A Critical Introduction*, London: Cassell, pp. 67–83.

Augé, Marc (1995) *Non-Places: Introduction to an Anthropology of Supermodernity*, trans. John Howe, London and New York: Verso Books.

Aumont, Jacques (2006) *Le Cinéma et la mise en scène* (Cinema and Mise-en-Scène), Paris: Armand Colin.

Aumont, Jacques, Bergala, Alain, Marie, Michel, and Vernet, Marc (1992) *Aesthetics of Film*, trans. Richard Neupert, Austin, TX: University of Texas Press.

Balázs, Béla (1972) *Theory of the Film: Character and Growth of a New Art*, New York: Arno Press.

Balio, Tino (1976) *The American Film Industry*, Madison, WI: University of Wisconsin Press.

Balio, Tino (1993) *Grand Design: Hollywood as a Modern Business Enterprise, 1930–1939*, New York: Scribner.

Balzer, Richard (1998) *Peepshows: A Visual History*, New York: Harry N. Abrams.

Barlet, Olivier (2000) *African Cinemas: Decolonizing the Gaze*, trans. Chris Turner, London: Zed Books.

Baron, Cynthia and Carnicke, Sharon Marie (2008) *Reframing Screen Performance*, Ann Arbor, MI: University of Michigan Press.

Barsacq, Leon (1977) *Caligari's Cabinet and Other Grand Illusions: A History of Film Design*, New York: New York Graphic Society.

Barthes, Roland (1997) "Rhetoric of the Image," in *Image–Music–Text*, trans. Stephen Heath, New York: Hill and Wang.

Basinger, Jeanine (1993) *A Woman's View: How Hollywood Spoke to Women, 1930–1960*, 1st edn., New York: Knopf [distributed by Random House].

Bazin, André (1967) *What Is Cinema?*, vol. 1, Berkeley, CA: University of California Press.

Bazin, André (1971) *What Is Cinema?*, vol. 2, Berkeley, CA: University of California Press.

Beck, Jay and Grajeda, Tony (eds.) (2008) *Lowering the Boom: Critical Studies in Film Sound*, Urbana, IL: University of Illinois Press.

Bellour, Raymond and Penley, Constance (2000) *The Analysis of Film*, Bloomington, IN: Indiana University Press.

Belton, John (1992) "1950s Magnetic Sound: The Frozen Revolution," in Rick Altman (ed.), *Sound Theory, Sound Practice*, New York: Routledge.

Belton, John (2002) "Digital Cinema: A False Revolution," in *October 100*, Spring, MIT Press; reprinted in Braudy, Leo and Cohen, Marshall (eds.) (2004) *Film Theory and Criticism*, 6th edn., New York and Oxford: Oxford University Press.

Bendazzi, Giannalberto (1995) *Cartoons: One Hundred Years of Cinema Animation*, Bloomington, IN: Indiana University Press.

Benjamin, Walter, *et al.* (2008) *The Work of Art in the Age of Its Technological Reproducibility, and Other Writings on Media*, Cambridge, MA: Belknap Press of Harvard University Press.

Benshoff, Harry M. and Griffin, Sean (eds.) (2006) *Queer Images: A History of Gay and Lesbian Film in America*, Lanham, MD: Rowman & Littlefield Publishers Inc.

Benveniste, Emile (1971) *Problems in General Linguistics*, Coral Gables, FL: University of Miami Press.

Bergman, Andrew (1971) *We're in the Money: Depression America and Its Films*, New York: Harper and Row.

Bergstrom, Janet (1999) *Endless Night: Cinema and Psychoanalysis, Parallel Histories*, Berkeley, CA: University of California Press.

Bernstein, Matthew (1999) *Controlling Hollywood: Censorship and Regulation in the Studio Era*, New Brunswick, NJ: Rutgers University Press.

Bernstein, Matthew and Studlar, Gaylyn (1997) *Visions of the East: Orientalism in Film*, New Brunswick, NJ: Rutgers University Press.

Biressi, Anita and Nunn, Heather (2005) *Reality TV: Realism and Revelation*, London: Wallflower.

Blaetz, Robin (ed.) (2007) *Women's Experimental Cinema: Critical Frameworks*, Durham, NC: Duke University Press.

Bogle, David (2001) *Toms, Coons, Mulattoes, Mammies, & Bucks: An Interpretive History of Blacks in American Films*, New York: Continuum [orig. 1973].

Bonnell, Victoria and Hunt, Lynn (1999) *Beyond the Cultural Turn: New Directions in the Study of Society and Culture*, Berkeley, CA: University of California Press.

Borde, Raymond and Chaumeton, Etienne (2002) *A Panorama of American Film Noir (1941–1958)*, trans. Paul Hammond, San Francisco, CA: City Lights Books [orig. 1955].

Bordwell, David (1985) *Narration in the Fiction Film*, Madison, WI: University of Wisconsin Press.

Bordwell, David (1989) *Making Meaning: Inference and Rhetoric in the Interpretation of Cinema*, Cambridge, MA: Harvard University Press.

Bordwell, David (1997) *On the History of Film Style*, Cambridge, MA: Harvard University Press.

Bordwell, David (2005) *Figures Traced in Light: On Cinematic Staging*, Berkeley, CA: University of California Press.

Bordwell, David (2008) *Poetics of Cinema*, New York: Routledge.

Bordwell, David and Carroll, Noël (1996) *Post-Theory: Reconstructing Film Studies*, Madison, WI: University of Wisconsin Press.

Bordwell, David and Thompson, Kristin (2008) *Film Art: An Introduction*, New York: McGraw-Hill.

Bordwell, David, Staiger, Janet, and Thompson, Kristin (1985) *The Classical Hollywood Cinema: Film Style and Mode of Production to 1960*, New York: Columbia University Press.

Bottomore, Stephen (1995) *I Want to See This Annie Mattygraph: A Cartoon History of the Movies*, Pordenone: Le giornate del cinema muto.

Bowers, Q. David (1999) *Nickelodeon Theatres and Their Music*, Blue Ridge Summit, PA: Scarecrow Press.

Bowser, Eileen (1990) *The Transformation of Cinema: 1907–1915*, Berkeley, CA: University of California Press.

Bowser, Eileen (1994) *The Transformation of Cinema: 1907–1915*, Vol. 2. Berkeley, CA: University of California Press.

Branigan, Edward R. (1984) *Point of View in the Cinema: A Theory of Narration and Subjectivity in Classical Film*, The Hague: Mouton.

Brantlinger, Patrick (1983) *Bread and Circuses: Theories of Mass Culture as Social Decay*, Ithaca, NY: Cornell University Press.

Braudy, Leo and Cohen, Marshall (2004) *Film Theory and Criticism: Introductory Readings*, 6th edn., New York: Oxford University Press.

Braziel, Jana Evans and Mannur, Anita (2003) *Theorizing Diaspora*, London: Blackwell.

Bresson, Robert (1986) *Notes on the Cinematographer*, trans. Jonathan Griffin, London: Quartet.

Breton, André (1969) *Manifestos of Surrealism*, Ann Arbor, MI: University of Michigan Press.

Brewster, David (1832) *Letters on Natural Magic*, London: Murray.

Brooks, Peter (1976) *The Melodramatic Imagination: Balzac, James and the Mode of Excess*, New Haven, CT: Yale University Press.

Bruzzi, Stella (2006) *New Documentary*, New York: Routledge.

Buchsbaum, J. (1988) *Cinema Engagé: Film in the Popular Front*, Urbana, IL: University of Illinois Press.

Burch, Noel (1973) *Theory of Film Practice*, New York: Praeger Publishers.

Burch, Noel (1979) *To the Distant Observer: Form and Meaning in the Japanese Cinema*, Berkley, CA: University of California Press.

Burch, Noel (1990) *Life to Those Shadows*, Berkeley, CA: University of California Press.

Burgoyne, Robert (1997) *Film Nation: Hollywood Looks at U.S. History*, Minneapolis, MN: University of Minnesota Press.

Burton, Julianne (ed.) (1986) *Cinema and Social Change in Latin America: Conversations with Filmmakers*, Austin, TX: University of Texas Press.

Butler, Judith (1990) *Gender Trouble: Feminism and the Subversion of Identity*, New York: Routledge.

Campbell, Jan (2005) *Film and Cinema Spectatorship: Melodrama and Mimesis*, Oxford: Polity.

Campbell, Joseph (1949) *The Hero with a Thousand Faces*, The Bollingen Series, New York: Pantheon Books.

Carroll, Noël (1996a) "Nonfiction Film and Postmodernist Skepticism," in David Bordwell and Noël Carroll (eds.) *Post-Theory*, Madison, WI: University of Wisconsin Press.

Carroll, Noël (1996b) "Notes on the Sight Gag," in *Theorizing the Moving Image*, New York: Cambridge University Press.

Carson, E., Dittmar, L., and Welsch, J. (eds.) (1994) *Multiple Voices in Feminist Film Criticism*, Minneapolis, MN: University of Minnesota Press.

Casetti, Francesco (1999) *Theories of Cinema 1945–1995*, Austin, TX: University of Texas Press.

Cavell, Stanley (1979) *The World Viewed*, Cambridge, MA: Harvard University Press.

Ceplair, Larry and Englund, Steven (2003) *The Inquisition in Hollywood: Politics in the Film Community, 1930–1960*, Champaign, IL: University of Illinois Press.

Cervoni, Albert (1963) *"Cuba Si!*, enfin," *France Nouvelle*, September 11–17.

Chanan, Michael (2007) *The Politics of Documentary*, London: British Film Institute.

Chatman, Seymour (1978) *Story and Discourse: Narrative Structure in Fiction and Film*, Ithaca, NY: Cornell University Press.

Chion, Michel (1994) *Audio-Vision: Sound on Screen*, ed. and trans. Claudia Gorbman, New York: Columbia University Press.

Chion, Michel (1999) *The Voice in Cinema*, ed. and trans. Claudia Gorbman, New York: Columbia University Press.

Chion, Michel (2007) *Écrire un scenario*, Paris: Editions Cahiers du cinéma.

Chopra-Gant, Michael (2008) *Cinema and History: The Telling of Stories*, London: Wallflower.

Christopher, Robert (2005) *Robert and Frances Flaherty: A Documentary Life 1883–1922*, Montreal & Kingston: McGill-Queen's University Press.

Collins, Jim (1989) *Uncommon Cultures: Popular Culture and Post-Modernism*, New York: Routledge.

Comolli, Jean-Luc and Narboni, Paul (1971) "Cinema/Ideology/Criticism," in Leo Braudy and Marshall Cohen (eds.) (2004) *Film Theory and Criticism*, Oxford: Oxford University Press.

Cook, Pam (ed.) (1994) *The Cinema Book*, London: British Film Institute.

Corrigan, Timothy (1991) *A Cinema Without Walls: Movies and Culture After Vietnam*, New Brunswick, NJ: Rutgers University Press.

Cowie, Elizabeth (1997) *Representing the Woman: Cinema and Psychoanalysis*, Minneapolis, MN: University of Minnesota Press.

Crafton, Don (1999) *The Talkies: American Cinema's Transition to Sound, 1926–1931*, Berkeley, CA: University of California Press.

Crary, Jonathan (1989) *Techniques of the Observer: On Vision and Modernity in the Nineteenth Century*, Cambridge, MA: MIT Press.

Culler, Jonathan (1982) *On Deconstruction: Theory and Criticism after Structuralism*, Ithaca, NY: Cornell University Press.

Curtis, David (1971) *Experimental Cinema*, New York: Universe.

Curtis, David (ed.) (1996) *A Directory of British Film and Video Artists*, London: John Libbey.

Dalle Vacche, Angela (1992) *The Body in the Mirror: Shapes of History in Italian Cinema*, Princeton, NJ: Princeton University Press.

Dalle Vacche, Angela and Price, Brian (eds.) (1992) *Color, the Film Reader*, New York: Routledge.

Davis, Glyn (2002) "Gregg Araki," in Y. Tasker (ed.) *Fifty Contemporary Filmmakers*, London: Routledge, pp. 25–33.

de Lauretis, Teresa (1991) "Queer Theory: Lesbian and Gay Sexualities," *differences: a journal of feminist cultural studies*, 3(2): iii–xviii.

de Lauretis, Teresa and Heath, Stephen (eds.) (1980) *The Cinematic Apparatus*, London and Basingstoke: Macmillan.

Deleuze, Gilles (1986) *Cinema 1: The Movement-Image*, trans. Hugh Tomlinson and Barbara Habberjam, Minneapolis, MN: University of Minnesota Press.

Deleuze, Gilles (1989) *Cinema 2: The Time-Image*, trans. Hugh Tomlinson and Robert Galeta, Minneapolis, MN: University of Minnesota Press.

Desser, David, (ed.) (1997) *Ozu's Tokyo Story* (Cambridge Film Handbooks Series), New York: Cambridge University Press.

Deuber-Mankowsky, Astrid (2005) *Lara Croft: Cyber Heroine*, Minneapolis, MN: University of Minnesota Press.

Dickson, W. K. L. and Dickson, Antonia (2000) *History of the Kinetograph, Kinetoscope, and Kinetophonograph [1895]*, New York: Museum of Modern Art.

Dixon, Wheeler Winston (1997) *The Exploding Eye: A Re-Visionary History of 1960s American Experimental Cinema*, Albany, NY: State University of New York Press.

Dixon, Wheeler Winston and Foster, Gwendolyn Audrey (eds.) (2002) *Experimental Cinema: The Film Reader*, London: Routledge.

Doane, Mary Ann (1991) *Femmes Fatales: Feminism, Film Theory, Psychoanalysis*, New York: Routledge.

Doherty, Thomas (1991) "Witness to War: Ron Kovic, and Born on the Fourth of July," in *Inventing Vietnam: The War in Film and Television*, Philadelphia, PA: Temple University Press, pp. 251–69.

Doty, Alexander (1993) *Making Things Perfectly Queer: Interpreting Mass Culture*, Minneapolis, MN: University of Minnesota Press.

Doty, Alexander (2000) *Flaming Classics: Queering the Film Canon*, New York: Routledge.

Douin, J.-L. (1998) *Dictionnaire de la censure au cinéma* (Dictionary of Censorship in Cinema), Paris: Presses Universitaires de France.

Dulac, Nicolas and Gaudrealt, André (2006) "Circularity and Repetition at the Heart of the Attraction: Optical Toys and the Emergence of a New Cultural Series," in Wanda Strauwen (ed.) *The Cinema of Attractions Reloaded*, Amsterdam: Amsterdam University Press.

Ďurovičovà, Nataša (1992) "Translating America: The Hollywood Multilinguals 1929–1933," in Rick Altman (ed.) *Sound Theory/Sound Practice*, New York: Routledge.

Durozoi, Gérard (2004) *History of the Surrealist Movement*, Chicago: University of Chicago Press.

Dyer, Richard (ed.) (1984) *Gays and Film*, rev. edn., New York: New York Zoetrope [orig. 1977].

Dyer, Richard (1993) *The Matter of Images: Essays on Representation*, London: Routledge.

Dyer, Richard (2005) *Heavenly Bodies: Film Stars and Society*, 2nd edn., London: Routledge.

Ehrlich, Linda and David, Desser (1994, 2008) *Cinematic Landscapes: Observations on the Visual Arts and Cinema in China and Japan*, Austin, TX: University of Texas Press.

Eisenstein, Sergei (1957) *The Film Form* and *The Film Sense*, New York: Meridian Books.

263

Eisenstein, Sergei (1988) *Selected Works*, ed. and trans. Richard Taylor, London: BFI Publishing.

Eisenstein, Sergei (1991) "Sergei Eisenstein: Selected Works," in Richard Taylor and Michael Glenny (eds.) *Towards a Theory of Montage*, vol. 2, trans. Richard Taylor, London: British Film Institute.

Eisenstein, S. M., Pudovkin, V. I., and Alexandrov, G. V. [1927] "A Statement"; Pudovkin, V. I. [1929] "Asynchronism as a Principle of Sound Film"; Clair, René [1929] "The Art of Sound"; all in Elisabeth Weis and John Belton (eds.) (1985) *Film Sound—Theory and Practice*, New York: Columbia University Press.

Eisner, Lotte (1973) *The Haunted Screen*, Berkeley, CA: University of California Press.

Eisner, Lotte (2008) *The Haunted Screen: Expressionism in the German Cinema and the Influence of Max Reihardt*, Berkeley, CA: University of California Press.

Ellis, Jack and McLane, Betsy (2005) *A New History of Documentary Film*, New York: Continuum.

Elsaesser, Thomas (1972) "Tales of Sound and Fury: The Family Melodrama" *Monogram* 4, 2–15.

Elsaesser, Thomas (ed.) (1990) *Early Cinema: Space Frame Narrative*, London: British Film Institute.

Everett, Anna (2001) *Returning the Gaze: A Genealogy of Black Criticism, 1909–1949*, Durham, NC: Duke University Press.

Ewen, Stuart (1977) *Captains of Consciousness: Advertising and the Social Roots of Consumer Culture*, New York: McGraw-Hill Book Company.

Ezra, Elizabeth and Rowden, Terry (eds.) (2006) *Transnational Cinema: The Film Reader*, New York: Routledge.

Ferro, Marc (1988) *History and Cinema*, Detroit, MI: Wayne State University Press.

Field, Syd (2005) *Screenplay: The Foundations of Screenwriting*, New York: Delta Trade Paperback.

Fisher, Lucy and Landy, Marsha (2004) *Stars: The Film Reader*, New York: Routledge.

Foucault, Michel (1971) *The Order of Things: An Archaeology of the Human Sciences*, New York: Pantheon Books.

Foucault, Michel (1982) *The Archaeology of Knowledge and the Discourse on Language*, New York: Pantheon Books.

Foucault, Michel (2002) *The Archaeology of Knowledge*, trans. A. M. Sheridan Smith, London: Routledge.

Freud, Sigmund and Breuer, Josef (1966) *Studies on Hysteria*, trans. from the German, ed. James Strachey, in collaboration with Anna Freud, assisted by Alix Strachey and Alan Tyson, New York: Avon Books.

Friedberg, Anne (1993) *Window Shopping: Cinema and the Postmodern*, Berkeley and Los Angeles, CA: University of California Press.

Friedberg, Anne (2002) "Urban Mobility and Cinematic Visuality: The Screens of Los Angeles—Endless Cinema or Private Telematics," *Journal of Visual Culture*, 1(2): 183–204.

Furniss, Maureen (2008) *Art in Motion: Animation Aesthetics*, London: John Libbey and Company.

Gabbard, Krin and Gabbard, Glen O. (1987) *Psychiatry and the Cinema*, Chicago: University of Chicago Press.

Gadjigo, Samba, Faulkingham, Ralph, Cassirer, Thomas, and Sander, Reinhold (eds.) (1993) *Ousmane, Sembène: Dialogues with Writers and Critics*, Amherst, MA: University of Massachusetts Press.

Gaudreault, André (1988) *Du littéraire au filmique* (From the Literary to the Filmic), Paris: Klincksieck.

Gehman, Chris and Reinecke, Steve (2005) *The Sharpest Point: Animation at the End of Cinema*, Toronto: YYZ Books.

Genette, Gérard (1969) "Vraisemblance et motivation (Verisimilitude and Motivation)," *Communications*, 11: 5–21.

Genette, Gérard (1991) *Fiction et diction*, Paris: Editions du Seuil.

Gillespie, David (2000) *Early Soviet Cinema: Innovation, Ideology and Propaganda*, London: Wallflower.

Ginzburg, Carlo (1992) *The Cheese and the Worms: The Cosmos of a Sixteenth-Century Miller*, Baltimore, MD: Johns Hopkins University Press.

Gladchuk, John (2007) *Hollywood and Anticommunism: HUAC and the Evolution of the Red Menace, 1935–1950*, New York: Routledge.

Gledhill, Christine (1991) *Stardom: Industry of Desire*, New York: Routledge.

Gomery, Douglas (1986) *The Hollywood Studio System*, New York: St. Martin's Press.

Gomery, Douglas (1992) *Shared Pleasures: A History of Movie Presentation in the United States*, Madison, WI: University of Wisconsin Press.

Gorbman, Claudia (1987) *Unheard Melodies: Narrative Film Music*, Bloomington, IN: Indiana University Press.

Grant, Barry Keith (2003) *Film Genre Reader III*, Austin, TX: University of Texas Press.

Grant, Barry Keith (2007a) *Schirmer Encyclopedia of Film*, 4 vols., Detroit, MI: Schirmer Reference.

Grant, Barry Keith (2007b) *Film Genre: From Iconography to Ideology*, London: Wallflower.

Green, Fitzhugh (1929) *Film Finds Its Tongue*, New York: G. P. Putnam and Sons/ Knickerbocker Press.

Griffiths, Robin (ed.) (2006) *British Queer Cinema*, London and New York: Routledge.

Griffiths, Robin (ed.) (2008) *Queer Cinema in Europe*, Bristol and Chicago: Intellect.

Gunning, Tom (1990) "The Cinema of Attractions: Early Film, Its Spectator and the Avant-Garde," in Thomas Elsaesser (ed.) *Early Cinema: Space Frame Narrative*, London: British Film Institute.

Gunning, Tom (1994) *D. W. Griffith and the Origins of American Narrative Film: The Early Years at Biograph*, Urbana, IL: University of Illinois Press.

Gunning, Tom (1995) "An Aesthetic of Astonishment: Early Film and the (In)Credulous Spectator," in Linda Williams (ed.) *Viewing Positions: Ways of Seeing Film (Depth of Field)*, New Brunswick, NJ: Rutgers University Press, pp. 114–33.

Gunning, Tom (1998) "Early American Film," in *The Oxford Guide to Film Studies*, Oxford and New York: Oxford University Press.

Guynn, William (1990) *A Cinema of Nonfiction*, Cranbury, NJ: Associated University Presses.

Guynn, William (2006) *Writing History in Film*, New York and London: Routledge.

Halberstadt, Ira (1976) "An Interview with Fred Wiseman," in Richard Barsam (ed.) *Nonfiction Film: Theory and Criticism*, New York: E. P. Dutton.

Hall, Stuart (1994) "Cultural Identity and Diaspora," in Patrick Williams and Laura Chrisman (eds.) *Colonial Discourse and Post-Colonial Theory: A Reader*, New York: Columbia University Press.

Hammond, John (1981) *The Camera Obscura: A Chronicle*, Bristol: Adam Hilger.

Handzo, Stephen (1985) "Appendix: A Narrative Glossary of Film Sound Technology," in Elisabeth Weis and John Belton (eds.) *Film Sound—Theory and Practice*, New York: Columbia University Press.

Hansen, Miriam (1999) "The Mass Production of the Senses: Classical Cinema as Vernacular Modernism," *Modernism/modernity*, 6: 59–77.

Hanson, Ellis (ed.) (1999) *Out Takes: Essays on Queer Theory and Film*, Durham, NC: Duke University Press.

Hark, Ina Rae (2002) *Exhibition: The Film Reader*, London: Routledge.

Havel, Vaclav (1984) "The Anatomy of the Gag," in *Modern Drama XXIII.1*, Toronto, ON: University of Toronto Press.

Hayward, Susan (1993) *French National Cinema*, London: Routledge.

Heard, Mervyn (2006) *Phantasmagoria: The Secret Life of the Magic Lantern*, Hastings: The Projection Box.

Heath, Stephen (1981) "Body, Voice," in *Questions of Cinema*, Bloomington, IN: Indiana University Press, pp. 176–93.

Hecht, Hermann (1993) *Pre-Cinema History: An Encyclopaedia and Annotated Bibliography of the Moving Image before 1896*, ed. Ann Hecht, London: Bowker-Saur with British Film Institute.

Hendricks, Gordon (1964) *Beginnings of the Biograph*, New York: The Beginnings of the American Film, pp. 59–65.

Herbert, Stephen (ed.) (2000) *A History of Pre-Cinema*, London and New York: Routledge.

Herbert, Stephen (ed.) (2004) *Eadweard Muybridge: The Kingston Museum Bequest*, Hastings: The Projection Box.

Hervé, F. (2001) *La Censure du cinéma en France à la libération* (Censorship of Film in France After Liberation), Paris: ADHE.

Higson, Andrew (2003) *English Heritage. English Cinema: Costume Drama since 1980*, Oxford: Oxford University Press.

Hill, Annette (2007) *Restyling Factual TV*, London: Routledge.

Hill, John (1999) *British Cinema in the 1980s*, Oxford: Clarendon Press.

Hillier, Jim (ed.) (1985) *Cahiers du cinéma: The 1950s: Neo-Realism, Hollywood, New Wave*, Cambridge, MA: Harvard University Press.

Hillier, Jim (ed.) (1986) *Cahiers du cinéma 1960–1968: New Wave, New Cinema, Reevaluating Hollywood*, Cambridge, MA: Harvard University Press.

Hillier, Jim (ed.) (2001) *American Independent Cinema: A Sight and Sound Reader*, London: British Film Institute.

Hjort, Mette and Mackenzie, Scott (eds.) (2000) *Cinema and Nation*, London: Routledge.

Hockings, Paul (ed.) (1975) *Principles of Visual Anthropology*, The Hague: Mouton.

Holm, Bill and Quimby, George Irving (1980) *Edward S. Curtis in the Land of the War Canoes*, Seattle, WA: University of Washington Press.

Holman, Tomlinson (2007) *Surround Sound: Up and Running*, 2nd edn., Burlington, MA: Focal Press.

Horkheimer, Max and Adorno, Theodor W. (1972) *Dialectic of Enlightenment*, New York: Seabury Press.

Hughes-Warrington, Marnie (2007) *History Goes to the Movies: Studying History on Film*, London: Routledge.

Huhtamo, Erkki (2004) "Peristrephic Pleasures on the Origins of the Moving Panorama," in John Fullerton and Jan Olsson (eds.) *Allegories of Communication: Intermedial Concerns from Cinema to the Digital*, Rome: John Libbey, pp. 237–8.

Huhtamo, Erkki (2006a) "The Pleasures of the Peephole: An Archaeological Exploration of Peep Media," in Eric Kluitenberg (ed.) *Book of Imaginary Media: Excavating the Dream of the Ultimate Communication Medium*, Rotterdam: NAi Publishers.

Huhtamo, Erkki (2006b) "Twin-Touch-Test-Redux: Media Archaeological Approach to Art, Interactivity, and Tactility," in Oliver Grau (ed.) *MediaArtHistories*, Cambridge, MA: MIT Press, pp. 71–101.

Huhtamo, Erkki (forthcoming) *Illusions in Motion: An Media Archaeology of the Moving Panorama*, Berkeley and Los Angeles, CA: University of California Press.

Huhtamo, Erkki and Parikka, Jussi (eds.) (forthcoming) *Media Archaeology: Approaches, Applications and Implications*, Berkeley and Los Angeles, CA: University of California Press.

Hunt, Lynn (ed.) (1989) *The New Cultural History*, Berkeley, CA: University of California Press.

Hyde, Ralph (1988) *Panoramania! The Art and Entertainment of the "All-Embracing" View*, London: Trefoil Publications in Association with Barbican Art.

Ivens, Joris (1969) *The Camera and I*, New York: International Publishers.

Jagose, Annamarie (1995) *Queer Theory: An Introduction*, New York: New York University Press.

Jameson, Fredric (1991) *Postmodernism, or the Cultural Logic of Late Capitalism*, Durham, NC: Duke University Press.

Jeancolas, Jean-Pierre and Marie, Michel (2007) *Histoire du cinéma français* (History of French Cinema), 2nd edn., Paris: Armand Colin.

Johnston, Ollie and Thomas, Frank (1995) *The Illusion of Life: Disney Animation*, Los Angeles, CA: Disney Books.

Kaplan, E. Ann (ed.) (1983) *Women in Film Noir*, New York: Methuen.

Kaplan, E. Ann (1990) *Psychoanalysis and Cinema*, New York: Routledge.

Kaplan, E. Ann (ed.) (2000) *Feminism and Film*, Oxford: Oxford University Press.

Keathley, Christian (2006) *Cinephilia and History, or the Wind in the Trees*, Bloomington, IN: Indiana University Press.

Kindem, Gorham Anders (1982) *The American Movie Industry: The Business of Motion Pictures*, Carbondale, IL: Southern Illinois University Press.

Klein, Norman M. (1993) *Seven Minutes: The Life and Death of the American Animated Cartoon*, London: Verso Books.

Kolker, Robert (2000) *A Cinema of Loneliness*, Oxford: Oxford University Press.

Konigsberg, Ira (1997) *The Complete Film Dictionary*, New York: The Penguin Group.

Koszarski, Richard (1989) "On the Record: Seeing and Hearing the Vitaphone," in Mary Lea Bandy (ed.) *The Dawn of Sound*, New York: The Museum of Modern Art.

Kovács, András Bálint (2007) *Screening Modernism: European Art Cinema 1950–1980*, Chicago: University of Chicago Press.

Kozloff, Sarah (1988) *Invisible Storytellers: Voice-Over Narration in American Fiction Film*, Berkeley, CA: University of California Press.

Kracauer, Siegfried (1947) *From Caligari to Hitler: A Psychological Study of the German Film*, London: D. Dobson.

Kracauer, Siegfried (1997) *Theory of Film: The Redemption of Physical Reality*, Princeton, NJ: Princeton University Press.

Kreidl, John Francis (1978) *Alain Resnais*, Boston, MA: Twayne Publishers.

Lacan, Jacques (2006) "The Mirror Stage as Formative of the *I* Function as Revealed in Psychoanalytic Experience," in *Ecrits: The First Complete Edition in English*, New York: Norton.

Landsberg, Alison (2004) *Prosthetic Memory: The Transformation of American Memory in the Age of Mass Culture*, New York: Columbia University Press.

Landy, Marcia (1996) *Cinematic Uses of the Past*, Minneapolis, MN: University of Minnesota Press.

Laplanche, J. and Pontalis, J.-B. (1973) *The Language of Psycho-Analysis*, trans. Donald Nicholson-Smith, New York: W. W. Norton & Company.

Lechner, Frank J. and Boli, John (eds.) (2008) *The Globalization Reader*, Malden, MA: Blackwell.

Lemaire, Anika (1979) *Jacques Lacan*, New York: Routledge & Kegan Paul.

Lewis, Lisa (1992) *The Adoring Audience: Fan Culture and Popular Media*, New York: Routledge.

Maarek, P. (1982) *La Censure Cinématographique* (Film Censorhip), Paris: Librairies Techniques.

Mahar, Karen Ward (2006) *Women Filmmakers in Early Hollywood* (Studies in Industry and Society), Baltimore, MD: Johns Hopkins University Press.

Mair, Victor H. (1988) *Painting and Performance: Chinese Picture Recitation and Its Indian Genesis*, Honolulu, HI: University of Hawaii Press.

Maltby, Richard (2004) *Hollywood Cinema*, 2nd edn., Oxford: Blackwell Publishing.

Maltby, Richard, Stokes, Melvyn, and Allen, Robert Clyde (2007) *Going to the Movies: Hollywood and the Social Experience of Cinema*, Exeter: University of Exeter Press.

Maltin, Leonard (1980) *Of Mice and Magic: A History of American Animated Cartoons*, New York: New American Library.

Mannoni, Laurent (1995) *Trois siècles de cinéma de la lanterne magique au Cinématographe* (Three Centuries of Cinema from the Magic Lantern to the Cinematograph), Paris: Éditions de la Réunion des musées nationaux.

Mannoni, Laurent (2000) *The Great Art of Light and Shadow*, trans. Richard Crangle, Exeter: University of Exeter Press [orig. French 1994].

Mannoni, Laurent and Campagnoni, Donata Pesenti (2009) *Lanterne magique et film peint: 400 ans de cinéma* (The Magic Lantern and Painted Film: 400 Years of Cinema), Paris: Éditions de la Martinière et la Cinémathèque française.

Mannoni, Laurent, Campagnoni, Donata Pesenti, and Robinson, David (1995) *Light and Movement: Incunabula of the Motion Picture 1420–1896*, Gemona: La Cineteca del Friuli/ Le Giornate del Cinema Muto.

Marcus, Millicent (1986) *Italian Film in the Light of Neorealism*, Princeton, NJ: Princeton University Press.

Mayne, Judith (1993) *Cinema and Spectatorship*, London: Routledge.

McArthur, Colin (1972) *Underworld USA*, London: BFI/Secker and Warburg.

McDonald, Paul (2000) *The Star System: Hollywood's Production of Popular Identities*, London: Wallflower.

McMahon, Robert (2003) *The Cold War: A Very Short Introduction*, Oxford: Oxford University Press.

Mekas, Jonas (1972) *Movie Journal: The Rise of a New American Cinema, 1959–1971*, New York: Macmillan.

Metz, Christian (1981) *The Imaginary Signifier: Psychoanalysis and the Cinema*, Bloomington, IN: Indiana University Press.

Metz, Christian (1990) *Film Language: A Semiotics of the Cinema*, Chicago: University of Chicago Press [orig. 1974].

Mhando, Martin (2000) "Approaches to African Cinema Study". http://archive.sensesofcinema. com/contents/00/8/african.html

Miller, Toby (2001) *Global Hollywood*, London: British Film Institute.

Mitry, Jean (2000) *The Aesthetics and Psychology of the Cinema*, Bloomington, IN: Indiana University Press.

Modleski, Tania (1988) *The Women Who Knew Too Much: Hitchcock and Feminist Theory*, New York: Methuen.

Moine, Raphaëlle (2008) *Cinema Genre*, Malden, MA, and Oxford: Blackwell.

Moley, Raymond (1945) *The Hays Office*, Indianapolis, IN: Bobbs-Merrill.

Moritz, William (2004) *Optical Poetry: The Life and Work of Oskar Fischinger*, Bloomington, IN: Indiana University Press.

Morley, David (1980) *The "Nationwide" Audience*, London: British Film Institute.

Morse, Margaret (1998) *Virtualities: Television, Media Art, and Cyberculture*, Bloomington, IN: Indiana University Press.

Mulvey, Laura (1989) *Visual and Other Pleasures*, Bloomington, IN: University of Indiana Press.

Murphy, Robert (2001) *The British Cinema Book*, London: BFI Publishing.

Musser, Charles (1990) *The Emergence of Cinema: The American Screen to 1907*, New York: Scribner.

Musser, Charles (1994) *The Emergence of Cinema: The American Screen to 1907. History of the American Cinema*, vol. 1, Berkeley and Los Angeles, CA: University of California Press.

Naficy, Hamid (2001) *An Accented Cinema: Exilic and Diasporic Filmmaking*, Princeton, NJ: Princeton University Press.

Naremore, James (1998) *More than Night: Film Noir in Its Context*, Berkeley, CA: University of California Press.

Naremore, James (ed.) (2000) *Film Adaptation*, New Brunswick, NJ: Rutgers University Press.

Naremore, James and Brantlinger, Patrick (1991) *Modernity and Mass Culture*, Bloomington, IN: Indiana University Press.

Neale, Stephen (2000) *Genre and Hollywood*, London: Routledge.

Needham, Joseph (1954–2004) *Science and Civilization in China*, 24 vols., Cambridge: Cambridge University Press.

Negra, Diane (2001) *Off-White Hollywood: American Culture and Ethnic Female Stardom*, London and New York: Routledge.

Neupert, Richard (2007) *A History of the French New Wave*, Madison, WI: University of Wisconsin Press.

Nichols, Bill (1991) *Representing Reality: Issues and Concepts in Documentary*, Bloomington, IN: Indiana University Press.

Nichols, Bill (2001) *Introduction to Documentary*, Bloomington, IN: Indiana University Press.

Nietzsche, Friedrich (1991) *Untimely Meditations*, trans. R. J. Hollingdale, Cambridge: Cambridge University Press.

Nowell-Smith, Geoffrey (2008) *Making Waves: New Cinemas of the 1960s*, New York: Continuum.

O'Brien, Charles (2005) *Cinema's Conversion to Sound: Technology and Film Style in France and the U.S.*, Bloomington, IN: Indiana University Press.

Oettermann, Stephan (1997) *The Panorama: History of a Mass Medium*, trans. Deborah Lucas Schneider, New York: Zone Books [orig. 1980].

Orr, John (1993) *Cinema and Modernity*, Cambridge, MA: Blackwell.

Paget, Derek (1998) *No Other Way to Tell It: Dramadoc/Docudrama on Television*, Manchester, UK: Manchester University Press.

Pasolini, Pier Paolo (1988) *Heretical Empiricism*, ed. Louis K. Branett, trans. Ben Lawton and Louise K. Barnett, Bloomington, IN: Indiana University Press.

Paxton, Robert (2004) *The Anatomy of Fascism*, New York: Knopf.

Perez, Gilberto (1998) *The Material Ghost: Films and Their Medium*, Baltimore, MD: Johns Hopkins University Press.

Perloff, Marjorie (2003) *The Futurist Moment: Avant-Garde, Avant Guerre and the Language of Rupture*, Chicago: University of Chicago Press.

Pfaff, Françoise (1984) *The Cinema of Ousmane Sembène*, Westport, CT: Greenwood Press.

Place, J. A. and Peterson, L. S. (1974) "Some Visual Motifs of Film Noir," *Film Comment*, 10(1) (January–February).

Reader, Keith and Vincendeau, Ginette (eds.) (1986) *La Vie Est A Nous!: French Cinema and the Popular Front, 1935–38*, London: British Film Institute.

Rees, A. L. (1999) *A History of Experimental Film and Video*, London: British Film Institute.

Reisz, Karel and Millar, Gavin (1953–68) *The Technique of Film Editing*, London and New York: Focal Press.

Renan, Sheldon (1967) *An Introduction to the American Underground Film*, New York: Dutton.

Ricci, Steven (2008) *Cinema and Fascism: Italian Film and Society, 1922–1943*, Berkeley, CA: University of California Press.

Rich, B. Ruby (1992) "New Queer Cinema," *Sight & Sound*, 2(5), September: 30–4.

Rich, B. Ruby (2000) "Queer and Present Danger," *Sight & Sound*, 10(2): 22–4.

Richards, Jeffrey (2000) "Fires Were Started," in David Ellwood (ed.) *The Movies as History: Visions of the Twentieth Century*, Sutton: Stroud, pp. 26–36.

Richie, Donald (2005) *A Hundred Years of Japanese Film*, Tokyo: Kodansha.

Robinson, David, Herbert, Stephen, and Crangle, Richard (eds.) (2001) *Encyclopedia of the Magic Lantern*, London: The Magic Lantern Society.

Rodowick, David Norman (1988) *The Crisis of Political Modernism: Criticism and Ideology in Contemporary Film Theory*, Urbana, IL: University of Illinois Press.

Rodowick, David Norman (1997) *Deleuze's Time Machine*, Durham, NC: Duke University Press.

Rosen, Philip (ed.) (1986) *Narrative, Apparatus, Ideology: A Film Theory Reader*, New York: Columbia University Press.

Rosenstone, Robert (1998) *Visions of the Past: The Challenge of Film to Our Idea of History*, Cambridge, MA: Harvard University Press.

Rosenstone, Robert (2006) *History on Film, Film on History*, Harlow, England: Pearson Limited.

Rossell, Deac (2008) *Laterna Magica—Magic Lantern*, vol. 1, Stuttgart: Füsslin Verlag.

Rossellini, Roberto (1992) *My Method: Writings and Interviews*, ed. Adriano Aprà, New York: Marsilio.

Rotha, Paul (1973) *Documentary Diary: An Informal History of the British Documentary Film, 1928–1939*, New York: Hill & Wang.

Roud, Richard (1983) *A Passion for Films: Henri Langlois and the Cinémathèque Française*, New York: Viking Press.

Royle, Nicholas (2003) *Jacques Derrida*, London: Routledge.

Russo, Vito (1981) *The Celluloid Closet*, New York: Harper & Row.

Said, Edward (1978) *Orientalism*, New York: Pantheon Books.

Salini, Laurent (1963) "Au pas cadencé" ("With a Rythmic Step"), *L'Humanité*, February 21.

Sargeant, Jack (1997) *The Naked Lens: An Illustrated History of Beat Cinema*, London: Creation Books.

Sarris, Andrew (1968) *The American Cinema: Directors and Directions, 1929–1968*, New York: Dutton.

Saunders, Dave (2007) *Direct Cinema: Observational Documentary and the Politics of the Sixties*, London: Wallflower.

Schaefer, Eric (1999) *Bold! Daring! Shocking! True!: A History of Exploitation Films, 1919–1959*, Durham, NC: Duke University Press.

Schaeffer, Jean-Marie (1999) *Pourquoi la fiction?* (Why Fiction?), Paris: Editions du Seuil.

Schatz, Thomas (1981) *Hollywood Genres: Formulas, Filmmaking, and the Studio System*, 1st edn., New York: Random House.

Schatz, Thomas (1988) *The Genius of the System: Hollywood Filmmaking in the Studio Era*, New York: Pantheon Books.

Schatz, Thomas (1997) *Boom and Bust: The American Cinema in the 1940s*, New York: Scribner.

Schivelbusch, Wolfgang (1986) *The Railway Journey: The Industrialization of Time and Space in the 19th Century*, trans., Berkeley and Los Angeles, CA: University of California Press [orig. 1977].

Schulte-Sasse, Linda (1996) *Entertaining the Third Reich: Illusions of Wholeness in Nazi Cinema*, Durham, NC: Duke University Press.

Sconce, Jeffrey (2000) *Haunted Media: Electronic Presence from Telegraphy to Television*, Durham, NC: Duke University Press.

Searle, John (1975) "The Logical Status of Fictional Discourse," *New Literary History*, 6: 319–32.

Sedgwick, Eve Kosofsky (1990) *Epistemology of the Closet*, Berkeley, CA: University of California Press.

Sergi, Gianluca (2005) *The Dolby Era: Film Sound in Contemporary Hollywood*, Manchester, UK: Manchester University Press.

Shohat, Ella and Stam, Robert (1994) *Unthinking Eurocentrism: Multiculturalism and the Media*, London: Routledge.

Silverman, Kaja (1983) *The Subject of Semiotics*, New York: Oxford University Press.

Sitney, P. Adams (2002) *Visionary Film: The American Avant-Garde, 1943–2000*, Oxford: Oxford University Press.

Slater, Daniel (1997) *Consumer Culture and Modernity*, Cambridge: Polity.

Smith, Jeff (1998) *The Sounds of Commerce: Marketing Popular Film Music*, New York: Columbia University Press.

Smyth, J. E. (2006) *Reconstructing American Historical Cinema*, Lexington, KY: University of Kentucky Press.

Sorlin, Pierre (1980) *The Film in History: Staging the Past*, Totowa, NJ: Barnes and Noble Books.

Spoto, Donald (1983) *The Dark Side of Genius: The Life of Alfred Hitchcock*, Boston, MA: Little Brown.

Sprengler, Christine (2009) *Screening Nostalgia: Populuxe Props and Technicolor Aesthetics in Contemporary American Film*, New York: Berghahn Books.

Stacey, Jackie (1998) *Star Gazing: Hollywood Cinema and Female Spectatorship*, reprinted edn., London: Routledge.

Staiger, Janet (1992) *Interpreting Films: Studies in the Historical Reception of American Cinema*, Princeton, NJ: Princeton University Press.

Staiger, Janet (1995) *Bad Women: Regulating Sexuality in Early American Cinema*, Minneapolis, MN: University of Minnesota Press.

Stam, Robert (1985) *Reflexivity in Film and Literature: From Don Quixote to Jean-Luc Godard*, Ann Arbor, MI: University of Michigan Press.

Stewart, Jacqueline Najuma (2005) *Migrating to the Movies: Cinema and Black Urban Modernity*, Berkeley and Los Angeles, CA: University of California Press.

Stokes, Melvyn and Maltby, Richard (1999) *Identifying Hollywood Audiences*, London: British Film Institute.

Street, Sarah (1997) *British National Cinema*, London: Routledge.

"Studio Slanguage," (1930), in *The Motion Picture Almanac*, Chicago: Quigley.

Sturken, Marita and Cartwright, Lisa (2001) *Practices of Looking: An Introduction to Visual Culture*, Oxford: Oxford University Press [new edition 2009].

Tarkovsky, Andrei (1987) *Sculpting in Time: Reflections on the Cinema*, trans. K. H. Blair, New York: Knopf.

Taylor, Richard (1983) "A 'Cinema for Millions': Soviet Socialist Realism and the Problem of Film Comedy," *Journal of Contemporary History*, 18: 439–61.

Taylor, Richard (1986) "Boris Shumyatsky and the Soviet Cinema in the 1930s: Ideology in Mass Entertainment," *Historical Journal of Film, Radio and Television*, 6(1): 43–64.

Thompson, Kristin (1988) *Breaking the Glass Armor: Neoformalist Film Analysis*, Princeton, NJ: Princeton University Press.

Thompson, Kristin and Bordwell, David (2003) *Film History: An Introduction*, 2nd edn., New York: McGraw-Hill.

Tomlinson, Doug (ed.) (1994) *Actors on Acting for the Screen: Roles and Collaborations*, New York: Garland.

Truffaut, François (1983) *Hitchcock*, New York: Simon & Schuster.

Truffaut, François (2000) "A Certain Tendency of the French Cinema," in Joanne Hollows, Peter Hutchings, and Mark Jancovich (eds.) *The Film Studies Reader*, London: Oxford University Press.

Trumpbour, John (2002) *Selling Hollywood to the World: U.S. and European Struggles for Mastery of the Global Film Industry, 1920–1950*, Cambridge Studies in the History of Mass Communications, Cambridge and New York: Cambridge University Press.

Urry, John (2007) *Mobilities*, Cambridge: Polity.

Vautier, R. (1998) *Caméra citoyenne* (Citizen Camera), Paris: Editions Apogée.

Vertov, Dziga (Denis Kaufman) (1984) *Kino-Eye: The Writings of Dziga Vertov*, selected by Sergie Drobashenko, trans. K. O'Brien, Berkeley, CA: University of California Press.

Vitali, Valentina and Willemen, Paul (eds.) (2006) *Theorising National Cinema*, London: British Film Institute.

Warner, Michael (ed.) (1993) *Fear of a Queer Planet: Queer Politics and Social Theory*, Minneapolis, MN: University of Minnesota Press.

Wasko, Janet (1994) *Hollywood in the Information Age: Beyond the Silver Screen*, Cambridge: Polity.

Weis, Elisabeth and Belton, John (eds.) (1985) *Film Sound—Theory and Practice*, New York: Columbia University Press.

Wells, Paul (1998) *Understanding Animation*, London: Routledge.

Westad, O. A. (2007) *The Global Cold War: Third World Interventions and the Making of Our Times*, Cambridge: Cambridge University Press.

Wexman, Virginia Wright (ed.) (2003) *Film and Authorship*, New Brunswick, NJ: Rutgers University Press.

Wilinsky, Barbara (2001) *Sure Seaters: The Emergence of Art House Cinema*, Minneapolis, MN: University of Minnesota Press.

Williams, Linda (2001) *Playing the Race Card: Melodramas of Black and White from Uncle Tom to O. J. Simpson*, Princeton, NJ: Princeton University Press.

Williams, Patricia and Chrisman, Linda (eds.) (1994) *Colonial Discourse and Postcolonial Theory: A Reader*, New York: Columbia University Press.

Williams, Raymond (1977) *Marxism and Literature*, Oxford: Oxford University Press.

Winston, Brian (1996) *Technologies of Seeing: Photography, Cinematography and Television*, London: British Film Institute.

Winston, Brian (2008) *Claiming the Real II: Documentary: Grierson and Beyond*, London: British Film Institute.

Wojcik, Pamela Robertson (ed.) (2004) *Movie Acting: The Film Reader*, New York: Routledge.

Wollen, Peter (1993) "The Last New Wave: Modernism in the Films of the Thatcher Era," in *Fires Were Started: British Cinema and Thatcherism*, Minnesota: University of Minnesota Press, pp. 35–52.

Wollen, Peter (2002) "The Canon," in *Paris Hollywood: Writings on Film*, New York: Verso Books.

Wood, Michael (2008) "At the Movies," *The London Review of Books*, 23, May 8.

Wyke, Maria (1997) *Projecting the Past: Ancient Rome, Cinema and History*, New York: Routledge.

Yewdall, David Lewis (2007) *The Practical Art of Motion Picture Sound*, 3rd edn., Burlington, MA: Focal Press.

Youngblood, Gene (1970) *Expanded Cinema*, New York: Dutton.

Zielinski, Siegfried (2006) *Deep Time of the Media. Toward an Archaeology of Hearing and Seeing by Technical Means*, Cambridge, MA: MIT Press [orig. German 2002].

Zimmermann, Patricia Rodden (1995) *Reel Families: A Social History of Amateur Film*, Bloomington, IN: Indiana University Press.

INDEX

Page numbers in *italics* indicate a substantial discussion. Page numbers and words in **bold** refer to entries in the Critical Dictionary.